Mountain Days at Home and Abroad

Walking, Running and Climbing: 40 years of adventures on mountains around the world

Bob Worth

With best wishes

BobWorth

Mountain Days at Home and Abroad

Copyright © Bob Worth 2013

Bob Worth has asserted his moral rights to be identified as the Author of this Work in accordance with the Copyright Designs and Patents Act 1988.

ISBN 978 1 48231 687 2

Cover photos
Front: Mt Everest from Kala Patar, Nepal (photo by Bob Worth)
Back: Author racing on the North Yorks Moors (photo by Cath Worth)

Dedicated to Cath and Molly,

Thank you for letting me go out to play.......

"Go and look behind the Ranges.......Go"
                                             (Rudyard Kipling)

Mountain Days at Home and Abroad

Contents

THE EARLY YEARS 9
  Early Mountain Competitions 10

THE MUNRO YEARS 18

  Section 1: Ben Lomond; Arrochar Alps; Tyndrum; Crianlarich &
           Loch Earn 18
  Section 2: Rannoch & Glen Lyon; Ben Lawers; Mamlorn;
           Bridge of Orchy 31
  Section 3: Cruachan Group; Glen Etive; Corrie Ba; Glencoe &
           Aonach Eagach; Appin 44
  Section 4: The Mamores; Ben Nevis & Aonachs; Grey Corries;
           Loch Treig & Loch Ossian; Loch Ericht to Loch Laggan 58
  Section 5: Drumochter 70
  Section 6: Tarf & Tilt; West of Cairnwell Pass 72
  Section 7: Glas Maol; Glen Doll; Lochnagar; White Mounth; Mt Keen .78
  Section 8: Glen Feshie; Western Cairngorms; Macdui & Cairn Gorm;
           Lairig an Laoigh; Eastern Cairngorms 83
  Section 9: Loch Laggan; Monadh Liath 95
  Section 10: Loch Lochy; Gulvain; Ciche & Kingie; Knoydart;
            Loch Quoich; South Glen Shiel; The Saddle 99
  Section 11: North Glen Shiel; A'Chralaig; Glen Affric; 110
  Section 12: Sgurr na Lapaich; The Strathfarrar hills;
            East of Achnashellach 117
  Section 13: Strathcarron; The Torridons 122
  Section 14: Slioch & An Teallach; The Fannaichs 126
  Section 15: Ben Wyvis & Beinn Dearg 133
  Section 16: Assynt; Hope & Klibreck 136
  Section 17: The Islands: Mull; Skye 139
  Note 1 - Munro's Tables 147
  Note 2 - Munro's Tables 147

SOME OF THE BEST LONG RUNS AT HOME 148

  A Long Day in the Lakes – The Lakeland 3,000's 148
  A Recce of the Bob Graham Round 150
  Scottish Islands Peaks Race 154
  The Mamores 3,000's 160
  The Cairngorm 4,000's 162
  The Crianlarich 3,000's 165
  The Round of Loch Mullardoch 168

RUNNING HIGH ROUTES IN EUROPE ... 172

Tour du Mont Blanc ... 172
Chamonix to Zermatt ... 179
Tour des Fiz ... 188
Corsican High Level Route (GR20) ... 192
King Ludwig Way ... 205
Jura High Route ... 211
Tour des Portes du Soleil ... 219
Tour de l'Oisans (GR54) ... 224
Tour du Beaufortain ... 234
Alpine Pass Route ... 240
Dolomites High Level Route – Alta Via 1 ... 251
Dolomites High Level Route – Alta Via 2 ... 259
Tour du Queyras (GR58) ... 270
Tour de la Vanoise ... 279

FURTHER AFIELD – WALKING, RUNNING & CLIMBING ... 291

Trekking in the High Atlas of Morocco – Jbel Toubkal ... 291
Around Annapurna – A Himalayan Journey ... 302
A First Alpine Holiday – Climbs around Arolla ... 318
The High Valleys of Everest and the Climb of Island Peak - 6,189m .. 329
The Everest Marathon ... 347
The Pindos Mountains of Greece ... 359
The High Tatra of Poland and Slovakia ... 366
Mongolia - Sunrise to Sunset ... 375
To the Top of Europe: Mount Elbrus – 5,642m ... 386
Mount Khuiten: Mongolia's Highest Mountain – 4,374m ... 397
Ecuador – Failure on Cotopaxi & Chimborazo ... 411

GLOSSARY ... 422
INDEX ... 424

List of Maps

Scotland and the Munros 16
Long High Routes in Europe 170
Tour du Mont Blanc 171
Chamonix to Zermatt 178
Tour des Fiz 187
Corsican High Level Route (GR20) 191
King Ludwig Way 204
Jura High Route 210
Tour des Portes du Soleil 218
Tour de l'Oisans (GR54) 223
Tour du Beaufortain 233
Alpine Pass Route 239
Alta Via 1 250
Alta Via 2 258
Tour du Queyras (G58) 269
Tour de la Vanoise 278
High Atlas of Morocco 290
Annapurna Circuit 301
The High Valleys of Everest 328

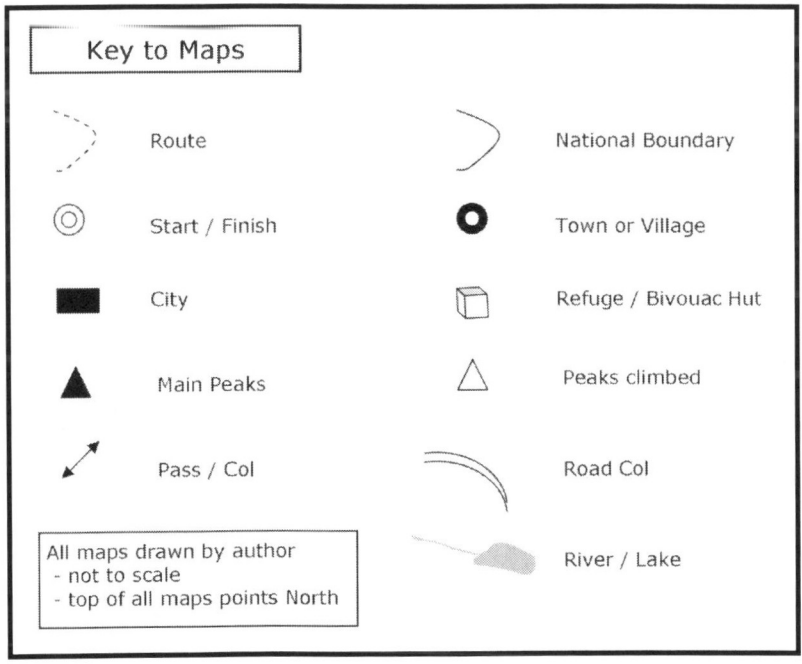

List of Illustrations

1: Peak Assault 2nd team: Jem, Bob, Stuart & Kevin 12
2: Enjoying another 'character building' day 15
3: Trainee at high-camp below Meall na Dige................25
4: Celebrating New Year on Meall nan Tarmachan 36
5: Stuart, Pete & Jem walking in to Jean's Hut 87
6: An Teallach 129
7: Abseil descent from The Inaccessible Pinnacle 142
8: On the Cairngorm plateau 163
9: Entering Italy on the Tour du Mont Blanc................174
10: Aig. de la Tsa, above Arolla..................................182
11: Ref. Alfred Wills, beneath the Rochers des Fiz 190
12: A crisp start to the morning on Corsica..................195
13: Neuschwanstein Castle, almost the end..................208
14: Tour de l'Oisans - difficult conditions for running......228
15: Trübsee, above Engleberg 243
16: Biv. Bocco, at the top of the Via Ferrata, Alta Via 1 ...256
17: Beautiful running terrain in the Dolomites................263
18: Easy running in the Soustra Valley, Italy 272
19: Monte Viso 274
20: Lac d'Ifni from Tizi n'Ouanoums 297
21: Chortens beneath Annapurna................................309
22: Rod on the summit of Zinalrothorn 326
23: Our tough little Sherpanis, always smiling..............338
24: Approaching the summit of Island Peak 342
25: Devout Tibetan 346
26: Looking down on the first few miles of the Everest Marathon route from high on Pokalde 353
27: Ama Dablam, a great back-drop to a marathon 355
28: Shopkeeper in Bhaktapur 358
29: Cath beneath the Astraka Hut 361
30: Morskie Oko Refuge..369
31: An early start on Elbrus.......................................394
32: Mount Khuiten from Nairandal..............................405
33: Cotopaxi from high on Iliniza Norte.......................416

(1) by the late Ray Batt, all other photographs from the author's collection.

THE EARLY YEARS

I think it was inevitable that I would enjoy long walks from quite an early age. I was brought up in Ashtead, Surrey, just to the south of London and remember walking two miles to primary school each day, playing in the school football team and running races against my elder brother; the winner received the pocket money that week! I joined the Cubs and moved up to Scouts as soon as I was old enough. For a few years the family entered local Challenge Walks; when I was 11 years old I walked a 39 mile event from Leatherhead to Worthing, I was the youngest to finish. That same year my sister walked the first 20 miles and she would only have been about eight years old. The previous year my brother had walked the Leatherhead to Worthing when he was 12 and that year he had been the youngest to finish.

"I can remember walking as a child. It was not customary to say you were fatigued. It was customary to complete the goal of the expedition." (Katharine Hepburn)

When I was 12 years old we moved north of London, to Broxbourne in Hertfordshire. I ran cross-country and played football for the school, I also started Race Walking, as my Dad had just gone back to it after several years out of the sport. I raced for Borough of Enfield Harriers and picked up medals at County and Area level, but at that age we weren't allowed to race any great distance, I think an hour was about the most I raced, which was usually about 7 miles.

With the Scouts I learned to sail and canoe, but the main thing was being given access to the big hills in Wales and Scotland. Hertfordshire Scouts owned a couple of mountain bases; Coetmoor Mill in Bethesda, North Wales, and the old railway station at Lochearnhead in central Scotland. Using these bases the Scouts ran an excellent programme of mountain training that started with a week-long *Initial Training Course*, leading to the *Hike Leaders Training Course*, then an *Advanced Techniques Course*, followed by the *Introductory Course for the Mountain Leadership Certificate*. At Lochearnhead we also had access to sailing on Loch Earn and white-water canoeing on the rivers at Killin and Strathyre.

Early Mountain Competitions

As well as the training courses the county also organised an annual mountain competition, *The Peak Assault*. The venue changed each year; the competition area was kept a closely guarded secret and disclosed only the week before the event.

The race was for teams of Venture Scouts or Rangers, the course only being revealed a couple of minutes before the staggered start. Unusually for a race, a standard time was given for each 'leg', penalties were added if you were outside the allotted time, so the trick was to arrive at the checkpoint a few minutes early, there was nothing to be gained from being too much quicker than the 'standard' time. As well as the navigation and endurance part of the exercise, teams were also tested on a range of mountain related topics and skills such as First Aid, mountain weather, speed and efficiency at pitching camp and preparing the evening meal.

My first entry into the Peak Assault was with the *George Hann VSU*, which at the time was mainly known as a caving unit. I was still quite young and was put in the 'B' team. The 'A' team were the older lads; the 'B' team were any others who just wanted a weekend away. No one had done any training and the gear had been thrown together at the last minute. The weather was superb in the Brecon Beacons that March weekend, almost a heat-wave; we struggled round half the course and eventually gave up, mainly due to lack of interest and the unseasonably hot weather.

By the following year I had joined the rival *East Herts Border VSU* and we entered a team of four, all of whom were pretty new to the game. At the end of February we held a training weekend in North Wales, based at Coetmor Mill in Bethesda, when we climbed Glyder Fawr, Glyder Fach and Y Garn in beautiful snow and fine weather.

The Peak Assault a couple of weeks later was run from Dolgellau and involved a long day over and around Cader Idris. We found all the check-points and finished about 10th from around 50 teams. We were pleased to finish well up the field and as we were all eligible for another two or three years we felt we could only improve.

The following winter, 1974, we again held a training weekend at Coetmor Mill at the end of February. It was another great weekend and we climbed Y Garn, the Glyders and Tryfan on good snow. Two weeks later we were back in Bethesda for the Peak Assault where we entered two teams; our 'A' team plus a mixed team for the first time. Because of the snow conditions the previous week the organisers decided it was safer to reduce the length of the course so we only had a fairly short run; from the Mill we headed south over Mynydd Perfedd to Y Garn, over ground we knew quite well. As it was, on the day conditions were ideal and we would all have liked to have been able to go further. We finished in around 5th or 6th place and were pleased to have improved again.

For 1975 we decided to train hard and from New Year until the competition in mid-March we were out virtually every weekend, hiking with 30 or 40lbs in our 'sacs. When we had finished we would do step-ups onto a bench, still with our 'sacs on. On the Sunday we would go for a long cross-country run, interspersed with stops for sit-ups and press-ups.

Once again we were booked into Coetmor Mill for a weekends training in February, the Saturday found us out on Moel Hebog and Moel Lefn, to the west of Beddgelert, in snow and strong winds. On Sunday we climbed Moel Siabod on good snow and in better weather.

The competition that year was down on Dartmoor, which meant a long drive down to the event centre at Dewarstone Cottage, and for the first time the event was a two-day affair with an over-night camp. This meant the choice of food and equipment was even more important and we took care to select the lightest gear we could lay our hands on.

We were drawn about 7th to start and by the first check-point on Trowlesworthy Tors we had already moved into a joint lead with three other teams. We led the way on a bearing to the second check-point and the other teams soon dropped away. Being a staggered start you never knew quite how well you were doing until the end of the day, but we guessed that we were going better than most.

We were in thick mist heading for 'three', a stone-circle, but found it spot-on. Unfortunately there were no marshals there so we went in search of them and discovered them about a mile down-stream at another stone-circle; they were at the wrong one. We then had to cross a mile of rough moorland to put ourselves back on course for number four, where we found we had been overtaken by several teams who had gone straight on from the missing check-point.

We were soon through check-points 4 and 5, and by the time we reached 6, on Green Hill, we were back in front. On the way out to Great Goats Head for check-point seven, we were surprised to find a letter-box memorial at Ducks Pool.

We were first to arrive at Nuns Cross Farm, early in the afternoon, which was a bonus as it meant we had the choice of the best place to camp. Teams kept coming in until well after dark. At the over-night camp each team had to complete a quiz on mountain related subjects such as weather and cloud formations, First Aid, Gaelic place names, and mountain rescue techniques. There was a heavy frost over-night and we were all up early for a mass start at dawn on the Sunday. We made good time back to Dewarstone Cottage, where we had an agonising wait as the results were read out in reverse order all the way from last in 50th place, up to the winners. It was a nerve wracking wait until they eventually called our name, we had finished second. Second was good but at the time we were all very disappointed not to have won, that was our best chance and somehow we had blown it, just one question wrong in the quiz made the difference.

1: Peak Assault 2nd team (L to R) Jem, Bob, Stuart & Kevin

The following year was to be the last Peak Assault for most of the team as we would soon be too old, so we again trained hard over the winter months. We had weekends at Coetmor Mill in January and February; the first weekend we climbed Snowdon by the Watkin Path; the following day we played on the snow to practice our ice-axe work. Unfortunately, in February the weather was terrible, rain lashed down the whole time, but it gave us good navigation training in thick cloud on the tops around Moel Eilios.

March saw us up in North Wales for the third time in just 6 weeks; that year the Peak Assault was back in Dolgellau. We entered our most experienced team yet, as well as a mixed team, and after finishing second the year before we had high hopes of going one better this time. However, almost unbelievably we went off course within about 15 minutes of starting, in fact before we had even left the road and were on the hill itself. By the time we noticed and rectified our error, then made our way to the first check-point, we were already down on time and we knew that any penalty points at all would put us right out of contention for the win. Feeling somewhat dejected we just ambled round the course for the next couple of hours as we had lost all interest in racing.

Several teams were suffering on the climb up Cader Idris and some were experiencing exposure symptoms, but as we were fit, well trained and well clad we hadn't found it particularly cold or windy. By mid-afternoon we realised with some surprise that despite our disastrous start we were still up with the leaders, so our competitive urge slowly came back and we then made good time to the over-night camp. It was only a short hike back to base the following morning and when the results were finally formulated and announced, we found that we had still managed to finish 6th without really trying.

We always eagerly looked forward to our winter weekends at Coetmor Mill in Bethesda and usually managed to do a fair amount despite the often poor weather at that time of the year. Some of my happiest memories are of coming down off Tryfan, the Glyders, Devil's Kitchen or Y Garn to the old shack at Ogwen for a steaming mug of tea and a hamburger. The weekends always seemed to revolve around food and drink, starting on the Friday night when we would stop at 'Greasy Lils', just off the A5 near Telford, for a big fry-up and mugs of tea. Everyone going to North Wales would stop there, or so it seemed, and we would often bump into people we knew.

We were young then and did silly things: ice-cold river crossings just for fun, not because we had to; something involving a traffic cone, a yellow flashing light and the Police; even a case of frostbite one winter, which confused the local Doctor in Cheshunt who had never seen it before. It was Martin's own fault, he thought it would be a good idea to wear his Mum's rubber washing-up gloves; they were certainly water-proof but they didn't exactly keep his hands warm.

Of all the memories of those early days in North Wales, perhaps the best is of the day in mid-December when we climbed Snowdon by the Pyg track and Crib Goch, crossed the summit, and then came back down via the Watkin Path. Half-way down, as we came to a deep, ice encrusted pool, someone said "That would be a great place to swim in the summer". Someone answered "Why wait for summer, what's wrong with now?" So two of us stripped off in the snow, jumped in and swam. It was freezing and took our breath away, so after a couple of minutes we dashed out, dressed quickly and then ran, in heavy mountain boots, all the way down the track back to the road.

We knew it would be a long wait for the minibus to come and pick us up so we decided to walk into Beddgelert and wait in the tea-shop. As it was a longish walk we started to hitch and almost immediately a car stopped for us. A very pretty girl in her mid twenties was driving and we chatted about our day and told her we were going to have a cup of tea in Beddgelert. She immediately invited us back to her place for tea and crumpets; 'her place' was actually the vicarage in Beddgelert. Unfortunately we had arranged to meet the others in the tea-shop so we had to pass on her kind invitation. When we did meet the others later they refused to believe that we had been picked up by the Vicar's daughter and invited back for tea and crumpets.

2: Enjoying another 'character building' day

Scotland and the Munros

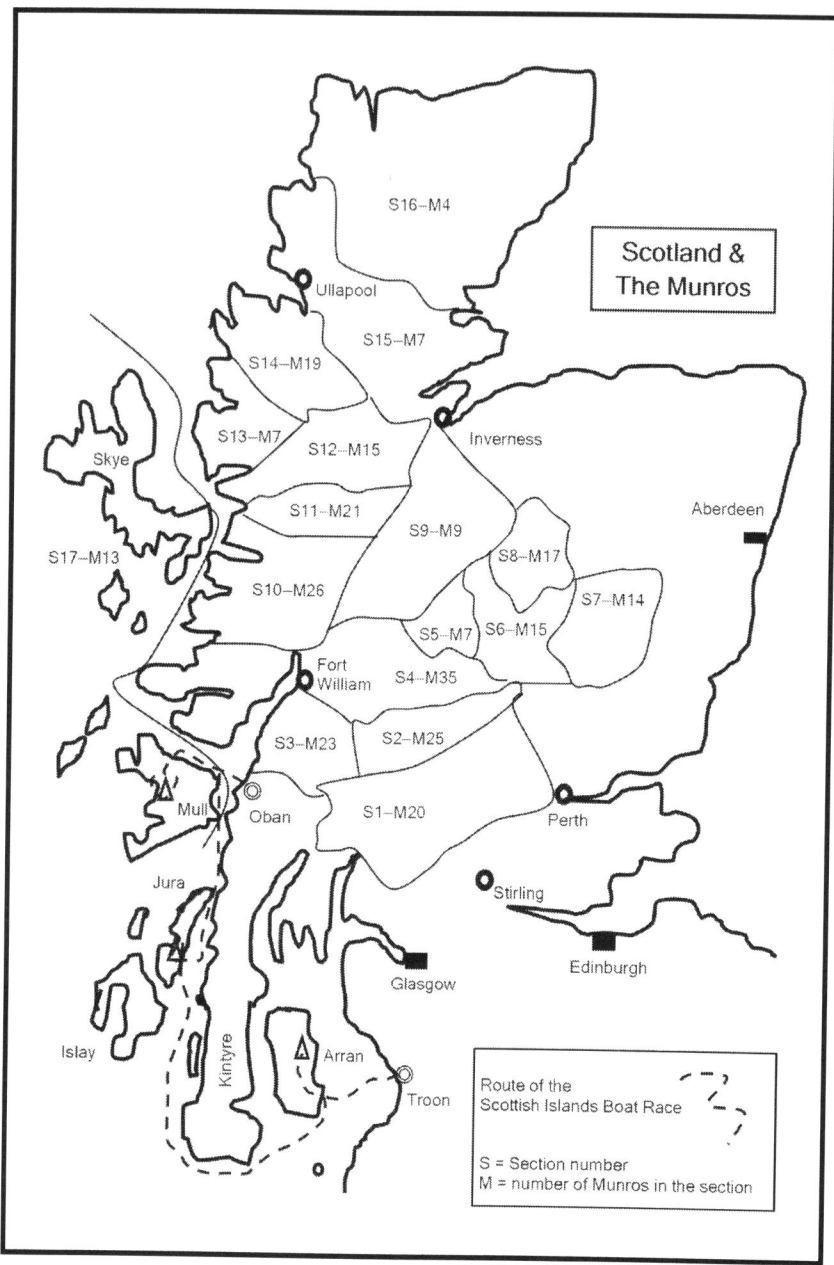

Section 1: Ben Lomond; Arrochar Alps; Tyndrum; Crianlarich & Loch Earn

Section 2: Rannoch & Glen Lyon; Ben Lawers; Mamlorn; Bridge of Orchy

Section 3: Cruachan; Glen Etive; Corrie Ba; Glencoe; Aonach Eagach; & Appin

Section 4: The Mamores; Ben Nevis & Aonachs; Grey Corries; Loch Treig & Loch Ossian;

Section 5: Drumochter

Section 6: Tarf & Tilt; West of Cairnwell Pass

Section 7: Glas Maol; Glen Doll; Lochnagar & White Mounth; Mt Keen

Section 8: Glen Feshie; Macdui & Cairn Gorm; Lairig an Laoigh; Eastern Cairngorms

Section 9: Loch Laggan; Monadh Liath

Section 10: Loch Lochy; Ciche & Kingie; Knoydart; Loch Quoich; Glen Shiel; The Saddle

Section 11: North Glen Shiel; A'Chralaig; Gleann Lichd; Glen Affric;

Section 12: Sgurr na Lapaich; Strathfarrar; East of Achnashellach

Section 13: Strathcarron; The Torridons

Section 14: Slioch & An Teallach; The Fannaichs

Section 15: Ben Wyvis & Beinn Dearg

Section 16: Assynt; Hope & Klibreck

Section 17: The Islands: Mull; Skye - Central Cuillin; Glen Brittle; Southern Cuillin

THE MUNRO YEARS

Section 1: Ben Lomond; Arrochar Alps; Tyndrum; Crianlarich & Loch Earn

Ben Lomond   3,192ft

Somewhat surprisingly I had my highest failure rate on Ben Lomond, having twice failed to reach the top, both times within a week of the other.

My first visit was a success though. I parked near Loch Dhu on the Aberfoyle to Inversnaid road and walked in through Loch Ard forest, which gave good fast going, over Duchray Water until another major stream was reached. Here the footpath heads away from the track and leads west along the stream, eventually coming out of the forest at a deer fence. From here a rough mile of moorland saw me onto Ben Lomond's south ridge where I joined the main tourist path and the steady climb to the summit began in earnest. The day was dull and overcast and gave only brief glimpses down onto Loch Lomond.

A final steepening of the path led me onto the rocky summit ridge which was followed for half a mile or so to the large cairn. After a quick bite to eat I returned along the ridge and dropped down to the saddle; here most people turn right for Rowardennan, I turned left back down to Loch Ard forest.

Sometime later I returned with my sister, to do the same route; it was between Christmas and New Year and with daylight hours short we decided to cycle in from the road and leave our bikes where the footpath leaves the forestry track. Unfortunately the weather was very, very cold; the forest roads were covered in ice, turning them into a skating rink. This made it very slow going and by the time we reached the footpath turnoff it was almost time to think about turning back; we didn't even start to walk towards the hill, instead we cycled back by a different route, coming out onto the road by Kinlochard. A week later, I was joined by another friend, and we decided to try the same route again. Much of the ice had thawed and we were through the forest in reasonable time but once we were on the hill we encountered deep soft snow. We made it to just below the summit ridge, when, in worsening weather, we decided we had better turn round if we wanted to get back to the car in daylight. That winter the score was Ben Lomond 2 : Bob Worth 0.

The more conventional 'tourist' route climbs from Rowardennan on Loch Lomondside. Every May there is a Hill Race from Rowardennan to the top and back; unfortunately it is always the week before the Scottish Islands Peaks Race, so rather than race I would often just run slowly up before the race started so I could watch and support my club-mates.

Beinn Narnain   3,036ft   **Beinn Ime**   3,318ft
Ben Vane   3,004ft

The round of these three peaks, forming part of the Arrochar Alps at the head of Loch Long, gives a long satisfying day with varied terrain and, given good weather, great views.

On my first visit I parked near Succoth and followed the main footpath steeply up through the forest, before emerging onto open hillside, where the obvious path continues steeply until a level track is reached; this then contours round to the west until it reaches the Allt a Bhalachain. This part of the route is usually pretty busy as it is also the main route up The Cobbler; not a Munro but nevertheless a great little mountain in its own right.

When I reached the huge Narnain Boulders I climbed a gully, passing some mountain goats on the way. The gully took me quite steeply up through broken ground to the col to the south-east of Beinn Narnain; from here a bit of a scramble led on up through some easy crags to the trig point on the summit. From the summit it didn't take long to drop down to the grassy plateau of the bealach beyond. The climb to Beinn Ime was just a long plod up a grassy ridge and on reaching the cairn and the large wind-shelter I surprised a chap who was sitting there reading a newspaper; this shows what an unusually calm day it was!

Leaving the summit I made my way carefully down the steep broken ground, avoiding the crags, to arrive beneath Ben Vane's south-western slopes. A fairly steep climb up the rough terraces gained height quickly and I reached the summit sooner than expected. Retracing my steps for the first part of the descent I then veered away to reach the foot of the crags forming Beinn Ime's east ridge. As I was now aiming for the Bealach a Mhaim again, I wanted to make sure I didn't lose any unnecessary height, nor did I want to climb any extra. It seemed a long way as I traversed beneath the crags of Beinn

Ime, until I eventually reached the footpath a short way above the forest. The final climb to reach the col seemed harder than usual, but once there it was downhill almost all the way on a good footpath back to the shores of Loch Long.

My next couple of times to the summit of Beinn Narnain were interesting as on neither occasion did I actually want, or plan, to go there. On the first occasion I was running in the Scottish Mountain Trial, a one day event for teams of two. We had run well to the first control beneath The Cobbler; the next control was on the far side of Beinn Narnain's south ridge, tucked away down in a corrie. We opted for the shorter, more direct route, even though it meant more climbing, i.e. we went up and over the south ridge. The mist was right down and we made a real mess of it. From the ridge the direct descent to the control looked impossible; we would have had to try to scramble down through horribly steep, wet crags that we couldn't see the foot of. We ranged back and forth along the ridge looking for a safe way down and before we knew it we were beside the cairn on the summit itself. This at least proved exactly where we were, but it still took several more precious minutes before we finally found a gully, which led us slowly but safely down. So much for our short-cut!

The second time, just four months later, was so much like the first that I still can't believe that I let it happen. It was on the first day of the *Karrimor Mountain Marathon (KIMM)*, we had again run well to the first control, in the glen between The Cobbler and Beinn Narnain. Now we had to find the second control, which was a long way round on the other side of Beinn Narnain, beside a stream below A'Chrois. We climbed up towards the Bealach a Mhaim and started up the north-western ridge of Beinn Narnain, we then tried to skirt round the crags, supposedly heading approximately north-east to pick up the ridge which would lead round to A'Chrois. The thick cloud meant we couldn't see far beyond arm's reach and we wasted a good deal of time searching for the ridge. We couldn't find it and by this time we no longer knew exactly where we were, the easiest option was to find the summit trig point, and from there set a bearing. This we did, and we found our ridge at last but only at the cost of perhaps fifteen precious minutes and a lot of wasted energy.

Under the circumstances, Beinn Narnain is not my favourite mountain!

Ben Vorlich 3,092ft

This Ben Vorlich lies just to the west of the top end of Loch Lomond; not to be confused with its namesake above Loch Earn. I climbed this one on a bright October day when we had enjoyed some early snow; conditions were superb, blue sky on a crisp, cold day and the snow down to about 2,000ft.

Parked at Ardlui railway station I set off across the hillside to cut over into the valley which leads up to Coire Creagach. The ground was wet and boggy lower down but as I climbed higher the going became easier; thankfully the frost had firmed things up. Keeping to the right-hand wall of the corrie I climbed steeply up the rough, broken terrain to join the crisp snow. I was soon up on the main ridge and then onto the north top of Ben Vorlich; from here the ridge led easily to the OS pillar on the main summit. The top was surprisingly crowded as everyone was out enjoying the unexpectedly good spell of weather. Across Loch Sloy the steep face of Ben Vane looked almost Alpine in its winter covering, and the sun glistened off Loch Lomond as it stretched away to the south.

To descend I dropped down to the east, to a ridge with the strange name of Little Hills, and from here I was able to cut directly down to the stream in the valley below. I followed this for a while, jumped across and further down veered off to return to the road just south of Ardlui station

Beinn Bhuidhe 3,106ft

I had been putting off visiting this hill as it seemed a long way to go for what looked like very little excitement. However, one fine November day I decided it was time to tick it off the list and give myself a run in a new area.

It was a beautiful early winter's day, but for some reason the whole of the valley was filled with thick fog. From the drive over the 'Rest and be Thankful' Pass I'd seen that the tops were clear and I hoped I would soon run into sunshine. Leaving the car at the head of Loch Fyne I jogged comfortably along the four miles of track, but I felt the thick fog getting into my chest, which wasn't good. I passed Glenfyne Lodge and was soon at the small cottage of Inverchorachan; from here I headed directly up the steep grassy hillside. Following a stream the ground was very wet and boggy, but the going turned better higher up when I entered the corrie beneath the summit ridge. By now I had climbed up out of the fog and had great views down the length of Loch Fyne and away to the sea. A cold wind had sprung up so I was glad to pull on another layer as I climbed the final craggy slopes to the OS pillar on the summit.

The descent was by the same route, but I stopped at a stream for a quick drink and a bite of mint-cake, to set me up for the return. It was dangerous to try to go too fast on the descent as the grass was steep and wet and my studs were worn fairly smooth. As I re-entered the fog I surprised a small group of ramblers; I came leaping down the hillside, going as it must have seemed to them, like a bat out of hell. They looked somewhat bemused as I grunted a breathless 'Hello' and was gone before they could react. Once back down in the glen I settled into a steady jog and the miles soon passed after an unexpectedly good day.

Ben Lui   **3,708ft**   **Beinn a'Chleibh**   **3,008ft**
Ben Oss   **3,374ft**   **Beinn Dubhchraig**   **3,204ft**

On my first visit to this group of hills I started from Tyndrum Station and walked in the four miles or so, along the land-rover track in Glen Cononish. From the old sheep-pens at the end of the track I followed the Allt an Rund for a short distance before crossing the stream and setting to work on the rough climb up the nose of Stob Garbh. It was fairly steep and in the drizzle and low cloud I couldn't see much, but after a rocky scramble I could just make out the drop down into the gully in the east face. The ridge was soon reached, which led easily round the rim of the corrie to Ben Lui's summit cairn.

From here a long descent of the ridge to the south-east, first over rocks, then on grass and heather, took me to the rough saddle above Coire Laoigh. The long 1,000ft climb seemed endless as I followed the edge of the corrie to eventually reach the top of Ben Oss. Pausing only briefly I continued through the rain, following the ridge north and gently down as it swung east to a saddle between Coire Buidhe and Coire Garbh. On the saddle I came out below the clouds for a short while and could see the black waters of Loch Oss far below me. I was now faced with one final climb, back into the clouds again, and round the ridge to Beinn Dubhchraig.

Leaving the summit I followed the north-east ridge, steeply at times, down into the forest. This in turn led to a track down by the railway line, where I came across a large stag, which had probably been hit by a train; it was a huge beast with a good head of antlers. The railway, and then a track, led me back to Tyndrum Station after a long, cold, wet day.

At that time I wasn't really 'collecting' the Munros, so I hadn't even thought of visiting Beinn a'Chleibh. This omission was rectified one superb winter's day when I walked-in down Glen Cononish to the end of the track. On firm snow I climbed up into the corrie on Ben Lui's east face and found a great little climb from there, out onto the ridge on my right, and round the rim of the corrie to the summit. As I'd been climbing I had watched a party climbing the steep Central Gully; they emerged through the cornice as I went past. From the summit I could almost run down the long slope to the west, down to the col, from where a short ascent took me to the cairn on Beinn a'Chleibh. From the cairn I had fantastic views out to Ben Cruachan and further west. It didn't take long to return to the saddle, before contouring round to the south of Ben Lui to reach the col from where I dropped down into Coire Laoigh and so back to the track for the long walk out.

I subsequently made several visits to these hills with Scout and Guide groups when I was instructing on courses at Lochearnhead Scout Station; it's a good place to have a reasonably easy wild camp. One such occasion was the time of the Royal Wedding between Prince Charles and Princess Diana. We decided to give the trainees a party to celebrate, so the night before the camp several of us carried in huge loads of tents, stoves, fuel and goodies for the party. Next day the trainees walked-in carrying only their own kit and some food; that year's course was a younger group than usual, hence the need for the leaders to act as Sherpas. The first day was taken up with simply walking in and setting up a small village of tents.

It was a glorious evening so after dinner John and I decided on a quick climb of Ben Oss, which towered above the camp. We climbed straight from the tents, steeply up the broken ground on the mountain's north ridge. We were both going at quite a pace and neither of us wanted to be the first to stop for a breather. The summit, being at the far, southern, end of the hill, was a long time in coming and only after several false summits. Once we made it though the view was fantastic, especially south, where Loch Lomond stretched away towards Glasgow and we thought we could even see the hills on the Isle of Arran. We returned at a more leisurely pace, down the steep hillside to our camp, only to find that in our absence the others had had their party, and they'd left none of the goodies for us!

On another occasion when we were camping with some young Scouts at the head of the glen, I had about an hour to spare before I had to leave to get a lift back to the Station. I dashed up Ben Lui via the ridge to the right of the corrie, round over the tops, and came back down the corrie's left ridge. After having worked up quite a sweat with this quick sprint up and over the summit, I enjoyed a deliciously cold swim in a small pool in the river before walking back out.

Ben Lui also featured one Christmas. My sister was looking after a friend's dog at the time and of course the dog came too. The usual walk in soon passed and we climbed Ben Lui easily enough from the Stob Garbh ridge. There was a little snow on the summit, which was fine, but an almost gale-force wind raged icily across the ridge. The poor dog was a pitiful sight as it was slowly being covered in a coat of ice and was often threatened with being blown away altogether. We were glad to leave the ridge and drop down into the shelter of Coire Laoigh, where we could recover from our battering and de-frost the dog.

Ben More   **3,843ft**   **Stob Binnein**   **3,821ft**
Cruach Ardrain   **3,428ft**   **Beinn Tulaichean**   **3,099ft**
Beinn a'Chroin   **3,104ft**   **Beinn Chabhair**   **3,053ft**
An Caisteal   **3,265ft**

Little did I think when I first climbed these peaks to the south of Crianlarich, usually just one or two at a time, that I would later do all seven Munros, plus a further four subsidiary 'tops', in one outing of less than 8 hours, it was a run of around 20 miles with 11,000ft of climbing and is recounted later in this journal.

Most of my early visits were made from Lochearnhead Scout Station, usually over New Year or Easter, and hence were often on snow. One New Years Day a friend and I were dropped at the old stone bridge on the A85. We climbed up through the forest in deep snow and started the long climb of Ben More. It was a superb day, although the soft snow made it slow going as we took it in turns to do the hard work breaking trail all the way to the top. The difficult conditions and the short daylight hours meant we had to miss out on Stob Binnein and instead we just plunged down the steep slopes to rejoin the road at Benmore Farm. With time to spare before we were due to be picked up we walked along the road to Crianlarich; sadly all the tea-rooms were shut but we had the bonus of the most magnificent sun-set, the snowy flank of Ben More turned from pink to gold as the sun went down.

We often used to take parties to the area for their three-day high camp. One Easter, when we had enjoyed a late fall of snow, I was camped with my group in a sheltered spot in the corrie between Stob Coire Bhuidhe and Stob Garbh. The morning was taken up with the walk in and pitching camp; in the afternoon we climbed Stob Binnein. The top few hundred feet were sheet ice, which is often the case here as the top seems to catch the wind, which quickly polishes any snow to ice and it can be lethal. We spent the following day on Stob Garbh and Cruach Ardrain; the conditions were very difficult, we either found deep snow, or ice, there seemed to be nothing in between. The most memorable part of this high camp was the loo; it had to be in the top 10 'Loos with a view', looking across to the majestic Ben More and Stob Binnein on the far side of the glen in perfect snow cover, with a bright blue sky overhead.

As a contrast, another Easter found us camped by the small lochan on the col below Meall na Dige. There were just one or two patches of old snow on the highest peaks and the sun shone brilliantly from a clear blue sky. We were all very sunburnt and were reduced to using margarine to see if it would like a sun-block; but it didn't. With the warm evenings and clear skies it was great to be able to stay out playing on the crags, climbing and abseiling until it was too dark to see.

3: Trainee at high-camp below Meall na Dige, making the most of the fine weather one Easter

That course was however quite exceptional, more usual was the weather for the week of the *MLC Introductory Course*. This time I was a trainee and for the three-day camp we started from Inverlochlarig and climbed up towards the head of the glen until we found a suitable place to pitch camp. It was a miserable day and as I had found out that our Instructor was pregnant I felt obliged to carry far more than my share of the kit. In the afternoon we climbed up to the col between Ben More and Stob Binnein; from the col we headed up Stob Binnein then out over Stob Coire an Lochain. Here one of the girls badly twisted her knee so half of the party were despatched down to the tents, while the leader and I, with the girls friend along for moral support, helped her back down to camp.

The following day was cold and wet but I scored extra Brownie points by preparing breakfast outside in the rain, which was served to my Instructor and Gail while they were still lying cocooned in their sleeping bags. We packed the tents and climbed on up the glen to the watershed, then traversed up and over the col between Stob Garbh and Stob Coire Bhuidhe. Once over the ridge we contoured round into Coire Ardrain and set up camp below the saddle between Stob Garbh and Cruach Ardrain. Thankfully the sun came out in the afternoon and we were able to do some easy climbs on the low crags beneath Stob Garbh's summit.

While at the Station one New Year, a friend and I were surprised when another of the leaders asked if we would care to join him and his girl-friend for a day on the hill. We agreed, mainly because at that time we were without transport. We drove round to Inverlochlarig and followed the good track up the glen until we reached Ishag Glen where we turned north and started climbing the south-east slopes of Beinn a'Chroin. It was only now that it dawned on us why we had been invited along; the snow was deep and soft and we were required to help break trail so his girl-friend wouldn't have too hard a time. It was however a good, if blustery day, and when we returned to his car we were pleased to see some nicely chilled beer waiting for us. We quickly forgave him for his deviousness.

I've spent many days over these hills, in all weathers and in all seasons. One of the first after I had moved up to Scotland I hitched to Crianlarich, climbed Ben More and Stob Binnein, then crossed over Stob Coire an Lochan and headed east to Meall na Dige. From there I followed the ridge to Stob Creagach and dropped down steeply into Monachyle Glen; a big climb up the far side of the glen brought me to The Stob and eventually, after some bog-trotting, to Lochan an Eireannaich at the head of Kirkton Glen. A pleasant stroll down through the forest brought me to Balquidder for the short walk out to the main road where I was able to hitch a lift home.

A later visit saw me, and a couple of running friends driving in to park at Inverlochlarig. We ran down to the farm and then turned up the land-rover track on the west side of Inverlochlarig Burn; this gave good running and we gained height easily. The last mile to the saddle was over rough ground, which slowed us a little, we were then faced with a steeper climb up to the bealach. From here a hard 1,000ft climb slowed us to the slowest of jogs until we finally reached the cairn on Ben More; it only took minutes to return to the bealach for the similar 1,000ft climb to Stob Binnein. From Stob Binnein we enjoyed easy running down to Stob Coire an Lochain, then east down to Meall na Dige. Here we took to a grassy ridge which dropped comfortably until, after a short plateau, a small rise took us onto Meall Monachyle. After a steep descent to the west we crossed the burn then contoured round the hillside to return easily to the car.

Ben Vorlich   3,231ft   Stuc a'Chroin   3,189ft

When I first climbed this pair of hills I had no idea that they would later be almost on my doorstep and they would be reduced to being mere training runs.

These are the nearest big hills to Lochearnhead and as such they receive countless ascents by trainees over the years. The usual, fairly unexciting, route for Ben Vorlich starts by the old stone bridge on the south side of Loch Earn, from where a good track leads through the grounds of Ardvorlich House and up into Glen Vorlich. After an easy walk you cross the stream and follow the obvious path on to the mountain's north ridge, which climbs steadily until just below the summit where you reach boulders and the final steep ascent to the cairn only takes a few minutes. If just climbing the one hill you can, rather than re-trace your steps take the ridge running off to the north-west and go out over the tussocks to Ben Our and then drop down to the footpath below.

We often used the slopes of Ben Vorlich to take parties in winter for ice-axe practice. One Easter on an *Advanced Techniques Course (ATC)* we had a casualty when one lad speared himself in his upper thigh with his axe; he did survive to finish the course though. Other memories of Ben Vorlich include a superb January day, when, in perfect snow conditions, two friends and I climbed the usual route up the glen but then climbed up into the corrie to the north-west and from there we had a good little snow climb up to the summit. On another occasion with my sister, we made it to within about 100 yards of the summit only to find the final cone covered in sheet ice; without crampons we were forced to turn back defeated.

I still have a photo taken when leading on an *Initial Training Course (ITC)* of a short-eared owl which I came across on the ground in Coire Buidhe, between Ben Vorlich and Ben Our. The owl didn't try to fly away; it just ruffled it's feathers to make it look twice as big, it's huge yellow eyes staring at me all the time.

One Christmas Eve, a few instructors were gathered at the Station prior to a course starting. A couple of us had endured a poor day out around Beinn Ime and Ben Vane; the weather was awful and we failed to make it to the top of either of them. Other parties had experienced a similarly dismal day. Everyone was showered and changed before it was realised that two lads had still not returned, although they should have been back from Ben Vorlich by 5pm. It was now 7pm and of course it had been fully dark for some time. Someone drove out to check the pubs and to drive up and down the roads to see if they were walking in, but they couldn't be found. Dinner was somewhat subdued and immediately afterwards we went off to change into warm kit to go out and search for them.

Two parties were dispatched to Glen Ample, one to walk in from either end of the glen; the third party, which I was in, was to search on Ben Vorlich itself. The weather, which had defeated most of us earlier in the day, had by now deteriorated still further and it was very dark. In an era before radios and mobile phones, we agreed a system of signalling with flares and set off from the roadside at Ardvorlich at about 9:30pm. Within minutes we were in deep, soft snow, with more snow falling all the time. It took an age to climb the track and to make some sort of attempt on the ridge to the summit. Eventually we decided it would be a miracle for us to find anyone on a night like that; the light from our head-torches was bouncing back at us off the wall of falling snow, and if we had gone on much further there could have been another six casualties to worry about. Reluctantly we turned about and retreated, still searching, back down to the main path.

As we reached the glen we saw a red light through the gloom and someone was waiting to tell us the good news that the two lads had come down to the road at Ardchullarie More, at the south end of Glen Ample; they had in fact reached the Station only minutes after we left. The two search parties headed for Glen Ample had been recalled in time, but we failed to see the flares and had spent almost 4 hours out in very dangerous conditions for nothing. We returned to the Station, cold and wet, only to learn minutes later that one of the minibuses had gone off the track in Glen Ample and we were needed to lift it back onto the track. We went out again, lifted the minibus back onto terra firma, and eventually went to bed around 3am after quite a night. Next day was Christmas Day and this passed in something of a blur. Looking back on that night it was probably one of the most dangerous moments of my life.

Stuc a'Chroin has also given many memorable days, often in conjunction with Ben Vorlich, which is usually climbed first; before dropping steeply down a rocky crest to the south-west. From here, in winter, I usually traverse to the right beneath the crags and then climb a snow slope to Stuc a'Chroin's summit ridge. In summer I usually go straight up the rocky buttress opposite; although this looks difficult it is in fact an easy scramble. The access routes to Stuc a'Chroin have become easier over the recent years as more land-rover tracks are appearing all the time.

Over later years I have done a lot of training runs over both Ben Vorlich and Stuc a'Chroin, both from the usual northern approach and also the longer way in, from Callander in the south. You can park at the Bracklin Falls car-park or at the farm at the road-end. A good route takes you to the old farm buildings at Arivurichardich, from where a climb up the rough tussocks sees you onto a saddle, then down to Glean an Dubh Choirein. After crossing the river you are now on Ben Vorlich's south ridge, which is followed easily to the summit. After a careful jog down the steep, rough south-west ridge and a quick scramble up onto Stuc a'Chroin, you then have an easy run along a superb grassy ridge for a couple of miles, all gently downhill, to the saddle where you rejoin the outward route.

Another favourite route, ideal for a fine summer evening, is to park at Ardchullarie More at the south end of Glen Ample, then run steeply up through the forest until you reach the land-rover track. This is followed for a short while up the glen, before turning off to the right and climbing steeply up the rough hillside to Beinn Each. From the top an interesting ridge undulates northwards for a while before turning east for the final steep climb onto Stuc a'Chroin.

A tough hill-race starts in Strathyre; it's about 13 miles with 5,000ft of climbing. From the village you climb steeply up into the forest on good forest roads; the angle then eases off a little as you climb to the edge of the plantation. Here you take to the rough open hillside, through the knolls before dropping steeply down into Glen Ample. A hard climb now takes you onto Beinn Each; the going then becomes easier as you follow the ridge north before the final steep pull up onto Stuc a'Chroin's summit. You re-trace your steps back to the ridge but instead of returning to Beinn Each you leave the ridge early and make a descending traverse to come down into Glen Ample at the same point you crossed the burn earlier. After a final steep climb up out of Glen Ample you are now just left with a fast finish down forest roads back to Strathyre.

Ben Chonzie   3,048ft

Ben Chonzie is definitely a mountain that is only climbed because it breaches the magic 3,000ft contour. It stands alone in uninspiring country to the north of Comrie; I climbed it one winter in the hope that the snow would make it more interesting. It was the day after New Year and freezing cold, but the sky was bright blue with not a cloud in sight.

A long drive up the Hydro Board road in Glen Turret ends at the dam at the south end of Loch Turret. From here a track leads along the east side of the loch to the far end, where it follows the feeder stream north through an interesting glaciated area, with mounds of moraine still clearly evident. An easy climb took me onto the snow covered summit ridge. The effect of the sun on the snow and ice was magical and I tried to take some photos but the strong wind and sub-zero temperatures kept freezing the camera and it refused to work.

From the top I followed the ridge south-west for a short distance to avoid a line of crags, then dropped down to the south to pick up the line of a stream which led me quickly back to the head of Glen Turret. That just left a short walk back alongside the loch to the dam.

Section 2: Rannoch & Glen Lyon; Ben Lawers; Mamlorn; Bridge of Orchy

Schiehallion   3,547ft

An uneventful little walk saw me up and down Schiehallion in poor weather, which meant I saw none of its famed views. The usual way up starts at a Forestry Commission car-park at Braes of Foss, from where an obvious track climbs up over open moorland. When you reach the hill you climb diagonally up to the ridge, to be faced with an unexpectedly long slog over boulders, which eventually leads you to the summit trig point.

A later visit in better weather was more fun as I ran up and down the same route. I was training for a '*KIMM*' and in good form and just cruised up to the summit ridge. Boulder hopping at speed was a more risky business, which brought some concerned looks from the many walkers. The descent along the ridge at speed was even more hair-raising but once off the boulders it was only a matter of minutes back to the car.

Creag Mhor   3,200ft   Carn Mairg   3,419ft

When I set out from Invervar in Glen Lyon I planned to climb four Munros, including Carn Gorm and Meall Garbh, but the atrocious weather made me change my mind half-way through the walk.

A path took me up through the forest and once out alongside the stream I crossed over and followed the Allt Coir Cheareaill up to a small bothy. Crossing the stream again I set off following a bearing up the grassy slope opposite, then up the ridge onto Creag Mhor. There was still quite a lot of old snow lying about and combined with the low cloud this made visibility poor to say the least. The rising wind was bitterly cold and I kept moving quickly down to the col to the north, still on a bearing, and then more slowly up onto Carn Mairg.

These hills are rather featureless and after having left Carn Mairg I seemed to be spending a long time going nowhere. I must have been quite some way along the ridge to Meall Garbh when, with the rain lashing down, I decided to call it a day; I dropped south to descend as quickly as possible, out of the clouds and out of the full force of the wind. The forest above Invervar eventually came into view and I splashed down the track back to the road to end a disappointing day.

Carn Gorm 3,370ft   Meall Garbh 3,200ft

Having failed to climb these two on my first trip, when I only made it as far as Creag Mhor and Carn Mairg, I had to make a return visit to Invervar.

I followed the track in, up alongside Invervar Burn and crossed to its west bank near the northern extremity of the forest. Here I took to the drab hillside for a long drag of a climb up onto Carn Gorm. Although far from perfect the weather was a lot better on this occasion and I had no trouble finding the north-east ridge leading out to the 'top', An Sgor. Continuing out to the north-east a short rise led to the stony summit of Meall Garbh.

I toyed with the idea of going on to the other two peaks that I'd climbed previously so as to complete the horse-shoe round of four Munros, but I had little enthusiasm for the area and instead just headed out to the 'top' of Meall Luaidhe, just a short distance away.

From the ridge I dropped down the grassy hillside to reach a stream, which I was following down towards Invervar Burn, when a terrible smell reached me. A few yards later I found the cause; in the stream was the bloated carcass of a large deer. I hoped that the people of Invervar didn't take their water direct from the hill as they do in Lochearnhead, and continued down to the burn and back out to the road.

The one highlight of the day was before I even reached Invervar. As I was driving there I had to cross the moor between Crieff and Kenmore; I spotted an owl hunting and stopped to watch for several minutes as the owl flew back and forth across the moors searching for food, it then swooped to the ground and presumably struck its prey, as it remained hidden from view thereafter.

Stuchd an Lochain   3,144ft

It must be said that this is not the most exciting of hills. From Glen Lyon I drove up to the dam at the east end of Loch an Daimh; from the dam I set off on foot, following a land-rover track a short way round the end of the loch before taking to the open hillside. It was a fairly steep climb up into heavy rain clouds. On reaching the crest of the ridge an old fence guides one along to the 'top' of Sron Chona Choirein. Leaving the 'top' I continued on along the ridge as it rounded the steep corrie to the north; a mile or so later a short rise found me beside the cairn on Stuchd an Lochain, with wild looking crags dropping steeply down into the gloomy corrie.

I planned on dropping down to the loch via the mountain's northern slopes but decided that the walk back along the lochside would be very wet after all the recent rain. Instead I stayed high and retraced my steps, back along the ridge, round to the cairn on Creag an Fheadain; from here I dropped straight back down to the land-rover track at the end of the loch. A few minutes later I was changed into dry clothes, drinking several cups of tea and eating sticky buns at the excellent tea-room at Bridge of Balgie.

A year or two later I was back in the area for the 'KIMM', which was being run from a camp-site on the south side of Loch Rannoch. The first day was a long one, over very rough terrain. We raced south from the lochside and passed just below Meall Buidhe, which lies to the north of Loch an Daimh. After rounding the end of the loch we had to virtually climb Stuchd an Lochain before dropping down to the over-night camp beside the wild Lochan nan Cat. Teams continued to arrive late into the night; as we cooked our evening meal and made several 'brews' we watched with some concern as the head-torches slowly descended the steep mountain to the final control. It was a cold, damp and rather gloomy place to camp on a wet October weekend and we were glad to leave next morning.

Day 2 started with a steep climb up into the mist to cross the ridge before dropping down to cross the River Lyon below the dam on Stronuich Reservoir. After making our way over the hills we crossed the Glen Lyon road at Innerwick to face one final climb, up into snow showers as we crossed the intervening ridge, which led us back down to the finish at the camp-site beside Loch Rannoch. Weather-wise the second day had been a lot worse than the first, and we were relieved to make it back to the finish with no navigational errors.

Meall Buidhe   3,054ft

This was an easy one to while away a lazy afternoon. Just driving there took longer than the walk itself.

I drove over the pass and down into Glen Lyon then followed the narrow road to the dam at the east end of Loch an Daimh. Taking straight to the hillside from the dam I climbed steadily up into the clouds and drizzle. Eventually I reached the ridge line and this led easily round to the mountain's south-east 'top'. From this 'top' the grassy ridge turned north and an easy mile soon passed before a short rise led onto Meall Buidhe itself. From the summit there wasn't much to do except return by the same way that I had come, back down to the car at the dam. The best part of the day was the home-baking and large pot of tea at the Bridge of Balgie tea-rooms.

Although not an inspiring hill on its own it looked as though there could be a good long run; from the dam up to Meall Buidhe; south-west over grassy ridges to Meall Cruinn and Creag Riabhach, crossing the river, the Eas Daimh, high up on the hill; then south over a different Meall Buidhe; round the south side of the loch onto Stuchd an Lochain; and then back to the dam.

Beinn Ghlas   3,657ft   Ben Lawers   3,984ft
Meall Garbh   3,661ft   Meall Greigh   3,280ft

This group of hills has given me many days of enjoyment in all weathers and all seasons; alone, with friends or leading parties; walking, running and skiing.

The easy way, and the way I first climbed Beinn Ghlas and Ben Lawers, is to start from the National Trust Visitor Centre, where you are already around 1,500ft up the hill. A well made and unmissable footpath climbs into the corrie, before climbing more steeply up the southern flank of Beinn Ghlas. Once onto the ridge proper the angle eases off and apart from one or two rocky outcrops, which are easily passed, there are no difficulties. From the summit the ridge narrows and drops to a col from where a steep climb leads up to Ben Lawers' massive cairn. It is said that the cairn was built so high in an effort to push the peak above the 4,000ft mark. Returning by the same route gives a shortish day but an enjoyable one. In winter conditions, with the tourist path covered in snow and ice, the peaks take on a whole new seriousness and I had a great day one November when the winter came early and the snow was in perfect condition.

The first time I completed the whole ridge, including Meall Garbh, Meall Greigh and the craggy 'top' of An Stuc (note 1), was on a glorious day one May. Starting at the Visitor Centre I was soon up and over Beinn Ghlas and onto Ben Lawers, which was still covered in snow. From here I followed the ridge north over rocks and boulders to a 'top', Creag an Fhithich, which looks down into a lonely corrie and a small blue lochan. A short descent to a col, where I disturbed a couple of deer, then a steeper climb led up onto another 'top', An Stuc. The descent from here calls for a little more care as it is steep and loose, but outside of winter it isn't dangerous and you are soon on the climb, on easier ground, to Meall Garbh. A short descent over rough tussocks leads to the last climb up easy grassy slopes onto Meall Greigh, over-looking Loch Tay. The problem with this route is that you are now a long way from home.

A descending traverse to the south-west to cross the Lawers Burn, near it's outlet from the lochan, enables you to pick up a land-rover track which traverses beneath Ben Lawers. On this occasion I then climbed north, up alongside a stream to regain the ridge between Ben Lawers and Beinn Ghlas. A short way below the ridge I disturbed a ptarmigan and found it's nest, complete with three eggs. From the ridge it was only a short climb over Beinn Ghlas and back down to the Visitor Centre.

At a later date, with a party of Scouts and Guides, I arranged for the coach to drop us off at Lawers Village on the road alongside Loch Tay, from here we were able to do the east/west traverse of the four Munros and be picked up from the Visitor Centre at the end of the day; a far easier way of doing the traverse. On this walk, around the time of the second May Bank Holiday, we arrived at the summit of Ben Lawers having seen virtually no one all day, only to find that we could hardly reach the cairn. There must have been over 100 people on top and we only found somewhere to sit some 50ft below the summit.

Meall a'Choire Leith 3,033ft   Meall Corranaich 3,530ft

The first time that I visited this pair of uninteresting hills was on a dull summers' day when I was happy to just have a short walk. Parking at the cairn on the watershed of the Lochan na Lairige pass I took to the heather and headed for the Allt Gleann Da-Eig. The deep heather made for slow going but once across the stream I started climbing into Coire Gorm, then up the grassy slopes onto Meall a'Choire Leith itself. From the cairn a ridge ran south down to a col at the head of Coire Gorm, an easy climb then led quickly up the grassy ridge to Meall Corranaich. From the top I followed it's south-western ridge for a short while before aiming back towards the car by the cairn.

A year or two later found me camped for a couple of days at the head of Gleann Da-Eig with a party of young Scouts. After a morning spent scrambling up the stream bed, we left the tents and made a rising traverse into Coire Gorm and then easily up onto Meall a'Choire Leith. From here we made our way down the ridge to the col and up the far side onto Meall Corranaich. I had my hands full trying to stop the kids going too fast down the steep grassy slopes back to camp. I knew that it would be very easy for one of them to slip and if they did, they would have gone a long way before stopping. However, they were blessed with the ignorance of youth and wanted to race down like madmen.

Meall nan Tarmachan 3,421ft

By starting near Lochan na Lairige you have already climbed over half way up this interesting little hill and there is only another 1,600ft to go.

My first visit was from the Scout Station at Lochearnhead while leading on one of the courses. We started by the large cairn marking the watershed of the pass and on a rather dreary winter's day climbed onto the mountain's long north ridge. This gave us an easy approach and after reaching the cairn we returned back along the ridge, teaching ice-axe and crampon techniques along the way.

I returned another winter, on my own; it was New Years Day, the snow conditions were superb and the sun was shining from a clear blue sky. From the dam at the southern end of the loch I ducked under the pipeline and climbed directly up the hillside. One or two steep little gullies linking the terraces gave some exciting moments and it didn't take long until I was up on the ridge and beside the cairn. The day was magical; I could clearly see far off Ben Nevis and away out to the Cairngorms.

4: *Celebrating New Year on Meall nan Tarmachan*

With crampons biting into the firm snow I followed the ridge south-west to the 'top' of Meall Garbh, continued to the col and along to the next 'top' of Beinn nan Eachan. I then headed out to take in the new 'top' of Creag na Caillich; this was shown on the first series metric maps as 911m (2,990ft) but has since been re-surveyed at 916m (3,005ft). As it was such a fine day I was in no hurry to return; instead of dropping down from the last top, I stayed high and retraced my steps back along the ridge, reaching Meall nan Tarmachan again just as the sun was starting to go down behind Ben More and Stob Binnein.

Unfortunately days like this are all too rare, it was certainly one to treasure.

Meall Ghaordie   3,410ft

"Quite the dullest hill in the Southern Highlands". That was the opinion of Irvine Butterfield writing in his *The High Mountains* guidebook and after a short afternoon spent on its slopes I must say that I have to agree with him.

I parked near the bridge over the River Lochay and set to work on the relentless climb up the grass and heather, making straight for the trig point on Meall Ghaordie's summit. To return I kept high to take in a couple of low tops but once on Meall Taurnic I didn't really have much option other than to just drop back down the hillside to the glen below.

I suppose any day on the hill is a good one, and at least I was out of the house for the afternoon in the fresh air. Other than that there's not much more you can say about Meall Ghaordie.

Ben Challum   3,354ft   Creag Mhor 3,387ft
Beinn Heasgarnich 3,530ft

This trio of peaks gave me a fine walk one summer. Starting from the end of the public road in Glen Lochay I had a long walk in down the track to Batavaime. From here I climbed up into the glen of the Allt Challum and was half-way up the steep craggy hillside, making my way towards Ben Challum, when I noticed a shepherd working three dogs away in the distance. I didn't want to be in the way and was fascinated by the superb control he had over his dogs, so I sat beside a boulder for 20 minutes while they cleared the area and moved out of sight. I then continued the grassy scramble up to the ridge which was followed for the short distance to Ben

Challum's summit cairn. A short detour along a narrow crest soon gave me the mountain's south 'top' too.

With quite a way still to go I returned over Ben Challum and followed the ridge north-west down to a col, from where a big climb led up to the ridge of Cam Chreag. Once over the ridge a short drop led to a further col beneath the 'top' of Stob nan Clach. This top was soon reached and a fine ridge led round the head of the deep corrie onto Creag Mhor.

After dropping down through broken ground to a wide saddle, a ridge rising steeply up the far side led me to the 'top' of Stob an Fhir-bhogda. Here the angle eased as the ridge turned north and led gently up to the summit of Beinn Heasgarnich. The rough descent of almost 3,000ft down to Badour in Glen Lochay played havoc with my knees; I was just settling in to the 5 mile walk-out along the track when a car stopped and two walkers offered me a lift. It had been a long hard day and I couldn't refuse.

I had visited Beinn Heasgarnich previously one Easter when leading on an *ITC* based at Lochearnhead. That year I was blessed with a really enthusiastic group; three Scouts and two Guides, and it was perhaps the happiest of all the courses I led on. For our three day high-camp I had brought them to Glen Lochay, where we camped in a delightful spot beside a burn above Batavaime. From the tents we climbed the steep grassy slopes and eventually came out onto crisp snow. They led the way to the 'top' of Stob an Fhir-bhogda and without any difficulty along the main ridge to Beinn Heasgarnich. We had lunch a short way below the summit in Coire Ban Mor, and then spent some time practicing with our ice-axes. I left them to enjoy themselves in the sunshine and snow, while I started to dig a snow-hole. They were surprised at how quickly one person could construct a reasonably sized shelter and they wouldn't believe me when I told them how warm it would be. They were glad that they wouldn't have to use it; instead I made them take us back to the tents by a devious route to give them more practice with the compass. The evening was spent singing songs, led by the girls, not around a roaring camp-fire but around a spluttering primus stove.

Meall Glas   3,139ft   Sgiath Chuil   3,016ft

The first time that I climbed Meall Glas was another of those occasions when I was camped in Glen Lochay for a three day high-camp when leading on a course at Lochearnhead.

It was New Year; there was no snow to be seen, just incessant rain and low cloud. From our tents near Batavaime we crossed the river and set to work on the climb up the north-west ridge of Meall Glas. It was an unexciting climb in almost zero visibility but once on the ridge you always knew roughly where you were; nevertheless we were pleased when the cairn appeared right on cue. We then followed the broad ridge round the corrie and out to the 'top', Beinn Cheathaich. From here we dropped down the north ridge, aiming for the bridge across the river, leaving a short walk back to camp.

Sometime later I returned to Glen Lochay on my own, parked at the locked gate, and walked-in down the track. Crossing the river at Lubchurran I made the seemingly endless trudge up the broad ridge to the 'top' of Meall a'Churain. From here the ridge levelled out and led to the Munro, Sgiath Chuil; which was half a mile away and just a metre or two higher. Things became a little more interesting on the steep rough descent to the col to the west, from where a long climb led up into the clouds, but once the ridge steepened I knew I was almost at Beinn Cheathaich, a 'top', and was soon beside the trig point. An easy mile or so along the ridge then brought me to Meall Glas. It was too cold to linger so I just dropped straight down to the north, aiming for the bridge at Badour. Once I was over the river I had a long walk-out back along the land-rover track to the car.

Beinn Dorain   3,524ft   Beinn an Dothaidh   3,289ft
Beinn Achaladair 3,404ft   Beinn a'Chreachain   3,540ft

Beinn an Dothaidh will always have a special place in my thoughts, and no doubt my sister Maggie's too. We both took a big fall there and were very fortunate to be able to walk away from it, but more of that later.

The peak of Beinn Dorain throws down a magnificent, almost perfect mountain shape when seen from the A82 as you cross the pass from Tyndrum. The usual route starts from Bridge of Orchy station; after crossing through the under-pass a good footpath climbs alongside the stream into Coire an Dothaidh. A further short steep climb leads to a broken ridge which is followed easily along to Beinn Dorain's summit cairn at the far end of the ridge. On my first visit there was still some late lying snow in the sheltered spots on the ridge and I enjoyed great views across to the Crianlarich peaks in the south and over to the wilderness of peaks to the south of Glen Coe. After retracing my steps back down to the saddle I then faced a steep climb to the summit of Beinn an Dothaidh. It didn't take long to return down to the saddle where the footpath took me back to the station.

I returned to the area one November when my sister and some friends were staying at Tyndrum for the weekend. I met them in their hotel on Sunday morning; several of the group were late down for breakfast, this had a knock-on effect in that we were also late in setting out for our walk. Initially we had planned to make a south to north traverse of all four Munros and to make things easier a car was dropped at Achallader Farm to save a long walk back. By the time we were ready to leave Bridge of Orchy station it was already late and we decided to miss the detour out to Beinn Dorain, instead we made our way up to the saddle and from there headed straight for Beinn an Dothaidh. It was a slow climb; one of the party complained of sore feet and turned back after just half an hour, the rest of us reached the summit and as we did the weather deteriorated, the clouds closed in and it was generally pretty miserable.

After a brief discussion it was agreed we should abandon the proposed route and just head down the ridge to the saddle to the east and from there drop down into Coire Achaladair and walk out to the farm where the car had been dropped off earlier. As we were now heading down there seems to have been a lapse in concentration and somehow we veered slightly off the ridge and found ourselves above steep slopes; broken ground that was a mix of crags and steep grass. The ground was saturated and covered in an inch or so of very wet slush.

Suddenly Maggie slipped and disappeared down the face of the mountain. It was so steep that she was hidden from view and as we heard no answer to our anxious shouts I un-strapped my ice-axe and started to descend a steep grassy gully. I had only taken a couple of steps when I too slipped on the slush; I tried braking with the ice-axe but it was useless and I found myself falling, sometimes free, then a bump, then free again. After several seconds I realised that this particular free-fall was lasting longer than the rest and I remember thinking 'I hope this doesn't hurt too much when I do come down to earth'. The next thing I knew was that I had landed in snow, so deep and soft, that I hadn't felt any bump at all on landing. Maggie quickly came over, somewhat surprised at having seen me hurtling through space to join her. She had been lucky too; we had both landed where the snow had slid down off the mountain, forming a deep soft cushion. The fall must have been around 150ft to 200ft.

> *"Climb if you will, but remember that courage and strength are naught without prudence, and that a momentary negligence may destroy the happiness of a lifetime. Do nothing in haste; look well to each step; and from the beginning think what may be the end."*

(Edward Whymper and plaque at Lochearnhead Scout Station)

The rest of the group traversed around the top of the craggy section and joined us; we then had a quick conference. Maggie was uninjured but possibly in a state of shock, as was I, who also had a few cuts and bruises, caused by my flailing ice-axe. Once we had confirmed where we were, we realised we had fallen into Coire a'Ghabhalach. The rest of the group took some of our kit from us and we slowly climbed to the col between Beinn Dorain and Beinn an Dothaidh, before making our way back to Bridge of Orchy.

We can't have looked a pretty sight as we waited in the hotel, drinking coffee while the car was collected from Achallader. The others insisted on taking me to hospital in Stirling before they continued on their journey down to Newcastle. I had a deep cut on my hand stitched and was given the all-clear. A few days later I went back to hospital and asked them to x-ray my hand; when they did it was found that I had a small break near the wrist and I was in plaster for the next few weeks.

Since then I have successfully done the route that we originally planned. The first was a long walk, again starting from Bridge of Orchy, up Beinn Dorain and Beinn an Dothaidh. This time I found the correct way down the ridge to the col above Coire Daingean; from the col a long grassy ridge climbed to the south 'top' of Beinn Achaladair and from there up to the main summit itself. A short descent to a narrow col then led to a climb out to the 'top' of Meall Buidhe, the narrow ridge winding round to the north-east for a final climb up onto Beinn a'Chreachain. From here it is a long way back to the station at Bridge of Orchy. Going down into the glen to follow the railway all the way back looked as though it would be hard work, so instead I stayed high and returned the way I had come. I passed round below Beinn an Dothaidh in an effort to see where we had fallen, but it all looked very different in summer.

The second time over the round of four Munros was done as a run. The day started in scorching hot weather and I had to wear sun-hat and sun-glasses right from the off; the sweat poured off me as I ran the now familiar path from the station up to the saddle and on up to Beinn Dorain. The descent back to the col gave me the chance to have a breather and let my pulse settle before the climb up onto Beinn an Dothaidh. I was soon down at the col to the east but as I started on the climb to Beinn Achaladair I realised that the weather was turning and by the time I reached Meall Buidhe I had to put my wind-proof on; as the day had started so well, that was all I had with me. On reaching the summit of Beinn a'Chreachain it was clear I should drop lower rather than return over the tops; it was a bad mistake not having anything to cover my legs as the cold wind, combined with the drizzle, was quickly chilling me. I followed the ridge back to the col between Meall Buidhe and Beinn Achaladair, before dropping steeply down to the north. It was steep enough to need care for the first few hundred feet but then the angle eased, as did the wind, and I contoured round the hillside, gradually descending and traversing until I reached a new plantation of trees alongside the railway. This forced me into an unexpected climb to go up and around it, but eventually I reached the station after a particularly good day, full of contrasts.

Beinn Mhanach   3,125ft

I wasn't expecting anything much from this lonely little hill, but the weather and snow combined to turn it into a surprisingly good day out.

I parked near Auch and walked down the road to the farm. Here the road gave way to a land-rover track, which led up the glen and under the sweep of the railway viaduct. It was a glorious spring morning and the three miles along the track soon passed. I stopped for a bite to eat near the ruins at the head of the glen; then the hard work began as I set to work on the steep grassy slopes leading to the 'top' Beinn a'Chuirn. It was uniformly steep and the ground quite wet from the recently thawed snow. A few hundred feet below the summit I came onto snow; it was perfect and just needed one firm kick to give a good step.

From the top I ran down the easy snow slope to the saddle, the crisp cold air and blue sky was magical. The sun had been to work on the snow leading to the summit of Beinn Mhanach and it was a harder job on this last short climb.

Sometimes the snow would support me, other times the crust would give way and I'd sink in. Once at the cairn I was able to make the most of the fine weather and have an unusually long lunch stop, enjoying the extensive views.

I started back down towards the saddle and then swung off to follow tongues of snow wherever possible, as these gave a good fast descent. All too soon I was back onto steep grass, which I zigzagged down to reach the track in the glen below. The walk-out was a pleasant stroll, there being no need to rush, and what's more, the sun was still shining!

Section 3: Cruachan Group; Glen Etive; Corrie Ba; Glencoe & Aonach Eagach; Appin

Stob Diamh   3,272ft   Ben Cruachan   3,695ft

My first time to Ben Cruachan was on a fairly dull summers' day. I started from St Conan's Kirk and walked in the three miles along the hydro-board road to the dam at the south end of Cruachan Reservoir. The long walk in was enlivened by watching a shepherd training four dogs, all of whom were working at once, although the youngest of the four didn't seem overly keen to do as it was told.

From the dam I took to the hillside and climbed diagonally up past the crags beneath Beinn a'Bhuiridh and on up to the ridge near the col, this then gave an easy walk up to the 'top' of Stob Garbh. A short descent to the north then gave a similarly short climb up to the cairn on Stob Diamh. Now in thick mist I set the compass to make sure I found the right ridge to take me out on a detour to another 'top' Sron an Isean. Leaving the top I passed beneath the summit of Stob Diamh and continued on along the main ridge, over the boulders and keeping an eye out for the crags dropping away on my right. This 'edge' guided me round to the spur of Drochaid Glas, which is another 'top'.

The narrow ridge continued round above the reservoir until a final steepening in the ridge took me up onto Ben Cruachan itself, the highest point of the horse-shoe. After a brief rest at the trig-point I made the short detour out to the west for the 'top' of Stob Dearg. From here I retraced my steps to the col, then contoured round to the south of Ben Cruachan to another col, which left just a short climb to the day's final 'top' Meall Cuanail. Continuing south the ridge then gave easier grassy slopes all the way back down to the dam and the long walk back to the roadside at Loch Awe.

I returned a year or two later, when the first snows of winter were covering the peaks; this time I started from the Visitor Centre in the Pass of Brander. It was a steep initial climb, up alongside a stream to come out onto the hydro-board road just below the dam. I decided to do the route in the opposite direction and from the dam a straightforward climb took me up the grassy slopes to Meall Cuanail. The short drop to the col beyond saw me onto the snow, which took me up the ridge towards Ben Cruachan. With shorter daylight hours and the worry of possibly being locked in the Visitor Centre car-park, I missed out the detour to the 'top' to the west and headed straight for Ben Cruachan's summit cairn.

The snow covered boulders made for slower going than usual and I didn't have the views I'd hoped for, nevertheless it was an enjoyable scramble along the ridge to Drochaid Glas and on up to Stob Diamh. I wasn't tempted by the eastern 'top' this time and instead just continued on the main line of the ridge to Stob Garbh. From here I dropped down to the col where I left the snow behind, and was back onto heather and grass for the descent to the dam. It didn't take long to drop down the steep footpath, cross the railway, and so back to the Visitor Centre, where thankfully the car-park gates were still open.

Beinn a'Chochuill   3,215ft   Beinn Eunaich   3,242ft

It was in October when I climbed this pair of peaks; starting from the track that leads to Castles Farm at the west end of Glen Strae. Almost a dozen Land-Rovers and Range-Rovers were parked nearby, which suggested that there was stalking going on somewhere nearby, but I decided to risk it.

A broad track led up the hillside, above the Allt Mhoille, and after a couple of miles or so I came to a junction in the track. This was the cue to take to the hillside for the undemanding climb to the ridge above. Once on the ridge it was followed easily out to the west to the cairn marking Beinn a'Chochuill.

With no sign of the stalking party I returned along the ridge with a clear conscience and dropped down to the col. A climb of around 900ft then saw me by the large cairn of Beinn Eunaich. After a quick bite to eat I followed the long south ridge which led easily down to regain the land-rover track a short way above the farm.

All in all it had been a fairly unremarkable day.

Beinn nan Aighenan   3,141ft

For some reason I omitted this peak when I climbed it's near neighbour, Ben Starav. I know it was another of those wet and cloudy days; Beinn nan Aighenan was off the main ridge, which would have meant a detour, it was also over a fold in the map, so it was not immediately obvious that there was another Munro here.

Rather than the long drive round into Glen Etive, I decided on an approach from the east, from Victoria Bridge. It was a fine summer day and I made good time along the land-rover track, past the small Climbing Club hut, through the forest, past the farm at Clashgour and over the river. Once across the river the track faded to a footpath which led west into the vast moors around Loch Dochard. After crossing the watershed I reached a bridge, crossed the River Kinglass and made my way up the valley of Coire na Caime. The hillsides were teeming with deer in this very remote spot and I was glad of the excuse of stopping to watch them as I had by now covered 10 miles and still hadn't even set foot on the mountain.

There was no path in the glen and as the river was almost dry it was quicker and easier to walk along the rock slabs which were showing in the river bed. A short climb then led out of the corrie and up onto the saddle beyond Beinn nan Aighenan. Once on the col it was a straightforward walk up to the summit. It was a rare day and I was able to sunbathe on top for a while but I was dehydrated and was keen to reach the stream for a drink. I headed off to the east before dropping down the craggy nose to take me back to the River Kinglass a short distance below the bridge. The good path then led back past the loch, along the river and eventually back to Victoria Bridge. I had my stove in the boot of the car, so the kettle was soon on while I changed out of my boots to end a long, hard, but very satisfying day.

Ben Starav 3,541ft   Glas Bheinn Mhor 3,258ft Stob Coir'an Albannaich 3,425ft Meall nan Eun   3,039ft

After the long drive down Glen Etive it was a relief to finally reach the parking place by the track which leads down to the bridge across the river near Coileitir.

The day was warm and promised to improve as I set off on a footpath alongside the river. After crossing a bridge the hard work started; a path led up an interesting ridge that climbed steadily to reach the trig point on Ben Starav. Ben Starav is another of those confusing mountains where the trig point is not on the highest point; here the true top, although only a metre or so higher, was a short distance along the ridge to the south-east. Unfortunately, as I climbed higher the clouds closed in and instead of improving, the weather rapidly grew worse; the wind built up and as the day wore on it brought driving rain.

After Ben Starav I had meant to take in Beinn nan Aighenan but 'out of sight, out of mind' as the saying goes. I couldn't see anything through the thick clouds, nor did I notice it on my map. I should have made a detour to 'bag' the Munro but it was hidden over the fold in my map, which was well wrapped up in my map-case to protect it from the hostile elements. It was only once I had returned home and had filled in the 'ticks' in the book that I realised that I had missed one out!

Instead I continued on along the undulating ridge to the grassy top of Glas Bheinn Mhor. From here a steep and slippery descent led to a col and a stiff climb up onto Stob Coir' an Albannaich. The big steep descent off Stob Coir' an Albannaich gave a few anxious moments but once on the col below I knew that the worst of it was behind me and made light work of the climb to Meall Tarsuinn, passed quickly over the top, and then up onto the ridge which led to Meall nan Eun.

From the cairn I returned to the col between it and Meall Tarsuinn before dropping quickly down into Coire Riabhach. It was very wet and generally pretty miserable as I tried to lose height as fast as I could. Eventually I picked up the footpath alongside the stream and this led easily down to the small farm at Glenceitlein above the River Etive. With just a mile to go, back along the land-rover track to the bridge near Coileitir, the sun decided to make a late but very welcome return, and I steamed along, both literally and metaphorically, as the sun dried me off.

Stob a'Choire Odhair 3,058ft   Stob Ghabhar   3,565ft
Creise   3,608ft   Meall a'Bhuiridh 3,636ft

One wet October weekend I walked in from Victoria Bridge up the *West Highland Way* as far as Ba Bridge. Here I headed up the stream towards Loch an Easain, then took to the steep hillside to climb Clach Leathad, disturbing several deer as I came out onto the crest of the ridge. From Clach Leathad, a 'top', I followed the ridge round the corrie and up a fairly steep, narrow ridge onto Meall a'Bhuiridh. From the top of the White Corries ski area I dropped carefully down the steep slopes to the south to regain my earlier route beside the stream, then down to the River Ba and back along the *West Highland Way* to Victoria Bridge.

Creise was climbed on its own when I was returning from a trip up north. With an hour or so to spare I stopped a short way down Glen Etive and made a quick dash up and down the rocky Sron na Creise ridge.

Towards the end of one winter I was back for the Stob Ghabhar group. I left Victoria Bridge and was soon at the club hut; the climb then started, up the footpath into Coire Toaig, from where I turned west and climbed the rough slopes of Aonach Eagach. At this point I came onto snow and watched a poorly equipped university party ambling along; they looked like an accident waiting to happen and I was pleased to get away from them. I quickly made my way up to Stob Ghabhar and out to the 'tops' of Sron a'Ghearrain and Stob a'Bhruaich Leith; from here I retraced my steps for a short way before contouring round to the north to pick up the outlying 'top' of Sron nan Giubhas. After a short steep descent I crossed the corrie and climbed the short distance to the saddle from where a ridge leads east for a short, icy scramble through the rocks onto Stob a'Choire Odhair. From this last summit I was soon down at the col to the south-east which gave an easy descent back to the track beside the Allt Toaig, down to the club hut and so back to Victoria Bridge.

I returned to the Black Mount group of hills for a long run one fine summer day. Starting at Victoria Bridge I ran in along the land-rover track to the club hut, here I turned north up the wet and sometimes boggy footpath, which climbed steadily up into the corrie. Leaving the path at about the 450m contour I took to the rough hillside for the climb up onto Stob a'Choire Odhair. It was good to have a bit of a rest on the rocky descent to the saddle before another rough scramble led to the 'top' of Aonach Eagach. From here it was good running terrain, along a rough ridge around the impressive corrie onto Stob Ghabhar.

Although the day was staying fine a cold wind had sprung up so I kept moving fast; out on a detour to the west, on good grass and a little old snow, so the 'tops' of Sron a'Ghearrain and Stob a'Bhruaich Leith were soon reached, then it was back towards Stob Ghabhar until I could contour round it's north ridge to collect the 'top' of Sron nan Giubhas. I followed an interesting ridge away to the north-west for a short while before dropping down to the saddle to the north. Here I found water for a long awaited drink, which set me up for the climb to another fine 'top' Clach Leathad. A blustery wind was making it difficult to run over the stony plateau but the next three tops weren't far away. A short rise led to Mam Coire Easain, from where a narrow ridge continued north out to Creise, and a little further, at the far end of the ridge another 'top', Stob a'Ghlais Choire. I had to return along the ridge to Mam Coire Easain from where I dropped down a rocky buttress to the east for a short, somewhat airy, run along a ridge before scrambling up the crest onto the day's final summit, Meall a'Bhuiridh, at the head of the Glen Coe ski area.

The steep descent to the south looks uninviting, but I had done it before, so after continuing a short way along the ridge I dropped down the hillside, constantly changing direction as I sought out the safest and most runnable line through the scree and boulders. Once in the glen below I traversed and descended at will, aiming for a corner of woodland; here I picked up a boggy footpath which led me out to the land-rover track. This is part of the *West Highland Way* and I passed dozens of heavily laden walkers as I ran the last few miles back to Victoria Bridge. It was a great route giving four Munros and six 'tops' in 21 miles of running with around 7,000ft of climbing.

Buachaille Etive Mor – Stob Dearg   3,345ft

I'd wanted to climb 'the Buachaille' by the Curved Ridge route, which is a long hard scramble, but on the day the weather was awful, with cloud down to the 1,000ft level. I decided it was too risky to go climbing alone up the east face to try to find the route, and instead set off from the car-park below the Devil's Staircase. The track led past the Climbing Club cottage at Lagangarbh and straight up into Coire na Tulaich. This gave a steady climb ending at a steep headwall, made up of loose scree, which opened out onto a col at around 3,000ft. From here, even in thick cloud, it was easy to follow the ridge which climbed through boulders first east, then north-east, to reach the summit cairn. There was no view and it was too cold to stop so I quickly retraced my steps back to the col.

Once at the col a long ridge snaked southwards and the going was quite good over the three 'tops' of Stob na Doire, Stob Coire Altruim and Stob na Bròige (note 1). I had hoped for good views off the last top, out over the long expanse of Loch Etive, but the cloud refused to lift so I just returned along the ridge to the first col, and dropped back down into Coire na Tulaich and back to the road.

I made another attempt to climb Curved Ridge one winter, when a couple of us 'went to have a look'. Unfortunately the conditions meant that the rocks were glazed with ice which really slowed us down and we decided to retreat to the Kingshouse. As it turned out this was a good move because within minutes we were being hammered by torrential, freezing rain. We were glad that we were on our way down and not still fighting our way up, and were thus spared to fight another day. That day came the following summer when we easily found the route and had a great time. We scrambled up Curved Ridge with no problems at all, and then carried on to complete the whole ridge, including all the 'tops' for another great day out.

Buachaille Etive Beag – Stob Dubh   3,129ft

The climb up to, and traverse of, the ridge was only ever going to make this a short day, so I stopped off to climb it when returning from a trip further north, rather than make a special journey for this alone.

From the road I set off for a short distance along the Lairig Eilde track, but after only half a mile I turned off and climbed the steep grassy flank towards the 'top' of Stob Coire Raineach (note 1). From here a short descent to the south led to a col, where a narrow ridge runs parallel to the Buachaille Etive Mor ridge; I continued on to the end and the main summit of Stob Dubh. The clouds were coming and going so that every now and again Beinn Fhada would loom up out of the mist. It didn't take long to return to the col from where a diagonal line took me back to the Lairig Eilde track and so back to the car.

Bidean nam Bian   3,766ft

This huge, sprawling mountain on the south side of Glen Coe surprisingly only boasts one Munro (note 1), although it has several satellite 'tops'. It is approachable from any number of directions and is almost guaranteed to give you a good day out.

My first time up Bidean nam Bian came one Easter when I was camped by the old bridge opposite Achnambeithach for five days as part of an *Advanced Techniques Course* based from Lochearnhead. The snow conditions were good above about 2,000ft. We followed the path up from Achnambeithach and climbed high into Coire nam Beith. When we reached the buttress of Stob Coire nam Beith we headed into the left hand glen to climb steeply but easily up the snow to the col between Stob Coire nan Lochan and Bidean nam Bian. From the col it was only a few minutes work to reach the cairn on the main summit. From here we returned to the col and retraced our steps down into the corrie; we stopped when we found a suitable spot as we weren't returning to the tents but planned to dig snow-holes for the night.

We were lucky to find an almost complete igloo in the corrie, this was finished off by one pair, one of whom had his arm in plaster and couldn't dig properly. The other pairs set to work and it probably took us a full two hours to construct our shelter, but it was a very good one. First we dug a tunnel, about four feet deep, down into a gently sloping bank of snow. We then started to dig horizontally to form a sleeping chamber, about 6' 6" by 4'. Only one of us could work in the tunnel at a time, the other hauled the debris out and tried to keep the entrance clear. We dug a pit at one end for the colder air to sink into, and once the 'door' was in place it was really quite cosy. One small candle was all that was needed to light the snow-cave and we passed a surprisingly comfortable night. Like the others though we were up quite early the next morning and we were all back down at the camp in the glen for breakfast.

That afternoon, as we stood outside the tents drinking tea, a snow storm came in. We could see right down the glen and watched in fascination as the valley turned from its sombre brown to snow white; the storm moved quite slowly, and it was perhaps five minutes before the snow reached us, covering all in its path as it headed off to the west. Since then I've returned on many occasions but the experience of your first snow-hole, like many other 'firsts', is never forgotten.

Another good trip some years later was with a mixed group of Scouts and Guides; it was late May and the weather was perfect. We climbed up into Coire nan Lochan and pitched the tents beside the lochans. In the afternoon, leaving the girls to sunbathe, I took the lads to find a reasonably easy scramble directly up the north face of Stob Coire nan Lochan. From the top we dropped down the ridge to the east towards Gearr Aonach and returned to camp. It was a beautiful evening and we enjoyed a swim in the icy lochan before dinner, after which we wandered around the high corrie until very late, reluctant to go to bed until it was fully dark.

The following day we all climbed from the corrie, up to the col to the north of Stob Coire nan Lochan, and then up to the summit. Here, two of the girls had had enough, so I returned with them to just above the camp; when I knew they were safely down I headed back to catch up with the others and we reached the summit of Bidean nam Bian together. From the main summit we headed out on a detour to collect the 'top' of Stob Coire nam Beith before returning to the cairn on Bidean nam Bian. It was a grand day for the traverse east out to Stob Coire Sgreamhach [note 1], then north along the narrow ridge to Beinn Fhada. From here we returned along the ridge to Stob Coire nan Lochan and back down to our camp. In readiness for Aonach Eagach the following day we packed our rucksacks and moved camp down into Glen Coe, at my usual spot above the road junction.

On a couple of occasions in winter I've climbed up into the 'Lost Valley' of Coire Gabhail, up along the stream, through the jumble of boulders which choke the narrow entrance, then out onto the flatter meadow, where, rumour has it, raiders kept their stolen cattle in days gone by. Continuing up the glen there is a good little snow climb up to the right to come out at the col between Bidean nam Bian and Stob Coire nan Lochan. It's a good walk over these two tops and round to Stob Coire Sgreamhach. I took a great photo here one March, looking south down the trough of Glen Etive, over Loch Etive which was bounded on both side by snow capped mountains, with Ben Cruachan in the far distance. It was mid-afternoon and the photo was taken into the sun, which gave it a magical effect.

With the various ridges and glens there are endless permutations for coming and going. One summer I parked in the lay-by near the start of the Lairig Eildhe footpath. After following the footpath for a short distance I took to the hillside and climbed obliquely up the terraces onto the northern end of Beinn Fhada. The ridge then gave a pleasant walk along to its top; it was a short scramble up onto Stob Coire Sgreamhach; round to Bidean nam Bian, down to the col to the north and back to the road via the 'Lost Valley'.

It's easier to be more adventurous when you're in company. One summer with a friend we climbed up into Coire nan Lochan and found a good scramble on Barn Door Buttress, which eventually led to Aonach Dubh and from here we walked part of the ridge. The scramble was fun; quite hard, but not desperate and quite exposed, but not too frightening. One thing's for sure, Bidean nam Bian is never a dull mountain.

Aonach Eagach -
Sgorr nam Fiannaidh   3,173ft   Meall Dearg 3,118ft

My first trip along the famous Aonach Eagach ridge also almost proved to be my last trip anywhere!

Having stayed at the Glencoe Youth Hostel I climbed straight up the hillside from there to gain the col to the south of the Pap of Glencoe. It was early April and I came onto snow as I climbed from the col, up the rocky ridge onto the western end of Aonach Eagach; here the ridge levelled off and I was soon by the trig-point marking Sgorr nam Fiannaidh.

Leaving the summit on the obvious ridge running away before me, I could clearly see that there was a large cornice overhanging the cliffs to the north side of the ridge so I made sure that I stayed well away, more to the right, south side of the crest. Suddenly there was a muffled crack and I was staring down to the bottom of the glen, just inches away from my right boot. I had almost been caught out by a double cornice, a strip of snow some 20 yards long had fallen away and I breathed a heavy sigh of relief that I had not taken another step to my right.

"I began to understand how they can risk their lives for the purity of it all, the purity of old rock and the new snow, of the crystaline air and the cleanliness of the very danger to which they are exposed. For there could be nothing mean about death in such a place, terrible perhaps, but never squalid."
(Anon)

The 'top' of Stob Coire Leith was reached without further incident but from here I was on to the famous pinnacles. The bright weather and firm snow made for an interesting scramble and I had no difficulties until I arrived at the top of a sheer drop; a short rock-face fell steeply to a deep notch in the ridge. Being on my own and without a rope, I cast about for an easier way down; I knew that I shouldn't have to climb down the cliff and that there must be an easier way. After a few minutes I decided that the only feasible route was a steep, almost vertical wall of snow that dropped a short way down the north face of the ridge. I thought if I could find a way down there I could reach a terrace which would take me round to the notch. Kneeling on the ridge I reached blindly down with my feet and kicked small toe holds. I lowered myself over the edge and kicked more holds; I then realised that these were easier to form and I'd found a chain of old steps. Once used to the pattern of where the steps were it was easy to climb down.

Safely landed on the terrace I took a few deep breaths to calm the nerves and hoped that there wouldn't be too much more like that. Thankfully there wasn't, and the next couple of pinnacles gave easy scrambling and soon led me up to the summit of Meall Dearg. From here I was able to relax a little and enjoy the walk out to the 'top' of Am Bodach, which marks the eastern end of the ridge. Dropping down into the corrie to the east I followed the stream back down to the roadside where I was able to hitch a lift back to the Youth Hostel. It had been a superb day but the collapsing cornice and the unnerving climb down the wall of snow had given me a little more excitement than I had bargained for.

Since then I have returned many times. One occasion was on a warm August afternoon; this time I set off on an east/west traverse, starting with the climb up into the grassy corrie above Allt-na-reigh. The 'top' of Am Bodach was soon reached and the whole traverse was a delight. The only drawback was that several times I had to wait as other walkers negotiated tricky steps; the fine weather had encouraged every man and his dog out onto the hills and there were frequent queues. After leaving Sgorr nam Fiannaidh I headed for the path down alongside Clachaig Gully, which gave a hard descent, so I arrived at the doorstep of the Clachaig Hotel in a rather hot and dusty state. After a swift pint the three mile walk back up through the glen soon passed.

Another good trip was with a group of Scouts and Guides as part of a three-day camp in Glen Coe. It was Whitsun and the weather was glorious as we set off from Allt-na-reigh on the now familiar climb up into the corrie. The whole traverse went well and they all enjoyed the scrambling and the sense of exposure. On the final top, Sgorr nam Fiannaidh, we had stunning views out to the west, along Loch Leven to Loch Linhe. Leaving the summit we followed a spur running out to the south, which dropped down steep grassy slopes; we were ok as it was dry, but I wouldn't recommend this way if it's wet. This route led us straight back to the tents and after striking camp we had time to swim in the ice-cold waters of the River Coe while we waited for the minibus to collect us.

I usually seem to be lucky with the weather on Aonach Eagach, or perhaps it's just that I only choose to go on the ridge when I know the forecast is good. One fine day in late September, on the spur of the moment I decided on a day in the hills. With many peaks out-of-bounds due to stalking I returned to Glen Coe. It was already quite late in the day by the time I reached Allt-na-reigh for an east/west traverse. The hills were quiet at this time of day and I made good time, arriving at the west end of the ridge just as the sun was starting to go down. The view out to the west was spectacular as the sun set over Loch Leven and Loch Linhe. As usual the camera was at home when I needed it most.

Sgor na h-Ulaidh   3,258ft

Parking in the lay-by on the A82, just up from Achnacon, I set off down the farm track alongside the river, and out to the cottages and farm buildings of Gleann-leac-na-muidhe. Leaving the farm I had to cross a very muddy field to reach the hillside; the mud was so deep and so wet it came over the top of my boots. Not a good start!

It was good to climb up onto drier ground; a steep climb over grass and heather then took me along the ridge of Aonach Dubh a'Ghlinne. From here it was easier going along to a 'top', Stob an Fhuarain, at the southern end of the ridge.

I followed the ridge as it ran off down to the south-west, this in turn led to a short rocky scramble up to the cairn of Sgor na h-Ulaidh. After a short rest on top I retraced my steps through the rocky section down to the col, contoured round below the top of Stob an Fhuarain and returned to the ridge of Aonach Dubh a'Ghlinne. The steep descent gave me the chance to look for a better route to the track to avoid the mud; that then just left a mile back down the glen to the roadside.

All in all it was an uneventful and rather unexciting day.

Beinn Fhionnlaidh 3,145ft

I was undecided how best to climb Beinn Fhionnlaidh as the guide-book had some uncomplimentary things to say about the Forestry Commission who had planted heavily in the area, thus making some approaches tedious and difficult.

However, I enjoyed the walk in through the forest from Invercharnan in Glen Etive. It was a roasting hot summer day and the heat was making me feel unusually lethargic and in no mood for a hard walk. The track led through the forest to come out at a deer-fence by a stream. The mountain was now only a couple of miles away and it was good to be able to see where I was going for once, without the need for a map and compass. Crossing the stream I surprised a couple of elderly Guiders who were paddling in the cool water; their trousers rolled up to the knee.

It was a straightforward climb to the summit, over steepish broken grassy slopes. A cool wind was blowing on top so I found a sheltered spot amongst the rocks around the trig point and spent a peaceful hour brewing tea and relaxing. One thing that did strike me was that there was no sign of any wildlife whatsoever. Usually in places like this I would have expected to see deer, hare, grouse and other bird life, but apart from two or three other walkers, nothing stirred, perhaps it was the heat?

The return down the hill took only a matter of minutes as I jogged back to the forest where I picked up the track back out to the road.

Beinn Sgulaird   3,059ft

I climbed this remote peak to the west of Loch Etive one weekend when returning from Glen Coe via the west coast route. My map tells the story of the walk quite graphically; it virtually disintegrated in the downpour!

"I dreamed of a great mountain to be climbed the next day, but the rain came down in torrents and washed it all away."   (Anon)

I left the car by a farm in Glen Creran and, already dressed in full water-proofs, I set off in a torrential downpour. Within minutes I was soaked; it wasn't long before I was up in the clouds and that was the most I would see for the next hour or so, just the inside of a very wet cloud.

I splashed my way up alongside a burn and took a very direct route aiming straight for the summit. It wasn't a day to be hanging around, just a question of up and down as quickly as possible. More by luck than good judgement I came out onto the ridge only yards from the summit cairn. Return was by simply retracing my steps, so it wasn't long before I spotted the farm again and was soon at the car where I could empty my boots and change into warm, dry clothes.

Beinn a'Bheithir -
Sgorr Dhonuill   3,284ft   Sgorr Dhearg   3,361ft

My first visit to this interesting horse-shoe ridge, which overlooks the sea-lochs by the Ballachulish Bridge, was made one dull summer day. Starting from the edge of the forest near Ballachulish House I followed the Forestry Commission track up the glen. At that time I didn't know where I would be able to leave the forest and take to the open hillside, but as I'd hoped, a path appeared which seemed to be heading in the right direction. I followed the path and it soon brought me out to the edge of the forest.

From here I aimed for the col between the two peaks, climbing steeply up the rough heathery hillside to reach it. This then gave a steep pull up the narrow ridge to the west, up onto Sgorr Dhonuill. The usual grey weather meant that I didn't have the views from the top that I had hoped for so I turned around and returned to the col. A narrow ridge then climbed steadily up to the trig-point on Sgorr Dhearg. Without stopping I dropped a short way down to the east and continued along another narrow ridge out to the 'top' of Sgor Bhan.

Retracing my steps I contoured round below Sgorr Dhearg and picked up its north ridge, which was crossed to its western flank for the steep descent back to the forest where a path soon led me back to the forestry road and down to Ballachulish House.

The following winter I returned for a more interesting ascent; it was a glorious March day when I left the car in Ballachulish village. After following the track south for a short while I turned off and started up the steep grassy slopes which soon gave way to snow. As I gained the ridge I watched a pair of ptarmigan running around like headless chickens. Shortly below Sgor Bhan I stopped to strap on crampons and then made fast progress on firm snow up to its cairn. From here it took only a few minutes to climb to Sgorr Dhearg, where I joined several other parties for a leisurely lunch in the sun. It was great to enjoy fine views for a change, with the combination of snow covered peaks, sea-lochs and dark forestry plantations.

I was enjoying myself so much that I almost ran down to the col beyond, which isn't wise when you are still wearing crampons and heavy boots! The 800ft climb up the easy ridge to Sgorr Dhonuill was a breeze and I passed quickly over the top and down the wide ridge running out towards the sea to the west. Once I was sure I had passed the worst of the crags I dropped down, working my way through small rocky outcrops and slabs, to the edge of the forest. Here I picked up a path that led me to the forestry track for the walk-out back to the road at Ballachulish House. The only problem with this route was the three mile walk along the busy A82 from Ballachulish Bridge to Ballachulish Village to collect the car.

Section 4: The Mamores; Ben Nevis & Aonachs; Grey Corries; Loch Treig & Loch Ossian; Loch Ericht to Loch Laggan

The Mamores –

Mullach nan Coirean	3,077ft	Stob Ban	3,274ft
Sgurr a'Mhaim	3,601ft	Sgor an Iubhair	3,284ft
Am Bodach	3,382ft	Stob Coire a'Chairn	3,219ft
An Gearanach	3,230ft	Na Gruagaichean	3,442ft
Binnein Mor	3,700ft	Sgurr Eilde Mor	3,279ft
Binnein Beag	3,083ft		

My first visit to the Mamores was on a wet day late one October. I left the car-park at the head of Glen Nevis and walked up through the gorge to cross the river by the wire bridge at Steall Hut. Passing beneath the impressive waterfall I followed the south side of the river, under the craggy nose of An Gearanach and round into Coire Ghabhail. It was a wet climb up alongside the stream, into thick clouds. Higher up in the corrie I took a bearing to take me into the boggy Coire an Easain from where a short rough climb took me up onto the main ridge. Once on the ridge I was soon up on the summit of Na Gruagaichean, quickly followed by its north-west 'top'.

Thankfully I came out of the clouds for a while when I dropped west along the ridge before climbing back up into the gloom by the summit of Stob Coire a'Chairn. From here I turned north off the main ridge and dropped to the bealach for a short rocky climb to the 'top' of An Garbhanach before continuing on along the ridge to An Gearanach. The rock on this section was greasy and made for slow going but from this last summit I hoped that my troubles were over. Unfortunately the descent didn't go quite according to plan; I started by following a faint path down towards Steall Hut but after losing the path I ended up in a narrow gorge and tried to contour round to the woods above the hut. The ground here was just as steep and wet and I spent far longer than I should have, struggling down, until I eventually reached the wire bridge.

A day or two later I was back in Glen Nevis, with the sky looking as though it may clear and give a good day. It didn't on both counts. Having camped in the corner of the forest near Achriabhach I followed the footpath up through the forest and out into Coire Dearg. Here I turned directly up the tussocks and climbed to the ridge which led me up onto Mullach nan Coirean. As I climbed higher, the wind increased and I had a real battle as I fought my way round the rim of the corrie and up onto the summit cairn. With the clouds closing in, but the wind now behind me, I hurried along to the mountain's south-east 'top' and then on up to Stob Ban.

This was harder now as the wind kept knocking me off balance as I crossed the rough blocks and boulders. I didn't stop and continued down to the col, before a short rough scramble took me up onto Sgor an Iubhair (note 1). I could tell that on a good day the round of the whole Mamores Ridge would be fun but this wasn't a good day, so I was content to just walk along as far as Am Bodach. From here I returned to Sgor an Iubhair, fighting against the wind, before dropping down to the col to the north. I warily made my way along 'Devil's Ridge' but even in these rather grim conditions it was nowhere near as bad as the name suggests. Only the climb to Sgurr a'Mhaim spoilt it as I again had to scramble over rough wet boulders to the summit cairn. A bearing took me down off the north-west ridge to a rough path that led all the way back to Achriabhach.

The peaks at the eastern end of the ridge were climbed a year or two later, in November, from Kinlochleven. A footpath led up the glen to join a land-rover track, this track was then followed for a short way until another footpath led off heading north-east. After a short distance I quit this path and took directly to the hillside to climb steeply up onto the main ridge, coming out between Na Gruagaichean and the south 'top' of Binnein Mor. I was soon on the south 'top' of Binnein Mor and from here brief breaks in the clouds gave me glimpses down to the lochs and reservoirs below. An easy ridge took me out to Binnein Mor then I followed the ridge down to the NNW. When I could see that the route would 'go' I contoured round the rough hillside beneath the worst of the crags to reach the lochan on the col; from here a short steep climb up through boulders took me to the summit of Binnein Beag. Leaving the cairn I returned to the lochan on the col and followed a path round into Coire a'Bhinnein; from here there was a short climb up to another lochan before a further short steep climb to the day's final summit, Sgurr Eilde Mor.

I thought I had plenty of daylight left and there was no real urgency as I dropped down the hill to gain the path by the lochan, and then dropped to the land-rover track beside Loch Eilde Mor. I set off on the walk-out back to Kinlochleven but when I saw a footpath marked on the map I quit the track and, thinking it looked more direct, took the footpath. The path soon petered out and I was left floundering about on steep ground, in stream gullies and amongst the trees. Night fell quickly and this made progress even slower. In places I had to climb down from tree to tree but eventually the lights of Kinlochleven appeared ahead of me and I emerged somewhat relieved and rather weary, onto a path that led me back to the roadside.

The 1990 *Rock & Run Mountain Marathon* was based in Kinlochleven and courses were run over the Mamores and Grey Corries. Running with Paul again, our course led firstly up and over Sgor an Iubhair, round below Sgurr a'Mhaim and down to a cunningly placed control above Steall Hut. Crossing the river we then had a big climb into Coire nan Laogh below Aonach Beag. From here a long, difficult leg took us up and over the Grey Corries ridge, where long tongues of old snow gave us a fast run down to the control; we then had to climb back over the ridge to a control on the flank of Meall Mor; we camped that night beside the Meanach Bothy. Early next morning we set off on a slightly shorter Day 2; the route took us up to the lochan beneath Sgurr Eilde Mor; over Binnein Beag; down to the north then up and over Stob Coire a'Chairn; along to Am Bodach and down to the finish in Kinlochleven.

A year or two later, as detailed elsewhere in this journal, I ran the whole ridge, including the eleven Munros and all six 'tops', in one long round of around 22 miles with approximately 11,000ft of climbing, in a little over seven hours.

Ben Nevis   4,406ft   Carn Mor Dearg   4,012ft

My first visit to Britain's highest mountain was one Easter when a group of us had travelled up from Hertfordshire for a week's climbing, followed by a week leading on a course at Lochearnhead.

For some reason, either the weather, lack of time or sheer laziness, we simply followed the 'tourist path' up and down, starting from the Youth Hostel in Glen Nevis. The snow came quite a way down the hill and a couple of the lads played on short plastic skis on the descent. When we were on the summit plateau a small helicopter had been buzzing around and it landed nearby, we found out that they were a French film-crew gathering some shots of 'The Ben'.

A couple of days later and now in a more adventurous frame of mind, three of us returned to climb one of the gullies on the north face. To try and save some of the walk in we persuaded Geoff to drive us as far up the hill as possible in his van, but once in the forest the tracks led away from the hill and our search for a short-cut was abandoned. We returned to the road to use the usual start from near the Golf-Club on the A82. In a field beside the road was the helicopter that we had seen on the summit; we were walking past when the pilot said something to the effect of "Are you going up the hill?" When we said "Yes" he surprised us by saying "Give me a hand to refuel and I'll give you a lift up to the CIC hut". We thought he must be joking, but he wasn't. Stuart helped him pump some fuel from a large drum, then it was "Hop in" and we were off.

Instead of having to walk the two or three miles up the glen, with a climb of around 2,500ft, we were whisked up there in a couple of minutes. We landed just above the hut and jumped out with grateful thanks. The amusing thing was seeing some of the crew who were working on the film; they had walked up carrying heavy loads, probably taking almost two hours, while we had been given a free ride. They did give us a funny look as if to say, who the hell are those guys?

We were a bit overawed by the huge cliffs all around us but there were a few steep, snow-filled gullies that looked more inviting than the rock. We roped up and set off on what at that time was probably the most serious winter route that any of the three of us had done. Although the weather was deteriorating rapidly we made reasonable time until just below the top. The exit was heavily corniced and Stuart and I had an anxious wait on poor foot-holds while Jem blasted his way through. One by one we emerged from the vertical world of the climb onto the windswept horizontal world of the plateau, where visibility was down to just a few yards. We carefully made our way across the plateau and back down to the Youth Hostel.

The next time I returned to 'The Ben' was to compete in the Hill Race which is held every year on the first Saturday of September. The race starts from the games park in Claggan and after a lap of the grass track you follow the road to Achintee. Leaving the road the route starts to climb the well constructed footpath, over a couple of metal foot-bridges, towards the half-way lochan. From here you cut the corners off all the zigzags and a rough run over the boulders of the plateau takes you to the marshals waiting by the summit. I climbed quite well but lost a lot of time on the descent; my glasses kept steaming up in the heavy mist and I couldn't see enough to move quickly over the slippery rocks. Once back on the 'tourist path' I was able to recover a few positions to finish in the top third a few minutes inside two hours.

A year or two later I was back to climb the Ben by way of the Carn Mor Dearg arête. I parked at Achintee and followed the 'tourist path' up to the lochan on the col. From here I contoured round into the glen of the Allt a'Mhuilinn and followed the footpath towards the CIC Hut. Just before reaching the hut I crossed the stream and climbed steeply up the far side. It was a hard slog but once out onto the ridge I soon reached the cairn on Carn Beag Dearg. The ridge was followed up to another 'top', Carn Dearg Meadhonach; the going was now quite straightforward along to Carn Mor Dearg itself. From here the cliffs of Ben Nevis, across the glen, looked superb; there was still a lot of snow in the gullies, despite it being August.

A narrow, rocky ridge then gave a pleasant scramble round the head of Coire Leis, past some fixed abseil posts. The scramble led up through jumbled boulders until the bivouac shelter on Ben Nevis came into view. I was soon among the dozens of walkers who had made their way up the 'tourist path'. It was the first time I'd been on top in summer and in good weather and was surprised by the number of flowers and memorial cairns; when I'd been up there before they had been covered in snow and hidden. I took the easy way down, cutting some corners to take a more direct line to the lochan, and so back to Achintee.

Aonach Mor 3,999ft   Aonach Beag   4,060ft

My first visit to Aonach Mor and Aonach Beag was on one of those wet and cloudy days that I had come to know so well. It was in the days before Aonach Mor became a major ski centre so I didn't have the present option of a ride half-way up.

I parked at the head of Glen Nevis and walked in through the gorge, round to the ruins at Steall. Here I took to the hillside and made a wet climb up alongside the Allt Coire Giubhsachan. I seemed to be climbing for ages and couldn't see through the thick mist to the col, but, trusting to luck, I hoped that I had passed the crags and started climbing diagonally to eventually come out on the col between the two peaks.

Knowing exactly where I was again eased my nerves and it didn't take long to climb the ridge to the north to reach the cairn on Aonach Mor. These weren't the conditions to make long detours to distant 'tops' so I turned about and returned to the col for the short scramble over the boulders up onto Aonach Beag. I wasn't in an adventurous frame of mind that day so I also ignored Aonach Beag's outlying 'tops' and instead just set my compass for the south-west ridge. As I descended, so the clouds rolled away and I almost enjoyed the boggy stroll back to the ruined cottage.

I didn't return for several years and this time I cheated somewhat; as I had a big hill-race the next day I didn't want too hard a day now. I took the gondola up to the top station then had a warm climb up onto the summit ridge. It was an easy walk along the ridge to tick off Aonach Mor, soon followed by Aonach Beag. From here I was on new ground as I followed the arête down to the south-east and out to the 'top' of Stob Coire Bhealaich. A rough path then led round the rim of the corrie to Sgurr a'Bhuic, which overlooks the Water of Nevis. Leaving this 'top' I had to retrace my steps all the way back to Aonach Mor itself. From Aonach Mor I sought out the faint path that led down to the saddle at the start of the north-east ridge. Once on the ridge it gave an easy walk over the 'tops' of Stob an Cul Choire and Tom na Sroine. A short rough descent off the final top took me down into the glen, leaving just a short climb over the tussocks, up and over the shoulder of the hill back to civilisation and the gondola station.

The Grey Corries -
Stob Ban   3,217ft   Stob Choire Claurigh 3,858ft
Stob Coire an Laoigh   3,657ft
Sgurr Choinnich Mor   3,603ft

This long range of mountains contains four Munros plus another eight 'tops' so a long hard day was in prospect. After staying the night at the Hostel at Roy Bridge I drove round through Spean Bridge up the minor road to the farm at Corriechoille. A five mile walk in down a good track took me to beyond the forest and then over the pass of Lairig Leacach to a small bothy. After a short rest at the hut the hard work began as I turned off the track and climbed the heather clad hillside to a saddle to the north of Stob Ban. A short steep climb from the col saw me on the summit. I then turned about and returned to the col and it's small lochan before climbing up into thick clouds around the summit of Stob Choire Claurigh. The top was made up of several hundred feet of large loose scree. With visibility down to only a matter of yards I wasn't sure what the weather was going to do for the rest of the day, but it didn't seem at all promising, so I decided to miss out the detour to take in two outlying 'tops' to the north and east; instead I set off west along the main ridge. Three 'tops' now followed in quick succession as the route followed the obvious narrow ridge, first Stob a'Choire Leith, then Stob Coire Cath na Sine and Caisteil.

By this time I was below the cloud once more but it remained dull with the cloud base always around the 3,800' level. A small rise brought me to Stob Coire an Laoigh, where the ridge made a dog-leg out to the 'top' Stob Coire Easain.

A big descent south-west down a narrow ridge then gave an even bigger climb up the far side of the col onto the day's final Munro, Sgurr Choinnich Mor; continuing south-west along the ridge brought me to its twin, Sgurr Choinnich Beag. I retraced my steps back to Stob Coire Easain as I needed to follow its north ridge down. One last 'top', that of Beinn na Socaich, part way along this ridge gave me an excuse for a stop to eat the last of my food, then followed a long descent taken at a jog, down easy grassy slopes to the river below. The path entered the forest and followed the course of an old railway back to the main track, which in turn led to the farm at Corriechoille.

Sometime later I returned to finish off the 'tops' in the area. It was a murky sort of day early one May when I set off up the land-rover track from Corriechoille. After only a few minutes a trials bike went noisily past, then another and another; for the next half an hour or so I had to walk on the edge of the path as motorbikes roared past me at regular intervals; by a stroke of bad luck I had found myself in the middle of one of the stages of the Scottish 6-day Trial.

Thankfully, instead of continuing up the glen to the bothy, as I had done before, this time I was after the 'tops'. A short while after leaving the forest I quit the track and climbed the open hillside, which led to a ridge, which in turn took me to the 'top' of Stob Coire na Gaibhre. The ridge then continued along, above the steep drop down into Coire na Ceannain and on to the north top of Stob Coire Claurigh. From here a narrow arête led out east to the rocky little 'top' of Stob Coire na Ceannain. Returning along the arête it didn't take long to scramble round onto the rough blocks and the cairn of Stob Choire Claurigh and from here I was back on my previous route which I repeated for another long day out.

Loch Treig -
Stob a'Choire Mheadhoin 3,610ft
Stob Coire Easain 3,658ft

These two peaks to the west of Loch Treig really give you two Munros for the price of one. They are both on a high ridge, the two tops are only about ¾ mile apart, and the drop between them is only about 400ft.

A narrow road leads to Fersit, which is at the head of Loch Treig, alongside the railway line. A track led for the first couple of miles down along the western side of the loch; when it ran out I took to the hillside for a rising traverse across rough ground, which led steeply up onto the main ridge. Once on the ridge I could hear deer bellowing in the glen below, it was October and the rut was just starting. A final short climb took me to the cairn on Stob a'Choire Mheadhoin. It was a stony descent to the col beyond, followed by a short climb along the edge of the crags up onto Stob Coire Easain.

To return I retraced my steps down to the col and crossed back over Stob a'Choire Mheadhoin. I stayed high on the ridge of Meall Cian Dearg before dropping steeply down grassy slopes on the north-eastern flanks, back to the track beside the loch.

Stob Coire Sgriodain 3,211ft   Chno Dearg   3,433ft

Situated on the east side of Loch Treig these two peaks are also best climbed from Fersit, at the end of a small track which runs south from the Spean Bridge/Loch Laggan road.

It was a fine day one May, and the snow still lay thick on the tops, when I set off across the railway and through the farm. A short way along the track I turned south and made my way across open moorland towards the shoulder. Half way up the ridge it became more broken, with short craggy outcrops and heather steps. This scrambling section was soon below me and the ridge levelled off for a while before the final climb to the summit cairn of Stob Coire Sgriodain. The snow on top was crisp and gave good going along to the mountains south 'top'.

I dropped down to the col beyond then made a short detour, heading south-east to take in another 'top', Meall Garbh, which was just a short distance away. The views were great from here, looking over to Ben Alder in the east, the Glen Coe peaks in the south-west, and Loch Treig and a host of other peaks to the west. After a quick bite to eat I returned along the ridge for a final short climb up to Chno Dearg. From here it left about 3 miles, all downhill across rough moorland to return to the farm at Fersit. The old snow on the upper 1,000ft gave a quick and easy descent as I ran, jumped and glissaded, but once the snow gave out the heather and tussocks were tiring and I was glad to reach the track to end another great day on the hill.

| **Carn Dearg** | **3,080ft** | **Sgor Gaibhre** | **3,124ft** |
| **Beinn na Lap** | **3,066ft** | | |

These three peaks are unusual in that the best way to approach them is by train; the nearest road access is miles away.

My first attempt at the round of Loch Ossian was a disaster. I caught the train at Bridge of Orchy for the short journey up over Rannoch Moor to Corrour Station. It was Easter and the weather was fine but cold, as I followed the track a short way down to the Youth Hostel, which is set in a lovely spot at the west end of Loch Ossian. I reached Carn Dearg already feeling tired and by the time I was down at the col beyond I just couldn't find the energy to climb Sgor Gaibhre. Instead I just dropped down to the Lodge at the east end of the loch. By now I was absolutely shattered and the three mile walk back along the lochside took me almost two hours.

I returned a couple of weeks later for another try and by now I had recovered from whatever it was that had knocked me out before. I made good time from the station at Corrour, down to the Youth Hostel and along the track which led south below Carn Dearg. Shortly after leaving the path, as I took to the deep heather, I came across a grouse doing its usual decoy trick of running around dragging a wing along the ground as though it were broken. I knew this would mean there were young around and sure enough I soon saw seven tiny bundles of feathers, which were running about in all directions trying to hide. I carried on upwards until I reached the ridge which soon took me to Carn Dearg's summit cairn, where I enjoyed extensive views out over Rannoch Moor. The north-east ridge gave a quick descent to the col at Mam Ban, from where a long plod up grassy slopes led to Sgor Gaibhre. There were more great views from here, out over Loch Ericht and the peaks around Ben Alder. After a brief rest I continued down to the next col where a short climb led to the 'top' of Sgor Choinnich.

A long gentle ridge then led out to the north-west to bring me out above Corrour Lodge; an easy jog and I was soon down beside the loch. I had to go along the track for a short way to by-pass a high deer fence then turned back above the forest towards Beinn na Lap. I knew I had plenty of time in hand to catch the next train so I stopped beside the stream, in a gully sheltered from the wind, and made a brew of tea.

Climbing on again I made my way up through the broken crags, passing several deer hidden among the gullies, until I arrived at the summit cairn of Beinn na Lap. Checking my watch again I set off down the hillside at a jog, now aiming for the west end of Loch Ossian. The final mile along the track saw me back at the station with half an hour to spare, so the stove came out again for another brew to pass the time and I could have made myself some money by selling teas and coffees to the other walkers gathering on the station platform.

Carn Dearg 3,391ft   Geal-Charn   3,656ft
Aonach Beag 3,647ft   Beinn Eibhinn   3,611ft

To make the long approach to these remote peaks easier, I cycled in from Dalwhinnie; about ten miles down along Loch Ericht, past Ben Alder Lodge and out to the bothy at Culra where I hid the bike.

The steep climb to Carn Dearg started from directly behind the hut; it was a stiff pull up the deep heather onto a ridge, which I followed as it climbed west, before it steepened again just below the summit cairn. Passing over the summit I dropped down to a saddle and a slight rise then led easily to the 'top' of Diollaid a'Chairn. On leaving this the ridge narrowed and gave great views down to high lochans, set deep into the corries on either side. A fairly steep rocky ridge then gave an easy scramble up to the plateau. By keeping to the north and following the line of the steep ground I soon reached the cairn marking Geal Charn's summit. After descending to a narrow col a short climb up an easy ridge took me to Aonach Beag.

From here I followed the cliff edge as it curved round the head of the corrie containing another small lochan; a rough descent led to a col and a steep climb soon saw me on the last of the day's tops, Beinn Eibhinn. The weather was deteriorating, I was in thick cloud with rain threatening, so I decided to miss out two subsidiary 'tops' which would have taken me further away from Culra, instead I set a bearing and dropped down to the stream far below. There was a lone tent pitched here in an ideal spot with only deer and mountain hares for company.

Once down in the glen I crossed the river and climbed a short way up the opposite hillside to reach a good path, which led easily to the Bealach Dubh, and from here a three mile stroll took me down to Culra Bothy. It didn't take long to cycle back to Dalwhinnie, although I stopped several times to watch herds of deer grazing on the moors beside the track.

Beinn a'Chlachair   3,569ft   Geal Charn   3,443ft
Creag Pitridh   3,031ft

A land-rover track leads south from between Loch Moy and Loch Laggan on the A86, it crosses bleak, open moorland to the ruined bothy of Lubvan. It was a wet and windy November day as I left the track at the bothy and started fighting my way through knee deep wet heather. Deer were calling through the low cloud and every now and again I disturbed fine looking stags, which didn't seem as wary as usual. The rain hammered down and I was well wrapped up as I climbed up the steep slopes to come out onto the summit ridge which took me to the cairn on Beinn a'Chlachair.

It was too cold and wet to stop so I continued along the ridge, the far end of which is made up of a line of steep broken crags. The clouds were still right down and visibility was virtually nil, which gave me a few anxious moments but I eventually arrived safely at the pass above the loch. Here I found an over-hanging boulder which gave me shelter while I had a bite to eat.

I was soon climbing again; a track led up to the col between the final two peaks, from where I just had to follow a compass bearing blindly, onwards and upwards to Geal Charn. I was just starting to lose hope of finding the summit cairn when both it and the trig point emerged out of the gloom.

Another bearing took me back down to the col for the short climb up onto Creag Pitridh. It was an easy scramble through broken crags up to the cairn. To descend I had to take yet another bearing to bypass the worst of the crags; I dropped down the heather clad hillside, back to the track in the glen, for the four mile walk-out back to the road.

Ben Alder   3,765ft   Beinn Bheoil   3,333ft

I climbed this pair of remote peaks on a glorious day one May. Leaving the car at Dalwhinnie I enjoyed a lovely cycle of about eight miles down along Loch Ericht, round past Ben Alder Lodge, to a shed near Loch Pattack. Leaving the bike hidden behind the shed I stripped down to shorts and tee-shirt for the short walk in to Culra Bothy.

From the bothy I followed the river for a short while, the route then climbed a fine ridge which gave an easy, though slightly exposed, scramble up onto the huge snow covered plateau of Ben Alder. I'd almost flown up the ridge, it was a great day and I was in top form.

Once at the summit cairn I had a short rest, then it was on around the edge of the corrie, passing above huge cliffs with large cornices, some of which were starting to peel off and were ready to come crashing down. The route then dropped steeply down to the south-east to the Bealach Breabeg, from where a short climb led me to the summit of Sron Coire na h-Iolaire, a 'top'. That left an easy walk along the ridge above Loch a'Bhealaich Bheithe to the summit of Beinn Bheoil.

From here it was easy going down the ridge, before dropping steeply down to the track by the loch. Once on the track it didn't take long to return to Culra Bothy and to collect the bike from beside Loch Pattack. It only took 40 minutes to return to Dalwhinnie, freewheeling most of the way, and that included a long stop to watch a large herd of deer grazing beside the track.

I climbed Beinn Bheoil again a few years later as part of the *Lowe Alpine Mountain Marathon*; the event centre that year was at the south end of Loch Laggan. We weren't told where the start was but were simply loaded onto coaches and after a short ride down the road we were dropped at Tulloch Station. We assumed that the start would be near here, but no, there was a fine old steam train waiting to take us down to Corrour Station.

The race started from near the Youth Hostel beside Loch Ossian and the course took us east over the rough moorland via the slopes of Carn Dearg, Sgor Gaibhre and towards Ben Alder. The weather stayed pretty good for the weekend so navigation went ok, although there were some tough route choices when controls were a long way apart. The penultimate control was actually on the summit of Beinn Bheoil; the final control was a nasty one in the middle of a wide area of peat hags, which left just a short run to Culra Bothy to the finish of Day 1 and the overnight camp. The following day was a little shorter but again had one or two tricky route choices as we headed straight up and over the Carn Dearg above the bothy. From here the course took us out over the slopes of Geal Charn and Creag Pitridh, round between the lochans of Lochan na h-Earba and so back to the finish at the south end of Loch Laggan.

Section 5: Drumochter

Geal-charn   **3,005ft**   **A'Mharconaich**   **3,185ft**
Beinn Udlamain   **3,306ft**   **Sgairneach Mhor** **3,251ft**

    These four peaks to the west of the Drumochter Pass are rounded, heather clad hills, which gave me a good day out one summer. I started from a lay-by on the A9, crossed the railway and climbed up the steep hillside towards Geal-charn. Where the ridge levels off there are several tall, slim, stone cairns, which are visible from the road; from the road these slim cairns look like people. It was a short climb from here to the summit, which was in cloud. From the summit an easy ridge led south, then once past the head of the Allt Coire Fhar, I had to bear left, eastwards, to climb the grassy slope onto the ridge of A'Mharconaich. The first cairn was not at the highest point; a further cairn about half a mile away at the far end of the ridge was about 9ft higher.

    I had to retrace my steps for a few minutes then followed the line of an old fence out to a col to the south-west. From the col the ridge continued heading south-west to reach the day's third peak, Beinn Udlamain. A large stone cairn gave some shelter from the cold wind while I ate my lunch and looked out over Loch Ericht and across to Ben Alder. With the cloud level dropping rapidly and rain threatening I continued down the south ridge to a broad saddle. The climb up to the trig point on Sgairneach Mhor was straightforward; I then took the east-ridge to avoid a line of crags and once below the crags dropped down to the track in Coire Dhomhain. This track led me back to the Drumochter Pass where I found a faint deer trod through the heather that took me the couple of miles back to the car.

Meall Chuaich   **3,120ft**

    This is a fairly easy Munro, involving just 11 miles and 2,000ft of climbing; most of the distance is on land-rover tracks. Rather than do it as a day's walk, which would have been a bit of a waste of time, I decided to run it one Friday evening when I was on my way further north for a weekend of Munro 'bagging'.

    It was almost mid-summer so I was able to set off from the road in vest and shorts at around 7pm on a glorious evening. From Dalwhinnie the track followed an aqueduct, crossed beneath the busy A9 before turning east into the hills and towards a small power station. Another mile, still on good tracks, led me to Loch Cuaich; here I took to the heather clad hillside but I soon found a path, which climbed steeply up to the summit. My lungs and legs were complaining by this time and I had to be careful near the top as there were rocks hidden amongst the heather.

Once at the cairn I had a brief rest to enjoy the somewhat hazy view and to let my pulse settle, before jogging slowly across the top then speeding quickly down the hillside back to the loch. From here it seemed a long four miles back to Dalwhinnie, retracing my steps along the hydro-board road, along the aqueduct and back to the car.

A'Bhuidheanach Bheag 3,064ft   Carn na Caim   3,087ft

These two peaks to the east of the Drumochter Pass are relatively easy as the pass itself is around 1,400ft, meaning that you are almost half-way there already. I climbed them early one winter when the first snows had just arrived.

I left the car at the Balsporran Cottages, crossed the A9 and set off up the hillside. First I had to cross a small ridge into the valley of the Allt Coire Dubhaig, there was a herd of deer here which I watched for a few minutes until they spotted me and took off up the slope. A steep climb took me up to Meall a'Chaorainn, from where I followed a faint line of tracks through the snow, across the featureless plateau to the trig point on A'Bhuidheanach Bheag.

Once again the day was cloudy and I had to go carefully on a bearing through the mist to pick up the cairns on A'Bhuidheanach and point 902m away to the north. The line of an old fence was a useful guide and it led me towards the cairn of Carn na Caim. From here I was someway away from the car and had two choices; I could drop down to the A9 and walk back along the road, or I could return over the tops. I didn't fancy the walk back along the busy A9 so I kept to the tops, only leaving the plateau once I had passed A'Bhuidheanach and the deep gully beyond. It was then just a question of a quick descent to the Allt Coire Dubhaig, where the deer were waiting for me again, before dropping down to the car at Balsporran.

Section 6: Tarf & Tilt; West of Cairnwell Pass

An Sgarsoch 3,300ft   Carn Ealar   3,276ft

These remote peaks are several miles from the nearest road so I used the bike, cycling in from the Linn of Dee, over White Bridge, past a ruined bothy then west along the north bank of the Geldie Burn. After some miles the land-rover track forded the river, I couldn't avoid wet feet but the river was fairly low during a rare, long hot summer, so it wasn't too bad. The ruin of Geldie Lodge was just a short way up the track and I left the bike padlocked there.

I set off on foot across knee deep heather, following the course of a stream, which led to the ridge of An Sgarsoch. From a small, deer filled, corrie I climbed into the cloud and onto the main east/west ridge, making a short detour to first take in Druim Sgarsoch. From here I turned about and retraced my steps west to the large cairn and wind-break on An Sgarsoch. After a brief rest I continued south-west, down to a col. From the col a steep grassy slope took me to the ridge which in turn led to the next summit, Carn Ealar.

From the cairn I had to follow a bearing which took me steeply down the hillside, through deep heather and areas of peat-hags where many deer were lying up. The course of a stream guided me back to the end of the land-rover track, which was followed back to the ruin of Geldie Lodge. Here I collected the bike and had an easy return back to the Linn of Dee, as it was gently downhill almost all the way.

Beinn Dearg 3,304ft

Beinn Dearg is a remote peak which requires a long walk in before you make it anywhere near the hill itself. I climbed it on a glorious morning one October.

Setting off from Old Blair I followed the land-rover track easily up through the forest and out onto open moorland. Where a footpath cut a corner, I took the shortest route, but the going was very wet and boggy, it would have been far quicker and easier to have stayed with the track. A short descent took me to a well maintained bothy, looked after by the MBA.

From the bothy a footpath continued northwards, dropping down to the Bruar Water and Bruar Lodge. I felt guilty going past the lodge; as it was October I thought that there may be some stalking going on, and the barking dogs made sure that I didn't go by unnoticed.

An enjoyable half-mile along the river was enlivened by the numerous birds flying back and forth, feeding just above the surface of the water. However, the hard work now began as I turned steeply up the hillside on a good path, which climbed above the burn. As I climbed higher the angle eased a little until the saddle was reached, then it turned steeper again as I climbed through the heather to Beinn Garbh. From here a broad ridge led round to the south, climbing up over a tiring boulder field to the big cairn on Beinn Dearg.

After a brief stop I continued on along the ridge, dropping slowly down to the south-west, ploughing through knee deep heather until, instead of the expected footpath, I came to a new land-rover track, which led easily along the burn to the bothy. Then it was just a case of switching off and with the mind in neutral, walking the six miles back over the moors, through the forest and back to the car. It had turned out to be a surprisingly enjoyable day.

Carn a'Chlamain   3,159ft

Glad of the chance of an easy day for once I left the car parked at Old Blair and cycled up the land-rover track through Glen Tilt until, after about 9 miles, I reached Forest Lodge.

After hiding the bike in the woods I followed the stalkers path as it climbed steeply up the heather clad hillside. The 1,500ft climb was quite fierce but eventually I came out onto easier ground and could now see the summit a little over a mile away, across the peat-hags. The path continued across the high moorland and after a short rise, passed beneath the summit of Carn a'Chlamain and up to the saddle between it and it's north top. After collecting the north top I followed the short ridge along to the main summit. Lunch was abruptly cut short by a violent squall of rain, so I lost no time in re-joining the path and dropping down to the glen. The long cycle back down to Old Blair was a wet one and all in all it was a very ordinary day.

Beinn a'Ghlo -
Carn Liath   3,197ft   Carn nan Gabhar 3,677ft
Braigh Coire Chruinn-bhalgain 3,505ft

It was May when I climbed this group of peaks; starting again with a cycle in from Old Blair, up Glen Tilt to the bridge just beyond Marble Lodge. Here I padlocked the bike and took to the footpath on the south side of the river. Before reaching the club hut I climbed away from the path, heading for a heathery ridge then down to cross the Fender Burn. A mountain hare exploded from my feet as I crossed the deep heather leading to the ridge. I then had a hard climb up to a col, where I turned right and followed the ridge a short way up to the cairn on Carn Liath.

I was feeling fit after having done a lot of walking and running in the hills over the recent weeks, so I jogged back down the ridge, crossed the col and set off on the long climb up to Braigh Coire Chruinn-bhalgain. Sitting in the sunshine by the summit cairn I chatted to a couple I had passed on my way up the ridge. They stoked my ego by telling me they considered themselves fit and strong walkers and they couldn't believe that they had taken twice as long as me to climb the ridge.

The ridge continued and again I jogged easily down to the next col from where a short steep climb led round above broken ground onto another ridge, which in turn led to the 'top' of Airgiod Bheinn. It only took minutes to leave the top and return along the ridge to another saddle from where I climbed to the boulder strewn plateau of Carn nan Gabhar. Three cairns stretched away along the ridge; the highest point was at the furthest, northernmost cairn, not at the trig-point which would usually be the case.

With rain now threatening on the wind I jogged north along the ridge before contouring just below the top of Meall a'Mhuirich. A very steep descent took me to a footbridge over the Allt Fheanach and then another bridge took me across the River Tilt. Neither of these bridges were marked on my map but both were very welcome. Once over the Tilt I was back onto a good land-rover track, which was busy with other walkers. I walked and jogged the four miles back to my bike and then enjoyed the free-wheel downhill all the way back to the road.

Glas Tulaichean 3,449ft   Carn an Righ   3,377ft

To climb this pair of Munros I parked at the Spittal of Glenshee on a weekend early in May. It was an easy walk in, down the track past the Dalmunzie Hotel, to join a path which followed the course of an old railway line, which once served Glenlochsie Lodge. From here I was surprised to find a new land-rover track which had only recently been bull-dozed out of the hillside, so I set off up the ridge not knowing quite where the track would lead me. Above about 1,500ft visibility was down to only 20 yards or so but the new track continued to climb the ridge in the right direction, so I kept faith with it. Soon after reaching the old snow, sensing higher ground to the right I stopped to take a rough bearing; I left the land-rover track and set off on the short climb up to the cairn and trig point of Glas Tulaichean.

Leaving the summit I followed my compass down along the north-east ridge for a short distance, then broke off in a more northerly direction to pick up a stream in the glen below. Crossing the stream I found the start of a stalkers path which contoured round beneath the slopes of Mam nan Carn and then turned north up to a small lochan on a col between it and Carn an Righ. I was temporarily below the clouds here but then had to climb steeply up into cloud again, on up to the summit of Carn an Righ. It was very easy returning to the col; I just linked the long tongues of old snow and was able to run quickly down, dropping something like 800ft in only a few minutes.

From the saddle I retraced by steps to the stalkers path and then on to the head of the stream where I crossed over to the col above Glas Coire Bheag. From here I dropped down into the heather filled corrie and eventually came out onto a good track in Gleann Taitneach, disturbing a couple of deer grazing beside the stream on my way down. Once in the glen it was simply a question of following the track back to the Dalmunzie Hotel, where I had to cross the river, and walk the final short distance back to the car.

Carn Bhac   3,098ft   Beinn Iutharn Mhor   3,424ft
An Socach   3,073ft

The round of these three Munros, along with their four subsidiary 'tops', makes a good horseshoe route around the head of Glen Ey. I left the car parked at Inverey and cycled in up the glen on a good land-rover track, which followed the Ey Burn about 5 miles up to the ruins of Altanour Lodge.

Leaving the bike padlocked to a tree I followed the footpath that led up through the rough moorland and climbed steadily, traversing the hillside to gain a saddle where the slopes eased for a little before steepening again for the final climb to Carn Bhac's summit, unmarked on the OS map. The clouds were down to a uniform level just a few metres above me, so although navigation was easy I had no real views to speak of. Rain was threatening so I moved quickly round to the summit's south-west 'top' where I felt I should use my compass for the long bog-trot across to Beinn Iutharn Mhor, whose summit was now hidden in the clouds. Once across the bleak moorland a short steep scramble brought me out onto a ridge which was followed to the big summit cairn.

It was by now too wet and cold to hang around so I jogged the descent to the col to stay warm. I briefly saw daylight at the col, but was soon climbing back into the clouds again on the short climb to the 'top' of Mam nan Carn. With the compass now a permanent fixture I followed it blindly to keep to the north-east ridge, which led down to a saddle before another short steep climb took me onto another 'top' Beinn Iutharn Bheag.

Descending from here I wanted to avoid the scree and crags shown on the map, but at the same time I didn't want to lose too much height, which I would only have to climb again later. As it turned out the scree was less of a problem than the map suggested and I dropped down to contour round the head of the middle of the three streams. A short rough climb took me to the final Munro of the day, An Socach, another summit not specifically marked on the OS map. In good weather it would have been a fine high level walk along an almost level ridge, out to An Socach's east 'top' about a mile and a half away; but this wasn't good weather, it was cold, wet and windy.

From this last 'top' a short ridge ran off to the north-west, which led me towards the head of Glen Ey and after passing to one side of Carn Cruinn, through the drizzle I could just make out the trees scattered around the ruined lodge. The descent to the lodge was over rough heather but at last I could put the map and compass away. Having the bike made it a gloriously fast and painless way of covering five miles after a long wet day on the hill.

The Cairnwell   3,059ft   Carn a'Gheoidh   3,194ft
Carn Aosda   3,003ft

This trio of unexciting hills were climbed on a miserable day one October. Two of the hills only just struggle to cross the 3,000ft contour and as the high point of the road is about 2,200ft you don't have much climbing to do.

From the car-park at the Glenshee ski-centre a short steep ascent, directly under a chair-lift, led up the heather, between ugly snow fences to the summit of The Cairnwell, which was just beyond the top of the lift. From here, in thick mist, I followed the ridge out to the north-west, then round as it passed above Loch Vrotachan to a couple of small lochans. A short climb then led over the indistinct lump of Carn nan Sac and a mile away to the west a bearing took me to the summit of Carn a'Gheoidh.

The weather was deteriorating so I happily ignored the other 'top', still further away to the west. Instead I returned back along the ridge to the twin lochans, round the head of the corrie and turned north across the heather for the short climb to Carn Aosda. Dropping down beneath ski-tows I was soon on the broad track which led easily back to the car-park.

It's not a walk I am ever likely to want to do again.

Section 7: Glas Maol; Glen Doll; Lochnagar; White Mounth; Mt Keen

Creag Leacach 3,238ft   Glas Maol   3,504ft
Cairn of Claise 3,484ft   Carn an Tuirc 3,340ft

In contrast to the three Munros to the west of the Glenshee ski area, this group of four peaks gave me a great day out early one summer.

I parked at a lay-by some two miles south of the ski centre and dropped down to cross the Allt a'Ghlinne Bhig. There was a good start to the day as I watched a heron fish in the stream, all too soon though it spotted me and took off. A steep climb up the grassy slopes of Meall Gorm soon had me warmed up and after crossing a low col I climbed on, up onto the boulders of Creag Leacach's south-west 'top'. An easy angled ridge then led to the main summit of Creag Leacach. Continuing on along the bouldery ridge I kept low down on the west side of Glas Maol, contouring out to the ridge which ran west to the 'top' of Meall Odhar. A short climb from here led to the grassy lump that is Glas Maol. After a hurried lunch by the cairn I jogged easily off to the south-east, then walked past an old 'pony hut' out to the 'top' of Little Glas Maol.

A good path led around and above the steep cliffs, contouring beneath Glas Maol to rejoin the main ridge; I kept to the path for as long as possible before bearing off to the north-east on another detour to collect the 'top' of Druim Mor, which lies opposite Little Glas Maol but with the deep trench of Caenlochan Glen in between them. It was easy walking from here to cross the high plateau to reach Cairn of Claise and a mile or two further across this fairly bleak landscape to Carn an Tuirc. This was the last of the day's eight summits but unfortunately I had been walking away from the car all day so I still had some way to go before a rest was in sight.

Dropping down off Carn an Tuirc to the north-west gave a direct route down to a path in the glen below. In my haste I put a foot wrong crossing some boulders; a rock rolled up and hit me on the leg. At first I thought nothing of it but I soon realised that it had made a deep puncture wound. I tied a dirty handkerchief round as a bandage, before making my way more carefully down to the track, alongside the stream and so back out to the road. The 3½ miles back over the pass and down to the car were painful as my leg was beginning to stiffen up but it had been a good long day and it wasn't surprising that I felt a bit tired.

Tolmount   3,143ft   Tom Buidhe   3,140ft
Broad Cairn 3,268ft   Cairn Bannoch   3,314ft

These four Munros are best climbed either from Glen Doll in the south, or from Glen Callater above Braemar to the north-west. As I'd climbed on Lochnagar the previous day, and stayed in Braemar overnight, it was easier to tackle them from the Braemar end.

A long approach up a good track took me to Loch Callater where I kept to the north-eastern shore; once at the far end of the loch the track faded away and I was left to struggle across boggy marshland. The glen narrowed and I passed between high cliffs on either side; the hills were teeming with deer, it was the middle of November and the rut was in full swing. The path now reappeared and led me up to the col from where a short climb took me onto Tolmount. I swung across the head of the corrie and saw a Land-rover parked a short way away. I expected to have an irate gamekeeper come dashing across to throw me off the hill but I didn't see anyone and was soon swallowed up by the mists around the summit of Tom Buidhe. From here I dropped back down to the north-east to regain the col I had been on previously.

From the col I was soon onto the 'top' of Crow Craigies and took a direct route across the moorland to another 'top' Craig of Gowal. From here it didn't take long to reach the boulder strewn summit of Broad Cairn from where I had great views down to Loch Muick and out to Lochnagar. The 'tops' of Creag an Dubh-loch and Cairn of Gowal soon followed and these led me out to the day's final Munro, Cairn Bannoch. Another 'top', Fafernie, was just a few hundred yards away to the west and after visiting this I set off towards Carn an t-Sagairt Mor. However, having been to the top of this one just the day before as part of the Lochnagar round, I joined the track that passed a short way beneath the summit. The track led north for a short while before dropping steeply down to the north end of Loch Callater; from here I was left with an easy walk-out back to the car.

Driesh 3,108ft   Mayar 3,043ft

These two peaks are found at the head of Glen Clova and are easily reached from the road-end at the junction of Glen Clova and Glen Doll.

A Forestry Commission road led across the river and up through forest, the road then narrowed to a footpath, very muddy after the recent heavy rain. Once out of the forest a couple of small muntjac deer came into view, but they were very nervous and soon hid themselves in the undergrowth. The path climbed the Shank of Drumfollow, up onto a col, from where a short steep climb led up towards the plateau and the summit of Driesh. The top is marked by a huge cairn and a trig-point.

I retraced my steps back down to the col and from here the way to Mayar was straightforward, just a mile away over easy ground. Once at the summit of Mayar I dropped north towards the head of Fee Burn. The descent into the head of the glen was quite narrow but further down the glen opens out and you cross into the forest on an amazing construction, designed to cross the high deer-fence with the minimum of effort. Once in the forest a good track led quickly back down to the car-park.

Since this first visit I've been back several times, often as a run. One good hard run left the car-park and took straight to the steep hillside to climb Driesh by The Scorrie before heading off to Mayar to complete the round. These two peaks were also included in the Angus Munros Hill Race I ran once. The race started at the car-park; we then climbed steeply up through the forest to Craig Mellon before dropping down to a shelter on Jock's Road; this track was followed up to Crow Craigies. A short climb took us to Tolmount and across the moors to Tom Buidhe; a long, rough traverse then saw us onto Mayar. Easy running led to Driesh from where we dropped down The Scorrie, waded the river and finished back at the car-park. It was a great race and everyone from my club, Ochil Hill Runners, ran well; packing three in the first ten we won the men's team race and Angela Mudge won the ladies race. Little did we know then that just eight years later Angela would be the World Mountain Running Champion!

Lochnagar-
Cac Carn Beag   **3,789ft**
Carn an t-Sagairt Mor   **3,430ft**
Carn a'Coire Boidheach   **3,650ft**

I'd been saving Lochnagar for a good day and thankfully it was bright and clear when I made the long drive down Glen Muick to the Visitor Centre and deer reserve at the far end. I set off from the road, past a small herd of deer in the woods, following a good land-rover track which climbed to around 2,500ft; a path then led me up to the col between Lochnagar and Meikle Pap, a small conical outlying 'top'. From the col the huge cliffs towering above the loch came into view, the tops were just covered in the first snow of the year.

As I climbed higher I entered heavy cloud and visibility dropped to only around 20 yards. It was easy to keep one eye on the cliffs to my right and climb round the edge of the corrie onto Cac Carn Mor; from here I followed the tracks of a fox across the snow out onto Cac Carn Beag, the highest point on Lochnagar. It's marked as a viewpoint on the OS map, but unfortunately I could see nothing. It didn't take long to back-track onto the plateau so I could make my way to Carn a'Coire Boidheach. As I left this summit I also left the snow behind as I crossed the bleak moorland over to Carn an t-Sagairt Beag, then down to a col to the south-west. Scattered about on the col is wreckage from an aircraft; I've come across several crash sites in the Scottish hills but this one contains the most wreckage that I've seen, one wing was almost complete.

I was soon onto Carn an t-Sagairt Mor before I retraced my steps, moving eastwards, taking in the 'tops' of Top of Eagle's Rock, Creag a'Ghlas-uillt and Cuidhe Crom on the way back. A blizzard swept in as I reached the cliffs of Lochnagar again but thankfully the wind was behind me and it blew me down the steep rocky ridge, across the col, and up the short steep climb of Meikle Pap. The huge boulders on the summit gave me some shelter from the wind and rain, before I dashed back down to the track below for the return to the Spittal of Glenmuick.

All in all it was another very good day on the hills.

Mount Keen 3,077ft

Mount Keen is the most easterly Munro and lies amidst a huge area of ancient deer forest, though the forests are no more. Whichever way you approach the mountain involves a long walk in so I decided to use the bike and left the car at the visitor centre car-park in Glen Tanar.

The morning was fine as I cycled a good track through thick forest. After about half an hour I came across a capercaillie; it was the first time I'd seen one in the wild, and was a great surprise. The capercaillie must be one of Britain's biggest birds, and is the size of a large turkey; it's related to the grouse and spends most of its time on the ground due to its size, although it does fly up into the trees to feed and find shelter. After stopping to watch and photograph the bird I continued on my way. The forest soon gave way to open moorland, the track crossing and re-crossing the Water of Tanar.

Leaving the bike padlocked to a footbridge I could see the summit of Mount Keen about two miles away to the south. Although it looked misty on top there was no snow in sight. However, by the time I was half-way up the top was covered in cloud and it had started raining. As I climbed higher the rain turned to sleet and then to snow; by the time I reached the summit cairn there was a real blizzard blowing and everywhere was already covered in an inch or two of fresh snow.

I stopped in the shelter of the cairn for a quick cup of tea and to put on more warm clothes, then turned to descend to the bridge and my bike. In the short time I had been on top enough snow had fallen to cover my upward tracks; thankfully the way was fairly obvious and once I'd dropped a few hundred feet the snow faded out and gave way to heavy rain, which stayed with me all the way back to the car.

Section 8: Glen Feshie; Western Cairngorms; Macdui & Cairn Gorm; Lairig an Laoigh; Eastern Cairngorms

Glen Feshie -
Sgor Gaoith 3,658ft   Mullach Clach a'Bhlair 3,338ft

For this pair of Munros and their five associated 'tops' I started about half way down Glen Feshie, parking on the eastern side of the river near a bridge over a stream. A forestry track led east up to the edge of the plantation. A footpath now climbed away through older, more open forest to the bare hillside. The heathery slopes of a 'top', Geal Charn, were directly in front of me and a steep climb soon saw me up onto the grassy summit. From here an easy ridge led round to the next 'top' of Meall Buidhe. Another short climb led up to the main ridge which I followed out a short way to the north to collect the next 'top' Sgòran Dubh Mor. The position was now far more interesting as the ridge dropped steeply away to the east, down into the narrow trough of Gleann Einich, with its loch nestling against the crags at the southern end. Leaving the top I followed the edge of the precipice up onto the summit of Sgor Gaoith. It was a lovely day and several other parties were out enjoying the fine spell of weather. It was fairly flat going along the wide ridge out to the 'top' of Carn Ban Mor.

A long gradual descent over the plateau brought me to the slight saddle from where a climb of only a few metres took me to the 'top' of Meall Dubhag; this little top is perched in the corner of the plateau, with steep slopes dropping away to the west and more especially the south, where a stream has cut back into the hillside. From Meall Dubhag I could see the day's final top away over on the other side of the corrie. Tussocks led round the head of the corrie to a land-rover track which gave easier going over the plateau. The summit of Mullach Clach a'Bhlair lay just a short way off the track. From the cairn I headed off down the south-west ridge, over Druim nam Bo, before dropping down into the corrie to pick up the land-rover track that led back down to the glen.

After crossing the river to its west bank, by a bridge that has since been washed away, the going was easier on a private road; then it was back over another bridge to the east side for the final half a mile to the road-end. That just left a walk of about 2½ miles back up the road to the car. It was a relief to take my boots off and join the picnickers who were paddling in the stream.

**Braeriach   4,248ft   Cairn Toul   4,241ft
Devil's Point 3,303ft**

These three peaks forming the high plateau to the west of the Lairig Ghru never fail to give a good day, despite the long walk in to reach them. Like the other Cairngorm peaks I have climbed them in all weathers and in all seasons.

One of my first visits to Braeriach was on a miserable November day; I'd waited until lunchtime in the vain hope the weather would improve and when the rain finally relented a little I set off from the camp-site at Coylumbridge. It was a lovely walk in through Rothiemurchus forest then out through the thinning pines to reach the entrance of the Lairig Ghru, near the Sinclair Memorial Hut, which has since been removed. I continued on up the Lairig Ghru until I found a suitable looking place to start the scramble up; it was steep and rough, and after an endless climb into thick clouds the angle started to ease and I came out onto the 'top' of Sron na Lairige. A short descent led to a col and the scattered wreckage of a crashed 'plane. From here a short climb took me up onto Braeriach's cairn, perched high above the deep corrie. Having had such a late start and with daylight fading fast I returned to the col and dropped straight down into the Lairig Ghru. I had to make it a quick walk-out and just made it back to the camp-site as night fell.

A more relaxed outing was made one summer when I again walked in from Coylumbridge, through the forest and up to the Sinclair Hut. This time I followed the path behind the hut which gave a far easier climb up to the ridge and along to the 'top' of Sron na Lairige, down to the col and up onto Braeriach. From here I headed on around the rim of the corrie onto Sgor an Lochain Uaine (note 1) and across the boulders up to Cairn Toul. Leaving the cairn I followed the ridge south, over the 'top' of Stob Coire an t-Saighdeir and started down the tussocks towards the col. In a grassy hollow I disturbed a small group of reindeer; there were two very young ones, probably only about a month old, and their mothers kept a very close eye on me; when I was too close they started to move menacingly towards me as though they were ready to charge. I retreated to a safe distance and watched them for a while before continuing on down to the col. From the col a short climb led up to the cairn on The Devil's Point.

It didn't take long to trot back down to the col and pick up the path that led easily down to the Corrour Bothy beside the River Dee. Seeing the bothy again brought back memories of a night we had spent there some years before. It was already dark as we came down off the tops and searched for the hut; when we saw lights and heard a noise like music we assumed they were coming from the hut and headed that way. However, when we reached the bothy it was to find it cold, dark and empty, so what were the lights and noises we were convinced we had seen and heard? It was only later that I read of the legend of the Big Grey Man of Ben Macdhui.

After crossing the bridge downstream of the bothy I was back on the main Lairig Ghru path which took me over the watershed amongst the boulders, and gave a pleasant stroll all the way back to Coylumbridge.

I've also made rounds of the peaks around An Garbh Choire as part of my runs over the Cairngorm 4,000's, one of those runs is described in detail elsewhere in this journal. I started on the ski road and ran in through the Chalamain Gap to the Sinclair Hut; up the ridge onto Braeriach; round onto Cairn Toul; dropped down to the Lairig Ghru; climbed steeply up on to Ben Macdui; which left an easy run over the plateau to Cairn Gorm and back down to Glen More.

Monadh Mor   3,651ft   Beinn Bhrotain   3,795ft

I first climbed these two peaks from the south; leaving the car at Linn of Dee I cycled in, crossed over the White Bridge and headed north along the Dee for a short way. After hiding the bike in the heather I continued on foot along the track until it petered out, then it was just a question of bashing through the heather, round into Glen Geusachan. A small herd of deer kept a wary eye on me as I passed between the two steep craggy hillsides. It was hard going and as I climbed higher I was soon into heavy cloud, this cut visibility to almost zero so I had to be careful where I turned off to climb steeply up to a small loch, Loch nan Stuirteag, on the saddle above. From the loch a ridge led south, up into a 'whiteout'.

The trail of a lone skier ran across my track as I climbed on a bearing up to the summit of Monadh Mor. There was no point in stopping so I continued south and was pleased when I spotted the narrow pass at the head of Coire Cath nam Fionn; continuing on, on a bearing, I was soon at the next summit of Beinn Bhrotain. From the trig-point, still in thick cloud, I took a fresh bearing which took me south-east and down off the snow. Crossing the bleak moorland the 'top' of Carn Cloich-mhuilinn now stood before me. I met my only other walker of the day on the summit, which either shows how bad the weather was, or just how big the Cairngorms are, so that you can still have the hills almost all to yourself.

After dropping down to the east I found a ridge which led almost all the way back down to the Dee. I was soon reunited with my bike and freewheeled most of the way back to the Linn of Dee. This was the first day I'd used my bike to access the hills like this; I only had a road bike but it convinced me of the benefits of cycling in to the foot of the hills rather than facing a long walk in and out. The following week I bought myself a mountain-bike which was used quite extensively on later hill trips.

Derry Cairngorm   3,788ft   Carn a'Mhaim   3,402ft

These two peaks lie either side of Luibeg Burn and to save a long walk in I cycled up Glen Lui to beyond Derry Lodge. A bridge was shown on the map at Luibeg, but it had gone, washed away, so I had to wade and push the bike through the river which, thanks to a dry summer, was unusually low.

When I reached the end of the woods I padlocked the bike to a tree and set off directly up the hillside towards Carn Crom. There were several deer lying just below the summit, they watched me warily but didn't run off as I passed close by. Once on Carn Crom the worst of the climbing was over and a long, broad ridge led easily up to the cairn on Derry Cairngorm. From here I made a detour from the planned horse-shoe route, to collect a couple of extra 'tops'. First Sgurr an Lochan Uaine, which overlooks the head of Glen Derry, then Creagan a'Choire Etchachan, from where I looked down onto Loch Etchachan. It was so hot I was tempted to drop down for a swim but I chickened out!

The summit of Ben Macdui came next; as expected it was swarming with people, the first I had seen all day. I headed south-east, over Stob Coire Sputan Dearg and out to the 'top', Sron Riach. These are both perched on the edge of a huge cliff which falls away to the green waters of Lochan Uaine. I now faced a big descent to a col over-looking the Lairig Ghru before a long drag took me up the narrow arête onto Carn a'Mhaim. A line of crags blocked a direct descent to the glen so I had to cut down the steep slopes to the north-east until I was safely below the crags, only then could I make my way downstream to Luibeg bridge and so back to the bike.

With the track running gently downhill all the way back to the road it didn't take long to reach the car to end another great day out.

Ben Macdui 4,296ft

Britain's second highest mountain forms part of the huge Cairngorm plateau and like many peaks it is an entirely different proposition in winter than it is in summer. I've twice tried to climb it on ski; the first time a group of us skied in from the Coire Cas car-park, over into Coire an Lochain and up onto the plateau. We made it quite close to the top before deteriorating weather made us turn tail; we returned via Lurchers Gully, which gave us some good downhill. Sometime later I tried again, this time skinning up over Cairngorm first, but again 'whiteout' conditions made life on top very difficult and instead we headed for the ridge along to Lurchers Gully and an easy descent.

5: *Stuart, Pete & Jem walking in to Jean's Hut, late afternoon (the hut is now removed)*

One of my first times to the top was one November when a group of us were renting a chalet in Aviemore for the week. Because of the short days at that time of year we decided to walk in late one afternoon and stay the night at Jean's Hut in Coire an Lochain, with a view to having an early start next morning. From the hut (which has since been removed) we climbed up out of the corrie and onto the plateau. It was a grey day with some snow about but the huge summit cairn wasn't too long in coming. After the usual celebratory photographs we headed back over the plateau, over Cairn

Gorm and back down to the road-end. Since that time I've run over the peak on countless occasions, in summer and in winter conditions. One such run, described elsewhere in this journal, was when I ran the Cairngorm 4,000's. By the time I reached Ben Macdui I had already run up Braeriach and Cairn Toul, crossed the Lairig Ghru, and climbed the Tailors Burn to reach the summit. The hard work was now over and that just left an easy run round to Cairn Gorm and the last few miles back down to Glen More.

I've also used the southern approach to climb Ben Macdui, although to save time I used the bike to just beyond Luibeg. A steep climb led up the ridge to Derry Cairngorm, then after a diversion to take in a couple of 'tops' the horseshoe led round onto Ben Macdui's sprawling summit. It was a warm summer day and the top was swarming with people, I even allowed myself a short rest in the sun by the cairn. Then it was on again, a big descent to the col, and steeply up onto a narrow ridge to Carn a'Mhaim before dropping down to regain the bike at Luibeg.

Cairn Gorm 4,084ft

This was my first ever Munro, but at that time I hadn't heard of the term and to me it was just a big hill. We were on a family holiday touring Scotland, when I was probably about 13. My sister and I, with our father, simply walked up the main tourist track in Coire Cas, beneath the ski tows. Meanwhile Mum and my brother took the chair-lift up; my brother had one leg in plaster following an operation on his foot. The climb left no lasting impression on me, but then again, an ascent of Cairn Gorm by this route in the summer is rarely going to provide much in the way of excitement.

Since that time I have run, walked, raced and skied to the top on countless occasions and have grown to love the area. In our late teens a group of us spent a lot of time in the Cairngorms; walking in October and November or teaching ourselves to ski over Christmas and the New Year.

A good route I've taken a few times in winter is to leave the Coire Cas car-park and climb up and over into Coire an t-Sneachda. From the corrie you climb up onto the ridge which, in the right snow conditions, can give a nice little walk, ending with a good scramble down into a dip before climbing to the plateau.

One ascent that I'll always remember was when I ran the Cairn Gorm Hill Race. We started on the road outside the camp-site in Glen More. The road gave a steep but fast ascent all the way up to the Coire Cas car-park; from the car-park we headed left and followed a footpath up through the heather and out onto the ridge. It had snowed heavily the day before the race, even though it was the end of June, and we were running on snow above 3,000ft. The race went up past the Ptarmigan Restaurant and on up the steps to the weather station by the cairn on the summit.

When racing at Dollar the previous weekend I'd lost several places on the descent so this time I was determined to 'go for it'. By the time I was back down at the Ptarmigan I had caught the chap in front and I chased him down into Coire Cas; I think I was airborne when I over-took him. My feet went from under me as I hurtled down the loose gravel track and I took off, coming to earth with a very big bump. I took the skin off both knees; both elbows; both hands; one shoulder and one cheek, but not the one on my face. Feeling more than a little shaken I picked myself up and walked the short way down to the mid-way station at the White Lady Shieling. Realising that nothing was broken and that it would take a long time if I walked all the way down, I started to jog the rest of the track to the car-park. By the time I reached the tarmac road I'd recovered from the shock and my confidence had returned so I switched back into racing mode, over-took many of those who had passed me while I was walking and raced down to the finish by the camp-site.

As I crossed the line, three or four ladies from the St Andrews Ambulance dashed over to support me as though I were about to collapse. When I looked at myself I realised why they were concerned. I was covered in blood; the running action had made a great job of spreading the blood around so that it had run all the way from my knees onto my socks and dripped off my elbows onto my shoes. I was a bit of a mess but after a shower things didn't look quite so bad; the kind ladies picked out the last of the gravel and patched me up. Since that time I've always been a cautious descender.

One March I was up in Aviemore with friends from the orienteering club, most of whom were downhill skiing, but a couple of us were on Telemark skis and we decided to go for a short tour. We skinned from the Coire Cas car-park straight up the hillside to the east, climbed the ridge past the Ptarmigan and from there it was an easy climb to the summit. We intended to go out to Ben Macdui but there were whiteout conditions on top which meant we had to ski slowly and navigate very carefully, not being able to see what was up and what was down. Once we had abandoned the idea of visiting Ben Macdui we headed for Cairn Lochan and found the ridge running north which in turn led us into Lurchers Gully and back to the car-park after an exciting day.

Another winter, a group of us had been skiing for a week at Cairngorm and we decided to have a night out in a snow hole. After skiing all day we dropped down to the car-park to collect our rucksacks and caught the last tow up the White Lady to the plateau. With about an hour of daylight remaining we were confident the five of us could construct a good sized shelter in the soft snow that was piled up along the snow fences by the uppermost ski-tow. What we hadn't taken into consideration was the sudden change in the weather. As we set to work to dig a cave the wind increased dramatically and within minutes it was blowing a freezing gale. Despite being well equipped and well prepared, it was impossible to complete our planned construction and instead we just ended up with a deep trench; using our skis and survival bags we were able to put a roof across one end. Stuart and Kevin were the lucky ones to squeeze in first and were reasonably sheltered under the roof, Pete and I were next in and were partially sheltered by having dug sideways into the wall, Jem was last in and he simply had the stars above him, but of course you couldn't see the stars through the blizzard.

It would have been virtually impossible to light the primus and cook dinner under those conditions so we shared some biscuits and lay huddled in our snow covered sleeping bags. It was a very long, very cold night, especially for Jem who was in the most exposed position, and it was he who gave in first. He left at some unearthly hour in the morning to ski alone down to the White Lady Shieling. As the rest of us prepared to leave a couple of hours later I couldn't find one of my ski-boots and was beginning to panic a bit, thinking it must be buried in the snow, we then discovered one of Jem's boots. As Jem had long since departed we realised he must have skied off wearing one of his boots, a white one, and one of mine, a blue one. We packed up and skied down to the White Lady Shieling to join Jem; surprising the restaurant staff who found us waiting on the doorstep for breakfast as they arrived.

As documented elsewhere, I've also run over the mountain several times as part of my solo runs over the Cairngorm 4,000's.

Bynack More   3,574ft

My first ascent of Bynack More started from the Coire na Ciste car-park, part way up the ski road. I set off across the heather, contoured round the hillside on a narrow deer track towards the small patch of woodland, crossed the ridge and dropped down into Strath Nethy. From here it was a long rough climb up onto the 'top' of Bynack Beg. Once on the ridge the going became easier and it didn't take long to reach the summit of Bynack More. Dropping south from the cairn I scrambled about on the granite tors for a while before continuing on, down to the broad saddle for the climb to another 'top', A'Choinneach.

I wanted to re-visit the small Fords of Avon bothy, so I dropped down the easy slopes to the east and followed the path to the hut. I'd been here twice before, once was on an energetic weekend; the first day I had walked from Coylumbridge through the Lairig Ghru to Braemar Youth Hostel; the following day I returned to Aviemore via Glen Derry and the Lairig an Laoigh.

The other occasion was when a group of us were staying in Aviemore for a week early one winter. We planned a two-day walk, over-nighting at the Fords of Avon bothy. The first day had gone to plan and we arrived at the hut tired and hungry. As we settled in our thoughts turned to food; the stoves, fuel and pans were unloaded from peoples 'sacs. We then waited for someone to produce the food. Slowly the horrible truth dawned on us; the food bags were still sitting on the kitchen table back in our chalet. All we had with us to feed six hungry lads was one small bag of salted peanuts that someone had left over from their lunch. A quick search of the hut turned up two *Oxo* cubes and a small candle. It didn't take long to prepare dinner that night, a cup of *Oxo* with a few peanuts floating in it. It was a somewhat hungry party that returned to Aviemore the following day having missed breakfast and lunch in addition to the previous nights' dinner.

On this occasion however I was well fed and I set off again, along the footpath heading for Loch Avon; from the east end of the loch I then made the short climb up to The Saddle. Just above here was a long snow slope in perfect condition. It was steep but quite safe and I quickly raced up it. From where I came out it didn't take long to reach the summit of Cairn Gorm before dropping down to the Ptarmigan for a well earned cup of tea. I returned down beneath the ski-tows into Coire na Ciste.

Beinn Mheadhoin   3,883ft

This was climbed on a glorious summer day from the Coire Cas car-park. I avoided the main path up Cairn Gorm and instead followed the ridge, beneath the ski-tows, out onto Fiacaill a'Choire Chais. This led easily up to the summit plateau and then gave me a pleasant stroll out to the south-west. I aimed for the stream which I knew I could follow safely through the gap in the crags at the head of Loch Avon.

An indistinct footpath led steeply down into the narrow glen and after crossing the river I made for the Shelter Stone, which in winter can be used for a cold and draughty bivouac. From here the path climbed up to the col and on up to the lovely Loch Etchachan. Climbing steeply to the east from the lochside I headed for Stacan Dubha, a 'top', which overlooks Loch Avon, then passed over the south-west 'top' and along the ridge to Beinn Mheadhoin, another mountain topped by rocky tors, similar to those on Bynack More and Ben Avon.

After scrambling about on the tors for a while I made a short detour out to another 'top', Stob Coire Etchachan before returning to Loch Etchachan and dropping down to Loch Avon. After passing around the west end of the loch I took the path along the north shore and followed this up to The Saddle, and on up into the corrie just below Cairn Gorm. Climbing out of the corrie brought me to the top of the upper-most ski-tow and from there it only took minutes to drop down to the Ptarmigan at the top station of the chair-lift. Following the ridge down through the snow fences I dropped down off the hill directly into the car-park, having carefully avoided the Tourist Path, and it's associated tourists, all day!

Beinn Bhreac   3,051ft   Beinn a'Chaorainn 3,553ft

One miserable Bank Holiday weekend in early May I set off from the car-park at the Linn of Dee to climb these two peaks which lie to the east of Glen Derry. A good track leads north from the road, through Glen Lui and up to Derry Lodge. A relatively tame herd of deer wandered among the trees down by the river and there were a couple of tents pitched in an idyllic spot.

As I came to the end of the woods in Glen Derry I turned east and headed straight up the hillside, climbing steeply onto the summit of Beinn Bhreac. The weather was horrible which meant I had to rely on map and compass to help me find the west 'top' of Beinn Bhreac, just half a mile away. There now followed a long stretch across the bleak Moine

Bhealaidh; a flat boggy area that was very, very wet underfoot. Another party kept appearing and disappearing through the gloom ahead of me but once on the firmer ground of the ridge leading to Beinn a'Chaorainn I soon passed them.

Leaving the cairn I kept a look-out for an easy descent route and managed to link together some long tongues of old snow, which took me steeply but quickly down into Glen Derry. Once down on the main Derry Lodge / Fords of Avon path I turned south and soon came across a side stream that fed into Derry Burn. In summer there are probably stepping stones here but today there was no way I could cross. I had to climb upstream for a good 400 yards before I could find somewhere safe to cross, even then I had to be very careful and had to wade waist deep through the icy water. A small group of walkers had come up from Derry Lodge but after seeing me cross they decided against it and turned round to go back the way they had come.

I walked quickly back down through Glen Derry and Glen Lui in an effort to warm up and dry out and was soon back at the car where I could at last empty my boots!

Beinn a'Bhuird   3,924ft
Ben Avon – Leabaidh an Daimh Bhuidhe   3,843ft

When I left the car to climb this pair of Munros and their many satellite 'tops' it was with the intention that it would be a long run and I was dressed accordingly. For some reason though I was tired after the first couple of easy miles, just running in on a land-rover track alongside Quoich Water in Glen Quoich. I briefly thought about turning round and returning to the car, but decided to press on and see how it went, although running now seemed out of the question.

The easy track continued to the head of Glen Quoich, crossed the river and then started to climb the ridge of An Diollaid. The track made for fast climbing despite me not being up to par and I was soon out at the south 'top' of Beinn a'Bhuird. From here it wasn't far to a rocky little top, A'Chioch, which is set above huge crags that drop steeply down to a small lochan below. The north top and main summit of Beinn a'Bhuird were reached easily, just by following the line of crags along. Feeling as I did, I willingly sacrificed the long detour out to the 'top' of Stob an t-Sluichd, leaving it for another day, instead I headed round the rim of the corrie to the next 'top', Cnap a' Chleirich.

Going north from here I came to a line of impressive crags ringing Garbh Coire and I followed the rim east along a narrow ridge which links the mass of Beinn a'Bhuird to Ben Avon. It was now only a short climb up the ridge to Ben Avon's high point of Leabaidh an Daimh Bhuidhe. The plateau is dotted with strange tors similar to those on its near neighbour Bynack More so I scrambled up one or two in passing as I headed out to Stob Bac an Fhurain. Still feeling weak I decided to 'pass' on the two 'tops' way out to the north and instead started to head for home.

On the way I took in the short climb of Mullach Lochan nan Gabhar, went out along the ridge to Stuc Garbh Mhor and contoured round to the tor on Stob Dubh an Eas Bhig. From here I headed south along an easy ridge to another 'top', Carn Eas, then sharply down to a saddle to the south-east for a short rise up onto the final 'top' Creag an Dail Mhor. From this last top I cut down the steep heathery hillside to a pass that led me down to Quoich Water. Faint deer tracks through the heather took me down alongside the stream, through a small patch of ancient forest and back to the land-rover track for the walk-out back to the road near Mar Lodge.

It was disappointing that I hadn't felt fit enough to visit all the 'tops' but after the way I felt at the start of the trip I looked on it not as three 'tops' missed but as two Munros and four 'tops' won.

Section 9: Loch Laggan; Monadh Liath

Beinn Teallach   3,003ft   Beinn a'Chaorainn   3,453ft

Beinn Teallach had only recently been promoted to Munro status, it was previously mapped at 2,994ft (913m) but a re-survey gave a revised height of 3,003ft (915m). My copy of *Munro's Tables* listed 276 Munros, so with the addition of Beinn Teallach this now made it 277.

A good forestry track headed north from the road at Roughburn Cottages on the A86, leaving the forest at a pleasant meadow on the Allt a'Chaorainn, a footpath then took me up the west bank of the stream beside another plantation. Once beyond the trees I quit the path and turned up the hillside, climbing up onto the ridge, which soon led me to the summit of Beinn Teallach. Among the rocks around the summit were three or four ptarmigan, they were well camouflaged, still in their winter plumage. From the summit I dropped down to the north, along a rough ridge, which brought me out at the head of the Allt a'Chaorainn by a cairn known as 'Tom Mor'.

I came across the fresh remains of a ptarmigan here, taken by a fox or perhaps an eagle. It was a long slog of a climb before I reached the ridge of Beinn a'Chaorainn; the top was covered in snow and huge cornices were ready to peel off into the steep corries to the east. The highest point was the central of three separate tops and after a short rest I continued on to the southern end of the ridge then just cut straight down the hillside to regain the track beside the stream in the glen below.

Creag Meagaidh   3,700ft   Stob Poite Coire Ardair 3,460ft
Carn Liath   3,298ft

I made the round of Coire Ardair one May Bank Holiday weekend. An un-missable path of railway sleepers, laid end to end, climbs up through the trees and sweeps round into the corrie and on up to the lochan at its head. I turned off a short distance before the lochan and struck directly up the hillside on a steep climb to the 'top' of Sron a'Choire. On the way up the climb I found a stag's skull, complete with two very impressive antlers. The skull was fairly clean and I was tempted to carry it back as a trophy, but it was heavy so I left it for someone else to find. By the time I reached the cairn on Sron a'Choire it was raining and the wind was building, so it was on with the full wet-weather gear and with map in one hand and compass in the other I pressed on, over Creag Mhor and along above the steep cliffs to Puist Coire Ardair. From here I headed out south on a long detour to 'bag' the 'top' of Meall Coire Choille-rais, which sits above another impressive corrie, and then out on a 'there and back' along the spur for another outlying 'top', An Cearcallach.

On returning towards the main massif, as I was concentrating on a bearing designed to bring me out onto the summit of Creag Meagaidh, a small bird flew up from my feet. Instinctively I looked down and there, only inches from my boot, was a tiny nest, just a scrape in the grass, with four eggs. When I described the bird, the nest and the eggs to someone at the B&B that evening we decided that it was probably a dotterel, and if so I was to consider myself lucky. Later, when I checked the reference books I found that in the 1970's it was thought that there were only around 50 breeding pairs left in Scotland although numbers are now recovering. I was lucky to have come across one with its nest and was very glad that I hadn't trodden on the eggs.

After finding the cairn on Creag Meagaidh I had to navigate carefully through thick cloud to find the pass known as 'The Window', which cuts a deep notch in the ridge. Once down at the notch I was out of the clouds at last and the rest of the afternoon stayed clear and dry. It didn't take long to climb to the summit of Stob Poite Coire Ardair then an easy walk along the broad grassy ridge took me to the mountain's east 'top', soon followed by Sron Garbh Coire and Meall an-t-Snaim, another 'top'. From the latter there was just one more short climb up onto the day's final Munro, Carn Liath. Leaving the cairn I dropped straight down the ridge back to the path of 'sleepers' in the glen below to end another long but interesting day.

Sometime later, looking for a short run, I was back to collect the 'top' at the east end of the ridge that I'd omitted on that first visit. I set off from the roadside at Aberarder Farm on a warm afternoon, ran in along the 'sleepers' and up through the forest. From the end of the forest I took to the steep hillside for a brute of a climb, straight up onto Carn Liath. Once at the cairn I was able to catch my breath and it was a lovely run along the top of the ridge, out over A'Bhuiheanach and along to the 'top', Stob Coire Dubh. From here I retraced my steps a short way along the ridge to a col, before plunging straight down the steep hillside on a knee jarring descent to the Allt a'Chrannaig. Once beside the stream the going became easier and it gave an enjoyable run back to the roadside.

Geal Charn   3,036ft

Not having the inclination to add this one to the round of the Monadh Liath peaks it meant a short trip up the A9 to 'bag' it separately.

I drove up past Laggan to the road-end at Spey Dam and walked in along a good track up into Glen Markie. Once beyond the end of the forest I crossed the Markie Burn and climbed steeply up the heathery hillside to Beinn Sgiath. On rounding the head of a narrow gully it left only a short climb up to the summit plateau, where a couple of families of ptarmigan ran about in confusion as I reached the large cairn.

It was a dry but grey day so I continued round the rim of crags to complete the horse-shoe of the corrie. It didn't take long to drop down into the glen to regain the track, which was followed alongside the river back to the dam to end a rather uneventful day.

The Monadh Liath -
A'Chailleach   **3,045ft**   **Carn Sgulain**   **3,015ft**
Carn Dearg   **3,093ft**

This group of hills gave a pleasant, undemanding walk one summer's day. After leaving the car at the road-end I followed the track north along the edge of the wood, up alongside the Allt a'Chaorainn until the track ended at the stream. Here I crossed over to the west bank and climbed diagonally up the heather clad hillside, past a small hut which is presumably used by stalkers, and on up the easy slopes towards the ridge. Just below the ridge I came onto an area of peat-hags; once through these I was soon on the summit of A'Chailleach.

It was great not to need a map and compass for a change; I could see to choose a good line down to the stream to the north, a short climb then led up to the undistinguished cairn on Carn Sgulain. The next few miles were across a virtual plateau, with old fence posts leading the way over Meall a'Bhothain to the shallow rise to the 'top' of Carn Ballach.

From here there was a negligible drop then re-ascent to the 'top' of Carn Ban; this was followed by a short detour out along a spur to the west to 'bag' Snechdach Slinnean. I only did this thinking that Snechdach Slinnean was another 'top' but I realised later that it had been demoted in the last re-shuffle of the lists. With the day continuing fine I contoured round below Carn Ban and out onto its south ridge which was followed easily up to Carn Dearg; this is a slightly more impressive summit due to the narrowness of the ridge. The narrow ridge continued to the mountains south-east 'top' where I enjoyed a long rest in the sun, knowing that the end was now in sight.

It wasn't a day for hurrying and I slowly made my way off the hill, dropping down to a col, then steeply down alongside a burn into Gleann Ballach. Following the advice of the guide-book I 'cut the corner' and contoured round; by keeping out of the bottom of the glen I avoided the worst of the boggy areas. As I dropped down to the bridge at Glenballach it was indeed wet, but this soon passed and the track led me comfortably back to the road-end.

A busy little tea-room in Newtonmore provided appropriate sustenance after a long hot day on the hill.

Section 10: Loch Lochy; Gulvain; Ciche & Kingie; Knoydart; Loch Quoich; South Glen Shiel; The Saddle

Sron a'Choire Ghairbh 3,066ft   Meall na Teanga 3,010ft

Situated above Loch Lochy this pair of Munros are best approached from the south, from a road known as 'The Dark Mile'. The route starts with a long walk in through thick forest up into Gleann Cia-aig. After climbing up into the glen for about three miles the path switches to the west bank of the stream for another mile and a half of bleak moorland. Just before the ruins of an old cottage I crossed the stream and followed the Allt cam Bhealaich up into the corrie. As I climbed up through the peat hags I disturbed several deer, the stags looked in good condition as this was early November and the middle of the rut; the sound of their bellowing kept me company all day.

I was able to pick up a good track which took me up to the saddle between the two peaks. First I climbed Sron a'Choire Ghairbh to the north; a good stalkers path climbed steeply up in tight zigzags until it petered out near the top and I followed a compass bearing to the top of the crags, which led me round to the summit cairn. Buried in the cairn was a tin containing a small book, so I added my name and a brief comment before returning across the snow to the top of the stalkers path, which quickly took me back down to the col.

A short climb up the heathery ridge then took me up to Meall Dubh, from where some careful navigation through heavy cloud saw me to the northern ridge of Meall na Teanga, which thankfully appeared right on cue. After a further short climb I was soon beside the summit cairn. From here I dropped down to the south-west and traversed along the edge of Coire Odhar Beag and Coire Odhar Mor. The more level ground here made for faster progress and when the ridge started to turn north I began to descend due west to return to the path just where it entered the forest. It was a pleasant stroll back down through the trees to the roadside.

Gulvain   3,224ft

The ascent of Gulvain involves a long approach of five miles before you even set foot on the mountain and unfortunately I had to do it twice.

My first attempt was on a wild February day. On the previous day I had intended climbing Sgurr Mor to the north of Loch Arkaig, but the roads were flooded and I couldn't get anywhere near it. On the Sunday it was still wet and windy as I walked in from the cottages at the west end of Loch Eil, heading for Gulvain. A good land-rover track led deep into the hills up Gleann Fionnlighe, following a river which tumbled over several small falls. Reaching the end of the track you have no choice other than to attack the steep grassy slope ahead of you, which climbs over 800m in about a mile.

With no sign of a path it was hard work climbing in an ever strengthening wind. Undecided whether or not to continue I slowly climbed higher, although by now I was finding it difficult to keep upright, but I eventually reached the south summit, a 'top', on the exposed ridge. On a good day the main summit would have been no more than a ten minute stroll away, but on that wild day I couldn't stand up and was being buffeted by winds, the like of which I'd never experienced before. I lay on the ground hanging on to the largest rocks I could find while thinking to myself that it was perhaps a silly way to spend an afternoon. A couple of futile efforts to progress along the ridge convinced me that if I were to be blown off the ridge I could actually be killed.

"The test of an adventure is that when you're in the middle of it, you say to yourself, 'Oh now I've got myself into an awful mess, I wish I were sitting quietly at home'. And the sign that something's wrong with you is when you sit quietly at home wishing you were out having lots of adventure."

(Thornton Wilder)

Once I'd accepted the idea of retreat I lost no time in dropping down onto the sheltered east side of the mountain. With no Munro to show for the day it seemed a long walk back to the car, already planning a return visit.

The return, a month or two later, was uneventful and somewhat easier as I took my bike to save the 10 mile grind along the land-rover track. One point to remember if you're on top with no visibility is that the top shown with a trig point on OS Landranger map 40 (Loch Shiel) is actually the lower, south summit. The end of the ridge, along with the higher north summit, is on sheet 41 (Ben Nevis).

Sgurr Thuilm   3,164ft   Sgurr nan Coireachan   3,136ft

These two peaks in the remote hills to the north of Glenfinnan give a natural horseshoe ridge walk around Coire Thollaidh.

I started from the Visitor Centre at the Glenfinnan Monument and followed the land-rover track up the glen and under the impressive curves of the railway viaduct. My map seemed to indicate that from here there was just a footpath up the glen, but a land-rover track continued up to some new buildings and beyond, in fact all the way to the foot of Sgurr Thuilm. It was therefore an unexpectedly easy walk in, past large areas of new forestry planting on both sides of the river. An open bothy at Corryhully looked palatial, it even had electricity.

Continuing up the glen I crossed the river where it forked and started on the ascent of Druim Coire a'Bheithe. The steep grassy slopes were hard going, very reminiscent of its near neighbour, Gulvain, but once out onto the ridge it gave an easy climb to Sgurr Thuilm.

The low clouds denied me any distant views but I could see just enough to make navigation reasonably easy; along the narrow ridge, over several intervening tops, and around the head of Coire Thollaidh. Here the path led up through rocky steps onto the summit of Sgurr nan Coireachan.

The ridge continued south, bounded by huge crags that dropped steeply into the corrie, before taking me onto Sgurr a'Choire Riabhaich. As I left the cairn here I dropped out of the clouds and could now see a reasonable route back to the glen. I slowly descended and at the same time traversed south, to eventually pick up a stalkers path that took me down to the land-rover track. It was an easy three mile walk-out, back under the viaduct, and down to the road.

I spent some time revising my map that day; adding on new buildings, tracks, several bridges and large areas of new plantations on both sides of the river.

"I am told there are people who do not care for maps, and find it hard to believe" (Robert Louis Stevenson)

Sgurr na Ciche   3,410ft   Garbh Chioch Mhor   3,365ft
Sgurr nan Coireachan 3,125ft

The long drive-in along Loch Arkaig gave me almost as much excitement as the day on the hill; the narrow single-track road was glazed with ice in parts and thick fog made driving very difficult.

It was mid-November and there had been some early snow, so I decided to cycle part way in to save some time. A good land-rover track took me all the way up to the cottage at

Upper Glendessary where I left the bike padlocked to a fence. Unfortunately the clouds had closed in and covered the tops as I followed the path about three miles up the glen, to where it turned a corner towards Loch Nevis. From this corner I started straight up the hillside to cross a spur. I was by now in thick cloud and walking on a bearing to traverse the rough ground that took me on to the col between Sgurr na Ciche and Garbh Chioch Mhor. A steep rocky gully would usually have been easy, but today the rocks were glazed with ice, which made things more than a little tricky. I had to take care but was soon up on the col. From the col I climbed left to avoid some difficult crags; a faint line of intermittent footprints just showed in places in the snow but I lost them crossing a boulder field. Without being able to see more than about 20 yards I had to guess where best to break through the steep crags, but at last the ground started to level out and I knew I must be almost on top. I found the old footprints again and followed these to the cairn on Sgurr na Ciche.

After a quick stop for tea and a *Mars Bar*, I turned about and returned to the col. An old stone wall led south away from the col and helped guide me up the ridge, which gave a bit of a scramble in places, up to the stony summit of Garbh Chioch Mhor. The wall continued along the narrow ridge and firm snow took me quickly to the 'top' of Garbh Chioch Bheag. From here the ridge dropped steadily through small crags to the Bealach nan Gall.

Across the far side of the col a bearing took me through the clouds in a north-easterly direction; some easy scrambling soon saw me beside the summit cairn on Sgurr nan Coireachan. Worried about the time I sought out the south ridge and followed this for half a mile; down off the snow and down out of the clouds. It was a rough descent but I was soon able to rejoin the track, headed back to Upper Glendessary where I collected the bike for the short ride out.

Sgurr Mor   3,290ft

As I had chosen to omit Sgurr Mor when I climbed the other Munros on the north side of Glen Dessary, it meant I had to make a long detour, out along Loch Arkaig, the following Spring. I decided the ascent of Sgurr Mor on its own would make a good run.

Parking at the road-end at the western end of Loch Arkaig I ran in, along the land-rover track to Glendessary. Here the hard work started as I took to the path which climbed steeply up alongside the stream. It was hot work as I climbed to the pass and once on the saddle I had to leave the path and take to the rough hillside for a big descent, down to the infant River Kingie.

I was now faced with a really hard climb; the sweat was pouring off me as I forced a good pace up the seriously steep grass and heather to gain the ridge at the col between Sgurr Beag and Sgurr Mor. Reaching the col gave me the chance to catch my breath, before climbing the final 800ft or so along the ridge to Sgurr Mor.

After a handful of jelly-babies I crossed the summit and followed the path down the ridge to the east. On reaching the new col I dropped down the steep slopes, zigzagging my way down to the river below. The water was ice cold and very refreshing, which revived me for the short climb up the heather and tussocks to regain the path at the saddle. From here it was good to be running properly again and the descent to Glendessary was taken at speed. The two miles back to Loch Arkaig were hard on the feet but gave a good 'warm down'.

It was a superb, high-mountain run of about 11 miles with some 4,000ft of climbing.

Gairich   3,015ft

Gairich lies on the south side of Loch Quoich and is great for a short day out. I started from the dam at the east end of the loch and followed the path, initially along the lochside, then across heather to the edge of a wood. From here a good stalkers path climbed the easy angled ridge. When the path ended at a pony stance cut into the hillside, the route continued up the ridge to a plateau and a lochan. Just below the summit the ridge steepened again and the path made its way through broken crags to the top.

As the rocks were wet and greasy the descent through the crags had to be taken with care but once I was down onto the broader grassy ridge I started to jog, then gathered speed so that I was soon hurtling down to the footpath by the woods, which quickly led me back to the dam. I camped that night on a soft grassy patch by the river where it emerged from beneath the dam.

A couple of years later I was again at a loose end for an afternoon; I ran the same route in foul conditions but once down below the clouds I could pick up speed again and was back at the camper-van in a little over the hour.

Knoydart -
Ladhar Bheinn	3,343ft	**Luinne Bheinn**	3,083ft
Meall Buidhe	3,107ft		

The Knoydart peaks were saved for a weekend that promised fine weather. It was a long drive-in along the north side of Loch Garry and Loch Quoich, down a very narrow road to the road-end at the small collection of farms at Kinloch Hourn.

Leaving the car I had a wonderful walk in along the shoreline and the six miles soon passed. During the walk I enjoyed fine views of Ladhar Bheinn, across the other side of Barrisdale Bay. There is a well maintained bothy at Barrisdale but I joined a couple of other tents pitched outside. After lunch and a brew, and with a somewhat lighter rucksack, I headed off for Ladhar Bheinn, the most westerly of the mainland Munros.

Across the river a stalkers path climbed up over the nose of Creag Bheithe and then led round into the narrow entrance of Coire Dhorrcail. Here a superb view opened up before me, the corrie opened out and huge cliffs formed an impressive headwall. From the path, I dropped down to cross the stream and started the climb onto the terraces of Druim a'Choire Odhair. The 'top' of Stob a'Choire Odhair quickly followed and after a short scramble I was soon up on the main summit of Ladhar Bheinn; a trig point a short way to the west is not at the highest point.

After a bit of a breather I continued on around the rim of the corrie, dropping down to a saddle, before climbing again to Aonach Sgoilte. From here I had a choice of two ridges; one heading north towards Loch Hourn, the other, which I chose, led east and dropped steeply down to the track over Mam Barrisdale. That left me just a mile or so back to the tent beside the bothy to end a long hard day.

Unfortunately the previous day's good weather didn't last and it was a bit bleak when I left the tent next morning. I followed the track south for a while, before a smaller path split off and climbed alongside a stream up into Gleann Unndalain and onto a col. The summit of Luinne Bheinn was hidden in the clouds as I climbed the ridge from the col; it was a lumpy sort of ridge which seemed to go on forever, then, out of the gloom the cairn appeared. It was too cold to loiter on top so I retraced my steps for a couple of hundred yards before dropping steeply down the hillside, out of the clouds and down to the saddle below.

A lone tent was pitched high in the corrie but there was no one about as I moved quickly past. I climbed onto another long, even lumpier ridge, which first led south, then turned west to climb into the clouds and drizzle once more. The situation should have been splendid but I could see no more than about 10 yards and could only guess at the views I was missing. From the summit of Meall Buidhe I retraced my steps back down to the col beneath Luinne Bheinn. A tiring traverse round under Luinne Bheinn saw me back down at the Mam Barrisdale, from where it didn't take long to return to my tent.

After a leisurely lunch at the tent it was just a matter of loading up the rucksack for the walk-out back to Kinloch Hourn. Yet another place I knew I would return to when I could.

Beinn Sgritheall   3,196ft

Situated above the north shore of Loch Hourn this peak was ideal for a short day. Starting from the end of the wood, beside the loch, I climbed the steep open hillside. A couple of deer raced out of the forest as I made my way towards the saddle high above the loch. It was a very, very hot summers day so I was pleased to have a short rest beside the lochan before setting to work on the long slog up the ridge to the summit. I'd forgotten to bring any water with me, and the climb had been a tough one in the heat, so I made a detour near the top, into a small gully where a tiny stream tinkled through the rocks. From the gully it was an easy walk up onto the north-west 'top' of Beinn Sgritheall, then only a short climb up onto the main summit.

Once on top I made the most of this rare occasion; I was on a summit with a great view and with plenty of time on my hands, so I lay in the sun for half an hour, looking out over the water to the mountains on Skye, across to the peaks of Knoydart and out to the Glen Shiel peaks. To descend, I followed the ridge east, down to a col and from here dropped down a steep grassy gully towards the road. Half-way down I cut off right to follow the line of a strange deep cut gorge, which led back to the road just half a mile east of the car.

Sgurr a'Mhaoraich 3,365ft

I climbed Sgurr a'Mhaoraich on the 1st May 1988 as my contribution to the *Boots Across Scotland* appeal to raise money for an injured climber. The aim was to put someone on top of every Munro at 1pm on that Sunday afternoon; to ensure success most peaks had at least two parties assigned to it.

From half-way along the north shore of Loch Quoich a good stalkers path climbed directly up the grassy ridge of Bac nan Canaichean. As I climbed higher the ridge turned west and narrowed and after passing over Sgurr Coire nan Eiricheallach I lost a little height to a col. Above here the ridge was covered in late snow and the conditions were terrible; almost gale force winds and virtually zero visibility. I scrambled over some rocky pinnacles searching for the summit cairn but I reached what I thought was the end of the ridge without finding the top. Retracing my steps, I carefully checked the top of each pinnacle and rocky outcrop but I still couldn't find the actual summit. Eventually, on my third try I found traces of old footprints in the snow and these led me to the cairn, which was no more than 100 yards away. I made it to the top just on the stroke of 1pm and met another couple there; I was pleased to hear that they too had had trouble finding the cairn in the awful weather. With no enthusiasm to go searching out the 'top' of Sgurr a'Mhaoraich Beag I about turned and retreated off the hill as quickly as I could.

Unfortunately the weather had been similar all over Scotland that day and two Munros remained unclimbed. Sadly the news came through that one of the participants had fallen when descending from Beinn Tulaichean and was killed. The appeal was a success though and several thousands of pounds were raised to assist not only the injured climber in his rehabilitation, but also funded vital medical equipment for the hospital in Glasgow that had treated him and radios for the Glencoe Mountain Rescue Team.

Gleouraich   3,395ft   Spidean Mialach   3,268ft

I climbed these two peaks one fine November morning. A well made stalkers path climbed steeply but easily up onto the south ridge; the ridge then levelled out and gave great views to the south and west, down over the windswept Loch Quoich. A recent fall of snow had left a good covering above about 2,500ft, but it was very soft which made the going a bit difficult over the rocky ground. As I progressed up the ridge a short sharp blizzard came out of nowhere and made visibility bad for a while but it had cleared again by the time I reached the summit of Gleouraich. A trig-point was shown on the map but I couldn't find one anywhere near the cairn, which was unmistakeably the top.

The route continued east, over the 'top' of Craig Coire na Fiar Bhealaich, before dropping steeply down a rocky ridge to the col. From the col a climb of around 800ft, above steep cliffs to the north, soon brought me to the summit of Spidean Mialach. I enjoyed a short rest beside the cairn while admiring the views north to the peaks of the South Cluanie Ridge and south down to Loch Quoich. Leaving the summit I jogged quickly down to the lochan I could see below, a footpath then led back down to the road a short distance from the car.

South Glen Shiel -
Creag a'Mhaim	**3,102ft**	**Druim Shionnach**	**3,222ft**
Aonach air Chrith	**3,342ft**	**Maol Chinn-dearg**	**3,214ft**
Sgurr an Lochain	**3,282ft**	**Creag nan Damh**	**3,012ft**
Sgurr an Doire Leathain	**3,272ft**		

The Cluanie Ridge is a Munro Bagger's paradise giving seven Munros in just eight miles and with only nominal descents and re-ascents between them. To avoid having a long walk along the road I left the car at the old bridge at the west end of the ridge, then cycled up the glen to the Cluanie Inn and up the land-rover track for a mile or so, where I padlocked the bike to a fence post.

From a bend in the track where it crosses the Allt Giubhais, I took to the hillside; the going was quite tough, through deep heather. As I climbed higher, so the conditions became easier, until I could pick up a faint path that led to a saddle on the main ridge, just north-west of the eastern-most peak, Creag a'Mhaim. By now the day was very hot and I had already used up half the water in my bottle. Once on the saddle there was only a short climb to the summit of Creag a'Mhaim but the 200ft climb took longer than it should have as the whole summit seemed to be balanced on a heap of unstable scree. It was an unnerving scramble but once on top I was able to enjoy the rest of the high-level traverse.

Dropping back down the scree to the col was fine and after that the rest of the ridge was mainly on short grass, which made for fast going. I was soon over Druim Shionnach and Aonach air Chrith and by this time the last of my water had gone. Being high up on a ridge like this meant there was no water within easy reach and in the exceptionally hot weather it was becoming a bit of a problem. The next part of the ridge was quite narrow and gave an airy traverse on to Maol Chinn-dearg. The following two summits came very quickly, and for little effort; first Sgurr an Doire Leathain, then Sgurr an Lochain. With the end of the ridge in sight and just one more peak left to climb, I decided to have a rest by the cairn. In the warm still air I soon nodded off and was virtually asleep; a slight rustle of stones roused me from my day-dreams and there, standing above me, was a bikini-clad beauty. I had to pinch myself to make sure I wasn't dreaming; I'd seen virtually no one all day and the way she seemed to appear out of thin air on this exposed peak was unreal. A couple of minutes later her companion joined her on the summit and I knew I was back in the real world so I packed my 'sac and headed off.

A small subsidiary top meant an extra drop and a climb of a few hundred feet, but I was soon on the day's final summit, that of Creag nan Damh. By this time I had had nothing to drink for quite a while and was glad to call it a day, so I dropped down to the north and picked up a short ridge running down to Sgurr a'Chuilinn. It didn't take long to then drop down the fairly steep broken hillside to the old bridge. Thankfully I had a litre bottle of lemonade in the car and this went down almost in one go. Duly refreshed I then drove up the glen to just beyond the Cluanie Inn to collect my bike, after a long but immensely satisfying day.

The Saddle   3,317ft   Sgurr na Sgine   3,098ft

It was late March when I climbed this pair of Munros; having driven up that morning, it was already quite late in the afternoon before I set off from the lay-by at the foot of the stalkers path in Glen Shiel. The path gave me a reasonably quick and painless climb as it cut across the face of the hillside to gain the broad saddle above. I hurried over the small rise of Meallan Odhar and around the head of the deep corrie; this landed me at the foot of the Forcan Ridge. It was an entertaining scramble up the narrow rocky arête, the way being complicated by a little snow that still covered the route.

Rocky pinnacles and greasy slabs were climbed or by-passed, and I tried not to pay too much attention to the fearsome looking drops on either side. Eventually though I arrived on the 'top' of Sgurr nan Forcan. From here the view along the rest of the ridge to The Saddle looked a little daunting. A tricky little descent to a narrow gap in the ridge led to a rough scramble back onto the crest, this was made more difficult by the old snow, but at last I made it to the trig-point on the summit ridge.

Keeping one eye on the time I quickly started down the steep grassy slopes to the south of the summit and traversed round and down to the Bealach Coire Mhalagain. From the small lochan a short steep climb took me up onto the ridge and this was followed round over the rocks to the north-west 'top' then to the cairn of Sgurr na Sgine itself. Worried about the time I hastily returned to the Bealach Coire Mhalagain and traversed back round onto Meallan Odhar; from here I was able to relax and wandered comfortably down the stalkers path to reach the roadside with a little daylight to spare.

Section 11: North Glen Shiel; A'Chralaig; Glen Affric;

The Five Sisters of Kintail -
Sgurr na Ciste Duibhe   3,370ft   Sgurr Fhuaran   3,505ft

Having driven through Glen Shiel many times I had long admired the Five Sisters of Kintail, which tower above Loch Duich, and it was a walk I wanted to save for a fine day.

Late one May, after camping at Shiel Bridge, I drove a short way up the glen to park at the old bridge, by the site of the battle. It was a beautiful morning as I climbed steeply from the road, following the edge of the forest, then alongside a stream, to eventually reach the ridge at a low col between Sgurr na Ciste Duibhe and Sgurr nan Spainteach. From the col it was only a short detour east, to take in the 'top' of Sgurr nan Spainteach. Returning along the ridge it was then only a short climb up onto Sgurr na Ciste Duibhe.

The views across Glen Shiel to the south, along the ridge to the other tops, and north out over Beinn Fhada made the steep climb worthwhile and for a change the map and compass stayed in the rucksack the whole day.

Continuing on along the ridge I passed easily over the 'top' of Sgurr na Carnach (note 1), dropped down to the bealach and then faced a short but steep little climb up to the highest of the five sisters, Sgurr Fhuaran. It was great to be able to laze by the cairn, looking further along the ridge and away down the whole length of Loch Duich. I soon grew restless, dropped down to the saddle to the north and continued on along the ridge to the last of the 'tops', Sgurr nan Saighead. From here impressively steep looking crags led along to the end of the ridge where I choose the western spur, which started to take me down towards Shiel Bridge. After a while I dropped down the steep grassy banks to the south to reach the floor of the glen about a mile north of the farm at Achnangart. The meadows alongside the river took me to the farm and the bridge out to the road; that just left a couple of miles on tarmac back to the car at Glenshiel Bridge.

The day certainly lived up to my expectations and gave a thoroughly enjoyable high-level ridge walk.

Saileag   3,124ft   Sgurr a'Bhealaich Dheirg 3,378ft
Ciste Dhubh 3,218ft   Aonach Meadhoin   3,284ft

My first visit to this group of Munros was on a wet October day; I climbed from the Cluanie Inn, up into the boggy An Caorann Beag and so onto the broad saddle of Bealach a'Choinich. It was more than a little grim; I couldn't even see the hill rising from just across the other side of the saddle. A bearing led me to the ridge, which climbed steeply before crossing over boulders as the ridge levelled out, and so on up to the cairn on Ciste Dhubh at the far end of the ridge.

With the growing wind now behind me I lost no time in returning to the bealach and, with compass still in hand, located the ridge running off to the south-west. The climb seemed endless, back into thick cloud and up to the 'top' of Sgurr an Fhuarail, then on around the ridge onto Aonach Meadhoin. When I'd set out I wasn't sure how far I would go, the four Munros were a possibility, but I was cold and wet and couldn't pluck up the courage to go any further. Instead I followed the spur that ran out to the south, dropped down to the stream and followed this down to the forest. The mile or so back along the road to the car was done in freezing rain, making me glad that I wasn't still slogging it out over the tops.

I returned to complete the route on a glorious day late one April, when snow still covered the tops. Setting off from a lay-by in Glen Shiel I made my way through a break in the forest, immediately climbing steeply up the rough hillside. It was hot, sweaty work and when I reached the snowline it became even harder as I struggled to gain a good footing in the steep soft snow. Eventually though I arrived on the ridge without mishap and climbed the short distance up onto Saileag. It was bliss to sit in the sun, enjoying the stunning views all around, while I got my breath back.

Once on the ridge the snow was firmer and I moved easily along, over Sgurr a'Bhealaich Dheirg and Aonach Meadhoin, and out onto the 'top' of Sgurr an Fhuarail. From here I dropped steeply back down to the road, about four miles east of the car.

A'Chralaig 3,673ft   Mullach Fraoch-choire 3,614ft

It was early one October when I climbed this pair of peaks which form the western branch of the North Cluanie horseshoe. Signs were posted by the roadside warning of deer-stalking so I thought I'd better play safe and asked at the estate cottage if my intended route was ok. There was no problem with the game-keeper and he wished me a pleasant walk, although this was starting to look unlikely as the rain was coming on and the clouds were clamped right down around the tops.

A footpath led up towards the pass at the head of An Caorann Mor and I followed this for some way. As I was about to cross one of the side streams I noticed a brown nylon tent bag, it looked full and I excitedly starting thinking what sort of light-weight tent I'd found; when I picked it up I was disappointed to find I'd only won a *Karrimat*. Nevertheless I added it to my rucksack and started up the rough hillside, climbing steeply to gain the ridge, which led easily out to A'Chralaig.

From here a fairly narrow ridge ran down to the north to the 'top' of Stob Coire na Cralaig, before twisting round above deep corries. The path wound through the rocky outcrops and up to the cairn on the summit of Mullach Fraoch-choire. After a short detour of only a few hundred yards I collected the mountains north-east top too.

From here I retraced my steps back over the main summit, along the interesting part of the ridge back to Stob Coire na Cralaig. Here I found the spur which took me down towards the watershed; thankfully as I lost height the clouds thinned and I could see to choose the easiest route. With tired knees I eventually regained the path in the An Caorann Mor, which led somewhat boggily back to the roadside.

Carn Ghluasaid   3,140ft   Sgurr nan Conbhairean   3,635ft Sail Chaorainn   3,285ft

These three peaks, forming the eastern arm of the North Cluanie horseshoe, gave me an unexpectedly hard walk one afternoon in November. It was after mid-day when I set off from the roadside and followed the old military road for a short distance before picking up the stalkers path which climbed steeply into the clouds. As the angle eased off a little an easy ridge took me to Carn Ghluasaid.

A ridge running out to the north-west then took me over the 'top' of Creag a'Chaorainn and on up to Sgurr nan Conbhairean. A short rest beside the cairn just made me wetter and colder so I hastened on along the ridge out to the north. Drifts of early snow covered the path in places but I was soon by the cairn of Sail Chaorainn. Continuing north I quickly lost count of all the knolls I was crossing and in the mist it was hard to tell exactly how far I was along the ridge. It was only when a brief break in the clouds gave me a glimpse down to Loch a'Choinich that I realised I had reached the last 'top' Tigh Mor na Seilge.

I returned along the ridge, following my own footprints through the snow, back over Sgurr nan Conbhairean. From the saddle just below I dropped down to the south, contouring and descending to finally come out onto the stalkers path which led me back to the roadside just as darkness was falling.

A'Ghlas-bheinn   3,006ft

When I left the car on a very wet November afternoon it was simply to go and visit the spectacular Falls of Glomach, the second highest falls in Scotland. I thought that with all the recent rain the falls would be in full spate and I wasn't disappointed. It was only after I had been out in the rain for about an hour that I thought I might as well take in A'Ghlas-bheinn while I was so close to it.

The walk started from a small parking place in the forest; a track climbed up along the stream and thankfully there was some shelter from the wind here. All too soon I was out of the protection of the forest and on a path across the open hillside; this climbed steeply, still following the stream up to the Bealach na Sroine. From here a short descent took me to the falls which dropped vertically from a lovely high mountain glen; roaring down between dark, dripping crags to the deep pool far below. It was only when I reached here that I decided that as I was already wet and cold, an extra half an hour to take in the summit wouldn't make much difference.

I returned to the bealach and then had a short steep climb up broken ground onto Meall Dubh, where some deer shifted uneasily as I passed. A flatter section followed, which the recent rains had turned into a long bog-trot. Another short climb led up into the gloom, over a small hump, before a final rise took me up onto the summit of A'Ghlas-bheinn.

The map showed crags on the southern side of the mountain so in view of the poor visibility and fast fading daylight, I retraced my steps part-way down the ridge before taking a bearing to head straight down the rough grassy slopes to the north-west. As I came out of the clouds I could see the path below me; once I was back on this I was just left with a rather wet walk back down through the forest.

Beinn Fhada   3,385ft

From the car-park in the forest in Strath Croe, I crossed the stream and followed a pleasant footpath around the hillside into Gleann Choinneachain. At the head of the glen I planned to climb up into the corrie of the Allt Coire an Sgairne and was pleased to find a good stalkers path here, although none was shown on my map.

The path climbed easily into the corrie, then zigzagged more steeply up towards Meall a'Bhealaich, until either I lost it, or it petered out. However, a knoll covered ridge led south to gain a large grassy plateau, which gave easy going up onto Beinn Fhada, also known as Ben Attow.

From here a good high-level walk around the edge of the plateau took me to the 'top' of Sgurr a'Dubh Doire. I then had to retrace my steps back towards Beinn Fhada, before contouring round beneath its summit, heading north-west out to another 'top', Meall an Fhuarain Mhoir, but not named on the map.

The steep slopes to the south would have given an alternative route for the return but they looked just a bit too steep so I decided to take the easy option and return the way I had come. It didn't take long to go round the rim of Coire Sgairne, where I regained the rough north ridge which led me back to the stalkers path for the return to Gleann Choinneachain and the stroll back to the car to end another excellent day on the hills.

Mam Sodhail	3,862ft	**Carn Eighe**	3,880ft
Beinn Fhionnlaidh	3,294ft	**Tom a'Choinich**	3,646ft
Toll Creagach	3,455ft	**An Socach**	3,017ft
Mullach na Dheiragain	3,210ft		
Sgurr nan Ceathreamhnan	3,771ft		

The eight Munros and sixteen 'tops' sandwiched between Loch Mullardoch to the north and Glen Affric to the south, were split into two trips for my first visits to these hills.

It was a superb day one April when I made the long drive down Glen Affric to the southern end of Loch Beinn a'Mheadhoin to tackle the five easternmost Munros. From the small car park at the road-end I followed a good track for a short way along the lochside towards Affric Lodge; here I turned up the hill on a stalkers path that climbed easily at first, then traversed the steeper ground up onto a broad saddle. As I climbed west from the saddle I moved onto firm snow which gave for fast going the whole day. It was bright and clear and navigation stayed easy as I could always see where I wanted to go.

I was soon up onto the 'top' of Sgurr na Lapaich; the ridge narrowed and led easily along to the next 'top', Mullach Cadha Rainich; a short climb on good snow found me by the large cairn on Mam Sodhail. From here the ridge turned to a north/south direction. The way south led out to some more 'tops', which I decided to leave for another time. I headed north, dropped down a short way to a col then climbed again to the trig-point on the next Munro, Carn Eighe. There were great views from here, where you really felt as though you were in the middle of nowhere.

From the cairn I had to do a long out-and-back; a fine ridge led a mile or so north, over a small 'top' Stob Coire Lochan, and along to Beinn Fhionnlaidh at the far end of the ridge. Again the 360° views were fantastic; out over Loch Mullardoch and across the snow covered mountains. After a short rest and a bite to eat I retraced my steps back to Carn Eighe and now headed east. Four 'tops' followed in quick succession as I moved easily along the twisting ridge; Stob a'Choire Dhomhain, Sron Garbh, An Leth-chreag and Tom a'Choinich Beag.

The great snow conditions gave me an easy climb up to the next Munro, Tom a'Choinich. Still heading east there was quite a descent down to a broad col, this left a long but easy climb up the ridge across the far side, first over Toll Creagach's west 'top' then up onto the day's final summit, Toll Creagach. From the cairn I headed south and the snow let me drop quickly down towards the stream; once off the snow the going became a bit rougher and slower but I was soon on the footpath which led back down to the lochside for the short walk back to the car.

For the three western Munros I again drove down to the southern end of Loch Beinn a'Mheadhoin to park at the road-end. Because of the long walk in and out I used my bike to save some time and energy. From the car-park I cycled over the bridge to cross the river and followed the land-rover track through the forest and a short way up the hill on the south side of Loch Affric. At the far end of the loch a bridge took me back over to the north side of the river and I cycled on for about another two miles until I reached a path that climbed away from the track. After hiding the bike I set off up the path which followed the stream into Coire Ghaidheil. The path, faint at times, took me up onto a col on the main ridge, where I turned left for a short steep climb to the summit of An Socach. On my OS map this is marked with a spot-height of 920m but is not given a name.

A fairly narrow ridge led off west and took me over the 'top' of Stob Coire nan Dearcag; a short while later I dropped off the ridge to the north, making my way down steep rough ground towards the lochan immediately below. Contouring as much as possible to save losing height unnecessarily, I fought my way across the tussocks and out onto the long ridge of Creag a'Choir' Aird. It was easier going along the top of the broad ridge, over the 'top' of Carn na Con Dhu and onto Mullach na Dheiragain. A short steep descent to the north took me to a narrow col from where a short climb brought me up onto the 'top' of Mullach Sithidh.

From here I retraced my steps back along the ridge, over Mullach na Dheiragain and Carn na Con Dhu, before facing a bit of a scramble up a rocky rib onto the final Munro of the day, Sgurr nan Ceathreamhnan. From the cairn a short drop down to the west led to a col and on up to Sgurr nan Ceathreamhnan's west 'top'. With the end now in sight I took the rocky ridge running off to the south and after descending for some way I dropped left down into the corrie of the Allt Beithe Garbh; the stream then led me back down to the main footpath in Glen Affric. A short distance along the path I came to the open Youth Hostel at Alltbeithe, although it's just a good bothy really, not a Youth Hostel as we know them. I stopped for a rest and a brew outside then, suitably refreshed, I set off on the two mile walk back to my bike and the eight mile cycle alongside Loch Affric to the car.

A year or two later I returned with a friend and included these eight Munros and all sixteen 'tops' in a long run around Loch Mullardoch; done over a weekend which included a high-camp in Coire Aird, half-way round. The detailed record of that run is included elsewhere in this journal.

Section 12: Sgurr na Lapaich; The Strathfarrar hills; East of Achnashellach

Carn nan Gobhar 3,251ft   Sgurr na Lapaich   3,775ft
An Riabhachan 3,696ft   An Socach   3,508ft

For my first time over the Munros to the north of Loch Mullardoch I drove in up Glen Cannich to park near the dam at the eastern end of the loch. It was a beautiful warm day as I set off along the lochside for a short distance before turning up the hill on a good footpath, which led easily but quite steeply, towards the ridge. It was a hot climb across the open hillside to the 'top' of Creag Dubh and from here I headed across rough ground towards Carn nan Gobhar. Among the tussocks I almost fell over a very young deer calf, it can only have been a few days old, it just lay in the long grass trying to hide. I passed by quickly so as not to frighten it or it's Mum and was soon on the rounded summit of Carn nan Gobhar.

From here the ridge dropped to a col to the north-west before climbing again, on rougher ground that gave a bit of a scramble, up round the head of the corrie to the trig-point on Sgurr na Lapaich. I made the short detour to collect the 'top' of Sgurr nan Clachan Geala, half a mile out to the south. After contouring back to the main ridge there was more steep ground, as I dropped south-west down to a col, before an equally steep and long climb up a narrow ridge that took me over An Riabhachan's north-east 'top', then a short way further onto the main summit of An Riabhachan. There were still two more 'tops' of An Riabhachan to go; the south-west 'top' lay a little further along at the end of the ridge, a short dog-leg to the north-west then took me to the west 'top'.

Another big descent took me down steeply to the south-west where the last climb of the day led me up a grassy ridge to the trig-point and cairn on An Socach; which isn't named on the OS 1:50,000 map, it's just marked as 1,069m. Leaving the cairn I headed straight down the rough hillside in a vaguely south-easterly direction, aiming for the corner of the loch. I soon picked up a stream, then a faint path, which led to an old hut and some sheep-folds.

Once down by the lochside it left quite a long walk back, along a fairly indistinct path. It was actually quite a sad occasion as the hillside above the loch was littered with dead deer; they seemed to have survived the winter but a cold wet spring must have meant that they couldn't find enough food. Within the space of just four miles I must have seen perhaps thirty carcases and the smell of death and decaying meat lingered in the air.

These four Munros were also included in my long run around Loch Mullardoch, which is detailed elsewhere in this journal.

Strathfarrar -
Sgurr na Ruaidhe   3,254ft   Carn nan Gobhar   3,251ft
Sgurr a'Choire Ghlais 3,554ft   Sgurr Fhuar-thuill 3,439ft

I had no problem accessing the private road running up Glen Strathfarrar from Struy; I'd taken my bike in case the gate was locked but thankfully it wasn't necessary.

I set off from where the Allt Choire Mhuillidh enters the river between the two small lochs and climbed, initially up a track, then a footpath, before taking to the open hillside. Although quite a stiff climb, it was straightforward and the summit of Sgurr na Ruaidhe was soon reached. A fairly fast descent then saw me down at the col to the north-west in just a few minutes.

No sooner had I dropped the 700ft then I had to immediately re-climb it, up a bouldery ridge onto Carn nan Gobhar. From the summit cairn it was easy to follow the ridge round and down to a narrow col, dividing steep corries to the north and south. Another climb of about 800ft brought me to the day's highest point, Sgurr a'Choire Ghlais. With the day staying fine, and the peaks all spread out along one central ridge, navigation was easy for a change and it was a very relaxed outing, enjoying the high-level walking to the full.

Continuing west, a short rise took me over the 'top' of Creag Ghorm a'Bhealaich, then another short climb took me onto the final Munro of the day, Sgurr Fhuar-thuill. As I descended from here I could see the stalkers path as it headed down the side of the corrie, but I passed by the top of this path and made a final short climb onto another 'top', Sgurr na Fearstaig. With the hard work over, and plenty of time to play with, I did a rare thing, I sunbathed on top.

Rested, I now headed for the stalkers path which took me down into the corrie and past a small lochan; it was quite a long way as I followed the stream back out to the road in Strathfarrar. Once on the road I walked and jogged the four miles back down Glen Strathfarrar to end another good day.

Sgurr Choinnich   3,276ft   Sgurr a'Chaorachain 3,455ft
Maoile Lunndaidh   3,304ft

I was staying at Gerry's Hostel near Achnashellach for a long weekend one March, the weather had been terrible; on the Friday night, while crossing Rannoch Moor, I passed two lorries that had been blown over just a few minutes earlier. The forecast was for more of the same, however I decided to give these three Munros a go, knowing that I could always cut the route short if the conditions deteriorated too much.

From the road a good track crossed the railway and the river, before climbing steeply through the forest to emerge into a bleak glen. Herds of deer shifted eerily in the mist as I walked silently through them. When the track followed the glen east, I turned off, crossed the river and tried to find the stalkers path leading to the Bealach Bhearnais. The heavy snow from the previous night was deep and soft, so I sank to my knees on the gradual climb, which was very tiring. Above the bealach the going became a little easier as the wind had blown most of the soft snow off the ridge. I'd planned the route in this direction in the hope that the wind would be behind me on the tops and only against me in the glen when I was on my way back. Even so it was very difficult to keep myself from staggering about; I could hardly keep my feet as I tried to follow a bearing up to Sgurr Choinnich.

There was almost a 'whiteout' on top and I was very glad to see the cairn; there followed a short steep descent to a col before a pull up onto Sgurr a'Chaorachain. I stayed close to the cliff edge and tried to keep the cornice in sight as visibility was almost non-existent. From here I wasn't sure how best to drop down to the twin lochans on the col to the north-east. It seemed very steep everywhere, with lots of snow on the faces, however, mid-way between Sgurr a'Chaorachain and the 'top' of Bidean an Eoin Deirg I found a rocky buttress which I scrambled down; then, once the angle of the snow alongside eased a little I crossed onto the snow and plunged down, up to my knees at each step.

A large boulder by the lochans gave me some shelter for a quick bite to eat; then I was climbing again with an occasional glance at the compass, to bring me out on the 'top' of Carn nam Fiaclan. More careful compass work led me to the narrow ridge, flanked by steep cliffs, until the ridge widened and took me to the cairn of Maoile Lunndaidh at the far end.

A bearing due north took me down to a col from where I cut left and followed a stream down into the glen. When the lodge came into sight I aimed straight for it, clambering in and out of peat-hags and crossing several boggy areas until I finally reached the river. Thankfully there were stepping-stones so I was able to cross and finally regain the land-rover track. After a long hard day, constantly having to be on the alert in 'whiteout' conditions, being buffeted by the wind and having to navigate carefully, it was good to be safely in the glen where I could relax for the five mile walk-out down through the forest and back to the hostel.

Sgurr nan Ceannaichean 3,003ft   Moruisg 3,026ft

The day following my ascent of the three Munros to the south of Gleann Fhiodhaig, the weather brightened so I enjoyed clear blue skies, but, as I could see from the way the snow was being blown off the ridge, the wind still raged just as strongly on the tops.

I followed the same track in from Craig, over the railway and the river, and headed up through the forest and along the Allt a'Chonais. At the corner, where the glen turned east, I took to the stalkers path, which climbed steeply up the hillside and onto the snow. I was relatively sheltered here and made good time on the long climb but as I neared the summit the full force of the wind hit me and I had a real struggle to make any progress.

Once on top of Sgurr nan Ceannaichean (note 2) I followed the ridge north, which led to a saddle, bounded on either side by deep corries. A further, broader, ridge across the other side then took me on firm, wind polished snow, to the summit of Moruisg.

With the day remaining fine, if somewhat windy, I could see to choose the easiest line down, aiming straight for the road to the north. As I left the snow behind the tussocky hillside became harder work, but it didn't take too long to reach the railway, cross the bridge over the River Carron, and out onto the road. That just left three miles or so back down the road to the hostel to end a shortish day.

Bidein a'Choire Sheasgaich 3,102ft   Lurg Mhor 3,234ft

This pair of peaks in remote country to the south of Achnashellach gave a long but enjoyable day one summer. A bridge was shown on my map, but it was very badly damaged; I started across it but then had second thoughts and in the end just waded the River Carron. I then had a bit of a fight through the forest on the far side but eventually I found the track I was after and this led to a fine stalkers path which climbed steeply up through the forest. The climb continued across open hillside; it was hard work on a hot and sticky day, but I soon arrived in the high corrie, which was teeming with deer. A short climb led to a narrow ridge and a scramble round onto a plateau. The path then dropped steeply down alongside the stream to bring me out at Bearnais Bothy. This is a small but well maintained bothy, dedicated to the memory of Eric Beard, a mountain runner who loved to run long solo rounds but tragically died while still very young.

After a short break I managed to stay reasonably dry when I crossed the Abhainn Bhearnais, there then followed a long slog across the heather and peat hags to climb into Coire Seasgach. As I climbed higher into the corrie the ground underfoot became a little easier, although the slope became steeper; finally I came out onto the ridge. A short distance along the ridge led to a final scramble through some rocky blocks and I was on the summit of Bidein a'Choire Sheasgaich (aka Cheesecake). Although the weather was fine, haze restricted the views so I continued to the south-east, with crags on my left and steep slopes to the lochan on my right.

Once at the col a grassy ramp led away up to the summit of Lurg Mhor. I deliberately missed out the 'top' of Meall Mor, just half a mile further along the ridge, knowing that would encourage me to come back another time. I returned down to the col and contoured round below the summit of 'Cheesecake' to regain its west ridge; dropped steeply down into the glen to cross the river and rejoin the footpath beside the bothy. From the south the climb wasn't quite so high to cross the intervening ridge and continue on the path back down towards Achnashellach. As it was now the end of the day it didn't matter if I had wet feet, so I ignored the broken bridge and just ploughed straight through the river and minutes later was back at the car drying off.

Section 13: Strathcarron; The Torridons

Maol Chean-dearg   3,060ft

The guide-book time for this decent little peak was 4 to 6 hours so I thought I would do it as a run, which would give me plenty of time for another peak in the afternoon.

Leaving the road at Coulags an easy path gave good running alongside the river, past an open bothy, to where a path turned west to climb steeply up to the col between Meall nan Ceapairean and Maol Chean-dearg. The full force of the wind hit me as I reached the col and it needed a very big effort to make any headway. Above the col it was a struggle to climb the rocky slopes, then I crossed the snowline and sank, sometimes up to my knees, in deep fresh snow. Within minutes it was blowing a blizzard. I knew the top was close so I kept up as fast a pace as possible, until the cairn loomed up out of the whiteness.

It was very windy and very cold on top so after checking my compass I quickly made my way back down to the col and then shot off down to the track in the glen. Once in the glen it was merely raining. The run back alongside the river was reasonably quick so I was soon able to warm up and by 11am I was back at Gerry's Hostel. After a bite to eat and a change of clothes I still had plenty of time to go off up towards Ullapool to climb Am Faochagach.

Beinn Liath Mhor   3,034ft   Sgorr Ruadh   3,142ft

It was a very wet and miserable November day when I set off from Achnashellach Station to climb this pair of peaks. A path led up through the forest to bring me out into a gloomy glen; a short while after a path junction I took to the hillside and set to work on the climb of Beinn Liath Mhor. In the low cloud and rain I couldn't see much of the hill and just had to meander up through the rough terraces and onto the boulders, hoping that I was taking the safest route and that I wouldn't come up against an unexpected cliff. Once I reached the eastern end of the ridge it was easy to follow the ridge along to Beinn Liath Mhor's large cairn at the far western end, a mile or so away.

In thick mist it needed some careful compass work to see me round to the col between the two peaks, avoiding steep crags at the head of the glen. The lochans proved useful landmarks and once I came to the path that crossed the col I took to the rough hillside again. Tongues of scree led up into the mist again, taking me to a rocky ridge, which I followed as it climbed to Sgorr Ruadh. Despite the low clouds I couldn't miss the lochans scattered about on the wide saddle to the south of the summit and from here it wasn't long before I found the path which led back down to the River Lair. This I just splashed across, as I was already so wet there was no point in wasting time looking for stepping stones.

I was feeling cold and wet and just a little fed up as I entered the forest above the station. All of a sudden the depression was lifted as I spotted a pine marten, the first time I'd seen one in the wild. It was only a brief glimpse but it was a beautiful little creature and the sighting immediately cheered me up. The previous few hours had been some to forget, but at the last moment it became a day to remember.

Beinn Alligin - Sgurr Mhor   3,232ft

This was climbed on a good day one October; the weather was reasonably clear and dry, but quite windy on top.

From the small car-park a short way down the north side of Upper Loch Torridon a boggy path headed across the hillside. The path started climbing straight away, up through sandstone terraces and into the steep Coir'nan Laogh. I followed the stream around, past it's source and up the headwall to arrive on the 'top' of Tom na Gruagaich [note 1]. From the cairn the main summit could be seen across the far side of the deep corrie, with the craggy 'Horns' behind.

It was a pleasant walk around the rim of the corrie, with views out to the north over a vast wilderness of lochs and moors. A short climb then led to the highest point, Sgurr Mhor. A sheltered spot gave the chance of a short break for lunch before dropping down the ridge to the north-east, which led round to a col. Here some easy scrambling started, up and over the rocky tors. All too soon I was over the exciting bits and now the ridge just dropped away in a series of terraces until I reached a path which led me down to a bridge across the Abhainn Coire Mhic Nobuil. This left an easy walk back along the river, through the woods and out to the road. It had been a short but very enjoyable day.

Liathach - Spidean a'Choire Leith   3,456ft
Mullach an Rathain   3,358ft

I was camped one August at the small site at the head of Upper Loch Torridon, hoping for fine weather for the long awaited ascent of Liathach. It was not to be though; as I drove up the road to the car-park I looked up at the towering mass, enveloped in thick cloud, and was very close to turning round and giving up there and then.

The walk in on the footpath round into Coire Dubh Mor was the only bit of the route I really saw all day. A cairn marked the turn off onto a faint path which led up through the heather and boulders. Things turned steeper as I climbed up through rough terraces until I finally gained the eastern end of the main ridge.

The clouds on top were thick and wet, but once on Stuc a'Choire Dhuibh Bhig it didn't take long to scramble along to Bidean Toll a'Mhuic. The next section was disconcerting as the ridge snaked around above huge cliffs; the going underfoot was very rough and over slippery blocks, eventually though a scramble took me up to the cairn of Spidean a'Choire Leith.

I knew of the pinnacles in the centre of the ridge and fully intended climbing them; however the almost zero visibility meant I couldn't tell if I was facing an easy 20ft scramble or a 200ft climb. If I made it up, would I also be able to make it safely down the other side? Reluctantly I opted for the path along the south side of the ridge, which by-passed the difficulties. However, this path was no easy 'cop out'; despite the mist I could sense the huge drop of almost 3,000ft down into the glen below. The narrow path clung to the steep hillside and was not the place for a slip. Eventually I emerged onto a grassy ridge, bounded on the north by fearsome looking crags and this was followed to the trig-point on Mullach an Rathain.

The day's excitement was far from over as although I had now traversed the ridge I still had to descend. I started out following the ridge that led off to the south-west and found myself dropping down into a scree filled, funnel shaped corrie. This became steeper and narrowed into a gully and I had several anxious moments as I clambered down through the mist. As I lost height the clouds thinned a little and at last I could see to choose a reasonable line down into the small hamlet of Torridon.

The camp-site was just a short walk back along the road. After a cup of tea I ran the four miles back down the road to collect the car. It had been a nerve wracking day, and that was without going over all the pinnacles; it also guarantees that I'll have to return to collect the two 'tops' I missed out, but hopefully next time it will be in better weather when I can see what I'm doing.

Beinn Eighe - Ruadh-stac-Mor   3,309ft

This is a huge mountain, shaped almost like a hand, with the 'wrist' to the south and the five 'fingers' running out from the north-west round to the east; between these ridges are spectacular corries. For such a big hill it's surprising that there is only one Munro (note 1), there are a further five satellite 'tops'.

It was a day or two after climbing Beinn Alligin that I set off from the car-park in Glen Torridon to follow the footpath above the stream, round between the towering walls of Liathach and Beinn Eighe. After a couple of miles a less well used footpath turned off to the north and climbed round the foot of Sail Mhor, before climbing again round to the lochan in Coire Mhic Fhearchair. This wild and remote corrie is one of my favourite places in Scotland, it is savagely beautiful.

From the southern end of the lochan I climbed the steep, rough south-west wall of the corrie; as I climbed higher I passed the scattered remains of a crashed bomber. Once on the ridge above I headed right and made the short detour to take in the 'top' of Sail Mhor. The tops were in clouds but once on the ridge navigation was reasonably straightforward. I returned to the col and enjoyed a short scramble through the crags to the next 'top' Coinneach Mhor.

From here I found the north ridge, which dropped steeply down to a narrow col; the ridge across the far side then climbed easily to the mountains principal summit, Ruadh-stac-Mor. It was too cold and damp to linger in the clouds so I was soon retracing my steps back to the main ridge. The narrow, rocky ridge dropped down to the south-east to another col before heading round the head of the corrie, through some small some rocky outcrops to the next 'top' Spidean Coire nan Clach (note 1).

There were still two more 'tops' to go, but these would have taken me further and further from the car and left a long road-walk back. If the weather had been fine I would probably have gone on, but as it was I decided to call it a day and from the cairn I searched for the short spur running south; this led down out of the clouds so I could pick a good line, down the steep rough hillside, reaching the road just to the east of the car-park.

Section 14: Slioch & An Teallach; The Fannaichs

Slioch   3,217ft

When I first saw Slioch from the car, while driving south down along Loch Maree, I was amazed that there was a 'walkers' route to the top; the final few hundred feet seemed to just rear vertically up from the ridge on which it stands. It became a hill that I desperately wanted to climb but in view of the possible difficulties, and it's fine position scenically, it was one I wanted to save for a fine day.

That day came a couple of years later when, after almost a week of heavy rain the skies brightened and the clouds rolled away. I started from Incheril, near Kinlochewe, and followed the path alongside Kinlochewe River, then along the north shore of Loch Maree until I reached the bridge over the Abhainn an Fhasaigh. After crossing the stream I headed away from the loch and climbed up into the narrow gorge of Gleann Bianasdail. Before long a cairn indicated the start of a faint path which climbed away from the glen, up the steep broken slopes and out onto Sgurr Dubh. From here I could see Slioch and the final approaches to it. A narrow ridge led easily up to a band of sandstone crags through which the path meandered fairly comfortably. Once through the crags the angle eased and an easy ridge took me to the trig point on the summit. As expected the view was fantastic; away to the sea lochs and surrounded by other high, remote mountains.

The north 'top' was only a short step away, above seemingly impregnable cliffs; then it was on, around the horse-shoe ridge to another 'top' Sgurr an Tuill Bhain. From here it didn't take long to drop down the steep heather terraces into the corrie and to follow the stream down into Gleann Bianasdail. That just left the short walk-out back along Loch Maree to the meadows by the river.

I had hoped for a good day out and Slioch certainly lived up to my expectations.

Beinn a'Chlaidheimh   3,000ft   Beinn Tarsuinn 3,070ft
Sgurr Ban   3,194ft   A'Mhaighdean   3,173ft
Mullach Coire Mhic Fhearchair   3,326ft
Ruadh Stac Mor   3,014ft

The round of these six Munros (note 2) in the remote Fisherfield Forest gives a long hard day and has the feel of a real expedition. On my first try I didn't even manage to reach the foot of the first peak. The weather had been wet for the whole of the previous week and I had a very wet walk in from the road at Corrie Hallie to the bothy at Shenavall. I looked at the river that afternoon and it was a frightening prospect; by the following morning it had risen even further and looked impossible. I spent a fruitless hour in the rain trying to find a safe place to cross but it was hopeless so I gave up.

About three weeks later I was back at Shenavall for another go; this time the river looked ok. I left the bothy reasonably early and had no problem wading the river before starting on the steep slopes that took me up the lowest of all the Munros, Beinn a'Chlaidheimh (note 2). I left the summit via a narrow ridge which led south over several bumps before dropping down a slope of loose scree to a col and two small lochans. Another hard climb up the rough, rocky slopes led to Sgurr Ban, only to quickly lose all the height gained, as I dropped to the next col below Mullach Coire Mhic Fhearchair. The climb to the summit was steep but the views made the hard work more than worthwhile.

A short detour along the ridge took me to the mountains east 'top' and beyond that the 'top' of Sgurr Dubh. After visiting these I contoured back beneath Mullach Coire Mhic Fhearchair and round onto the horse-shoe ridge again. From Meall Garbh an easier climb took me to Beinn Tarsuinn, at the head of Gleann na Muice. Leaving the summit I followed the ridge a short way before dropping steeply down to a broad saddle. It was a long way across the saddle before I could start on the climb to A'Mhaighdean, generally regarded as being the most remote of all the Munros. A scramble up through a series of small crags saw me on the summit. Thankfully for a special day like this the weather was fine and visibility was good so it was easy to pick the best line down to the col to the north-east. Here I hid my rucksack and made the short scramble up through the scree and rocky steps to the cairn on Ruadh Stac Mor.

From this final summit I dropped back down to the col, eventually found the rock behind which I'd hidden my 'sac, and continued down to the path which leads away from Fuar Loch Mor. Once on the path I was soon down to the main track and I followed this across the plateau and down into Gleann na Muice Beag. A good path followed the stream down to the river crossing and led me back to Shenavall. After a short stop at the bothy for a brew and a bite to eat, I had the six mile walk-out back to the road followed by a long drive home.

I didn't know it at the time but the last 10 miles of that route was to be done several more times, but in the opposite direction, as part of what became my favourite hill race, the 25 mile *Great Wilderness Challenge,* which takes you through the hills from Dundonnell to Poolewe.

A piper sets the field off from the road at Corrie Hallie and you start climbing immediately; up a rough track to a saddle and the 1st check-point. From here a sometimes wet and boggy footpath leads down to the bothy at Shenavall and the 2nd check-point. After crossing the river you have to cross a rough and usually wet marsh which leads to an easier second river crossing near Larachantivore. Once across this river a footpath leads upstream then branches off up into Gleann na Muice Beag. This is the second big climb; fairly steady at first then more steeply up zigzags for the last few hundred metres; up onto the plateau and the 3rd control. From here good running on a fine path takes you below Ruadh Stac Mor and A'Mhaighdean before descending steeply to the 4th check-point at Carnmore. I always feel that the race only really starts when you reach this point.

Still on a good path you pass beneath a small hill and cross a narrow causeway between Dubh Loch and Fionn Loch. One year waves were crashing over the causeway, soaking us with spray as we ran across. The route then follows the sandy beach of Fionn Loch for a short distance, which is always hard work, then climbs gently away from the water. The next few miles, although on a path, can be wet and boggy and this hurts when the legs are starting to go; it's tough out to the 5th control near Loch an Doire Crionaich, and even tougher from here to the woods by Kernsary. The final check-point in the woods is a welcome sight and you are then back onto a firm land-rover track. The puddles here can be deep enough to swallow a tired runner but eventually you come out onto a tarmac private road which takes you the last mile or so into Poolewe and the finish by the bridge.

My best result came when I was very fit after a good summer; I had a great run to finish 2nd, coming home inside 3 hours, which I was very happy with for such a tough, hilly and boggy 25 miles.

An Teallach -
Sgurr Fiona 3,474ft   Bidein a'Ghlas Thuill 3,484ft

My first visit to the famous An Teallach ended in failure. It was a cloudy, wet, windy day one November and I set off up the track from Corrie Hallie not knowing quite what to expect. After climbing up the track for a mile or so I dropped down to cross the stream then took to the hillside, making my way easily across the interesting sandstone slabs and terraces. It wasn't too long before I came out at the cairn on the 'top' of Sail Liath. So far so good, but here my troubles began. The tops were covered in snow; there was almost zero visibility; I'd never been there before; and the rocky towers all seemed very big and very steep. I started out along the ridge but I'm not really sure how far I managed. The further I climbed, the harder it became, and not wanting an 'epic' I finally decided to call it a day and return the way I knew was ok.

Shortly before reaching Sail Liath again I came across a narrow gully, which dropped steeply down to the lochan in the wild corrie below. Seeing old footprints in the snow gave me confidence to go for it, so I strapped on my crampons and stepped over the edge, disappearing rapidly down the gully, which turned out to be far easier than it had looked from above. It seemed a long walk down the corrie to the roadside but it had been a good day even though I hadn't made it to the highest summits.

6: An Teallach

It was a year or two later before I could return to An Teallach, this time it was during the month of May. I again started from Corrie Hallie and walked a short way up the track before crossing to the open hillside where the terraces gave easy access to the steep slope leading to Sail Liath. From here the ridge is narrow and climbs over several pinnacles, giving good scrambling, but all these could be passed using a path which keeps low on the south side beneath the difficulties. Unfortunately I was again cursed with thick cloud, which made route finding very difficult. I kept to the crest of the ridge for as long as possible, but eventually, at one seemingly impassable tower, I dropped down to find the 'easy' path. This took me round beneath the summit of Sgurr Fiona and I came out onto a saddle to the west of the peak. An eerie climb then led up through the mist to Sgurr Fiona's cairn. It wasn't the weather to stop so I headed down to the col to the north, from where I had glimpses through the clouds of Loch Toll an Lochain far below. A short climb then led up onto Bidein a'Ghlas Thuill, the highest point on the traverse.

In the poor weather I saw no point in making a detour to take in the 'top' of Glas Mheall Liath and instead I continued north from the trig-point to collect the 'top' of Glas Mheall Mor. From here a scree slope led down across the moorland and eventually I picked up a path which followed the stream down to the road about half a mile west of Corrie Hallie.

As it was still early I treated myself to a pot of tea at the Dundonnell Hotel before driving round to the road-end at Badrallach on the north side of Little Loch Broom. From here I had a lovely 12 mile run, following the cliff top path out to Cailleach Head and back. What it was to be young and fit then!

A'Chailleach 3,276ft   Sgurr Breac 3,281ft

This easy pair of Munros was climbed on a fine day in mid-May. I parked off the road and walked-in down the landrover track to the ruined lodge at the east end of Loch a'Bhraoin. After crossing the outlet stream by a footbridge, I followed the path for a short way before taking to the open hillside for a short grassy scramble up between small crags. This took me to the spur of Druim Reidh, and after a levelling off of the ridge it led easily to the 'top' of Toman Coinich. This 'top' is on a ridge equi-distant between the two Munros so you have no choice other than to visit one and then retrace your steps, before going out to the second.

I dropped the short way down to the col to the west and an easy climb then led up to A'Chailleach. After a short rest I returned to the col and contoured round just below the summit of Toman Coinich to gain the col to the east, from here it was only another short climb up onto Sgurr Breac.

As I made my way down the steep eastern ridge towards the col, I was looking across to the Fannaichs group of hills, which were my target for a couple of days later. Before reaching the pass though I veered away to the north-east to drop down steep hillside and pick up a good footpath beside the stream.

The glen gave me an enjoyable walk out; down past small groups of deer to the loch, followed by a short walk out to the road.

The Fannaichs -

An Coileachan	3,015ft	**Meall Gorm**	3,174ft
Beinn Liath Mhor Fannaich	3,129ft	**Sgurr Mor**	3,637ft
Meall a'Chrasgaidh	3,062ft		
Sgurr nan Clach Geala	3,581ft		
Sgurr nan Each	3,026ft		

This was another rare opportunity to grab seven Munros in one outing. Situated on the north side of Loch Fannich, some six miles from the road at Grudie, I knew I was in for a long day so I took the bike and cycled in along the hydro-board road to about a mile short of Fannich Lodge.

The weather outlook was not promising and I battled against a gale force wind the whole day. On leaving the bike I started the steep climb straight up to the first Munro, An Coileachan. As I had feared, the wind made it very hard going and the cloud base was down to about 2,000ft, so I didn't have the bonus of any views. Once on top though, apart from the wind, it was easy walking, and there were no difficulties with navigation, in spite of the low cloud. The route went down to the saddle then climbed to the south-east 'top' of Meall Gorm and easily along to the summit of Meall Gorm itself. A short distance before the cairn I came to a small, stone built shelter; the wind whistled through the gaps in the walls and roof, but it was nevertheless great to have the chance of a brief rest from being buffeted by the wind.

After crossing over the 'top' of Meall nam Peithirean I contoured round below the snow covered top of Sgurr Mor as I tried to find it's north ridge, which led me out on a short detour to the rocky summit of Beinn Liath Mhor Fannaich. Retracing my steps back along the ridge towards Sgurr Mor I passed another little stone shelter. The cairn of Sgurr Mor, the highest peak of the day, is perched on the edge of a steep drop into the corrie below. From here there is another 'top' to be crossed, Carn na Criche, before making a further dog-leg to climb easily out onto Meall a'Chrasgaidh, just a few hundred feet above the saddle.

This was the furthest point and I was now on my way home via just two more peaks; the ridge was both steeper and narrower but it was an easy scramble up to the trig point on Sgurr nan Clach Geala then I was soon on my way down to the col some 1,000ft below. One last climb of the day saw me onto the summit of Sgurr nan Each.

It didn't take long to drop down off the summit, heading for the track alongside Loch Fannich, but as I followed the streams down into the glen the going underfoot became very heavy; part way down I came into an area of deep peat-hags where I disturbed several deer. Once down by the lochside I was glad to be re-united with my bike; in rain, and with the wind now behind me, the ride back down the hydro-board road to Grudie took less than 30 minutes, it was gently downhill almost all the way.

Fionn Bheinn   3,062ft

There's not really a lot to say about this grassy lump, except that it is over 3,000ft and that it is a Munro. I climbed it one wet and windy November afternoon when most sensible people would have been at home in front of a warm fire, watching television.

> "Once more unto the breach dear friends .... once more"
> (Henry V - Shakespeare)

A short distance east of Achnasheen a track leads up the hill, through a small area of woodland before heading out onto the open hillside. The clouds were down to around the 1,500ft level, but as long as I went uphill in a vaguely north-westerly direction I assumed I'd find the summit. After plodding up through the mist and rain I eventually reached the summit ridge, and this led easily along to the OS post on the summit.

A more direct line, diagonally down the hill, surprised some deer as I came splashing past and within a few minutes I was back at the car and drying out. What fun!

Section 15: Ben Wyvis & Beinn Dearg

Ben Wyvis - Glas Leathad Mor   3,433ft

Having seen this mountain on so many occasions when I was driving past on my way further north, I finally felt that I should stop and climb it.

The walk in through the forest from the roadside at Garbat would have been a nice start if it hadn't been so wet underfoot; as it was a boggy track led up to the fence and the open hillside. I was now faced with a real slog of a climb, up the steep grassy flank onto the 'top' of An Cabar. Thankfully that was all the hard work over and done with in one go and it was a pleasant, though somewhat breezy, stroll along the gentle ridge and up to the trig point on Glas Leathad Mor, the highest point on Ben Wyvis.

Continuing north it didn't take long to drop down to the col for the short climb to the 'top' of Tom a'Choinnich. I debated going for the remaining 'top' but this would have meant a four mile detour, just for a small grassy lump, and as I had a long drive home it was left for another time.

From Tom a'Choinnich I dropped down into the corrie to the south; stopping a short way below the summit ridge to watch a pair of ptarmigan with their young, this sighting was really the only bright spot in an otherwise boring day.

It was a long descending traverse to take me back to one of the few breaks through the thick forest. That just left the same boggy track, back down to the roadside at Garbat.

Am Faochagach   3,120ft

Am Faochagach gave me a surprisingly hard walk one November afternoon; I had already run up Strathcarron's Maol Chean-dearg that morning, in a blizzard, which was my only excuse.

From Black Bridge on the A835 Ullapool Road I had a three mile walk in along a land-rover track to the dam at the southern end of Loch Vaich. It was a dull afternoon, the clouds were right down and rain showers kept coming and going. After following the western shore of the loch for about a mile, I turned away and followed the course of the Allt Glas Toll Mor. I came onto fresh, soft snow at around the 1,500ft level and with the low cloud this made ideal 'whiteout' conditions. Steering by compass I climbed above the stream and onto Meall Gorm, from where I was able to follow the edge of the corrie round for the short climb up onto Am Faochagach.

Conditions were difficult; the soft snow was very tiring making it slow going, and in a whiteout I was in no mood for further exploration. Instead I just turned about and followed my footprints, which were rapidly being covered over, back across Meall Gorm. From there I set a rough bearing to take me into the shallow glen carved by the Allt Glas Toll Mor, and once I found this I could put the map and compass away and simply follow the stream back down to the lochside. At the end of a long day the walk back from the dam to the road was hard work and I was glad to reach the car and change out of my wet boots.

To this day I've no real idea what Am Faochagach looks like or what the views are like. Maybe I'll go back another time to see what I missed, but then again, maybe not.

Beinn Dearg   3,547ft   **Cona Mheall**   3,214ft
Meall nan Ceapraichean   3,205ft
Eididh nan Clach Geala   3,039ft

It was mid-May when I climbed these four Munros on a round of Gleann na Sguaib. I set off from Inverlael, on the Ullapool road, entered the forest but then missed the turning where I should have crossed the river. As it was I had an unnecessary struggle through dense forest to reach it's boundary, which I followed to the river, where I was able to cross using boulders. Once over the river a good track led easily up alongside it, past some small waterfalls, until it reached a lochan at the head of the glen. From here the path climbed much more steeply to the saddle below Beinn Dearg.

Above the saddle everything was still covered with snow, but it was firm and an old stone wall led up towards the summit cairn. With no views and a long day ahead, I quickly ran back down the snow to the saddle. From the saddle I had a bit of a battle in strengthening winds as I climbed the boulder strewn slopes out to Cona Mheall. Turning at the summit the wind now helped to push me along as I jogged back down to the saddle, which I was now crossing for the third time. The wind then helped push me up the climb to Meall nan Ceapraichean, where I put up a couple of ptarmigan.

From here I now had to aim NNE, to collect the 'top' of Ceann Garbh, before running easily down old snow towards the pass above Lochan a'Chnapaich. Finding a reasonably sheltered spot in a deep gully I had a quick rest and a bite to eat, as by now the force of the wind was making walking very difficult. The final climb onto Eididh nan Clach Geala was straightforward and on easy grassy slopes but once on top I just had to descend without stopping. The wind on the summit was so strong that I had to keep moving; if I stopped the wind just blew me over. I was down on all fours at times, scuttling along, trying to lose height quickly; trying to find a more sheltered spot.

Although not marked on my map, I was pleased to see a good path leading down from beside the lochan; by the time I reached here the wind had moderated so it was a reasonably easy walk back, downhill all the way to rejoin the morning's track in the glen below. This time I made sure I found the correct route through the forest and was soon back at the roadside. A couple of minutes later I had a brew going in the telephone box in an effort to try and thaw out.

Seana Bhraigh   3,040ft

This one was done as a fairly long run of almost 18 miles, although much of it was on good tracks. I started from the phone-box at Inverlael on the Ullapool road and ran easily through the forest, crossed to the north of the river and took the footpath which climbed more steeply to the forest's edge.

From here the path continued climbing, steeply up a heathery spur, before bearing off to drop down to cross the stream to the north. The climb from the stream was more gradual and still on a good path, which led into a narrow gap, past a string of small lochans and beneath a short stretch of crags. Unfortunately the weather now started to deteriorate and I had to navigate carefully over the marshy plateau, around the craggy rim of Cadha Dearg until I found a short climb up very wet ground to a small summit. I contoured round to reach the saddle to the north-west and from here it was only a few more minutes to the cairn on Seana Bhraigh.

The route finding had been tricky in the clouds but the return was much easier as I recognised some of the terrain. It was an easy run back to the path, into the gap, past the lochans, down and then across the stream to regain the heather shoulder. In no time I was back down in the forest for the last couple of miles out to the road. It had been a great run.

Section 16: Assynt; Hope & Klibreck

Conival   3,234ft   Ben More Assynt   3,273ft

I arrived at Inchnadamph on a wet and windy October afternoon and rather than search out a sheltered spot to camp, in a rare moment of extravagance I decided to stay at the Inchnadamph Hotel. The hotel is clearly aimed at the hunting, shooting and fishing crowd; it was probably splendid 50 or 100 years ago but now it seemed old and rather shabby.

The following morning the weather showed no signs of improving as I crossed the river at the road and followed the land-rover track east, along the River Traligill. After a short while the track climbed away from the river and led me to the farm buildings at Glenbain. From here a muddy footpath continued on up the glen, before dropping down to cross the river at a ford. My route however headed up the glen, without crossing the river; I climbed steadily at first until I could sense the saddle through the clouds above. A long steep climb over rough ground brought me out onto the ridge which runs north off Conival. From the saddle the going became rockier, up a fairly narrow arête, until Conival's summit cairn emerged from the clouds. Brief breaks in the weather gave glimpses down into the wilderness of lochans and peat-hags away to the north.

Not being a day to hang about I quickly left the cairn and dropped steeply down a short way to the east to pick up a narrow ridge. The wind here was incredible; it was being channelled through the gap between the two peaks, but by moving carefully I was soon at the foot of the short climb, which led over boulders to the summit of Ben More Assynt.

The mountains south 'top' lay almost a mile away on a fairly narrow ridge, whose sides fell away steeply into the gloom. A warning in the guide-book not to descend too soon off the ridge appeared valid; it did look very tempting to just drop straight down from the 'top' towards Dubh Loch Mor, however, I carried on for another half a mile and found a friendlier looking gully, which took me steeply down and brought me out at the southern end of Dubh Loch Mor. Out of the clouds at last and sheltered from the wind, I now had the chance to stop for a brief rest and a bite to eat. After that I contoured round the head of the glen to reach the rocky cleft beneath Conival's south-western flank, which brought me out above the River Traligill once more.

I had carried my head-torch with me in case I decided to search out some of the caves marked on the map, but I was wet and cold, and just made my way down the heather clad hillside and followed the river back out. Part way down, the river disappeared into a cliff, leaving a virtually dry river bed for half a mile or so, until the river re-emerged and here I rejoined the land-rover track for the final mile back down to the road.

In spite of the weather it had been another great day in the mountains.

Ben Hope   3,042ft   Ben Klibreck   3,154ft

I decided to combine these two peaks with a hill race one April weekend. The Ben Rha race was on the Saturday afternoon and was only a fairly short one; about 7 miles with just 850ft of climbing. I managed to hang on and pick up my first ever hill running trophy, which was a bit of a surprise and made the long journey north worthwhile.

Ben Hope and Ben Klibreck are about 15 miles apart and are not really feasible to climb in one outing, unless you can leave a car at either end; both outings are reasonably short though and can easily be done the same day.

The day after the race I left Tongue and drove down alongside Loch Hope to leave the car by a cow-shed part way down Strath More. As I wanted to climb Ben Klibreck later and then faced a very long drive home, I ran Ben Hope, going fast and light. The initial slopes were very steep and took me quickly up through a gap in the crags to reach a grassy terrace; from here it was head down, hands pushing down on my knees, and aim straight for the summit cone. A line of cairns showed the way but it was a beautiful clear day, I could see for miles and there was no chance of going astray. The run back down the steep but easy slopes was great fun. I surprised a couple who were slowly making their way up the ridge; they gave me a look as though I was an escaped lunatic and I was back at the car in not much over an hour.

After a change of shoes, a drink and a bite to eat I drove the short way down through Altnaharra to park off the road by a foot-bridge over the River Vagastie. The day was staying fine, though hazy, as I crossed the empty moorland and passed a couple of lonely lochans before setting to work on the steep climb up onto Creag an Lochain. Here I turned north to follow the obvious ridge toward the summit of Meall nan Con, the main top of Ben Klibreck. The last few hundred feet of climbing were over boulders but it wasn't long before I was resting beside the shelter by the cairn.

Thinking of the long drive home I couldn't linger and dropped quickly back down to the north/south ridge before cutting diagonally down the open hillside above Loch nan Uan. A large herd of deer watched me nervously and when I came too close for comfort they raced off. Initially I had only seen about 50 or so, but more and more kept appearing from a fold in the hillside until almost 300 beasts were on the move, a magnificent sight. A bit of a slog across the moor brought me back out at the roadside to end a grand day, capturing the two northernmost Munros.

Section 17: The Islands: Mull; Skye

Ben More (Isle of Mull)   3,169ft

In view of its unique island situation I should have saved Ben More for a fine day but no, my usual bad luck with the weather prevailed. Rather than take the car over on the expensive ferry from Oban, I left Onich early one morning and took the ferry across Loch Linnhe. I then had a race against the clock, down narrow, twisting roads to Lochaline. The small ferry was waiting and I drove straight on and within a few minutes we were off on the short crossing of the Sound of Mull.

The day was dark and stormy as I drove across the island and part-way down the south side of Loch na Keal. On a reasonably small island like Mull I would have expected a 3,000ft mountain to stick out like a sore thumb but with thick cloud down to about 500ft I couldn't see it and had no idea what it looked like.

I started from near the farm of Dhiseig and set off across the open moorland. Once in the cloud I had to take a bearing to bring me out onto Ben More's northern shoulder. After a steep climb the shoulder levelled out and a long line of cairns marked the route all the way to the summit. After some time, climbing gently all the way along the rubble strewn ridge the trig-point, surrounded by a low stone wall, appeared out of the mist.

A short stop was sufficient to check the map and swallow a *Mars Bar* before I turned about and retraced my steps back along the line of cairns. As I dropped down off the shoulder I came out below the clouds and could see the car by the roadside about a mile and a half away; looking out to the west I could also see that the long awaited storm was rapidly approaching. Watching the front coming in up Loch na Keal I set off at a jog, racing the oncoming rain. Unfortunately the front was quicker than I was and it caught me while I was still about 400yds from the car. The rain hammered down so hard that it hurt and within seconds I was soaked to the skin.

Since then I have been fortunate to return to Mull again when competing in the *Scottish Islands Peaks Race*. Mull is the first of the islands after leaving Oban, followed by Jura, then Arran, before finishing in Troon. We landed in Salen, ran in along the road then turned east along Loch Ba to pick up a good stalkers path which led up the glen onto a grassy ridge. From here the climb traverses under the rocky knob of A'Chioch and out onto Ben More's summit. A run down to the west to rejoin the road then left a long road run back to Salen to meet up with the boat again. This gives a run of about 4½ hours depending on whether you are lucky enough to run it all in daylight or not. One of the races is described in detail elsewhere in this journal.

Isle of Skye:
Am Basteir 3,069ft
Sgurr nan Gillean 3,167ft
Bruach na Frithe 3,143ft

I was keen to complete the traverse of the Cuillin Ridge in one go but, not having climbed there previously and being well aware of the ridges reputation, which meant rock-climbing skills were required, I decided to join a group and for the first time be 'guided' on the Scottish hills. A local guide, G. offered a week's training culminating in a traverse of the ridge, however, it quickly became apparent that he had no interest in the group making the traverse. I think he had too many clients; there were five of us with him for the week, plus another couple who joined us for the weekend.

However, it was a beautiful day when we drove round from Glen Brittle to the Sligachan Inn to try the northernmost peaks. From the Inn a wet footpath took us across the moor, alongside a stream, passing through a narrow gorge towards Coire a'Bhasteir. We were soon at the foot of the northern ridge of Sgurr nan Gillean, the Pinnacle Ridge.

One look at the crags and pinnacles was enough to convince me that I had been right to join a guided group; I would never have gone up that way on my own. We scrambled after G. for a short way then stopped to rope-up. It was soon clear that G. knew the route like the back of his hand; with the security of a rope we climbed the towers and pinnacles quite easily and all too soon we arrived on the small rocky summit.

The descent was by the narrow west ridge; we had a short abseil down a steep chimney, before contouring round to the scree. From here we regained the ridge for the short scramble onto Am Basteir. Returning to the bealach to the east we traversed round beneath Am Basteir to reach the bealach on its west side. From here terraces led up onto the ridge and after crossing a mass of scree we reached the trig-point on Bruach na Frithe.

With the sun still beating down relentlessly we were all very thirsty so we raced back down to the Bealach nan Lice, traversed to the Bealach a'Bhasteir and dropped down into the rocky Coire a'Bhasteir. The little stream rushing out of the corrie was cool and refreshing and set us up for the walk-out, back down through the rocky gorge to the moorland path which took us back to the doorstep of the Sligachan Inn.

We had to re-hydrate and the famous old inn was the obvious place to do so. At the bar we met Walter Poucher, the renowned mountain photographer/writer; he was then in his 90's and we were somewhat surprised to see him sitting at the bar wearing make-up and gold lamé gloves.

Sgurr a'Mhadaidh 3,010ft Sgurr a'Ghreadaidh 3,197ft Sgurr na Banachdich 3,167ft

For this trio of peaks, which make the round of Coire a'Ghreadaidh, we started from part way up the glen, a short way beyond the bridge over the River Brittle. A faint path dropped down to cross the river before climbing across the heather and up into Coir' a'Mhadaidh. From here G. led us up an easy scramble known as Foxes Rake. As ever, once we were actually on it and climbing, it was a lot easier than we first thought when we were looking up at it from below. Another scramble up a steeper chimney took us out onto Sgurr a'Mhadaidh's north-west ridge, which was followed more easily to Sgurr a'Mhadaidh's main summit.

The clouds were down so we didn't see much and in the cool wind we were pressed to keep moving swiftly along. We headed off south, down the narrow arête, with steep drops off to both left and right, until we came to An Dorus (The Door), a deep notch in the rocky ridge. We had a steep climb up the far side but it was enjoyable scrambling, if a little exposed. After a further short traverse we dropped to another notch, before climbing up into the gloom once more. We kept to the east side of the crest as we continued up the ridge until the way was blocked by a fearsome looking crag. This was where having a guide proved useful, as G. led us round and up via a series of ledges until we were beside the cairn on Sgurr a'Ghreadaidh.

While we had a short break the clouds thinned a little and we could just make out Loch Coruisk far below. Moving on again the ridge remained very narrow along to the south 'top' of Sgurr a'Ghreadaidh; if any ridge is 'knife-edged' then this was it. I read later that this is perhaps the narrowest and most exposed part of the whole Cuillin Ridge!

After leaving the 'top' we dropped a little height and things became easier for a while, but that was just to lull us into a false sense of security. We now came to a series of little pinnacles, which we scrambled up and abseiled down, it was exciting ground and being on a rope meant we could move with confidence. Some easy slabs then took us to the 'top' of Sgurr Thormaid.

Continuing south along the ridge we dropped a short distance before facing the final climb up scree and boulders that saw us up onto the cairn of Sgurr na Banachdich. From the summit we were on easier ground and heading downhill; G. took us off west along a narrow but easy ridge out to the little top of Sgurr nan Gobhar and from here it was each man for himself as we sought out our own lines down scree and rocks, dropping as quickly as we could to the heather and the final walk-out back to the Youth Hostel.

Sgurr Dearg – Inaccessible Pinnacle   3,254ft

The Inaccessible Pinnacle was perhaps the main reason I'd chosen to climb with a guide; every guide-book you read says that this is a real rock-climb and should not be treated lightly. In addition to the five of us, we were joined by another couple of clients for this day, one of whom hoped to complete his round of the Munros with our proposed ascent of the pinnacle.

7: Abseil descent from The Inaccessible Pinnacle

So it was a big group who set off from Glenbrittle House and followed the footpath up alongside the stream to the waterfalls of Eas Mor, before heading across the heather, past the loch and up towards Coire Lagan. We then struck up the rough, bouldery hillside and onto the west ridge of Sgurr Dearg. From here it was an easy scramble along to the cairn on the 'top' of Sgurr Dearg itself. We had a rest and looked over to The Inaccessible Pinnacle, a narrow, blade-like crest of rock that rises just 20ft higher than Sgurr Dearg.

It didn't take long to drop down to the base of the pinnacle and walk round beneath it. From the foot of the east ridge, a couple of us scrambled up the 150ft 'Moderate' rock-climb; I was actually half-way up before I realised that this was it, it was too easy and a bit of an anti-climax really. The weather was lovely and we could see for miles, I guess it would have seemed much harder if the clouds had been down, an icy gale blowing and the rocks wet and greasy. Today though it couldn't have been better and a couple of us romped up it in no time. Meanwhile G. was roping up the others and they climbed more slowly, until we all just managed to squeeze onto the narrow summit block. The 'completionist' was congratulated but G. wanted us off and down in order to make room for the other climbers who were gathering at the foot of the pinnacle; our guide wasted no time in rigging an abseil down the shorter, western face.

Re-grouping and putting away the climbing gear we continued south-east along the ridge, over An Stac, to then drop steeply down the easy screes into Coire Lagan. Below the lochan we picked up the footpath which led us down to Loch an Fhir-bhallaich. Here the party split up, some descending, while I and a couple of the others stopped for a dip in the inviting waters before returning to the Youth Hostel. The swim was a lovely way to end an exciting day, with the 'hardest' Munro now out of the way.

Sgurr Alasdair 3,309ft   Sgurr Mhic Choinnich 3,107ft

This day was another scorcher; in brilliant weather we followed the path from Glen Brittle, up past the waterfall, round above the loch and into Coire Lagan. Here we crossed to the right-hand wall of the corrie and climbed up the steep but easy slabs which led to The Cioch. A stiffer climb, this time protected by the rope, took us to the top of the huge boulder. Relaxing on this tremendous view-point we had an early lunch while gazing out over the hills and over the sea to Rhum.

All too soon we had to move on; we climbed down off the boulder then an easy scramble led up to the ridge which we followed to the 'top' of Sgurr Sgumain. From here it wasn't far along the ridge to Sgurr Alasdair, the highest point on Skye. We had to climb one short wall of rock which blocked the path, but I don't know if this was the 'bad step'. I remember it being little more than 6ft high, one pull and you were up and over quite easily.

Enjoying the fine weather and 360⁰ views, we dawdled along. We had a tricky little scramble out to the 'top' of Sgurr Thearlaich and an equally hard scramble down the other side. G. then led the way to the narrow corridor known as *Collie's Ledge* and a short way along this he roped-up to lead King's Chimney, a 'Difficult' rock-climb. We followed up the corner and across the wall to come out virtually on the summit of Sgurr Mhic Choinnich.

Leaving the top we continued along the narrow, rocky ridge, down to the col below An Stac, here we dropped down the rough screes all the way to Coire Lagan. The weather again persuaded the more hardy of us to stop for a swim in Loch an Fhir-bhallaich, before continuing back down to Glen Brittle to end another fantastic day and a great week.

Sgurr Dubh Mor   3,089ft

This peak will always be a little bit special because it was my 'last' Munro. It wouldn't have been if an earlier walk had gone to plan; that time I climbed Sgurr nan Eag but in the appalling weather I decided to forget about Sgurr Dubh Mor and Sgurr Dubh na Da Bheinn and instead just concentrated on descending safely.

It was about three months later, 15th June 1990, when I next found myself camped at Glen Brittle. Thankfully the weather was kinder and I enjoyed the walk in from the campsite, climbing the familiar boggy path, which led round into Coir'a'Ghrunnda. This corrie perhaps ties with Coire Mhic Fhearchair on Beinn Eighe as being my favourite spot in Scotland.

The easy angled slabs of rock gave exciting scrambling, although as you rarely had to use your hands perhaps it should still be called walking. The lovely high loch gave a good excuse for a rest then it was on again for a short scramble up the rough path which leads to Bealach a'Garbh-choire. From this rocky col on the narrow ridge, a faint path led up, around huge blocks to the 'top' of Sgurr Dubh na Da Bheinn.

From the cairn a short scramble down through crags led to a narrow col, across the other side of which the path could be seen winding its way up through easy rocks to Sgurr Dubh Mor. Once on top, the last of my 277 Munros, I celebrated with a cup of tea and some flapjack. The views were worthy of the occasion, simply magnificent. I looked down to the wild Loch Coruisk; across to Sgurr Alasdair; down to the sea and the small islands; and across to the Inaccessible Pinnacle. Although

I've been fortunate to visit many beautiful parts of the world, Scotland will always take some beating.

> *"Great things happen when men and mountains meet"*
> (Blake)

I stayed some time on the summit until a cold wind made me move on again. A short scramble down to the col, followed by the scramble up and over the 'top' and I was soon back at the bealach and then the loch. In clear weather it was so much easier; then came the fun of the Coir'a'Ghrunnda slabs and all too soon I was back on the wet footpath across the moors and heading down to the camp-site.

It was a very special day.

Sgurr nan Eag   3,037ft

One March, with bad weather on the mainland, I decided to cross over to Skye for a couple of days in the hope of finding better weather there. But of course Skye was no better.

The clouds were clamped right down and it was grey and miserable when I set off from the camp-site at Glen Brittle. The boggy path crossed the moors and the plan was that I would turn off up into Coir'a'Ghrunnda. I seemed to have been walking for a very long time, with no break in the hillside to indicate the entrance to the corrie, and eventually, through the gloom I realised that I could just about see the sea and the island of Soay, not far away to the south. I had come a good mile too far, so rather than retrace my steps and search for the way into the corrie, I found myself facing an unexpectedly hard climb up a mixture of heather, boulders and scree to join the ridge near Sgurr a'Choire Bhig. The scrambling was not hard, but it was dangerously loose, and in the thick mist I really had no idea what I was getting myself into.

Eventually I reached Sgurr nan Eag and from here I had more anxious moments as I continued along, down the ridge to the Bealach a'Garbh-choire. Here I was faced with a choice of either an easy-ish descent into the corrie, or further unknown scrambles above steep drops and through thick mist. I regret to say that I took the easy option and dropped down to Loch Coir'a'Ghrunnda. The mist started to clear as I had lunch by the loch and I considered climbing back up to the bealach to continue along the ridge, but having started to descend my heart was no longer in it, and instead I sought out the cairns which marked the way down the slabs. I kept losing the route, but as I dropped lower, the mist thinned, and I finally regained the path I'd used earlier that morning.

The eroded, boggy path gave me time on the walk out to plan a return visit to 'bag' Sgurr Dubh Mor, having missed out on it this time.

Bla Bheinn   3,044ft

Bla Bheinn stands alone, somewhat away from the main Cuillin ridge, and I made the long drive round to the head of Loch Slapin on a miserable November day.

The weather was wet and windy as I set off from the lochside, up a good track which roughly followed the Allt na Dunaiche. All too soon I was up in the clouds and once I was in Coire Uaigneich I couldn't see more than a few yards; and what's more, what little I could see I didn't like. There seemed to be steep buttresses, running with water, and in the strengthening wind I only wanted a walk, not to have to start scrambling up an unknown route.

Continuing up I came out onto snow, this hid the path, but thankfully from time to time I could just make out some old footprints, which led me to the fairly narrow summit ridge. I carefully made my way to the south 'top' first then carried on along the arête to the trig point on Bla Bheinn's main summit. The conditions on top were pretty desperate and I was keen to descend as quickly as possible so after swallowing a *Mars Bar* I re-crossed the old snow and dropped down into the corrie where it was more sheltered. That just left a trudge back through the puddles to the car.

In better weather I would have gone on from the summit out to Clach Glas and Garbh-bheinn but given the conditions it would have been foolish to go on; I was happy to call it a day, drop down and dry out.

Note 1 - Munro's Tables

When I completed the Munros in June 1990 I based this on the Munro's Tables as they stood at that time, which was the 1984 revision. This listed 276 Munros; to these I added Beinn Teallach, as it had recently been re-surveyed at 915m, making 277 Munros in all. There was a later revision of the Tables in 1997; this demoted one Munro, Sgor an Iubhair in the Mamores, and added eight new ones, giving a total of 284.

The 'new' Munros are: An Stuc on Ben Lawers; Stob Coire Raineach on Buachaille Etive Beag; Stob na Bròige on Buachaille Etive Mor; Stob Coire Sgreamhach on Bidean nam Bian; Sgor an Lochain Uaine between Cairn Toul and Braeriach; Sgurr na Carnach on the Five Sisters of Kintail; Spidean Coire nan Clach on Beinn Eighe; Tom na Gruagaich on Beinn Alligin.

Note 2 - Munro's Tables

Since the 1997 revision, more accurate GPS aided measurement has established that two former Munros do not quite breach the magic 3,000ft mark, these are: Sgurr nan Ceannaichean near Achnashellach and Beinn a'Chlaidheimh, which was one of the 'Fisherfield Six'.

Thus at the time of writing there are now 282 Munros, all of which I climbed in my initial round.

(*Munro's Tables and Other Tables of Lesser Heights* published by The Scottish Mountaineering Trust)

SOME OF THE BEST LONG RUNS AT HOME

A Long Day in the Lakes – The Lakeland 3,000's

The whistle blew at 2am and we were off. Somewhat surprisingly, rather than walking, almost everyone started off at a comfortable jog on this 'walk' which was organised by a local group of the *Ramblers Association*.

We filed through the deserted streets of Keswick at an easy pace, across the park, then out onto the hillside where most slowed to a walk. The broad scar of the Latrigg track was easy to see in the dark so there was little need for a head-torch. As we climbed higher we looked down on the lights of Keswick, while above us we saw a patch of mist just covering the summit, otherwise the night was cool and clear. As we continued the climb, by-passing the top of Little Man, the first of the fast runners passed us, already on their way down. Not too long after them, we too arrived on the summit of Skiddaw (3,054ft) where we handed our numbered discs to the marshals to check-in. Dawn was breaking as we jogged easily back down the track, still without needing our head-torches, which stayed in the bottom of our 'sacs all day.

By 4:30 we were back, almost where we'd started; we checked in at the Moot Hall and set off on the 10 mile stretch down past Derwent Water, along Borrowdale, to Seathwaite. We walked and jogged down the road, out to Seathwaite Farm where most people took the track via Stockley Bridge up to Styhead, but we crossed the river at the farm and followed an alternative route up past the waterfall of Taylorgill Force. The people camping 'wild' beside Styhead Tarn had a rude awakening to a glorious morning, as dozens of walkers and runners streamed past so early.

From the pass a colourful line of those in front pointed out the way ahead, up the Corridor Route onto Lingmell Col. We then crossed over and contoured round to the scree at the foot of Lords Rake. The scree was a bit worrying with so many people around but there was worse to come. As we climbed into and up the rake a group of four were just ahead of us, two of them were quite slow and were very careless with their feet. Moving out left onto the West Wall Traverse, the group stayed in front and continued to knock fist sized lumps of rock down onto us; we endeavoured to catch some of these before they did too much harm below. As we climbed out of Deep Ghyll the wind hit us so we didn't linger in checking in at the summit of Scafell (3,162ft). The leader had surprised the summit marshals by coming up so fast that they were still in their sleeping bags when he arrived.

From the summit the choice was either down to Foxes Tarn and traverse round to Mickledore or to go straight down to Mickledore via Broad Stand. We decided on the route via Foxes Tarn and we were glad we did; when we passed the foot of Broad Stand and looked up we saw a traffic jam and several people were dithering on the steep face. From the col at Mickledore it wasn't far up over a boulder-field to the summit of Scafell Pike (3,206ft).

Still on rocks and boulders we soon crossed Broad Crag and Ill Crag and moved down towards Esk Hause, where we were pleased to meet a friend who fed us *Lucozade* and *Mars Bars* to keep us going. It was good to reach grass again and we had an easier run down to Angle Tarn. From here we contoured round to Stake Pass followed by a short climb up on to High Raise, where there was another check-point. Here we enjoyed a short rest while we re-grouped after the climb. The next section was about three miles, gently downhill on fairly good going alongside Wyth Burn; we jogged all the way down to Steel End at the foot of Thirlmere, where we met up with our support again.

After another quick break to eat and drink in preparation for Helvellyn we left the road at Wythburn Church and climbed steeply up through the trees; the path then zigzagged up the hill to finally bring us out onto the ridge near Nethermost Pike. From here we had great views all round and we could see most of the day's route. The angle eased as we followed the ridge up to the summit of Helvellyn (3,116ft) which, as usual, was very crowded. From the top we now had an easy run down to the north-west to a patch of scree, which we crossed carefully; once past the worst of the scree we ran comfortably down the close cropped grass to come out at the road at the foot of Helvellyn Gill. From the final check-point it just left us with a six mile jog back along the road to Keswick to finish in a time of around 14½ hours.

All in all it was another great day in the hills; we had been very lucky with the weather, it made navigation easy and yet it was not too hot for us to keep moving fairly quickly the whole day. The route is approximately 46 miles with around 11,000ft of climbing.

A Recce of the Bob Graham Round

A mid-September weekend saw me meet up with my sister and a few of her friends for a recce of the famous Bob Graham Round; a round of 42 Lakeland peaks, covering some 72 miles with around 27,000ft of ascent. We were all relatively inexperienced at this sort of long distance endurance event, and with the nights already drawing in we decided to run it over two days, staying overnight at Wasdale Head. The plan was that we would try the round properly, looking to complete within 24 hours, the following June, once we were really fit.

We left Keswick on a clock-wise round just after 4am, heading for Skiddaw, the first of the 42 peaks. It was a beautiful night, very dark but without a cloud in sight as we climbed the wide scar of the path by torchlight. However, within half an hour, as we contoured round Little Man, the clouds closed in and a freezing wind came up from no-where. We reached the summit of Skiddaw just before 5:30, put on all our warm gear and snatched a quick breakfast.

We had expected it to be day-light around the time we left the summit, but the heavy cloud meant we had to navigate carefully by torchlight, north-wards a short way down the ridge, before taking another bearing to take us down to the track below Great Calva. It seemed a long slog up through the heather, as we climbed through the clouds and came out at the summit cairn.

Day-light came as we waded the ice-cold stream between Great Calva and Blencathra but we were still in thick cloud and worked our way by compass across featureless moorland. This section from Skiddaw to Blencathra was proving to be very tiring and time consuming; we had to take direct routes across the fells, any paths always seemed to be going in the wrong direction for us. On reaching the summit ridge we followed this along to the summit proper. The descent from Blencathra was quite steep as we rapidly made our way down the rocky Halls Fell Ridge. Half way down, the rocks gave way to easier grassy slopes where we could run safely down to the road in Threlkeld. Here we met our support and we all took the opportunity to refuel.

The climb to Clough Head was again straight across country with only occasional faint traces of a path. The summit cairn eventually loomed up out of the cloud and from here we jogged along the ridge ticking off Great Dodd, Watsons Dodd and Stybarrow Dodd. The climbs up to each summit were negligible; the navigation was relatively straight forward and we enjoyed the easier conditions underfoot. After a short drop down to Sticks Pass, it was upwards again onto Raise, then Helvellyn itself, which was already very crowded. As we approached the summit the clouds parted at last and we could now see for miles.

We followed the crest of the ridge south, crossing Nethermost Pike and Dollywagon Pike, before dropping steeply down to Grisedale Tarn. Here we looked up at the steep flank of Fairfield with some trepidation; before we tackled the climb we took the opportunity of mixing some poly-bags of *Staminade*, which we filled from the tarn and drank on the spot, while stretched out in the warm sun.

We were soon on the move again and the steep climb didn't take as long as we had feared as we went directly up onto Fairfield's summit. It was an easy jog down to the col, then up to Seat Sandal, which gave another short stiff climb, following an old stone wall. From the summit we went off directly down the ridge to cross the road at Dunmail Raise.

We hadn't worked out a detailed schedule for the day but I knew we had been slower than expected on the Keswick to Threlkeld section; however, we estimated 5 hours for the section from Threlkeld to Dunmail and we were pleased to see that we had made it bang on time. We took the opportunity to have a longish stop with plenty to eat and drink. By the time we were ready to leave it was already 3pm, with a maximum of five hours daylight left. It was a long section from Dunmail to Wasdale Head, taking in 15 summits, the hardest being Scafell and Scafell Pike, which we wouldn't reach until almost the end of a long hard day, and in the dark. Unless we could pick up the pace it was starting to look as though we would need to re-think our plans.

From Dunmail we climbed straight up the horrendously steep fellside. After touching the cairn on Steel Fell, we jogged off towards Calf Crag, following a pleasant undulating path. Unfortunately, from here we struggled across open fell, which seemed never ending, until we finally arrived on top of High Raise. It was now we realised that time was against us and we reluctantly agreed that we should just make straight for Wasdale Head. It meant we would miss several summits around Langdale, Bowfell and the Scafell area. The general consensus was that it would be too risky finding ourselves in the dark on the tricky boulders of Scafell Pike, followed by an ascent and descent of Scafell by torchlight.

Once the decision had been made we seemed to speed up a little and we ran off down High Raise to Stake Pass, on past Angle Tarn beneath Bowfell, followed by a short climb up to Esk Hause, then down again to Sprinkling Tarn. By this time the sun was just setting behind Yewbarrow and the light was fantastic, throwing all the ridges into sharp relief. It was a beautiful sight to end the day as we made our way to Styhead and down to Wasdale Head, where we were booked into a B&B for the night.

Next morning, Steve, who had been troubled by a bad back, decided to call it a day; in his place we were joined by Chris, who had run over from Seathwaite in time for breakfast. With a fresh pair of legs in the team a quick pace was set on the steep 1,800ft climb to Yewbarrow's summit. From here the ridge gave good runnable ground, contouring below Stirrup Crag before another climb up onto Red Pike. The low cloud meant more map and compass work to take us to Steeple, and then the trig point on the shapely summit of Pillar, standing at the head of Mosedale.

As we dropped down from Pillar the clouds cleared again; we had great views down onto Ennerdale Forest, and we had a good fast run down to Black Sail Pass. We took a direct route up Kirkfell and the narrow gully round on the left gave us a quick and painless climb to the summit cairn. Leaving Kirkfell we kept up a good pace down to the col from where we looked up at the 1,000ft climb to Great Gable. Keeping to the left of the ridge we enjoyed a bit of a scramble to emerge amongst a crowd of people milling around the summit.

After only a short rest we moved off and were soon onto Green Gable, from where we had a long run out over the tops of Brandreth, followed by Grey Knotts, then down to the road at Honister Youth Hostel. This section had again gone to time; we arrived five hours after setting off from Wasdale Head.

With the end in sight we enjoyed a brief rest and a bite to eat before the final big climb; we set off up Dale Head, the track initially following the fence, then taking a direct line to the summit. Short grass gave good running along Hindscarth Edge and around onto Hindscarth itself, which stands a short way off the main ridge. From the summit we dropped down to regain the main ridge, which we followed as it turned north and led us to our final peak, Robinson. The best running of the day now followed, and we dropped easily down the track, which eventually led back to the road at Little Town.

I was sorry not to have managed all the peaks but we had covered the bulk of the route and gained a far better understanding of what we should expect if we were ever to try the round for real in the future.

As it turned out, injuries and old age meant I never did make an attempt on the Bob Graham Round, one of the biggest regrets of my life.

Scottish Islands Peaks Race

When the *Rock & Run Mountain Marathon*, which was to have been held on Skye, was cancelled, I was lucky to be invited at short notice to join a boat entered in the Scottish Islands Peaks Race. The *Glasgow Herald* described the event as 'possibly the most arduous event in the Scottish sporting calendar' while *The Times* went one better and called it 'the most gruelling event in the world'.

We met in Oban and looking at us we did not look likely participants in what promised to be a tough few days. Bill was skipper and owner of 'Lady Shamrock', a *Shipman 28* yacht, which is usually based in Crinan; the other two sailors were Bill's brother-in-law, Andrew, and a family friend, Hamish. The rest of the five man team was made up of two runners; Alan and myself. It was unfortunate that we had only come together the week before the race; it would have been a lot easier if we had run and sailed together beforehand.

A briefing was held early on race day to go over the route and some rules; for the runners it was relatively simple and what I was used to, but for the sailors it seemed to be far more complicated and several long-winded arguments broke out. An STV camera crew were out and about interviewing the leading contenders, clearly that didn't include us.

The start gun sounded at noon and 54 pairs of runners streamed away from the Sailing Club for the opening 10km run; out over a moorland road, before dropping back down to the coast, past the Sailing Club, along the sea-front and down to the beach in Oban. Andrew was waiting on the beach with the dinghy and rowed us out to 'Lady Shamrock', which was already under way. It was a bit of a struggle climbing onto the moving boat, but once safely on board Alan and I went below to keep out of the way leaving Bill and Andrew to sail us out of Oban harbour; Hamish meanwhile had bravely wrapped himself around the rear stay and was giving a stirring performance on the bagpipes. This was easier said than done, as the boat was keeling over in a keen Force 4 wind.

The fleet made a fine sight as we raced out; there was a wide range of craft from small mono-hulls like our 'Lady Shamrock', to a 70ft schooner and a large ketch, along with several large catamarans and hi-tech trimarans. The wind was variable so for a while we made little headway around Lismore Island and we were forced to watch as the leaders, already well ahead of us, split up, some keeping to the south side of the

Long Runs at Home

Sound of Mull, while the majority headed further north towards the mainland peninsular.

The 20 mile sail to the small harbour of Salen on the north coast of Mull took us almost 5 hours; Hamish then rowed Alan and I to a derelict pier. After a compulsory 'kit-check', for which we had a 'time-out' of 5 minutes, we set off, starting with a four mile section on the road, heading south-west across the island from Salen to Knock. We then turned onto a forest road, following the south shore of Loch Ba. It was a lovely evening and gave superb running in beautiful country. The first control was at the edge of the forest, from where a stalkers path led up into Glen Clachaig. After a couple of miles we crossed the stream and climbed more steeply up to an obvious col. During the climb we could see a couple of other teams some way ahead and I was constantly urging Alan on in an effort to close the gap.

There was a cool wind blowing on the col and a long climb then followed on good ground, alongside a small rocky outcrop. A'Chioch loomed up out of the mist and we contoured round below to the south, crossing an unstable scree slope, before another short climb took us up to the col beyond. Once above the col we were soon scrambling up the rocky ridge to the summit of Ben More, a Munro, and the highest point on the island.

Quickly punching our control-card we made our way by compass off the summit by way of the mountains north-west ridge. After an easy couple of miles we came out below the mist and aimed off towards control 3, which was down by the road; an unexpected electric fence a couple of hundred yards from the road gave me a nasty shock when I mis-timed my jump. Once on the road we had a run of about seven miles back to Salen, which we reached in the dark, 20 minutes before midnight.

Hamish was waiting for us at the final control, handed us our life-jackets, and rowed us out to the 'Lady Shamrock'. Bill, Andrew and Hamish had all taken the opportunity to have a couple of hours sleep and to eat a hot meal while anchored off Salen; they had left soup and a stew ready for Alan and I. The sailors took us carefully out into the Sound of Mull, while Alan and I ate, then immediately went to bed to try to recover in time for the next running 'leg'. During the long night sail Bill, Andrew and Hamish took it in turns to go below for a couple of hours rest as only one or two were usually needed on deck at any one time. At one stage, when rounding Mull and turning south into the Firth of Lorn the wind dropped and the tide turned against us, so they rowed for a while to stop us losing ground.

Saturday dawned grey and foggy and we saw little all day, except for a lone seal, as we made our way down amongst the islands, past the famous Gulf of Corryvreckan, which can be a dangerous place of whirlpools and strong currents. Unfortunately I felt really ill going down this stretch and was forced to stay below for most of the day, unable to eat or drink. The 60 miles of sailing took us just over 18 hours and we arrived at Craighouse on Jura's east coast at 17:50.

Again, Hamish did the honours and rowed Alan and I to the pier where we scrambled up the ladder. Having been sea-sick several times during the day and eaten nothing, I quickly ate a couple of bananas and some chocolate while we jogged along the track to the check-point at the distillery. A couple of other teams were there, but they were checking out having already completed their Jura run, thus they were around 6 hours ahead of us. The leading boats had already been and gone.

We left the distillery and ran north along the shore road for a mile or so before turning off onto open hill-side. This area is remote and seldom visited so there are few paths here, this made it hard going as we headed up into the mist, unable to see any real features of note, which meant careful navigating by map and compass. We seemed to have been going for far too long and I was starting to feel concerned; eventually though, keeping faith in the compass we found the lochan, with its small island, which I had been aiming for.

This gave us confidence and we were able to pick up the pace so we were soon at the foot of Beinn a'Chaolain, the first of the three Paps of Jura. We had been warned that the Paps were all scree covered, with no obvious paths up them, and in mist it was difficult to find the best line. However I knew a reasonable route led up from near the col and as it turned out we were able to follow a grassy rake for most of the way, only coming out onto loose blocks a few feet below the summit ridge.

The control was on the summit cairn and after quickly punching our control-card we lost no time in descending to another col some 1,000ft below. I tried to keep the pace quite fast as I didn't want to be on the hills in the dark; I was keen to be up and down the second summit, Beinn an Oir, as soon as possible. The sight of the lochan in the col below proved that we were in the right place and we scrambled up a rocky ridge, being over-taken near the top by a pair from a rival boat. They were going well and although we were together leaving the summit it was disappointing that we couldn't keep pace with them on the descent. The route wasn't obvious and we had to keep seeking out the safest line in the fast fading daylight. After another 1,000ft descent we crossed the col and climbed 1,000ft to Beinn Shiantaidh. Again we had to seek out the easiest way, trying to keep to the grass or heather, rather than the ankle breaking scree, and by luck or good judgement I found us a good route and the final climb didn't take too long, even by the light of our head-torches.

Coming down was slower as it was hard to see if a drop was 2 metres, 20 metres or even a potentially fatal 200 metres. It seemed interminable coming through the scree but at last scree gave way to heather and the going became easier. Unfortunately Alan and I now managed to lose each other for 10 minutes or so. I had been out in front searching for a route and stopping every so often to look around and make sure that Alan was ok and keeping up, this time however when I looked around there was no sign of his head-torch. I called out, wandered right, left, up and down, but could see no sign of him. After several minutes of searching I was left with no alternative but to fear the worse and I had to start back up the hill, climbing an extra 200ft or so, to look for him.

Eventually I heard a call from below; how he sneaked past me I don't know, nor could I understand how he hadn't heard me when I had called out. After warning him not to disappear again we finally dropped below cloud level and even in the dark it was just possible to make out the shape of the coastline and the whereabouts of the final check-point. However, that was still two miles away, across rough moorland, and we were pleased when we finally saw the bridge just ahead of us. Once on the road we were left with a run of around three miles back to Craighouse. A pair of runners was just setting off as we returned to the jetty; we wished them well and didn't envy them their running in the dark.

It was just after 1:30 on the Sunday morning when we climbed down into the dinghy and made our way back to the boat. Again the sailing team had eaten and slept while we had been out on the hill, and they had left a pot of soup on the stove for us. The boat was underway and we were preparing to leave Craighouse Bay when there was an almighty crash; the soup went flying as did almost everything else that wasn't tied down. Bill quickly started the engine to reverse us off the reef and we were soon sailing away with no apparent damage. We started the pump but there was little water, we had been very lucky.

We were now faced with the longest sailing leg of the trip, 80 miles or so, round the potentially rough waters off the Mull of Kintyre to Arran. I was a bit apprehensive having felt so sea-sick when we sailed from Mull to Jura, but the tablets seemed to work and the weather was kinder to us. After almost 10 hours in bed, we runners spent the afternoon relaxing while the sailors worked the boat as hard as they could. Later the wind dropped and it took us several hours to pass on the landward side of Sanda Island and across to the south end of Arran. The strange lump of Ailsa Craig sat up out of the water, the top covered in a layer of cloud, so that it looked like cream poured over a Christmas Pudding.

We had hoped to make Lamlash by around 6pm, which would have given us the chance to run up and most of the way down Goatfell in daylight. Unfortunately the light winds meant that it wasn't until almost 10pm that we came into the bay. Then, just to make things interesting, the wind picked up and the cloud ceiling dropped; we almost flew into the bay, going far faster than we had done all day. With a strong wind and a strong tide, we wanted to launch the dinghy as close to shore as possible, but the water was shallow close in, and crowded with other small boats; it was only after a few scary moments that Alan and I were safely off and Bill was able to motor away to anchor for the night.

On checking-in we were told there were seven teams on Arran, some boats had in fact already reached Troon and finished; a few were still behind us and a few more had retired. We hoped to be able to catch some of the teams ahead so we could make a race of it, but we met six of the teams on their way back before we had even reached Brodick. The run took us off the main road, around a hill and down into Brodick via fields and country lanes. By now it was dark, cold and misty and we envied the teams who were already down and off Goatfell. We jogged quietly through the grounds of Brodick Castle and found the track up Goatfell, which initially climbed gently through dense forest, then out onto more open ground, before climbing steeply onto the mountain's east ridge.

There was a check-point on the ridge, which took a bit of searching for in the dark and mist, but we were lucky and soon picked it out and punched the card before going on up to the summit itself. It was around here that we saw the other remaining team, they were on their way down and were around 30 minutes ahead of us. The top of Goatfell is rocky and the path was not obvious in the dark, however we knew that 'up' must take us to the summit cairn and eventually we located it and found the control and the marshal in a small tent. Alan was having trouble with his head-torch, which kept failing; new batteries didn't solve the problem so a loose connection was diagnosed but we couldn't cure it and he had to make do with a small hand-torch for the descent.

The hardest part of the run followed as we tried to find our way down off the summit; our torch beams bounced back at us off the mist, at times it was easier to switch the torches off and then, in the dark, we could see a vague outline of the area around us. After some worrying minutes we were happy that we were on the right track and made our way back down to the control on the east ridge. Once off the ridge the going quickly became much better and the track easier to follow, this took us back down towards Brodick Castle, which we reached just as dawn was breaking.

The Arran leg was all part of the game; having to set off on a run no matter what time of day the boat reached the island; some teams may be able to complete all three runs in daylight, others may be unlucky and have to do all three in darkness. On Arran we were unfortunate in having to do the worst part in the dark and in bad weather.

The run back along the country lanes and through the fields was refreshing in the early morning light and we scrambled into the dinghy just after 5am on the Monday morning. Bill took us out past Holy Island and across the Firth of Clyde towards the finish at Troon. Once in the outer harbour Hamish and I boarded the dinghy for the last time and we were towed alongside until Bill had to veer away, leaving Hamish the shortest possible distance to row into the inner harbour. We tied up at the pontoon and the two of us ran the 200 yards to the club-house and the finish.

Bearing in mind that we were virtually the smallest boat in the fleet, we were quite pleased to finish 37th out of 54; we were amazed to see that the winning boat took just 37 hours, they reached Troon in the early hours of Sunday morning, just as we were leaving Jura. It was a great event, and one I was to do again.

The Mamores 3,000's

The round of the Mamores was something I had set my heart on as on the four occasions I had previously visited the area to 'bag' the Munros, each day had without fail been miserably wet and windy and I'd seen hardly anything of the range. To do the whole circuit of 11 Munros and a further 6 satellite tops would be a long day of around 22 miles with about 11,000ft of climbing.

Late one May, towards the end of a two week holiday that had included the Scottish Islands Peaks Race and a good run in the Bens of Jura Hill Race, I decided to give it a go on the promise of a fine day by the Met Office.

Starting at the bridge at Achriabhach in Glen Nevis, I ran down the road a short way to a footpath that led up through the forest. It was not an encouraging start when I made a poor route choice after leaving the forest half-way up the glen. I should have cut straight up the hillside but it looked steep and a long way, so I lazily decided to continue up the glen to see if there was an easier way around the corner; but of course there wasn't. I still had a steep climb to reach the summit ridge, and by coming this way I also had a section of loose scree and gravel to contend with. However, I eventually reached the ridge and that left just a short jog around the edge of the corrie to come to the first Munro of the day, Mullach nan Coirean.

From here a gentle descent over good runnable ground led to the mountain's south-east top. Big crags dropped away steeply to the north and I had superb views across to Ben Nevis and away to the peaks of Glencoe in the south. The main ridge crossed a couple of saddles before turning south, across rough blocks of quartzite to the rocky Stob Ban, reached in exactly 1½ hours. I now faced a careful descent to the east, which took me down to a small lochan where I was glad to be able to refill my water-bottle, knowing it would be some time before I had another opportunity. From the lochan a grassy scramble led up to the 'Devil's Ridge', a narrow arête which runs north off the main ridge; this meant a detour to take in the 'top' of Stob a'Choire Mhail and the Munro of Sgurr a'Mhaim.

From here I re-traced my steps back to the main ridge for the climb to the Munro of Sgor an Iubhair (note 1). A 500ft dip south-eastwards was followed by another 600ft climb to Am Bodach, where once again the ridge changes direction. This time heading off north-east, where a big drop led to a col and then a steady pull up to Stob Coire a'Chairn; which was reached in a little over 3 hours.

From here another detour is called for; an outlying spur runs north to the rocky slabs of first An Garbhanach and then to the higher An Gearanach. I ran back over the intervening summit to regain the main ridge once more, now heading off south-east where a drop of some 700ft leads to the easy ascent of Na Gruagaichean's north-west 'top' and then only a little further, to the main summit itself. With the ridge once again running away north-east on good terrain I soon reached the south 'top' of Binnein Mor. The way to the main summit lies along a rocky ridge, which meant slower going for a while. From the Munro it was again necessary to re-trace my steps, down to the col, but instead of climbing back to the summit of the south top I cut around the head of the corrie along terraces that brought me out at the same height on the ridge just a short climb from the 'top' of Sgurr Eilde Beag. From here it started to feel as though the end was in sight, just two more Munros to go, but they were both sited off the ridge which meant there was still plenty of hard running to come.

I dropped steeply down to the north before heading round to the lochan, from where a stiff climb on tiring legs led me to Sgurr Eilde Mor. The day was staying fine and after only a brief stop to check the map I dropped back down towards the lochan where I was pleased to find a footpath that led me down to the stream at the head of Coire a'Bhinnein. I quickly mixed a poly-bag of *Gatorade* to wash down the last of my food.

Suitably refreshed I ran round to the lochan lying in the saddle between Binnein Mor and Binnein Beag, from where a steady pull up the rocky cone took me to the final summit of the day, Binnein Beag. Here I sought out the steep gully I remembered using during a previous *Rock & Run Mountain Marathon*, and again it gave a fast descent to take me back level with the lochan from where I dropped quite quickly over tussocks down to the Water of Nevis. I crossed the river and was soon on the main path back to Glen Nevis.

To my dismay, as I entered the car-park at the road-end, the ice-cream van was just leaving; I made my weary way the final mile or so down the road, to reach Achriabhach in a couple of minutes over 7 hours.

The Cairngorm 4,000's

For two or three years I'd been toying with the idea of running the round of the four 4,000ft peaks of the Cairngorms; the round gives a superb run of about 23 miles with 7,300ft of climbing; the four tops are the four highest Munros, except of course, Ben Nevis.

The only decision to make is which way round to run it; clockwise, taking in Cairn Gorm first; or anti-clockwise starting with Braeriach. As the section from Ben Macdui to Cairn Gorm and back down the hill to Glenmore is the easiest to run, I decided to go anti-clockwise, which meant I would have the harder running out of the way first.

The weather was cool and overcast, with heavy cloud covering the summits as I left the car-park part way up the ski-road. From the road the track led down to cross the river, followed by a short steep climb up to the Reindeer pens. I then jogged easily along the well made footpath, following the river towards the rocky defile known as the Chalamain Gap. Here the good path deteriorated; I scrambled through the large boulders but once I was through the 'gap' the path reappeared and I was soon losing height as I made my way down to the Sinclair Memorial Hut (which has since been removed) at the northern end of the Lairig Ghru.

From the site of the hut I was on a long climb up a ridge onto Sron na Lairige. Here I climbed up into thick cloud and had to keep one eye on my compass, as I headed for the narrow col where the ridge swings west and out towards Braeriach. I now had to contend with drizzle as well as the low cloud; then a large flock of ptarmigan exploded from beneath my feet, which made me jump.

From the col an obvious track led up past the scattered remains of a wrecked aircraft and I soon arrived at my first summit. Once on the plateau it was fairly fast going over the rock strewn gravel. I kept close to the edge as I ran round the corrie; the clouds were still closed in and by watching the edge carefully I was able to keep my bearings. An easy climb led up over Angels Peak and then after a short descent and re-ascent I was soon on Cairn Toul.

From here I was unsure of the best way to descend into the Lairig Ghru; the choice was either to continue south along the ridge, then drop down to a track near the Corrour Bothy and to cross the Dee by a bridge, or alternatively to just take my life in my hands and drop straight down from the cairn, through the crags in as direct a line as possible. I knew the first way, which was a couple of miles longer than the alternative, but as the river was likely to be low and easily crossed, I decided to risk it and take the shorter route.

With visibility down to no more than 10 yards I cautiously picked my way down the scree and boulders into Coire an t-Sabhail. Once over the lip of the corrie the going became easier as I kept to the bank of a stream; deep heather then led me down to the Dee in the Lairig Ghru below. After the recent almost drought conditions it was easy to cross the river and keep my feet dry, but in reality they were already soaked from ploughing through the knee deep heather.

Next came a long hard climb, up the Tailors Burn, which was swarming with frogs. I was soon back into the clouds again but I knew from a recent visit that the summit of Ben Macdui lay just a short distance to the left, once I had passed a line of crags and the angle of the boulder field started to ease. The summit of Ben Macdui is one massive boulder field; several large cairns and rock wind-breaks are dotted about, as well as the huge summit cairn itself. After a final drink and a *Mars Bar* I set my compass and ran easily off to the north towards a pair of lochans.

8: On the Cairngorm plateau

From here a good track led across the plateau to the abrupt edge above the wild Coire an Lochain and Coire an t-Sneachda, both of which we had climbed in the previous winter. It was exciting running along the edge with brief glimpses through the mist, down into the corries and crags below. One last climb and the weather station on the summit of Cairn Gorm came into view; I didn't stop as the summit was swarming with tourists despite the rather grim conditions.

Following the line of cairns, I jogged down a paved path to finally come out of the cloud at the Ptarmigan Restaurant by the top chair-lift station. The descent was straightforward, down the main path, where I couldn't help remembering the time I ran the Cairngorm Hill Race and fell heavily on the descent. This time, on tired legs, I ran more carefully down the steep gravel path, past the half-way station, through the car-park to the road. Here I struck directly down the hill to avoid the long loop taken by the road and so I arrived back at the car in a little over 5 hours.

"...and in the darkest hours of urban depression I will sometimes take out that dog-eared map and dream awhile of spacious days and perhaps a dried blade of grass will fall out of it to remind me that I was once a freeman of the hills."

(AH Sidgwick)

The Crianlarich 3,000's

To start my second round of Munros I decided on a long run over the group of hills to the south of Crianlarich; this would give me a 20 mile run taking in 7 Munros and 4 satellite 'tops' with a total ascent of around 11,000ft.

The day started warm and dry but unfortunately the cloud was down to about 2,500ft when I left Crianlarich. A clock-wise round seemed sensible, so the hardest climbs would be out of the way early; this meant tackling Ben More, the big one, first.

Starting from the railway station, the couple of miles along the road went quickly as I headed out to Ben More Farm. A track climbed a couple of hundred feet then turned south up the glen, so here I took to the open hillside for the unrelenting climb of just over 3,000ft, up the uniformly steep grassy slopes. I was soon up among the clouds where visibility was down to just 10 yards, this didn't matter too much as I just had to keep heading up. Further up I came to the remains of an old stone wall and a faint path followed this ever upwards towards the summit.

It was a very long steep climb; my heart and lungs were complaining and my calf muscles were screaming for mercy but thankfully another couple of minutes saw me at the summit cairn. By compass I found the right way down off the summit, which is ringed by crags. After a short while the slope became easier and I was able to run swiftly down to the col, from where a climb of 1,000ft took me up onto Stob Binnein. The slopes to the north and west of this peak are bare and lie at an angle of about 45 degrees; in winter, when they are covered in snow and polished by the wind, they are turned into a dangerous skating rink where accidents can and frequently do happen.

Without stopping I headed south, down onto a grassy ridge which gave great running out towards the 'top' Stob Coire an Lochain. From here I now had to make a detour out to the east to take in another 'top' Meall na Dige. A short steep descent brought me to the col where I recognised the broken stone wall and then the small lochan. To find the summit cairn I had to use my compass carefully to see me through the broken ground to the top.

I now retraced my steps, back to the col and up onto the ridge near Stob Coire an Lochain. A steep and rough descent to the west saw me down to a stream where I was glad to have the chance of a quick drink before continuing down, then cutting right, beneath a line of crags, aiming for the watershed of the Ben More / Inverlochlarig glen. At last I emerged out of the mist to see where I was for the first time for a long while and thankfully I was spot on, directly beneath Stob Garbh. Before crossing the burn I made up a poly-bag of *Staminade* and grabbed a bite to eat; then it was onwards and upwards again. A steep grassy gully climbed through the crags and back into thick mist. It was hard going to the summit of Stob Garbh, another 'top', and careful navigation was needed to keep to the ridge, which led south through boulders to the next Munro, Cruach Ardrain.

Finding the correct way off the summit needed concentration but once I found the south ridge it was good to be running again, along an easy grassy ridge out to Beinn Tulaichean. When I met a walker I was flattered to be asked if I was "doing a Hugh Symonds", who, earlier in the summer had completed a monumental run over all the British Munros, not just Scotland but down through the Lake District and Wales and across to Ireland in one continuous journey.

By now I had been on the go for almost 4 hours and there was still a long way to go as I left the cairn and retraced my steps a short way along the ridge before dropping due west down the open hillside towards a stream. Picking up a faint track I contoured round below the crags of Stob Glas and eventually came out onto a marshy saddle below Beinn a'Chroin. I was beginning to feel the pace by now and was glad to have a short stop by a stream where I mixed another poly-bag of *Staminade* and forced down a piece of flapjack.

The 1,500ft climb to Beinn a'Chroin was next, so I was soon up and climbing once more; the slope was steep and grassy as I aimed for a ridge high above me. The cloud was still right down so I couldn't see the top, I just kept climbing, expecting to see the summit cairn and eventually it loomed up out of the mist. From here the summit ridge continued west out to another 'top' at the far end. The next leg was a bit tricky as I had to find my way through a barrier of crags. I kept faith in my compass even though it felt wrong, and after a while picked up a faint path which led in zigzags down to a col below An Caisteal.

From the col, I had to make a detour out to the next Munro, Beinn Chabhair. A descending traverse took me below a line of crags onto a saddle at 2,000ft. From here there was no path and I had to strike directly up the rough hillside but at last I could see where I was; the clouds had parted and I was in the sunshine for the first time that day. After touching the cairn I was soon rushing back down, back the same way to the saddle below. Now I had just one more big climb to go; 1,200ft up to An Caisteal. Glad that I was able to see at last I spotted a good route, up into a grassy corrie and surprisingly quickly up onto the final summit.

I checked my watch and found I'd been out for almost 7 hours; I knew I had a race on my hands if I wanted to reach Crianlarich inside 8 hours. In bright sunshine I stripped off everything that decency would allow and ran quickly north along a grassy ridge called Twistin Hill. At the lowest point on the ridge I dropped down into the glen. Not a fast descender at the best of times, as I was tired I took it carefully over the tussocky grass until I reached the River Falloch.

I had hoped for a good track here but instead found just a vague path, which often disappeared into a boggy morass. At one point I plunged in up to my knees in a vile smelling bog and had to waste precious minutes washing myself off in the river. Then it was on again, with one eye on the watch, until half a mile from the road I crossed a fence and joined a bulldozed track. At last I was able to run properly again; over the river, under the railway, and so out onto the road. From here it was just 1½ miles back along the road to Crianlarich. It wasn't exactly a sprint but I was able to maintain a reasonable pace back into the village to reach the station in 7 hours 56 minutes.

The Round of Loch Mullardoch

In a moment of weakness I agreed to a long run in the hills, mountain marathon style, with a hill running/orienteering friend, Martin. We decided to run around Loch Mullardoch, which lies to the north of Glen Affric; this would give us 12 Munros and 21 satellite 'tops' in approximately 45 miles of running with around 17,500ft of climbing.

Late one Friday evening we parked at the dam at the east end of the loch and with about an hour of daylight remaining we set off to try and gain a little height before finding a place to camp. This way we hoped to out-wit the dreaded midges, which were already out in force. We found a good spot, high up in the corrie and hoped that we would be safe.

As soon as we woke next morning we realised that this wasn't the case. The whole of the outside of the tent was covered in millions of the little beasties. No sooner had we stepped outside when we were immediately covered in swarms of the wee xxxxxx's!

"Be not afraid of moving slowly, only of standing still."
(Chinese Proverb)

It was impossible to try and cook breakfast and swat at the same time, so we hastily packed the kit and climbed up out of the corrie and over our first summit of the day, Toll Creagach. After following the ridge for a while we dropped down to the south to find water and stopped to cook a late breakfast. Temporarily refreshed we were soon ticking off the peaks, over Tom a'Choinich and sundry other 'tops' until we reached Carn Eighe. Here we had to make the first of many detours off the main ridge to 'bag' Beinn Fhionnlaidh; we dropped our 'sacs just below the summit to be collected on the way back.

Back on the main ridge Mam Sodhail came next, but a top two miles away on an outlying spur added both distance and height before we regained the central ridge line. It was a lovely warm day, there was little water to be found without losing height and our meagre supply of jelly babies was soon gone.

A big descent to the bealach gave an equally big climb up the other side onto An Socach, below which is the remote Alltbeithe Youth Hostel. However, the relative comforts were not for us, we still had some way to go. Martin was setting a good pace and I was starting to feel the strain and was tiring on the climb up the unpronounceable Sgurr nan Ceathreamhnan.

In the unaccustomed energy sapping heat it was hard to find the strength for another detour to take in two 'tops' on the northern spur but after these we knew that a good rest was in sight. With one final climb we were up onto Mullach na Dheiragain and after the satellite 'tops' we could at last drop down into the corrie to the north. This gave us a superb high-camp and we spent an hour or so watching a large herd of deer grazing their way up the hillside towards us. When they finally did scent us or our *Pasta Choice* they slowly retreated to a safe distance.

The following day started well; no midges in sight and the first mile or so was all downhill. It was of course too good to last and after crossing the river, which flows from the west end of the loch; we faced a long climb of almost 3,000ft. A good stalkers path took us easily up part of the way; it then petered out and left us with a soul destroying slog through knee deep heather and tussocks until at last we reached more runnable high ground leading to An Socach.

The second day was far shorter with only four Munros and a handful of tops and these all lay on one main east/west axis, running parallel to the loch. A good run brought us to An Riabhachan followed by a craggier section over-looking high mountain lochans. Sgurr na Lapaich came next; we thought the name seemed familiar and realised that we had crossed a peak of the same name the previous day when running the ridge on the south side of the loch.

We reached Carn nan Gobhar together but with just one more summit remaining I began to run out of steam and Martin steadily pulled away. The rough descent was tiring and we were glad to pick up a footpath which followed the stream down to the lochside; that just left a final long mile back to our start point below the dam.

Long High Routes in Europe

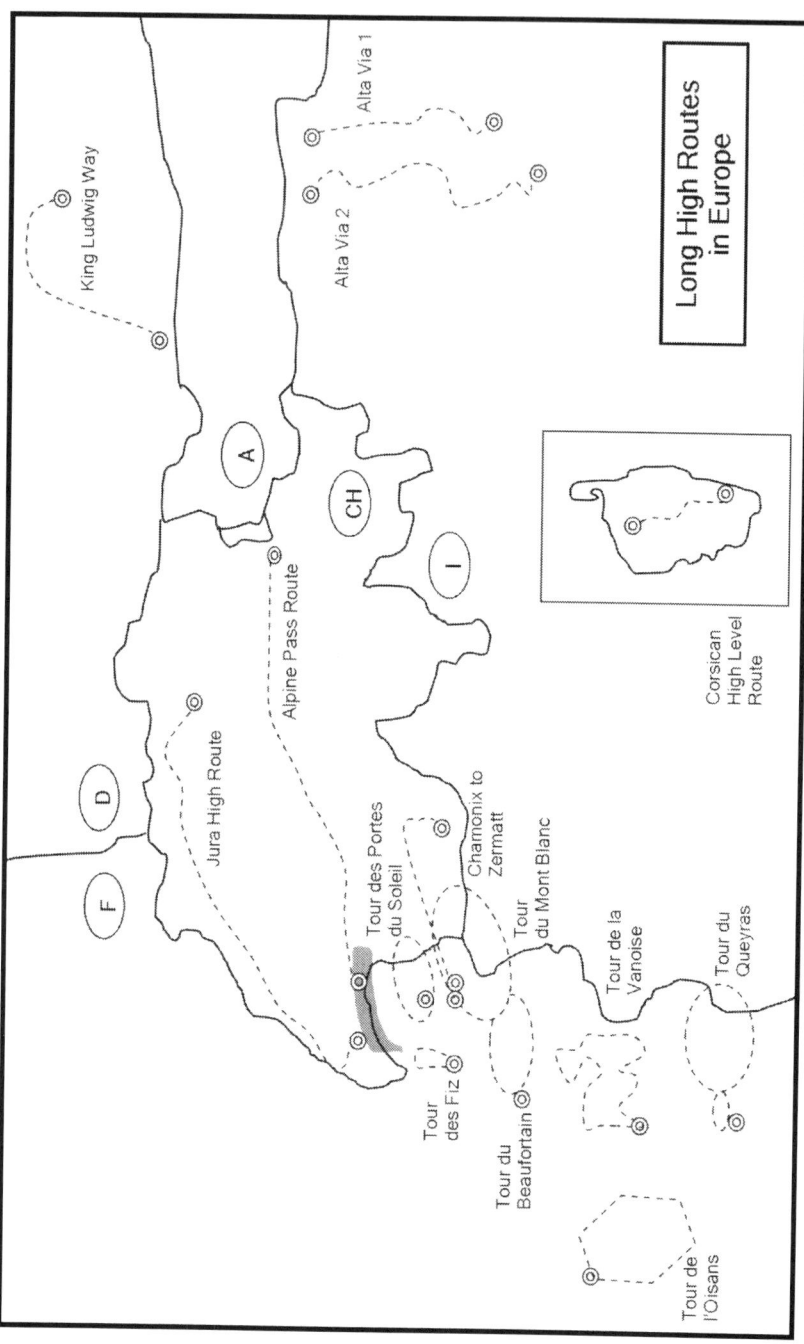

Tour du Mont Blanc

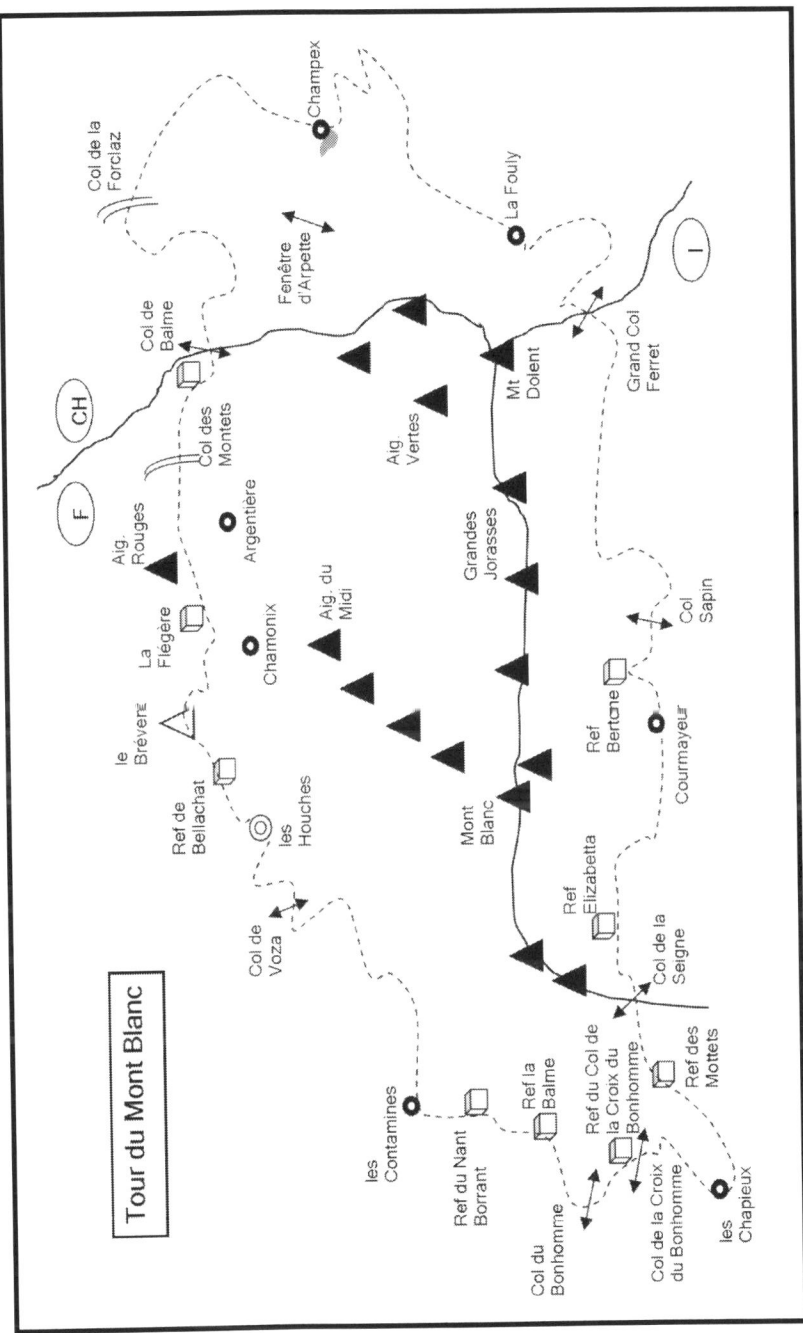

RUNNING HIGH ROUTES IN EUROPE

After working in Banking for about 18 years, first in London, then more recently in Scotland, I realised I couldn't go on doing the same job for another 25 years until I retired. I was 36, single, bored and needed a change. The answer was to resign, sell my house and car and buy a camper-van. After a couple of weeks touring round the remote parts of the far north of Scotland I headed to the Alps for the next eighteen months, during which time I ran, skied or cycled every day.

All the tours in the following section were run solo, as part of that trip, apart from two (a) I walked rather than ran the Corsican High Level Route; I needed to be self sufficient in food and with winter approaching I had to carry a heavier rucksack, which meant running was out; and (b) I ran the Tour de la Vanoise with my wife Cath, a few years after completing the other routes.

Tour du Mont Blanc

This is perhaps the best known of all the 'Tours'; I decided to run it 'anti-clockwise', starting from beside the gondola station at Les Houches, from where a good path climbs steadily up to the Col de Voza. I overtook a couple of English girls on the climb; they were running the tour as training for the *KIMM* which was a couple of months away. I soon reached the bar on Bellevue but it was too soon to stop so after dodging the narrow-gauge train, which climbed past full of camera wielding tourists, I moved on across the alp. From here a big descent took me down through forest to cross the torrent rushing from beneath the Bionnassay Glacier. I then faced an abrupt climb up towards the snout of the glacier; one or two sections of ladder had been fitted on the steeper parts to assist. It was a glorious day when I reached the Col de Tricot; as I was standing on the col, taking in the view and catching my breath, I felt a tickle on my leg, looking down I was surprised to see a sheep licking off the salty sweat.

From the col a very muddy and slippery descent took me to the chalets at de Miage, it's a magnificent grassy alp with a dozen picturesque chalets bedecked with colourful window-boxes. High, snow covered mountains and the glacier towered above. I then faced another short climb up and out of the corrie to cross the ridge by the Chalets du Truc. A good track gave me a gentle run down to the village of Les Contamines.

Although in France, Les Contamines felt very Swiss; it was all window-boxes and flags and had a pretty little church. A short road section led south from the village, up into a wooded gorge; the track here crossed great slabs of rock which gave easy going, up past a natural rock bridge which has been carved by the torrent over thousands of years. There is another pretty little church up here, Notre Dames des Gorges. The climb now started again and it was onward and upward once more to the refuge at Nant Borrant. Still climbing I passed another private refuge and shortly after this I moved onto snow. On rounding a ridge the col came into sight, although it was still some way ahead, and it was near here that I overtook an American lad carrying his mountain bike. The 4 inches of soft snow were no problem in studded fell shoes but he was wearing ordinary trainers and didn't appear to be very happy.

I finally arrived on the Col du Bonhomme; there is a small shelter here for emergencies, it wasn't needed today but it must be blessed by many on a wild day. The refuge was still a mile or so away, at the Col de la Croix du Bonhomme; it is potentially difficult to find but with a clear sky and footprints to follow through the snow, I was soon there. The old hut had been enlarged by building a new one around the original, and it was fairly busy. Almost two hours later a very tired American arrived; still carrying his bike. The view from the hut balcony was of an unbroken rim of mountain peaks, with just a glimpse of the village of Les Chapieux far below.

Next morning it was already hot enough for me to have to wear a sun-hat and sun-glasses when I left the refuge just after 8am. Initially the path crossed the still frozen snow slope, before dropping down through a lovely grassy alp, where sheep and cows grazed peacefully. I soon saw my first marmots of the run, the high pitched squealing from the sentries warning the others of my approach. Once down at the small hamlet of Les Chapieux I found myself in a narrow valley where I was back into deep shade and it was suddenly very cold, so I pushed on hard up the short road section in an effort to stay warm. Shortly after passing a dam, the huge bulk of the Aiguille des Glaciers revealed itself, and the day's next objective, the Col de la Seigne, could be seen just to its right.

After breaking away from the road and back into the sunshine I reached the farm and chalets at Mottets. A large bowl of strong black coffee set me up for the remainder of the climb to the col. The way was straightforward and I was only back onto snow for the last few hundred metres. The col is the frontier with Italy and a gentle jog took me down beneath stunning rock and ice scenery to the Refuge Elizabetta.

Below the refuge is the Lac de Combal; a strange area that looks as if it must be dry more often than it is flooded. Just before a bridge at the east end I headed up a footpath that climbed steeply up to the right, past several ruined chalets; then I was high enough to look across to the Glacier du Miage, which every now and again calves ice-bergs into the small Lac du Miage at its foot.

A good high-level running route, again with marmots for company, now led effortlessly round towards the ski area which covers the Col Chécrouit. An ice-cold ice-tea was a great reward for reaching here, the path then dropped steeply down through forest to come out on a road that looks out over the entrance to the Mont Blanc tunnel, with Chamonix just a 15 minute drive away.

9: *Entering Italy on the Tour du Mont Blanc*

I ran through Courmayeur, stopping briefly outside the Guides Bureau to down a litre of milk. The day was again to end with a big climb, so I left town, ran through Villair and climbed on a steep path up to Le Pré and the Refuge Bertone. I spent a lazy couple of hours enjoying the sun and when another Brit arrived a little later, although I didn't know him, we found we had a number of mutual friends and acquaintances. There were just four guests staying at the refuge and we enjoyed a superb meal, all home grown including the salad and the goose.

Day 3 dawned cloudy and unsettled and I was away just after 8am. A good climb led up onto a grassy ridge, which was very reminiscent of Scotland, past several small tarns and knolls below Tête Bernarda; then, turning south past Tête de la Tronche I dropped down to the broad Col Sapin. It only took minutes to descend from the col to the ruins at the head of the valley and rather than follow the guide-book I kept to the route shown on the map, which meant another short sharp climb to cut up and over the col opposite. I watched a couple of birds of prey here, before starting on the long descent of the wild and lonely valley beyond. Further down I picked up a good path which took me down to La Vachey.

I had to follow the road for a short distance up the Italian Val Ferret, until I reached the chalets at L'Arnuva, where I took the opportunity of a quick bowl of coffee to warm me up. This was the road-end and from here the path was quite busy as it climbed to Pré de Bar, just below the Grand Col de Ferret. Unfortunately the weather remained cloudy and grey and a little rain was starting to fall.

On reaching the col, with my shoes wet from the sodden snow, I crossed into Switzerland and dropped down into a grassy corrie where a good path gave easy running, initially contouring then falling away more steeply down to the valley floor. I was soon through the small village of Ferret and once across the river a pleasant woodland path followed the stream down valley to La Fouly, another small village that gave me the chance to re-stock with hill food.

On leaving the village, a long, mainly downhill stretch followed, through mature pine forests. In places the path had fallen away and had been re-built; either carved into the cliff or built out on logs overhanging the edge, handrails had been provided for the weak at heart. This easy section continued for some miles until the path took a sharp right turn and I was suddenly running along a knife-edged ridge. This was the lateral moraine from the Saleina Glacier which has now retreated several kilometres.

The path led me down to the delightful village of Praz de Fort and then to Issert. Here a finger-post tells you that it is just 1½ hours to Champex, but that is all uphill, perhaps a bit too steeply for the end of a long hard day. After an hour I emerged by the lake-side at Champex, which looked rather dreary in the low cloud and drizzle. A dortoir at an SAC inn proved a good place to stop for the night; I could have gone on for another half an hour up the hill but there was a choice of routes for the following day and I wanted to see what the weather was going to do before I committed myself.

Unfortunately it was as I feared on Day 4; it had rained all night and it was still raining in the morning. I knew it would have snowed higher up, making the higher option too dangerous, so the lower route it had to be. An easy downhill stretch started this long last day, along lovely forest trails over a carpet of pine-needles. The climbing then started and I was going well, perhaps because of the effect of the four big bowls of strong black coffee I'd had for breakfast. But the caffeine buzz wasn't to last and it was only when I heard the cheerful sound of cow-bells that I knew I must be approaching the upper limit of the forest. Sure enough a few minutes later I came out onto open pastures from where I contoured round the hillside to a small chalet and this in turn led to a big descent to the road col at Col de Forclaz.

The col gave me an excuse to stop for a *Coke* and an ice-cream and after a few minutes rest I picked up the path which cut down across the road zigzags to Le Peuty. Again I took the map route rather than the guide-book route and thus faced another 3,000ft climb, steeply up through mature pine forest then across open hillside. The clouds were clamped right down so I could see none of the famed views, there was however a brief clearing as I approached the chalets at Les Herbages which allowed a quick glimpse of the 'hotel' on the col above. Knowing that I was nearly there I pressed on and celebrated crossing back into France with a coffee at the Col de Balme Hotel. 'Hotel' is perhaps too fine a word for it but it was nevertheless a welcome stop and I was glad of the chance to warm up. Down the far side from the col I came out into the ski-tows of Le Tour, and a long downhill stretch on good runnable tracks soon found me by the roadside at the Col des Montets.

Unfortunately this coincided with quite a downpour so I had to don full water-proofs before crossing the road and setting off on the climb up towards the Aiguilles Rouges. Thankfully the storm was short-lived and I climbed quickly to the obvious rock-band several hundred feet high. The path eventually made its way by a cunning route up the cliff with the assistance of several iron ladders, metal and log-steps and handrails. This superb high-level path then gave great running along to the ski-lift at La Flégère, from where the path continued on, on more of the same sort of ground. It felt strange cruising along up here in almost zero visibility, until after a few more miles the upper station of Plan Praz suddenly loomed up out of the mist.

I was now growing concerned about the time; I knew the last few miles would take me down through dense forest, which would make night fall even quicker, however, I pressed on. I climbed up to the Col du Brévent and then still further over a rocky ridge to reach the summit of the Brévent, the top of which is now desecrated with a ski-station. It was gone 6pm so I hurriedly set off on the knee-jarring descent of around 5,000ft. I could climb all day if I had to but it was these long descents that really hurt. My feet felt battered, bruised and blistered; the ETA's didn't give enough protection on such ground.

After a very quick stop at the lonely chalet Bellachat for a final couple of ice-teas, I set out again into the cold, wet, mist. It was down, down, down, past a tricky section by a waterfall, which was protected by cables, until at last I could hear the muffled sound of traffic in the valley far below. Still dropping steeply through the forest the smell of wood-smoke came to me, and in a few more minutes I was out at the roadside for a final mile back to the van at Les Houches.

According to the guide-book the route is only about 120 miles but in reality, with all the zigzags, I'm sure the run was a bit further than that. There is around 33,500ft of ascent but more critically, the same amount of descent.

Guidebook: Tour of Mont Blanc by Andrew Harper
             (Cicerone Press)

Map: Sheet 8   Massifs du Mont Blanc / Beaufortain
             (1:50,000 Didier et Richard)

Chamonix to Zermatt

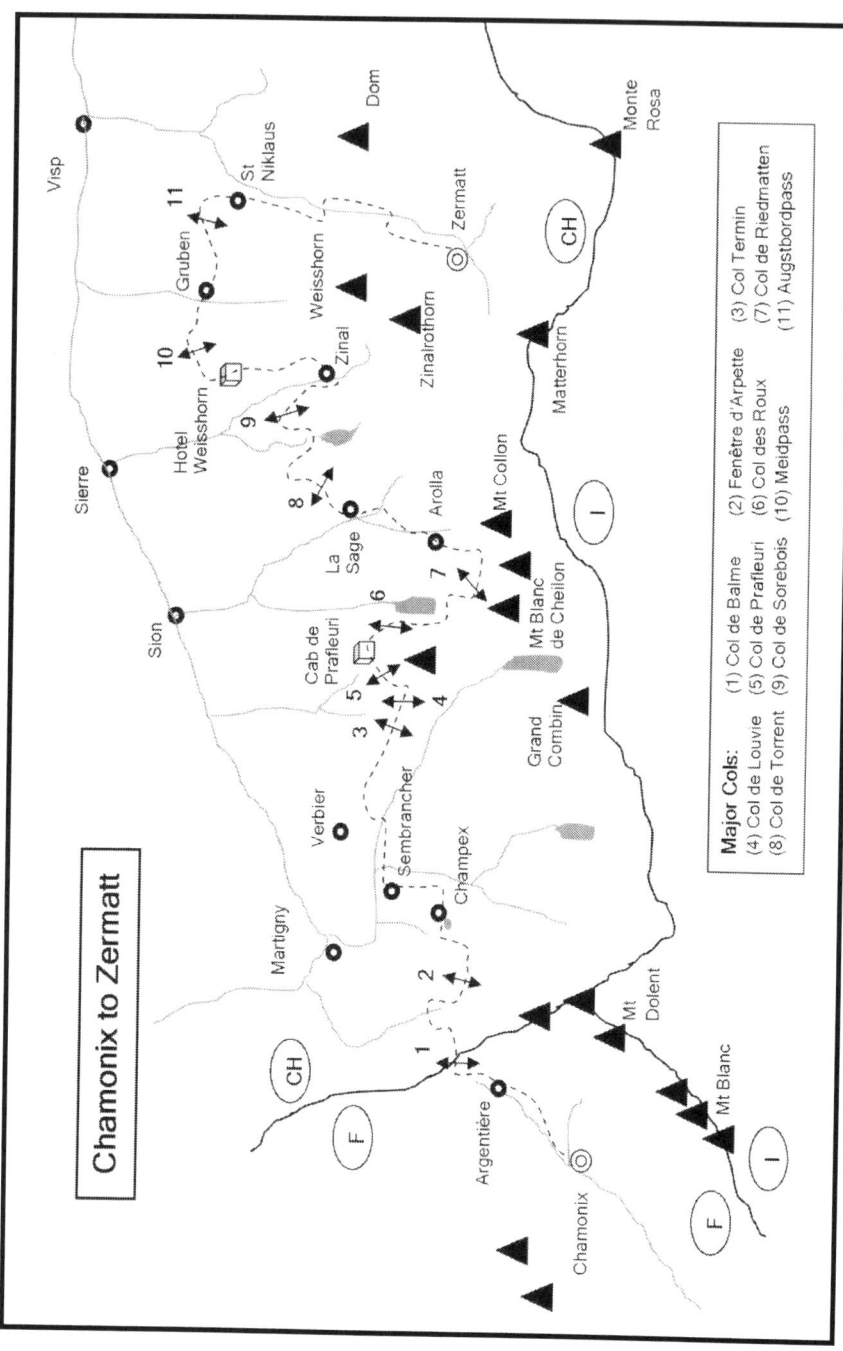

Chamonix to Zermatt

A little apprehensive that my severe blisters from the Tour du Mont Blanc (TMB) hadn't had time to heal sufficiently after just five days rest, I left Chamonix on a glorious morning, bound for Zermatt.

The first part of this route is similar to the end of the TMB in that I first had to cross the Col de Balme and drop down to Champex. An easy trail led from Chamonix up the valley to Le Lavancher and up to Argentière; from here the track climbed to the small ski-centre at Le Tour. This gave me superb views across to the Aiguilles Rouges on the north side of the valley and I could pick out my route of a few days before. From Le Tour a track climbed steeply up alongside the télécabine but thankfully I was soon able to join a grassy footpath which took me up to the old hotel on the Col de Balme. As the weather was fine I was glad to take the opportunity of following the high-level route to Champex, which for safety I had missed out when on the TMB. From the col a good path led off north-east to contour round beneath the Pointe de Midi. It was a wonderful situation giving fine views north and down to Trient in the valley below; the footpath then turned a corner and suddenly the two glaciers, des Grandes and du Trient, came into view. This was high-level running at its best.

A trough outside the chalet at Les Grands gave me the chance to refill by water-bottle, I then enjoyed a lovely descent through superb forest, which was a wonderful mixture of colours. The track continued down to cross the torrent issuing from the Trient Glacier, then up to a little 'buvette' where I stopped for a quick *Coke*. The second big col of the day now loomed ahead of me; it was hot work as the sun beat down from a cloudless sky. As I climbed higher I could look down onto the bare ice of the glacier, the path then turned away and it became calf-achingly steep, despite the zigzags. Finally I reached the boulder field which told me that the top wasn't too far away.

I had a couple of minutes rest on the col, the Fenêtre d'Arpette, and as I left so too did another party. Dropping down from the col to the east is very steep and the rock, very loose. When the party following knocked a rock down, just missing me, I excused it as an accident. When the second rock came bouncing towards me I thought they were being careless. When the third rock came crashing down I was starting to feel upset and when the fourth was a very near miss I was ready to catch the rock and throw it back up at them! Thankfully the worst of it only lasts a few hundred metres and I was soon away from them, although the rocky terrain still needed care for some way yet.

Eventually the track led down to kinder ground and it gave good running down the valley to the Refuge d'Arpette, where a welcome ice-tea eased the dust from my throat. An ideal footpath then led away through the forest, alongside a little brook, to come out just above Champex. The difference between my visit on the TMB and this one couldn't have been more obvious; now there was a perfect blue sky, people were out and about, the lake looked clean and inviting and the cafes and bars looked very tempting.

However, it was too early to stop for the night so I pressed on for Sembrancher. It was difficult to find one route and stick to it; there were so many paths to choose from among the terraces and fields. On reaching Sembrancher I looked for somewhere suitable to stay; and at first it didn't look very promising, until eventually someone told me of the Station Hotel. This was ideal as they had just refurbished and opened a small dortoir in the attic; it was cheap, clean and I had it all to myself.

Day 2 dawned fine again although the sun didn't reach the floor of the valley until I had already been going for an hour. The path from Sembrancher led up into the forest for a short way, before dropping down to the rifle-range at Le Châble. After passing through the village the hard work started; way-marks led steeply up the narrow streets to Cotterg, which is the real, working Switzerland, not the parts tourists usually see. I climbed up past an old water-mill, through orchards of apples and plums, before reaching a small chapel at Les Verneys; a peaceful spot overlooking the valley.

From here the footpath again climbed steeply, through beautiful forest, over a carpet of pine needles. Another remote hamlet, Clambin, high above the forest, gave me the opportunity to refill my water-bottle as the day was now very hot. It was good to briefly re-enter the cool of the forest as I climbed up to the ski-tows near Les Ruinnettes. From here the footpath contoured easily until it picked up the line of a 'bisse' which led almost to the door-step of the Cabane du Mont Fort. The hut sits on a spur at the head of a large corrie; unfortunately the corrie is now filled with a massive cable-car station.

After a bowl of soup at the hut I was soon off again to find the first of the afternoon's three cols. A narrow footpath could be seen contouring round the hillside across steep scree; this path is called the 'Sentier des Chamois' and I scanned the hillside for any signs of the elusive beasts. The path was quite exposed at times, but not difficult, one or two sections were protected by lengths of cable. As I rounded a corner I came across a group of five chamois, they were startled but didn't run too far. Shortly after this I reached a steep, loose section of path, but again this was well protected. A continuing traverse then led round to the broad Col Termin.

From here I had great views back to the Mont Blanc range and the Grand Combin; below the col to the east I could see the green waters of the Lac de Louvie far below. Leaving the col I contoured northwards, out along another high-level path into a wild and rocky valley which ended in a basin of boulders and scree. The sound of running water made me sacrifice a few metres of height as I sought out the stream and mixed a poly-bag of *Gatorade*. A final rough scramble over the boulder-field took me to the Col de Louvie; from here it opened out onto a whole new valley dominated by the glacier known as the Grand Desert, which tumbles down off Rosablanche.

It was a rough and rocky descent to the glacier itself, which was awash with melt-water streams; it took ten minutes to cross the glacier and I was soon back onto the moraines, which led me to several small tarns. The path then led down to pass below the small glacier that flows from Grand Mont Calme, just where it calves into two small green tarns. A short scramble took me up to the third col, the Col de Prafleuri, where again wide new vistas opened up before me. I could see the Pigne d'Arolla and Mont Blanc de Cheilon, above the Dix Glacier. I knew this area well having climbed those peaks a few years earlier. It was another steep and rocky descent from the col, which led down into a wilderness of moraines, transformed over the years by quarrying; the stone from here was used to build both the first and second Dix dams.

At last, after another long hard day I reached the Cabane de Prafleuri. The guide-book warned that there was usually no resident guardian and you needed to carry your own food. Thankfully the guide-book was out-of-date and whilst you could self-cater, the guardian soon rustled up a fantastic four course meal and she couldn't have been more helpful. It was a great place to spend the night and after an equally good breakfast I was away early for the short climb to the Col des

Roux, just above the hut. On arriving on the col I was met with the fine sight of two ibex standing on the skyline above.

A long descent now followed; down across pastures and past a couple of lonely chalets and cow byres to pick up a fine track alongside Lac des Dix. It was fast going here, past a family of marmots and round to the south end of the lake. A high-wire suspension bridge crossed the inlet in the south-east corner and a path then climbed steeply above the moraine of the Cheilon Glacier. A rising traverse took me past a herd of around twenty chamois that were grazing in the screes.

The col was now above me, and the track swung left to climb steeply to the Col Riedmatten, at around 10,000ft. From here a short rocky descent led to a more open grassy bowl with a few scattered ski-tows, a good path then led easily down through the pines into Arolla.

I followed the way-marks past an army base and out on an undulating footpath which took me through delightful forest to a fine lake, named somewhat unimaginatively 'Lac Bleu'.

10: Aig. de la Tsa (top centre) above Arolla

Since leaving Arolla my left foot and shin had been feeling very sore so I took the opportunity to give it an ice-cold bathe in the lake in an effort to take away the swelling. It must have happened a few minutes above Arolla when I turned my ankle on a tree root in the forest; at the time I'd thought nothing of it but now it was very sore and was rather worrying. The steep descent through forest down to the road at La Gioulle was particularly trying but I discovered that it only hurt on the downhills; it was fine going up or on the flat. Unfortunately the next three miles were downhill all the way to Les Haudères.

The path wound pleasantly down through the woods to reach the pretty village of Les Haudères, it was tempting to stop here but I decided to push on a little further so that part of the next climb was out of the way. A narrow footpath climbed up the hillside to the farming village of La Sage. The village was over-run with the Swiss Army, they had filled the dortoir but luckily I found a room at the Hotel du La Sage, although the army were also staying here; they had even laid plastic sheeting to cover the carpets and installed a command telephone in the bar. After another fine meal and a half hour spent doctoring my feet and ankle I turned in looking forward to sleeping in a real bed for the first time for several weeks.

Day 4 dawned cloudless and I was away before 8am. A short section on the road led to Villa and from here a footpath climbed 3,000ft across beautiful grassy alps to the Col de Torrent. This was reached easily in 1hr 50 mins against a guide-book time of four hours. After a short rest I dropped gently down the far side of the col, round a high mountain lake and down towards Lac de Moiry; which was an unbelievable colour of turquoise. The high dam is a popular spot for tourists so I was pleased to be able to stop for a coffee before climbing up towards the day's second col, the Col de Sorebois. First though I had to negotiate an electric fence, much to the merriment of a toothless old dear who finally pointed me in the right direction. The path was faint initially but as I climbed higher the way became more obvious, finally zigzagging up to the grassy col.

Wide new horizons again presented themselves, with views across to the Weisshorn, Schalihorn and my first alpine 4,000m peak, the Zinalrothorn. Unfortunately, climbing up to the col from the east was a messy network of ski-tows and the way down was on a broad track to the mid-station of Sorebois. The descent then steepened as it dropped down to the village of Zinal in the wooded valley below. The day's third big climb now started; the footpath climbing steeply up through the cool shade of the forest. Near the tree-line the path levelled off to contour along the hillside for mile after mile. On this short stretch alone there must have been a dozen different varieties of butterfly, several types of cricket and I saw a few small lizards too. Looking back there were amazing views of the Weisshorn and the Matterhorn plus countless other high snow peaks. Unfortunately as the afternoon wore on the sky started to cloud over, though it stayed warm. I reached the Hotel Weisshorn in the late afternoon; this is a fine old Victorian hotel that stands alone on the end of the ridge, far above the valley.

The next day dawned dull and the weather prospects didn't look promising as I looked down from my bedroom window onto the cloud filled valley below, the high peaks were also swallowed up by the clouds. On leaving the hotel I had to drop a little to the east before climbing steadily up through grassy pastures to the narrow col at Meidpass. The descent to the east was far rockier as the path zigzagged down past the Meidsee to continue on to some chalets just above the timberline. Unfortunately the morning remained unsettled with clouds still drifting around the tops but it was quite warm and the cool of the forest was welcome on the descent to the village of Gruben.

After a quick snack I now faced a big climb of about 3,500ft to the final col of the route. Initially the way up from Gruben was steep but on a good footpath, which wound up through the forest above the hotel. I saw several squirrels on this stretch; what I noticed most about them was how noisy they were, I couldn't ever remember actually hearing squirrels back home. Shortly after leaving the forest the angle of the slope eased a little to give good going over grassy alps. Higher still and I came out into a wild, rock strewn corrie, although the path remained good, only going onto rocks once I reached the small tarn that lay just below the pass. This final pass, the Augstbordpass, gave a good excuse for a short rest while I tried to sort out the route below.

The eastern side of the col was far more barren and severe with almost nothing to be seen except for grey rock. There were however a few small patches of old snow, one of which was partly covered in red algae which made the snow look rose-coloured. Several hundred feet were descended into this rocky wasteland before the footpath bore off to the right to climb round the side of the corrie, still on huge blocks of rock. The deep trench of the Mattertal could now be seen ahead and a little later I reached a cairn on the shoulder; as you turned the corner at this cairn you suddenly had before you a fine array of snow peaks and glaciers. Fortunately, the weather was improving and I could see through the haze to the long glaciers falling down off the Ulrichshorn opposite.

There was no rush so I spent some time at this idyllic spot just enjoying the peace and quiet. Eventually though I felt I should move on and I rejoined the path which now traversed the hillside before dropping down in tight zigzags to the small hamlet of Jungen, a delightful old farming community. Only the ski-gondola from St.Niklaus reminded you that this was the 20th century. I resisted the temptation to take the easy way down and continued on the descent, first through pleasant forest then across more open hillside. In all the descent from the Augstbordpass is close on 6,000ft so my knees and feet were somewhat weary as I came down past several way-side shrines into St.Niklaus.

The guide-book suggested somewhere to stay; they were full but the landlord kindly made a couple of quick phone calls then led me through the streets to a house where an old lady was waiting to greet me and take me in.

The final day was only to be a short one as I just had to go up the valley to Zermatt. From St.Niklaus the route first takes the old road alongside the river to the small village of Mattsand, you then leave the road and on a good footpath continue above the river to Breitmatten; here I had to walk a short section on the new road as landslides had made the other side of the river impassable. On reaching Randa you can take to the riverside again as a good track leads up the valley to Täsch, which is not a pretty place, it seems to mainly be a large car-park as this is as far as they allow cars, keeping Zermatt a traffic-free town. A steady climb up alongside the railway, sometimes actually on the roof of the railway tunnel, passing a couple of firing ranges, you then turn one last corner and there it is; the mighty Matterhorn in all its glory. The High Level Route officially ends at Zermatt railway station, which is where this path comes out, but as it was still early, after finding a place to stay I decided to end the run at the Riffelberg, a good vantage point for the Matterhorn. Without a rucksack the 3,000ft climb felt good, climbing steadily up through beautiful forest before coming out at the pastures of the Riffelalp. Hordes of tourists poured off the train as I jogged to the hotel for a well deserved beer and a cream cake.

The route is a similar length to the Tour du Mont Blanc at about 120 miles but it has a little more climbing at 36,500ft. I had hoped to run it in four days but it actually took a little over five, this was for a number of reasons; my feet were still sore from the TMB, my ankle hurt the afternoon below Arolla, I was carrying a heavier rucksack with more safety and 'bivvy' gear, and the terrain made running harder. I thought though that it was perhaps a better route than the TMB as it took me into the heart of Switzerland, away from the tourists and into the working villages, that is until the finish in vibrant Zermatt. I expected Zermatt to be expensive and it certainly could be if you were prepared to pay, it could also be very reasonable and the Tourist Office were happy to provide me with a list of 'budget' places to eat and stay.

Guidebook: Chamonix to Zermatt: The Walkers Haut Route by Kev Reynolds   (Cicerone Press)

Maps: Sheet 5003 Champex-Lac / Trient
Sheet 5006 Zermatt / Saas Fee
(1:50,000   Landeskarte der Schweiz)

Tour des Fiz

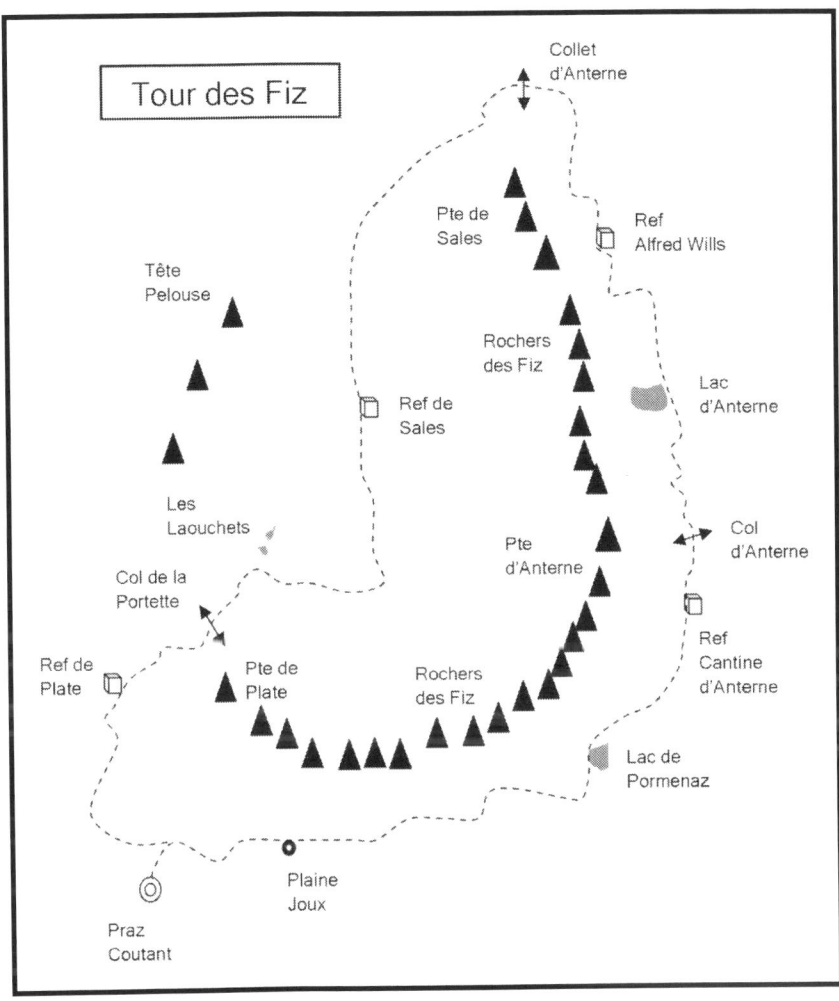

Tour des Fiz

On the drive up towards the Chamonix valley I had been impressed by a small range of seemingly vertical crags; at the time they carried a light covering of snow, which emphasised the clearly defined rock strata. Later, when in the Chamonix Guides Bureau I found a description of a two and a half day tour of these peaks, which are the Rochers des Fiz. It took me an hour to translate the route into English and after looking at the map I decided it would make a good days run, carrying just a bum-bag with some wet/cold weather gear.

It was a long drive up countless hairpin bends to the start at Praz Coutant; this is a strange place as virtually all the properties are either nursing homes or sanatoriums. Thankfully the *Meteo* were right again and it was a glorious morning as I jogged slowly up the steep track, through mixed woodland. After leaving the dense forest behind the way became more open and I could see the almost sheer cliffs towering above me. What wasn't obvious at this stage was where the weakness lay so that I could climb them.

The path zigzagged steeply up into a corrie then made its way up a narrow gully before traversing left on an airy pathway. The path then cut back right, close to a small cable-way which is used to re-supply the hut and chalets above. From here I arrived onto a plateau and a short way further, hidden in a sheltered hollow, I found the CAF hut, the Refuge de Plate, and half a dozen other small chalets. The hut and the chalets were already closed up for the winter, although the hut did have a long ladder leading up to its 'winter-room', which was in the attic and thus could be reached even when the hut was snowed in. The terrain up here was quite unusual, there were large slabs of rock which gave an excellent running surface; it would probably be paradise for a geologist as it looked as though the slabs were once the sea-bed.

From the hut I followed a faint path that led away to the right, first across rough ground then across grassy slopes which took me up to a narrow col, the Col de la Portette. The situation here was very impressive, there was absolute silence, no sound whatsoever until a couple of alpine choughs flew close above me so that I could hear their every wing-beat. Below me the new corrie seemed even more desolate than the last. I ran quickly down the far side, along short cropped grass towards two small lakes, from here I cut across a rock shelf, where I had marmots for company, then on down to a broad meadow at Grand Pre.

The way led easily down to the small summer settlement of Chalets de Sales; it was like a ghost town as everywhere was locked and shuttered. As I only had a very small water-bottle with me I took the opportunity to have a long drink at the spring before continuing down into a narrow gorge. Here I hit an unforeseen problem......Cows! The footpath was narrow; below was an almost sheer drop to the river, whilst above the path it was a steep mix of loose scree and gravel. There were about 30 cows ahead of me on the path, all of whom possessed very sharp looking horns. Whenever I tried to pass the tail-end one it would break into a semi-gallop, barging into the others in front, which caused them to run on as well. Only a couple of days previously I had read in the paper of a woman who had been trampled to death by a herd of cows so I was reluctant to do anything too rash. It took me several anxious minutes to eventually pass them all without casualties on either side.

After passing a couple of small waterfalls the gorge opened out and I knew I needed to turn off somewhere around here. In the French guide it told me to turn right on reaching 'une platitude'. The French/English dictionary simply told me that the translation of 'platitude' was 'platitude' which wasn't much help. Looking up 'platitude' in my English dictionary it told me that it meant 'a commonplace remark'. This still wasn't much to go on so I hoped it wasn't a vital piece of information and pressed on. A plank footbridge led across the stream where I found some faded paint marks which suggested that I was on 'a' route if not necessarily 'the' route.

With the roar of a large waterfall deep in the forest to my left, I kept right again and climbed, quite steeply at times, up around the north ridge of the Pointe de Sales onto the Collet d'Anterne. From here good running over grassy meadows, beneath towering cliffs, led to a stream crossing; after crossing a marshy area a short climb then led up through some rocks, behind which lay the Refuge Alfred Wills. The hut was closed but I stopped for a quick bite to eat before continuing with another short steep climb up the hillside beyond. On reaching the ridge, ahead of me in the grassy hollow I found the Lac d'Anterne; it's outlet stream runs underground and only emerges from beneath the rocks some 600ft lower and almost a mile away. Continuing south along the lakeside I was overshadowed by the huge wall of rock which is the Rochers des

Fiz; another easy climb then took me to the final col of the day, the Col d'Anterne. Here I surprised two sunbathing beauties, so I tried to look cool as I jogged up the final few metres to the pass.

From the col a fairly fast and steep descent leads down to the Refuge d'Anterne. From the hut a glorious path took me over the grassy alp to Lac de Pormenaz, where frogs hopped noisily into the lake as I approached. The path then dropped steeply down towards the river; there was one short tricky section but this was protected by cables. Once down and across the river a track led through the forest to the ski-station of Plaine Joux.

11: Ref. Alfred Wills, beneath the Rochers des Fiz

On this last stretch the views were superb as I could look across to Mont Blanc and the first stage of the TMB; the climb to the Col de Voza and the ridge to Bellevue. After a short jog down the road I was able to re-enter the forest on a footpath that dropped down to Praz Coutant, eventually picking up the same path that I had used to leave the village that morning.

The route is only a short one but it does nevertheless give a very worthwhile mountain run through magnificent scenery. It is about 20 miles with around 7,500ft of climbing.

Guidebook: photocopy available from the Guides Bureau in Chamonix (in French)

Map: Sheet 8 Massifs du Mont Blanc / Beaufortain (1:50,000 Didier et Richard)

Corsican High Level Route (GR20)

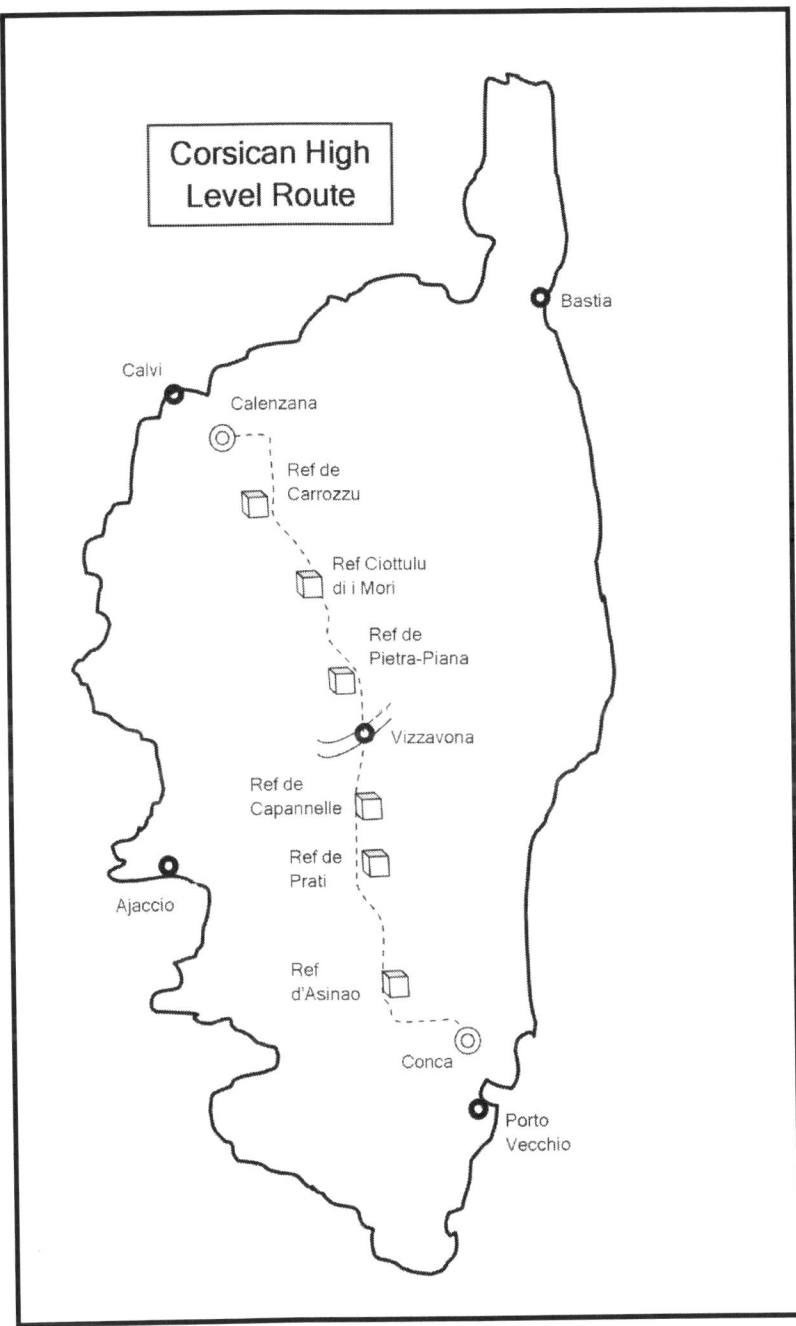

Corsican High Level Route (GR20)

I caught the evening ferry from Nice to Bastia, on the north-east coast of Corsica, where I arrived early the next morning. From here I took the train round to Calvi on the north-west coast. I hadn't been able to buy any maps before I came over so I had to wait in Calvi for the shops to open after lunch; while I waited I had a coffee and read in that morning's paper that a German had been missing on the GR20 for the past four days, two ground teams and a helicopter had been searching for a couple of days but there was no sign of him.

The route officially starts at Calenzana, and with no local buses I had an eight mile road walk up to the village. After an hour of walking the thunder started rumbling, the heavens opened and within minutes the road was under almost an inch of muddy water; changing into full waterproofs I plodded on. Finding a Gîte d'Etape, run by the National Park, on the outskirts of the village, I settled in and dried off. The rain continued all afternoon but by 9pm the stars were out, which looked promising for the morning.

Day 1 on the route and I was up early and away by 7:30. The 1:100,000 map, which was the best I could find for the northern half of the island, gave little detail and the first part of the route had changed from that shown in the guidebook. I was more than a little confused so I tried not to lose the way-marks. Initially the way led up from the church, through the village and across an area of head-high bracken and undergrowth, which, being wet from the previous days' downpour soon soaked me. The path climbed steadily up and over a ridge from where there were great views out to Calvi and the coast. After traversing round a valley, which was covered in vines, then climbing onto rockier terrain I reached a col; a short way down the far side I entered pleasant forest and contoured round the head of the corrie. From here more difficult, rockier ground took me up towards the ridge and across a further low col. The open country here made for faster going and I could see the Refuge di l'Ortu di u Piobbu across on the other side of the corrie. A small herd of four ibex grazed nearby; the male of the group was a magnificent specimen, very powerful looking with a huge head of horns.

The call of a goat-herd echoed across the corrie and just before I reached the hut a herd of perhaps 200 tiny goats came crashing down the rocky gully to quickly disappear into the undergrowth below. After passing the refuge the path led round through forest into another rough and rocky corrie, traversing below some rock slabs I then climbed through boulders on an obscure route to reach the ridge at a rocky crest. The view from here into the corrie beyond was unexpected; there were huge rock spires and towers that the map only hinted at.

The ridge was followed for a while, climbing steadily up to the east; the red and white way-marks then took off down beneath the ridge on the far side. Clouds were drifting in and covering some of the tops but thankfully I could see vaguely where I was meant to go. The way led up onto the crest of the ridge again, before heading down on ground similar to Jake's Rake on Pavey Ark in the Lake District.

A further short climb, up into the clouds, took me onto the Col de l'Inominata at around 2,000m. From here a long steep descent to the south dropped down to a stream. The roof of the Refuge de Carrozzu came into view but it was another half hours work to continue down the rocky track, across a recent stone-fall, and through the forest. I ran down the last ½ mile, reaching the refuge about 30 seconds before the skies opened and the rain fell in torrents.

I'd only been walking for 7½ hours; 3pm was early to stop but with just three hours of daylight remaining I knew it would be hard going to reach the next hut before dark. The rain settled it and I moved in, sharing the hut with three Frenchmen and four Germans. Later that evening, when I went out to check on the weather, I disturbed a large fox rummaging through the rubbish.

It was another early start on Day 2, which began with a short descent through forest; the path then climbed up across rock slabs and along a stream before crossing the river by a suspension bridge. Then the fun started as the path led up alongside the river, crossing more rock slabs, which were wet and slippery from the previous days' rain. After passing the worst of the difficulties way-marks led up into the corrie, climbing all the while, sometimes up rock slabs, sometimes up loose gullies, until I reached a flatter area covered in dwarf pines, and eventually a small blue lake, Lac Muvrella. From here it wasn't far up to the col; I then had to descend a short way to pass round under the summit of Muvrella before regaining the ridge where it ran off to the south.

Next came a steep descent of some 2,000ft over rocky ground, which brought me out at the ski station of Haut Asco. The skiing didn't look too exciting; there wasn't much in the way of either pistes or tows. From here it was a long, reasonably straightforward climb, initially through sparse forest then onto more open ground up to the Col Perdu. The map again gave no indication of the view from the col. It was certainly very impressive; the col is a narrow gap on an airy ridge from where a very steep descent of 700ft takes you down into the Cirque de la Solitude, a remote corrie, seemingly hemmed in on all sides by towering cliffs with no obvious exit. This section is generally regarded as the crux of the whole route and a good head for heights is essential.

There were cables to assist but I found it easier to down-climb the whole way. Thankfully the route was over sound rock and there were usually holds when you needed them; one section followed a darker vein of rock, similar to the basalt dykes on Sgurr nan Gillean on Skye.

On reaching the foot of the corrie a similarly steep climb up the far side is again protected by cables and a short section of ladder. After several hundred feet the route bears left and you eventually come out at the col of Bocca Minuta, seemingly almost within spitting distance of the Col Perdu, which was left almost an hour before. Although the weather was poor and overcast the clouds stayed just high enough to enable me to see where I was going in the Cirque de la Solitude, which was just as well as the route finding here was crucial. From the exit col a faint path dropped steeply down, through rock slabs and boulders, into the valley below. Half-way down I came to the Refuge Tighjiettu; now on a better path the way led down into ancient pine forest near a small mountain farm.

It was easy for a while from here, contouring through the forest before heading up again on a climb of some 1,800ft, up into a dismal gloom. It was very disconcerting not knowing how far it was to the col above but eventually, after a section of steep scrambling, the path started to bear left around the head of the valley and I reached the Col de Foggiale. By now visibility was down to only about 10 yards and the drizzle had turned to rain, so I was pleased that the Refuge Ciottulu di i Mori was only another 15 minutes away. A short traversing climb led through a maze of low scrub, which hid the way-marks, but the hut loomed up out of the mist at about 3:30pm. The next hut was said to be a further six hours away so this meant another early finish but I didn't mind as I was cold, damp and hungry.

There were a couple of French lads in the hut and from them I learned two interesting things. They were a day behind their schedule because two days earlier they had found the body of a Frenchman; they reported it to the Police and had to show the helicopter crew where to recover the body. Apparently the man had gone astray, followed a river down it's right-hand side rather than the way-marked left bank, and had fallen to his death. With this death, and the German who was still missing, the GR20 was living up to its reputation of being the hardest of the GR's. The second important thing I learned was that the small shop at Vizzavona had closed for the season, as had all the hotels, so there was no accommodation or food to be had there. This was bad news as I had intended re-stocking there; fortunately they told me of another hotel a short way off route that carried a small stock of groceries and I was promised that this was open all year.

After a somewhat disturbed sleep, it sounded as though two mice were running around the hut wearing clogs, I was up early and away before 7am. It was a glorious morning, sunshine and a bright blue sky, which soon burned off the heavy over-night frost.

12: A crisp start to the morning on Corsica

The path led easily around the hillside before dropping steadily down to the river below. The river was crossed on boulders, re-crossed, and the way then entered mixed forest. Passing some old stone buildings the route continued on a good path which led gently down to the road. From here I had to make a short detour a mile or so up the road to the Hotel Castellu di Vergio, where thankfully I was able to re-stock on most of what I needed. As it was out of season the hotel had run down its stock so much of what I bought was tinned and therefore heavy, but they did have some tasty sausage and some good bread, which saw me through to the end.

From the hotel I returned a short way down the road before dropping down into the forest to regain the route of the GR. The next few miles were some of the easiest as a good footpath contoured through mixed forest. I had company from time to time; first cows, then goats and later some semi-wild pigs. You could always tell when there were pigs around as the ground had been disturbed. All too soon the path started climbing again up to the Col de St Pierre. The col was marked on the map as a view-point but the earlier blue skies had long since given over to the usual clouds so I saw nothing other than two camouflaged hunters who were lying behind rock shelters beside the shrine.

The climb continued up the ridge on open ground before bearing left into the forest, keeping just below the ridge line. The path was hard to follow but it then made its way back over the ridge to drop steeply down to the east; below me I could just make out the lake, Lac de Nino. As I dropped down out of the clouds the lake was soon reached and an enjoyable path crossed the meadow at its southern end before following the stream down to a forest of ancient pines.

An easy traverse led round to the stone enclosures and huts at the Bergerie de Vaccaja and from here I could see my next objective, the Refuge de Manganu, which was some way ahead across on the other side of the open corrie. After crossing the river a short rocky climb brought me to the hut at about 1:15. I passed the hut without calling in; the guide-book gave a time of six hours for the section from here to the next hut and with just four and a half hours of daylight I knew I would have to move quickly. The first half hour or so gave a good steep scramble, up past a couple of waterfalls and out onto a grassy plateau. From here the angle eased as the route continued to climb over rocks and boulders to the Breche de Capitello. This was now supposed to be a fine horseshoe ridge walk but I had no views other than the dripping rock in front of me.

I had to keep a careful look-out for the way-marks as it would have been something of a disaster if I were to lose the route, however some short sections of scrambling cheered me up and helped keep me warm. After a further short climb I reached the Col de la Haut Route; at 7,245ft the highest point on the route. The steep descent off the far side, searching for the path in almost zero visibility, was a little trying at the end of a long hard day but the slope then eased and led more gently down through boulders. At last I came to the white-painted rocks of a heli-pad and the Refuge Pietra-Piana was now only 50 yards away. There were already some Germans and an Englishman in the hut so it was nicely warmed up when I settled in and changed out of my wet clothes.

After another mouse disturbed sleep I decided to make the following day an easy one, simply moving on down to the next hut at l'Onda, which was only about four hours away; a double stage would have taken me to Vizzavona where I had been assured everywhere was shut for the winter and to try for three stages seemed to be pushing my luck. The weather was so bad next morning that I had trouble finding the path away from the hut, but I finally found the route, which resembled a stream more than a path. The path wound through stunted bushes and eventually entered open forest. I joined the other Englishman from the hut and together we walked down the valley in pouring rain until we reached the Bergerie de Tulla.

On sticking our heads round the door we were invited in by two old Corsicans. They gave us seats by the fire, throwing on more logs to help us dry out. After chatting for some minutes we were offered whisky (it was still only 10:30); not being a whisky drinker I refused but was then offered a pastis, which I was pleased to accept. More chat followed, we were then given coffee, next they brought out some bread and a large chunk of their home-made cheese; with the cheese came some red wine, made just a few miles down the valley. After a couple of glasses of this and the pastis I had warmed up and was ready to head out into the rain again. During our chat I'd been told that there was a refuge open at Vizzavona and in view of the weather they suggested that we take a lower route, missing out l'Onda altogether. We decided to take their advice and after much shaking of hands and expressions of mutual admiration for our new found Corsican friends we made our way, somewhat less steady on our feet than when we'd arrived.

The path followed the roaring river down through pine forest and we finally came out at a minor road, the other chap went left, while I headed right, about 4km up the road to Vizzavona. I fully expected a quiet afternoon, resting and drying my kit but of course there was nowhere to stay. Everywhere was locked and shuttered and I had no option but to go on to the next refuge; so much for my easy day.

After crossing the road I set off on the climb, up through forest, quite steeply at times and in worsening weather. The Col de Palmemte was reached in about an hour and a half; once again the promised views were denied me so I pressed on, dropping a short way down to the east and then following the footpath easily southwards. The path more or less contoured round the hillside for several miles, in and out of numerous side valleys, past a couple of closed Bergeries, before climbing steeply up through forest to come out at a road. From here it was only a few minutes' walk on a rough path to the Refuge de Capannelle. There were some untidy ski-tows and a closed bar and restaurant, but I had a warm welcome from the French and German couples in the hut and they kindly made me tea as I changed out of my wet things. It was a surprise to find myself here, one stage over the half-way point after four days, whereas when I had set out that morning I fully expected to still be one stage north of Vizzavona.

Day 5 dawned wild and windy but the two old Corsicans from the day before had said that the weather would improve so I set off anticipating a full day. The first couple of hours were in the shelter of the forest and on a fine footpath where I was able to make good time, contouring round the hillside past a collection of old stone buildings that wouldn't have looked out of place in Nepal. After several wet river crossings I came to the more open plateau of Gialgone; there were several groups of hunters near here, at this time of year they lie in wait near the high passes to shoot at the birds as they migrate south.

A steep descent led to a suspension bridge over the Marmano River, which rushed through the narrow gorge. Shortly after this the path started climbing to reach the forested shoulder at the Col de la Flasca. I dropped down again to join a good forestry track which led out to the road at the Col de Verde. The wind was still gusting strongly but it was staying dry so I continued on, up the track across the road until the way-marks led to a steeper footpath which climbed in zigzags up into the mist. With the mist came rain, this then became a torrential downpour. While I was in the trees I was reasonably comfortable but as I climbed higher the trees thinned out and I had a real fight on my hands to reach the Col de Prati. By now it was hard to stand and the rain had turned to stinging hail. Life was no longer fun and I was delighted when the Refuge de Prati emerged in front of me.

This was still some four hours short of my planned stop but after waiting two hours the weather had if anything deteriorated even more. I had no choice but to stay there for the night. As I only had food for another two days things looked a little bleak and I couldn't afford to simply sit out the storm at the hut. Not surprisingly I had the hut to myself. There was no dry wood left and I couldn't light the few sodden branches I'd carried up with me. I moved the kitchen table closer to the stove and slept on the table, keeping one ring of the gas cooker on all night. I managed to stay fairly warm and dried my kit but it was a sleepless night, the constant roaring of the wind shook the hut to its foundations and almost tore the door from its hinges.

Day 6 and when I looked out I expected to find clouds racing past the window; I had almost made up my mind to quit and to just concentrate on finding a safe way down. However I was pleasantly surprised to find blue sky and a weak sun. The wind continued unabated though and with the wind-chill factor the temperature was well below freezing. My revised plan was to simply try to reach the Refuge d'Usciolu, some five hours away. Luckily the route finding was fairly easy for once as I was able to see where I was going. The faint path led up onto a lovely rock ridge, initially keeping just below the crest on the east side, which was fine as it gave some shelter from the full force of the wind. Later I had to cross to the western side and then there was a short stretch on the very crest of the ridge itself. Where the wind was hitting the ridge full on the rocks were glazed with a thin veneer of ice, which meant I had to be extra careful with my footing, which was far from easy as the wind was making me stagger uncontrollably. I found out later that winds of 185kph (almost 120mph) were recorded at this time. Other than the wind the route was very enjoyable and gave me some easy scrambling. After a few miles I started to drop down to the Col de Lapato, passing on the way a small cross erected in memory of a German walker killed near here a few years before.

Entering some woodland just above the col gave me some temporary shelter from the wind and I was soon climbing up the other side on an indistinct path through the trees. Thankfully the path generally stayed on the east side of the ridge, where I could move reasonably easily, until it crossed again to the west where I encountered more ice-glazed rocks. I arrived at the Refuge d'Usciolu at about 11:30 and as visibility was still good and the rain holding off I decided to take a calculated risk and go for the next hut, which, according to the guide-book was eight hours away. With just six and a half hours of daylight remaining I hoped that after 24 hours of unceasing gales the wind would soon start to die down. It didn't!

From the refuge I regained the ridge line, passing just under the crest; either to the east, easy and fast; or to the west, icy, windy and slow. Another couple of miles of this ridge gave enjoyable going but I was growing concerned about the weather, which seemed to be changing for the worse again. I came quickly down off the ridge onto a pleasant forest path, with the trees now a splendid mix of autumnal colours. The path was hard to follow across an open forested plateau, but I kept one eye on the compass and was soon crossing an open section of moorland, jumping one or two streams until I reached the suspension bridge over the River Casamintellu. Several of the wooden planks looked rotten but I survived the crossing and started on the climb of Monte Incudine. This was the bit that had been worrying me, climbing a 7,000ft peak at the end of the day, when the weather and visibility were invariably at their worst. I had however reached this spot far quicker than I'd thought likely given the conditions, and I was delighted to see that only the top few hundred feet were in the clouds.

From the bridge the path climbed quite steeply up through woodland, bearing left and eventually out onto open hillside, where I followed a burn up into a small valley and from there up to a col on the mountains north ridge. On reaching the col I was again hit by the full force of the wind; I staggered up into the clouds and round the rim of an exciting looking corrie. Thankfully the route was well marked and after a bit of a battle, sometimes on all fours, I reached the tall cross which marked the summit.

A narrow ridge led away to the south-west and after descending this for about 10 minutes the way-marks turned abruptly left and plunged down towards the Refuge d'Asinao. I fully expected the descent to be steep but not quite as dramatic as it was. As soon as I turned off the ridge the mountain just fell away in a series of rocky slabs; thankfully the path zigzagged carefully down, giving a little easy scrambling into the sheltered corrie. The whole day had gone far better than I could have hoped when I left the refuge that morning and it was only 4:30 when I let myself into the d'Asinao hut. An American lad was already there, but there was no stove in the hut and it was freezing cold, the wind finding its way through every crack. After a bowl of soup I retired to bed for a couple of hours to thaw out; I crawled out of my sleeping bag later to cook my dinner but was back in bed by 7:30. Although I was cold I was in a happier frame of mind as I knew that with just two stages left to reach Conca, nothing was going to stop me now; with virtually no food left I had to finish the following day anyway!

Day 7 and I awoke after another disturbed sleep and realised at once that I couldn't hear anything; after two days listening to the constant roaring of the wind it had at last stopped. It was almost 7:30 before I left on a reasonably clear morning; the path continued down towards the river, across rock slabs and boulders. It was a difficult river crossing on slippery boulders but once across the far side I soon entered forest and the next few miles passed quickly on a good path. From here there was a choice of route; I could either take the slightly longer but easier route or the shorter but more entertaining route called the 'variente alpisme'. With the weather not immediately threatening I decided on the extra climbing of the 'variente'; I turned off the main track and climbed steeply up through thinning forest towards the magnificent rock scenery of the Cornes d'Asinao. On reaching the ridge I followed the crest south before dropping down beneath sheer cliffs.

The next hour or so gave some good walking, with a little exciting scrambling thrown in; one short slab, which was running with water, was thankfully provided with a chain for protection. Two ibex made the ground look easy as they cantered off, then all too soon the road at the Col de Bavella came into sight. It took me another half an hour to clamber down the rocky path until I passed below the last of the cliffs, where there were some rock-climbers in action. It was in this area that the missing German had last been seen and there were Police posters on several trees on either side of the road, appealing for information.

After a short stretch on the road I took to a footpath that dropped down to cross the river at a forestry bridge. Almost immediately the path started to climb again, up to another rocky crest and a narrow col, the Foce Finosa. By now the rain had returned so I was back in full water-proofs as I continued on down the far side into dripping forest, slowly losing height to reach the last refuge of the walk, the Refuge Paliri. It would have been good to stop but by now I was out of tea, coffee and soup and I had nothing to brew up with other than a little dried milk.

After leaving the refuge the path continued to lose height; I passed through an area that had recently been devastated by fire, a further climb then led up to some rocky spires giving me a final easy scramble. On crossing the ridge the path dropped down into burnt forest again; it was hard to follow the path as many of the burnt trees had fallen and blocked it, you had to either climb over or under them. It was slow and frustrating going and by the time I was through my face, hands and clothes were black.

However, the route remained interesting, staying high above the wooded valley, then, after one last corner, I reached the Col d'Usciolu. From here the end was in sight, I could see the small hill town of Conca directly below. The path zigzagged steeply down, through low scrub to emerge at a road from where it was only another ten minutes down into the village and the finish of the GR20 at the small church. On my way through the village an old couple asked if I had seen anything of the missing German and there were more Police posters appealing for information.

Although the walk was now finished I still had some way to go that afternoon. There are no hotels or any other accommodation in Conca and there are no buses either. I set off on the four mile walk down the road to Ste.Lucie de Porto Vecchio, which is on the main road that runs up the coast from Porto Vecchio to Bastia. On reaching Ste.Lucie de Porto Vecchio I was told that there was nowhere to stay in the village but there was somewhere open at Pinarellu, another three miles further away on the coast. When I found that hotel it was of course shut. I resigned myself to walking the three miles back to the main road and hitching twelve miles to Porto Vecchio. I started hitching and almost immediately a car stopped. After explaining my predicament the driver pulled up outside a house just 100 yards away, there was a block of holiday apartments to the rear and a restaurant alongside. I was given an apartment and assured that although the restaurant was closed I could eat with the family.

They made it clear that they thought me irresponsible to have gone on the GR20 alone but they seemed quite impressed with the time, only 6½ walking days, plus a half a day storm-bound at the Prati hut. They told me that a Legionnaire holds the record of around two days; but that was carrying no pack and no food.

The following morning my host kindly drove me round to Porto Vecchio, gave me a bottle of local wine and made me promise to return to the island for a more leisurely stay. I caught the afternoon bus to Ajaccio and that evening took the ferry back to Nice.

The distance is advertised as being about 115 miles with around 33,000ft of climbing and if that's right then the route took longer than originally planned. Going earlier in the year with more settled weather and more daylight, it would have been easy to combine more stages. I could also have got away with carrying a lighter rucksack, which would have allowed me to run the route rather than walk it.

Guidebook: The Corsican High Level Route by Alan Castle (Cicerone Press)
GR20 – A Travers la Montagne Corse -FFRP (in French)

Maps: Sheet 20 Corse Nord 1:50,000
Sheet 23 Corse Sud 1:50,000 (Didier & Richard)
Sheet 73 Corse Nord 1:100,000
Sheet 74 Corse Sud 1:100,000 (IGN)
(7 or 8 sheets at 1:25,000 would be required to cover the whole route, expensive but probably worth it, especially if the weather is bad)

King Ludwig Way

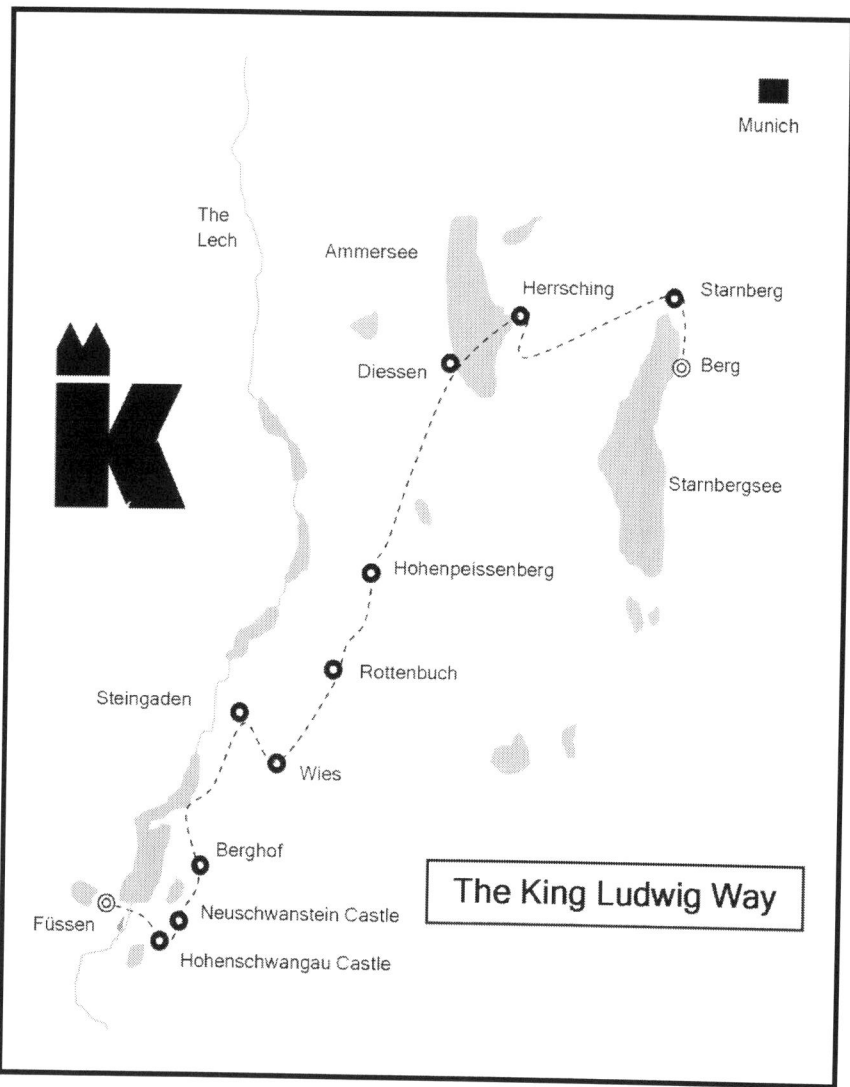

King Ludwig Way

Not a 'Haut Route' as such but I was looking for an easy run to start the new season after having spent the previous four months skiing. The King Ludwig Way, 76 miles through Bavaria from Lake Starnberg to the fairytale castle of Neuschwanstein near Füssen on the Austrian border, seemed to fit the bill nicely. It was all low level and was sure to be free of snow by mid-April.

The King Ludwig who gave his name to the walk was King Ludwig II of Bavaria, who succeeded to the throne, aged just 18, on the death of his father in 1864. He befriended Wagner and funded his operas, had little time for state affairs and instead indulged in his passion for building splendid palaces. Eventually he was declared insane and forced to abdicate. Just three days after his abdication he was found dead, floating in Lake Starnberg. He was a strong swimmer and an autopsy showed no water in his lungs, which ruled out drowning; to this day nobody knows how he met his end.

The route started a short distance down the east side of Lake Starnberg, at Berg. Opposite a small chapel in the woods there is a cross set a few yards out into the lake which marks the spot where the King's body was found. It was a beautiful morning as I set off, carrying just a light rucksack and feeling a little apprehensive. Whilst I was fit from four months skiing, I hadn't done a huge amount of running. Also I hadn't run for ten days as I had a broken rib; the result of a silly accident in near 'whiteout' conditions on my penultimate days skiing. Dosed up with painkillers and hay-fever tablets I was glad I wasn't going to be drug-tested.

The first few miles went quickly and easily, as I knew where I was going following a recent recce on my bike. The route led up along the lakeside, through the trees and reeds up to Starnberg, past piers and boat-yards, rowing clubs and yacht clubs, under the railway and out onto the town's main street, now adorned with a 40ft blue and white striped maypole that depicted the town's local trades.

It didn't take long to leave town and pick up a good footpath alongside a stream that led to the Maisinger Schlucht; a wooded gorge with a delightful river flowing through it. Signs along the path warned of the dangers of unexploded bombs in the woods! After crossing the road in Maising a track led off across the fields to a small lake, the Maisinger See. This is a Nature Reserve, full of noisy wildfowl; I also saw a couple of what I think were young grass snakes. After crossing the path they dropped into a small pond, swam across and then climbed out the other side to disappear into the undergrowth. A little further as I passed by the reed fringed lake I heard the tap-tap-tap of a wood-pecker, then I saw it clearly as it carried on its business quite undisturbed by my presence.

Flower filled meadows led to the hamlet of Aschering and a track led me off into the cool of the forest where a couple of deer ran off shyly; the run was fast becoming one long nature trail. The route was easily followed through the trees; all major junctions were marked with the now familiar blue K with a crown above. Leaving the forest a track led across more meadows to Andechs, passing several wayside shrines on the way, which led pilgrims to the Monastery set on a small hill-top nearby.

The day had now warmed up even more and we were enjoying something of a heat-wave. A wooded section gave some shelter from the sun as the path followed the top of a gorge then dropped down through the trees to the small lakeside town of Herrsching. Unfortunately I had to wait two hours for the next ferry across to Diessen; time spent watching the ducks, swans, coots and greylag geese. The ferry crossing took 25 minutes, so it was after a break of almost 2½ hours that I finally started running again. In that time my legs had stiffened up and it was hard work until I warmed up and was running freely again. I headed up the main road to Diessen Monastery, then off across the flower strewn meadows to a nature trail in the forest. Deep in the woods a mineral spring issued from beneath a small shrine so I took the chance to mix a poly-bag of *Gatorade* to keep me going. Still in the forest I ran past a small chapel; then I was back onto farm tracks leading through meadows and forest, with butterflies rising on thermals and newts dropping into the streams.

Several kilometres of tracks through forest led to Wessobrunn; another small hamlet dominated by its maypole, church and monastery. For me it was important as I could buy myself another couple of *Cokes*. Following the way-marks through the village I then had a short sharp descent to cross the Schlittbach; a climb up the far side took me through more rolling forest and meadows, past farms and hamlets, before re-entering delightful mixed woodland, where more small deer skipped away.

On reaching Hetten I had to buy yet more to drink to set myself up for the short stiff climb up to the summit of the

Hohenpeissenberg; a small hill, adorned with a church, a weather station and a TV mast. From here, far off in the haze, I could see snow covered Austrian peaks. Starting to feel the strain, I headed off down to the village with its ubiquitous blue and white maypole then picked up a farm track across the fields. This took me over a railway and into more meadows and forest, always gently rising and falling, always interesting.

The next section through the Ammer Gorge was perhaps one of the best of the run. It was a great path, much of it on steps and board-walks: down to the river-side and a roofed-in bridge, then without crossing the river a steep climb led up through the trees, still on a narrow footpath, up and down more steps, along narrow and sometimes airy board-walks, with the river roaring past below. More small deer trotted away as I puffed past, then I came out into meadows again and I knew that the day's end was in sight. A pleasant run between wood and field took me through Moos to the monastery at Rottenbuch where I finally ground to a halt in the village square.

It had been a long hot day, about 43 miles in 7½ hours, and I had drunk nearly a gallon of various things, yet that still wasn't enough. This was my first night out of the van for about six months and being in a proper bed for once I couldn't sleep.

Next morning I was away from the Gasthof before eight. I left the village through the arch-way in the old walls; slowly worked the aches and pains out of my system and back into running mode. It was a pleasant start, through meadows out to another small lake and along a field path to Wildsteig. A farm lane then led to Holz, where there is a lovely little Baroque chapel, then on to Wies, where there is another important Baroque church. From here there was a choice of routes; I opted for the longer 'Steingaden loop'. After a quick stop for a *Fanta* the way led across a wooded marsh, over several kilometres of duck-boards and forest track. More deer and a huge slow-worm were seen here.

I soon reached the small village of Steingaden and was glad to be able to buy another 1½ litres of *Fanta*. More easy running along farm tracks, through small hamlets and remote farms took me to Prem, from where a quiet track led along the embankment on the eastern side of the Premer Lechsee, a man-made reservoir. This part of the route was also shared by the Lech High Level Route, which runs from Landberg to Füssen. Cuckoos called out from the woods alongside, then a rising track across open meadows was hard work but I finally dropped down to reach Berghof. Unfortunately the only shop had shut just minutes earlier so I had to make do with a polybag of *Gatorade*, mixed and drunk at the village fountain, much to the amazement of two old ladies who watched my every move.

Leaving Berghof the way led easily through open fields, past Hergratsriedsee, another small lake teeming with wildfowl; an arm of the Forggensee then reached up to the lane. On reaching the hamlet of Brunnen the path turned along the embankment of the Mühlberger stream and now I had my first sight of the twin castles of Neuschwanstein and Hohenschwangau. These slowly came nearer as I continued on along the stream, with dozens of squirrels for company. At the foot of the Tegelberg cable-car several colourful parapente canopies were spread out in the landing zone in the field; three or four more were lining up above, ready to come in to land.

Suddenly the path started climbing into the Pöllat Gorge; a steep and narrow cleft in the rock through which the river roared in mighty falls. The footpath is actually bolted onto the wall of the gorge in places. The Marienbrücke footbridge came into sight high above the gorge and in one last effort I ran the steps that led up to Neuschwanstein Castle.

13: Neuschwanstein Castle, almost the end

The path was busy with tourists and I hate to think what they thought of the sweating, gasping figure that ran past them down the steep tarmac road, dodging in and out of their horse-drawn carriages. I made my way beneath the towering walls and turrets and moved on to the next castle, Hohenschwangau. From here I found the narrow footpath known as the 'Alpenrosenweg' which took me above two delightful lakes which nestled amongst the trees; the Alpsee and the Schwansee. The Austrian border was now just a mile away and snow covered peaks towered over me. A footpath took me down through the forest to the Schwansee, then I had one last climb, up and over a wooded ridge where the roar of the Lech Falls came up through the trees. I was soon down at the road for the last few hundred metres to the bridge over the Lech, through the town walls and so into Füssen and the finish.

The second day was somewhat shorter, about 33 miles, making 76 miles covered in a total running/walking time of around thirteen hours. Although there were no big hills it was always gently rolling countryside and I guess there was around 4,000ft of climbing, but with 100m contour intervals on the map it was hard to be precise. The route turned out to be far better than anticipated, always interesting, either due to the trees and flowers, the farms and churches, or the ever present birds and wildlife.

Guidebook: King Ludwig Way by F & C Speakman
            (Cicerone Press)
            The King Ludwig II Hiking Trail
            (Starnberg Tourist Information)

Maps: Sheet 180   Starnberger – Ammersee
      Sheet 179   Pfaffenwinkel - Schongauerhand
      Sheet   4   Füssen – Ausserfern
      (1:50,000 Kompass Wanderkarte)

Jura High Route

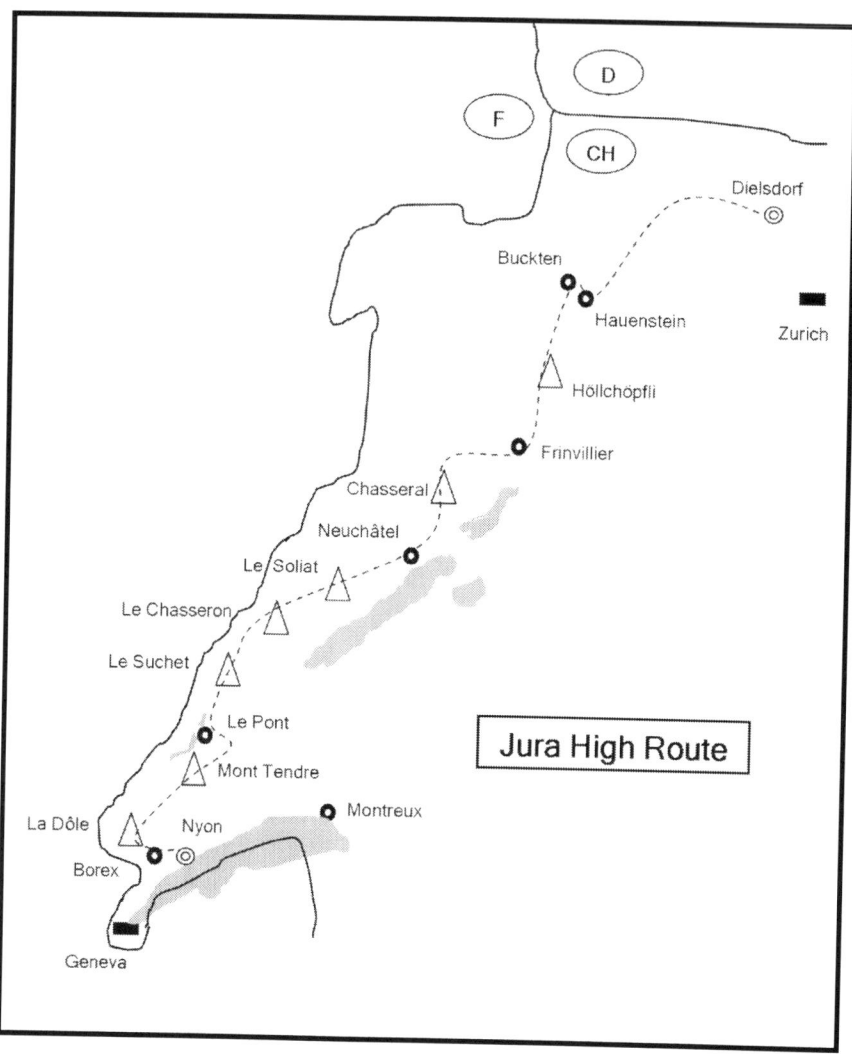

Jura High Route

The Jura High Route is a 300km, long distance footpath that runs from Dielsdorf (about 15 miles north-west of Zurich) to Borex (about 20 miles north-east of Geneva). The route passes over several summits of over 5,000ft but I hoped the snow would have gone and that the paths would be runnable by early May.

The route starts at Dielsdorf Railway Station, where red and yellow way-marks took me through the village and up a steep lane between vines and gardens to the hill-top village of Regensberg. This is a delightful old place with fountains in the square and houses dating back over 400 years. On leaving Regensberg the route led up into forest, the first of many over the next few days, where deer watched nervously from among the beech trees.

The track climbed a narrow wooded ridge, which then dropped down a steep concrete staircase to take me into the small town of Baden. Complicated route finding through the town took me over an old timber covered bridge, alongside the river and into the modern shopping precinct. A finger-post in the centre of the arcade directed me to Platform 1 of the station from where an under-pass eventually took me out to the western side of town. It was good to climb into forest again, sometimes on broad forest tracks, sometimes on narrow footpaths, but all junctions were clearly marked, either by a 'Hohenweg' sign or the familiar red/yellow diamond. Dropping down from the ridge I ran past a rocky outcrop with a couple of shallow caves where small deer and squirrels kept me company.

The route now led down to cross the River Reuss near steep weirs; pastures then took me into Brugg, a pleasant old town on the River Aare. It didn't take long to start climbing again on a footpath among the trees, along to a small village where I took the chance to buy something to eat and drink, knowing that I was about to enter a long dry woodland stage. As I continued along the track a kestrel hovered above me, it was a splendid sight and only a few feet above my head. I re-entered the forest and on a mix of tarmac, forest track and footpath I climbed up onto the ridge again. It now started to rain, not quite heavy enough to warrant stopping to put on water-proofs but the damp weather brought out huge numbers of big fat slugs and massive snails. There were so many that it was hard to put my feet down without squashing at least one.

Open meadows and forest fringed glades were strewn with wild-flowers and these led me down to Staffelegg.

I was soon back into the wilderness of pastures and meadows, then climbing again, initially on a forest track, then more steeply on a rough footpath to regain the ridge among the beech-woods. Unfortunately any views were lost in the clouds, but glorious running through forest then open meadows led down to a narrow road where way-marks guided me round a farm. The farm dog went crazy as I cautiously walked by him; just when I thought I was safe the dog flew through the fence and stood snarling at me, the old farmer and his wife eventually took pity on me and called the dog to heel. I hurried away up the hill, following a line of telegraph poles across the fields; these led up to the wooded ridge again before dropping down through more pastures to the small hamlet of Hauenstein. As luck would have it, it was Ruhetag, and both the Gasthof and the hotel were closed that afternoon. There was nowhere else ahead on the route for several hours so I had to jog down the road to the north searching for somewhere to stay. Two places in the next village were also closed so I had to continue down the road to Buckten before finding somewhere that could take me in.

Day 2 dawned somewhat overcast again and rather than retrace my steps back up the road to Hauenstein I made my way to Laufelfingen. Here I found a footpath that climbed up alongside a stream, into the woods then across pastures to regain the ridge at Challhöchi where I re-joined the main High Level Route. A good track led along the ridge here; the track was engineered by the Army in 1915 and several Swiss regiments who helped construct it had carved their insignia into the rock-faces along the way. From down below came the sound of gun-fire and explosions as modern day soldiers played war-games.

Good easy running led along the ridge then down through forest and pastures to cross the road at Bärenwil. A trough gave me the chance to refill my water-bottle before climbing on a narrow footpath up into the forest then out onto the crest of the ridge. Grassy pastures led along the crest with views down to a mist shrouded ruined castle on my right, whilst to my left was the Mittelland, the agricultural plain stretching all the way from the Jura to the Alps. Climbing steadily the narrow ridge entered mixed forest, a beautiful section then led along the ridge to Roggenflue, a view-point above a steep limestone cliff. From here a big and fairly steep descent took me down to the small town of Balsthal; the kiosk at the railway station provided *Mars Bars* and *Coke* to refuel me for the next few miles.

On leaving Balsthal the route took me steeply up through forest to regain the crest of the ridge. This is a favourite launch site for hang-gliders; there were wind-socks for them on the ridge along with a map of where to land. Still climbing, but less steeply now, the path led along the ridge-top through open forest. At one point I ran past a huge slab of limestone; bolts and daubs of chalk proved that this was a popular climber's crag. The path then swung through a narrow gap in the rocky crest to continue along and out onto pastures beneath another long line of crags. This was the cue to change to the second of the four maps I needed for the route.

After several miles along the ridge I came to the small farm of Hinterer Weissenstein where I was glad of the chance to stop for a quick coffee; immediately afterwards I was climbing again, following the wooded crest out onto a broad grassy ridge, Stallflue, which is topped by a large metal cross. The view south from here was similar to that from my then, home hills, the Ochils; down a steep grassy escarpment to the patchwork of fields in the plain below, with the river winding round in lazy ox-bows. I should also have been able to see the distant Alps but haze and low cloud denied me. As I jogged along, sometimes in woods and sometimes through meadows, it was always interesting. I think I spotted a female capercaillie and there were squirrels everywhere. The track then led down through fields full of horses, many with young foals by their side. It was here I realised that the signs no longer read 'Hohenweg' but had now changed to the French 'Chemin des Crêtes', a sure sign I was making good progress along the route.

A gentle descent took me through a pleasant, park-like area that was buzzing with crickets, and led to Frinvillier where the only accommodation was a roadside hotel. The landlord could hardly believe I had only taken two days from Dielsdorf; Frinvillier is usually six stages. The guide-book suggests 14 days are needed for the route; when I'd set out I thought I would need five or six days, but after reaching here in two I was confident that I would now be able to finish within five days. When the landlord heard what I had planned for the following day he said I would need at least six hours to reach the next top, Chasseral, but if I had a mountain-bike then I could perhaps reach it in four.

Day 3 was again warm but cloudy and the climb started almost on leaving the hotel. From the roadside a footpath climbed in steep zigzags through the trees. I came out into grassy meadows, back into forest, and across more flower-filled meadows. A faint trail through the dew wet meadow showed the way, other than that there was no sign of a path on the ground. I soon passed a Swiss Alpine Club hut, but unlike the Alps the Jura huts are locked and you need to book ahead to arrange for a key. A little later I passed a wooden chalet for cross-country skiers, the Jura being a popular ski-touring area.

The 3,000ft climb was fairly gradual and brought me out onto the crest of the ridge once more. A radio mast loomed up out of the mist and I was soon on Chasseral, having taken less than half the six hours predicted by the locals. One or two patches of snow still lay in the sheltered hollows and a few ski-tows climbed up from the grassy southern slopes. The restaurant at the ski-lodge gave me an excuse for a coffee stop before continuing on along the ridge, following the edge of the limestone crest.

A long and sometimes rough descent now took me down through an untidy area of tree-stumps, rocks and roots, all very slippery and hard to run. Then it was down through pastures and scattered farms, through a brief rain shower and into the small village of Chaumont. Passing the funicular railway that links the village to Neuchâtel down on the lake, I entered forest again; a steep path then took me down, cutting across the forestry tracks. It was hard on the feet and knees and seemed to take an age before I finally reached the road which skirted round the northern edge of Neuchâtel. A local stopped me for a chat; he pointed to a mist shrouded Le Soliat and told me it would take eight hours to reach there. It did look high and a very long way away, but I was planning on spending the night there and counting on no more than four hours to reach it.

Pairs of fighter jets flew noisily over the lake and at last the sun tried to come out as I ran through vineyards, crossed the railway at Bôle and then dropped down into the Gorges de l'Areuse. The river-worn rocks channelled the water through the deep gorge from where I started another 3,000ft plus climb. Sometimes on track, sometimes on road, but usually on good forest paths, the trail led ever upwards, eventually quitting the forest to cross pastures and forest fringed meadows, passing a lonely farm or two until I reached the edge of an escarpment that fell away sheer to the north. Continuing around the edge of the cliffs I came across a small herd of seven or eight chamois with their fearsome looking horns. After another mile or so I came out onto the plateau-like top of Le Soliat. Here huge cliffs dropped away and I looked down into the amazing limestone cirque of Creux du Van. The cirque is almost a mile across; sheer cliffs fall for more than 1,000ft to a broad band of scree, criss-crossed by animal tracks; below the scree the valley floor is heavily forested.

A short jog around the edge of the cirque took me past more chamois and across the fields to the Ferme du Soliat. The dortoir here is above the cattle-shed, so the sounds and smells of the cattle drifted up throughout the night; it was a great place to stay though, good wholesome food and very cheap.

I was away to a reasonably early start on Day 4, leaving the farm in a light mist and drizzle. Easy running led through cow-filled pastures, the sound of their bells ever-present. In a couple of places I passed deep sink-holes in the limestone then I was soon climbing the ridge to the next top, Le Chasseron, crowned by the usual triangular trig-point on legs. It was a fine spot; steep cliffs fell away to the north-west with more gentle grassy slopes to the south-east. I continued on along the edge of the escarpment before dropping down beneath ski-tows, which led to a rough track that took me steeply down into the village of Sainte-Croix.

I left Sainte-Croix in a torrential downpour. The route climbed steeply at first to regain the ridge; thunder and lightning crashed around me as I followed the path across forest fringed meadows. The next few miles were on a quiet country lane, passing camouflaged machine gun posts and lines of concrete tank traps; the French border was only a mile away.

Leaving the road a pleasant footpath led on up to the ridge and over a grassy top, Le Suchet, it was then down once more through flowery meadows and more anti-tank defences to the hamlet of Ballaigues. I needed another quick stop here for a *Coke*, then it was on again, over the main road and down into forest. The way-marks took me over a small dam, along to the goods siding and out of Vallorbe railway station. A short stretch on the road took me to the edge of town from where I headed up a steep wooded valley past several fish farms; just upstream of which is the Source de la Orbe, a pretty area of caves and streams, where the waters emerge from their journey underground.

I now faced a very steep climb on a rough footpath that led up through forest to eventually come out onto a forest road beside the railway, near to where the railway disappears into a tunnel. The track continued on then dropped down to the small village of Le Pont which sits between two lakes, Lac de Joux and Lac Brenet, where I found a B&B for the night.

Unfortunately Day 5 had a hungry start; it was a Sunday and the B&B wouldn't serve breakfast until 8:30, which would have meant I wouldn't be able to leave until at least 9. I made do with a swig of water and two chocolate biscuits and set off just before 7:30. Thankfully the previous day's storm had moved on and patches of blue sky promised better for later on.

It didn't take long to regain the track in the woods and this in turn gave easy running through pastures, where an old couple were out early picking mushrooms. After crossing the road I started on the climb of Mont Tendre. It was fast, enjoyable running across open meadows, with views back through the trees to the twin lakes of Le Pont; a long level forest path let me cruise along, past a couple of farms and up onto Mont Tendre's summit, adorned with the usual metal trig-point. This is the highest point of the Swiss Jura at around 5,550ft and as usual I had the summit to myself. There were a few patches of snow still lying among the rocks. After a brief rest I dropped down to the south, crossed through a dry-stone wall and continued down on grassy tracks into forest before emerging at the road at the Col du Marchairuz where I stopped for my long over-due breakfast.

Fed and watered I followed an indistinct path from the col until it came out onto a broader path which gave great running on easier terrain so the miles passed effortlessly. I was a little surprised to find two old guys here, setting up an alpenhorn, which one then started to play. Continuing on along the ridge a short climb led to the rocky tor of the Crêt de la Neuve; around the summit cross were masses of colourful wild-flowers.

From here the trail continued indistinctly through grassy meadows, passing in and out of wooded areas until I came to the ruins of a 12th century convent. By now the sun was shining and I enjoyed a *Coke* and a slice of apple pie at an inn in the centre of the village of St. Cergue. Suitably refreshed and with just one of the fourteen stages remaining I followed the way-marks past the ski-tows and camp-site and started on the final climb of the journey. It was 2,000ft, quite steeply up a grassy footpath, then more easily across pastures. I stormed up the hill safe in the knowledge that it was the last one and came out at the Col de Porte, with the final summit just half a mile away, around the rim of a huge cirque. A short while later I was on top of La Dôle; the summit is cluttered with a giant 'golf-ball' type radar dish, a cable-car to service it, a weather station and ski-tows.

After a brief rest I returned to the col and dropped steeply down a loose path to the foot of the cable-car. The road from here swings down in a series of long loops but my route was more direct, straight down the steep forested hillside. It was hot, thirsty work and a spring in a small clearing gave me the chance to top-up my water-bottle before I plunged downwards once more. The descent was hard on my knees and my feet were feeling every stone through the soles of my running-shoes but at last I could see daylight and I knew I was reaching the edge of the forest. A minor road led directly into Borex; as I jogged along I looked up and there was Lac Leman and beyond it the high snowy peaks of the Alps.

The Jura High Route officially ends at Borex but there is no accommodation and only an intermittent Post-Bus service, so I had no choice but to continue on, down the busy main road into Nyon, a large town on the lakeside from where I caught the train back to Dielsdorf.

The route is officially 299 kilometres but with diversions to find accommodation on Day 1 and Day 5, I made it about 308km, or just over 190 miles in all, with around 31,000ft of climbing. It was an interesting journey; although there were few big climbs it was always rolling along comfortably. Being a limestone range there were very few surface streams and in hot weather it was important to take every opportunity to refill my water-bottle from taps or troughs when I found them.

Guidebook: The Jura–Walking the High Route by Kev Reynolds (Cicerone Press)

Maps: Sheet 1   Aargau, Basel, Olten
      Sheet 2   Delsberg, Biel, Solothurn
      Sheet 3   Chasseral, Ste-Croix
      Sheet 4   Lausanne, St.Cergue, Vallee de Joux
      (1:60,000 Wanderkarte des Jura – Kummerly & Frey)

Tour des Portes du Soleil

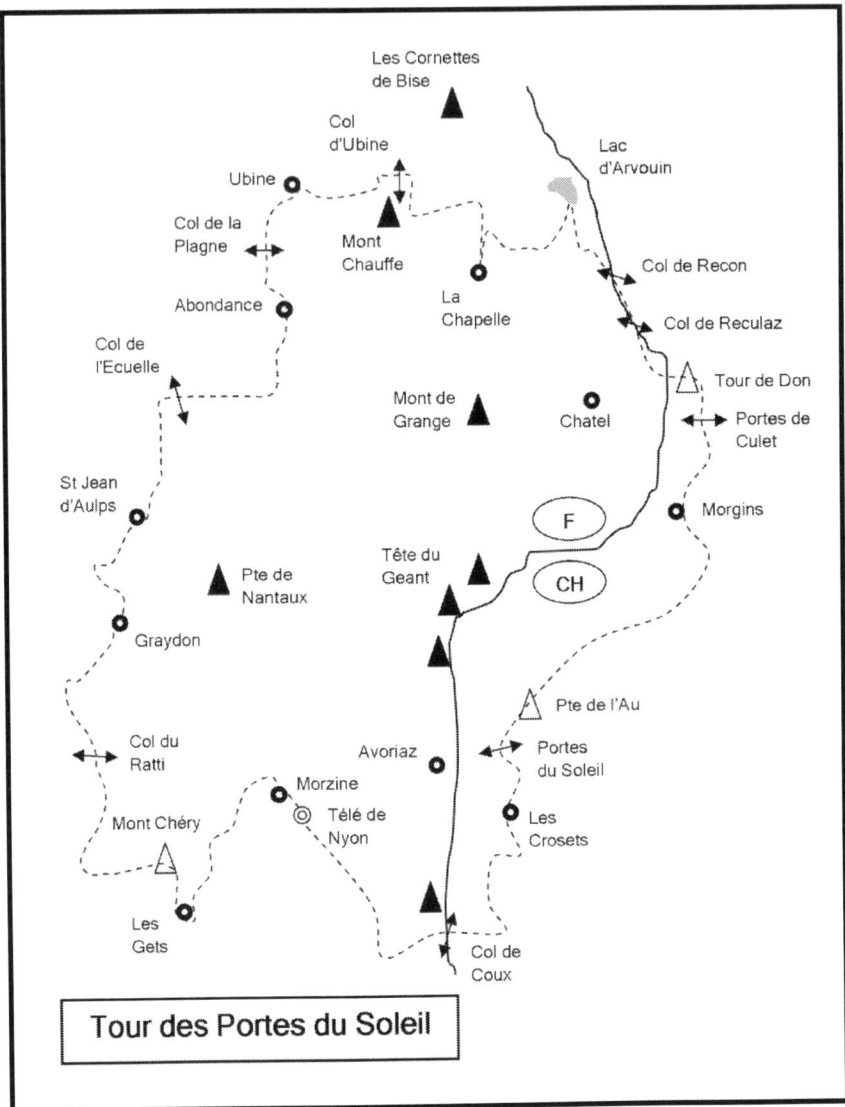

Tour des Portes du Soleil

I arrived in Morzine towards the end of May; the first thing I noticed as I drove up the road in the pouring rain was that there was a lot more snow now than when I had tried to ski there in February. However, next morning when the rain had stopped, it soon became clear that the snow was fresh and a couple of days of bright sunshine quickly pushed the snow-line back up the hill.

The route is not specifically sign-posted or way-marked; it is shown on a local map for walkers and mountain bikers, but the map was virtually useless to navigate by. A slightly different route was shown on the IGN 1:25,000 map; this is a good map but it only covers the three quarters of the tour that's in France, the remaining quarter of the tour is over the border in Switzerland; unfortunately the map turned to black and white and any over-printing, such as for routes, simply stopped at the border. Knowing that the Swiss are very efficient at sign-posting their paths I assumed I would find a way through.

From the start at the foot of the Téléphérique de Nyon I headed off along the river a short way into Morzine, from where a track climbed away up the hill, following a ski piste. I climbed steadily up through the trees, over a ridge and jogged down into Les Gets. The first big climb started here; underneath the cable-car the track led through meadows and forest and climbed quite steeply up to Mont Chéry, amongst a clutter of ski tows.

From the summit I had a good view across to my next objective, the Col du Ratti; first though I had a steep descent on a narrow footpath down to the road at Col de l'Encrenaz. From the road a lane led up to a farm, a faint footpath then took me out along an obvious ridge, this gave good fast running under an already boiling sun. As I climbed higher I kept down to the left of the ridge which took me to the small Col de la Basse; steep grassy slopes then led up through colonies of playful marmots to the Col du Ratti.

There was a lot of snow still lying in the sheltered corrie on the far side of the col and I involuntarily ducked when a small avalanche set off a rock-fall, which thankfully was a safe distance away. The route wasn't obvious here as snow covered the track, but I was able to use a long tongue of old snow to cut a big loop off the track and lost a lot of height very fast. Then it was on, dropping down a rough footpath into the valley to the small farms and church that make up the hamlet of Graydon, where I had a brief stop to buy a *Coke* and refill my water-bottle from the trough. A track now climbed easily through forest up onto the crest of a ridge, which was followed for a while before another steep descent through mixed woodland brought me out onto a tarmac road. The road took me down to the small village of St. Jean d'Aulps. As I'd hoped, I reached here before the shops shut for their usual long lunch break and I called in at the 'boulangerie' for another couple of cans of *Coke* and a couple of sticky pastries. Serving behind the counter of the 'boulangerie' was undoubtedly the most beautiful girl in the world, she was absolutely stunning and I was very embarrassed when the sweat dripped off the end of my nose onto the sparkling clean glass counter!

Leaving the village a road climbed steeply to the hamlet of Mont d'Evian from where a rough track climbed into the cool of the forest, passing scattered farms, until I eventually reached the Col de l'Ecuelle. Climbing on from the col a path took me to the Pointe des Follys and its associated ski-tows. My toes, still sore from running the Jura High Route the week before, felt the stony descent down a land-rover track on the far side, before a pleasant contouring path led through forest then farmlands and into Abondance.

A steep road climbed out of the village for a short way before I turned off onto an over-grown footpath; this soon met a rough track which climbed through forest and up to the grassy Col de la Plagne. A delightful grassy path climbed away from the col, through the trees and wildflowers, giving easy running, before dropping down to the farm buildings at Ubine. This lonely little settlement sits in a grassy corrie beneath towering cliffs that culminate in the impressive Mont Chauffe. My path now led along under the cliffs and up to the Col d'Ubine. From the col a very steep descent took me down to the forest where a stony track continued the descent until I could pick up a footpath alongside the river, which in turn led me out to the road on the outskirts of La Chapelle where I soon found a bed for the night.

Day 2 was a little overcast to start with as I climbed a short distance back up the road to cross the river, the road then contoured round the hillside to a small farm. From here a footpath took me steeply up through forest, gaining height quite viciously at times, until I came out into an open corrie that was ringed by rocky peaks. The path climbed through a narrow gap in the ridge opposite to reveal a hidden corrie, which was filled by the beautiful Lac d'Arvouin. Leaving the lake I headed off across the hillside on a level track, which gave good running round into the next corrie where I faced a further climb. The grassy path led easily up and out onto a narrow ridge which was the border between France and Switzerland. Great running along the crest of the undulating ridge, all the while following the boundary stones, took me through forests and pastures, over the Col de Recon, over the small Pointe de Recon, and down to the Col de Reculaz. A grassy run then led into Switzerland itself, climbing easily to the small summit of Tour de Don. The ridge-top path made for fast, easy going before dropping down to the tree-lined Col de Conche. A short distance from here was a remote chalet where I willingly called a short halt to re-fuel.

On the climb to the Portes de Culet I disturbed several basking lizards. From the col a steep grassy track led down off the hill to join a minor road that I followed to the village of Morgins. It was just gone noon on what had turned into another boiling hot day; as I jogged past the church a dog leapt into the water trough to cool off; other than the dog and me, no one else stirred.

"Only mad dogs and Englishmen go out in the midday sun"
(Noel Coward)

I joined the dog and splashed water over myself to cool off before I started on the long climb to the ridge above. A short stretch of road led to a footpath which climbed steeply through the trees, then across more open ground to the small hamlet of Madze from where I climbed to the crest of the ridge. This now gave me a long, undulating ridge run, passing the tops of several ski-tows that climbed up from the eastern side. In places the path could only just be followed through the dense scrub. Eventually, after crossing more snow I reached the summit of the Pointe de l'Au, at 2,152m it was the highest point on the tour.

Unfortunately the day now started to cloud over and although still very warm it looked as though a storm was on its way. I hurried on down to the col called the 'Portes du Soleil' and then ran easily down the track into Les Crosets. A brief stop here for a couple of ice-cold *Fantas* set me up for the climb up out of the valley and onto a broad grassy ridge. A good track took me round into the head of another valley from where I could see the next, and almost final objective, the Col de

Coux, after which it would be downhill almost all the way to Morzine. First though I had to reach the col. The track I was on seemed to go down some way to a farm before climbing again to the col. When I saw the option of a traverse across the hillside I thought it would save me quite a bit of descent and re-ascent. At first the contouring path was well defined but then it just disappeared and I was left floundering about on a steep hillside covered in loose blocks and scree. As usual the short-cut proved to be a poor choice and I was glad it was only the marmots that witnessed my mistake, I could hardly stand upright on the unstable mass let alone try to walk or run. Eventually the rocks gave way to grass, which although steep, was a little kinder on my ankles and my nerves. Finally I reached the path that led to the col; there was a lot of snow on this side of the pass but I knew from a run a few days before that the other side was clear.

From the col I was back into France and on familiar ground again. I dropped down into the corrie on a good footpath, which became a track on entering forest. A gentle jog took me to the road, then, once across the river an easy run along the riverside path found me back at the cable-car station on the outskirts of Morzine.

I was pleased to be back among the big mountains again after my 'warm up' runs on the King Ludwig Way and the Jura High Route. The Tour des Portes du Soleil proved to be an unexpectedly good route of around 70 miles with 21,000ft of ascent.

Guidebook: None

Maps: Sheet 3528ET Morzine/Massif du Chablais 1:25,000 IGN
Cartes des Promenades à pied et en VTT   1:36,000

Tour de l'Oisans (GR54)

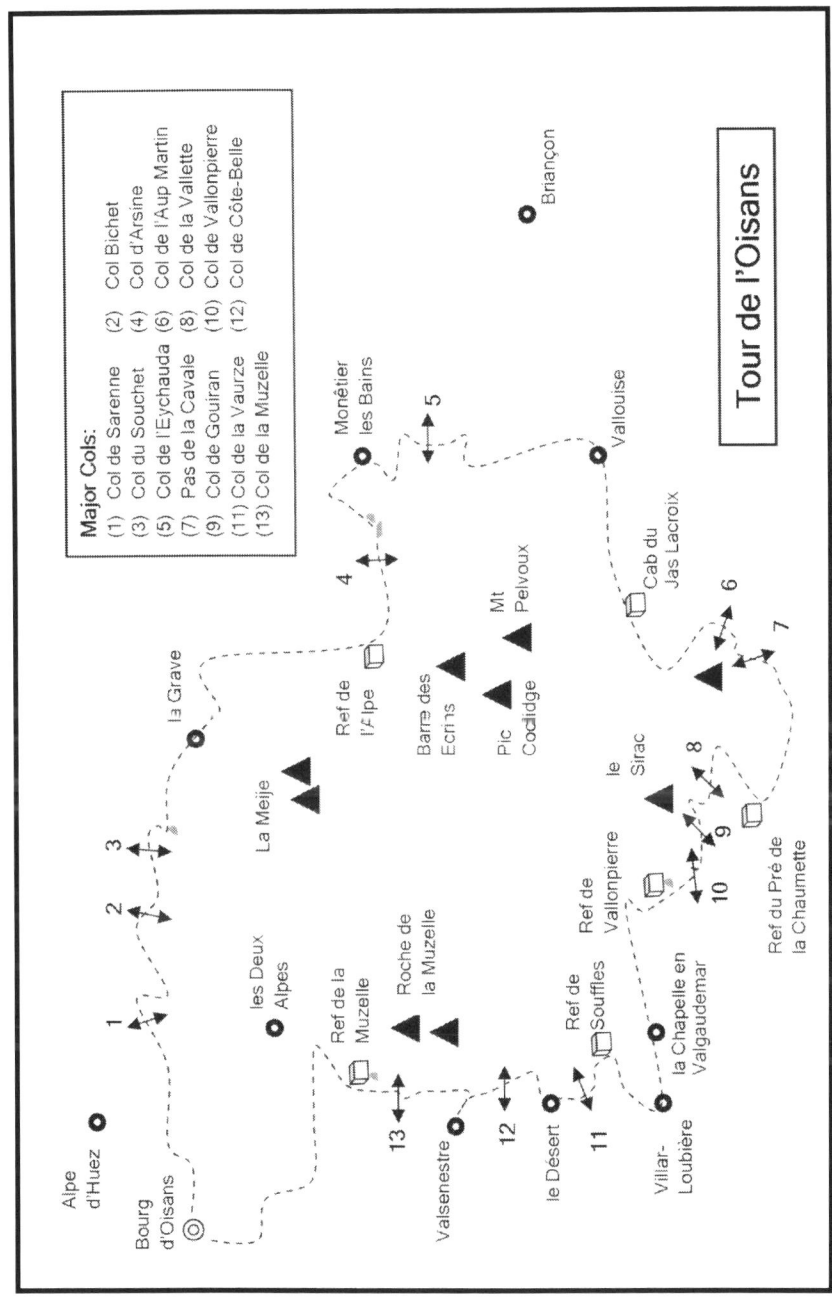

Tour de l'Oisans (GR54)

I'd originally planned on running the Tour du Queyras next but after recceing in the area for a few days, and running up to some of the high cols, I decided there was still far too much snow. I then spent a few days running and cycling in the Dauphiné area, including cycling the famous Alpe d'Huez climb, and thought that perhaps the Tour de l'Oisans was 'on', although it was clear that the snow was still quite deep in many places.

I left Bourg d'Oisans early on a cold, grey day, ran through the town and picked up the footpath near the foot of the Alpe d'Huez road. The path was immediately interesting as it climbed steep slabs, gaining height quickly to eventually come out on a woodland path that climbed to the hamlets of le Châtelard and le Rosay. From le Rosay a path led through fields, round a shoulder and dropped down to cross the Sarenne by a small stone bridge. A rough track then climbed steadily alongside the river, finally joining a road which crossed a grassy corrie and led to the first col of the route, the Col de Sarenne.

The road dropped down the far side of the col and at the first hairpin bend I took to the narrow footpath that headed down in tight zigzags. By the time I regained the road a steady drizzle had set in. I passed through Clavans le Haut, dropped into the woods and down into Clavans le Bas. After refilling my water-bottle at the fountain it was on again, down an overgrown footpath to a bridge. Another steep, wet, overgrown path took me to the delightful little village of Besse. Thick cloud meant I could see very little as I climbed round a grassy corrie towards a col, not named on my map, but understood to be the Col Bichet. This opened out onto a huge bowl and apart from the rain it gave good running.

After a wet river crossing, the path continued across the grass, climbing easily to the next col, the Col du Souchet. In almost zero visibility I now managed to lose the route and I unexpectedly found myself beside a small lake. Careful examination of the map showed it to be Lac Lerie, a mile off route, therefore an extra two miles running. I finally regained the way-marks and these led round the hill to some ski-tows, which signalled that I was nearing civilisation again. A very steep and slippery descent took me down to the river and after crossing it a short climb brought me into the pretty village of le Chazelet.

I dropped down onto another overgrown footpath; the rain was falling steadily and my light-weight water-proofs were no longer water-proof. I plunged down through the soaked undergrowth, feeling very cold, and was pleased to come out onto a wider track which took me into la Grave. I was concerned that the weather would stay bad for the whole of the Tour; one of the drawbacks of going 'light-weight' is that you don't have much margin for error.

Thankfully on leaving la Grave there was another big climb and this soon warmed me up again; a steep path climbed up into forest before dropping down to the riverside near Villar d'Arêne. Although it was still raining heavily it was a pleasant path along the river, climbing gently all the while. As the river turned south the path started climbing more steeply into a narrowing glen. Marmots and a fine chamois raced away as I neared the Refuge de l'Alpe; pushing on through the rain and clouds in a very 'Scottish' looking glen I reached the Col d'Arsine. I had run up to here from Monêtier about a week earlier, to check on the snow, so the rest of the day's route was familiar to me and I was able to put the map and guide-book away for a while.

There was a little snow to the west of the col then I was down into a rough corrie with two or three small lakes nestling beneath the Glacier d'Arsine. The corrie narrowed at its exit and after a short steep section of path I was soon down at the Lac de la Douche. From here it was an easy run down through forest; I was pleased to see some blue sky for the first time that day and I even started to dry off. A gîte at Monêtier les Bains gave me quite a feast that night.

Day 2 started with another glimpse of blue sky which I hoped promised better for later on. From the gîte I crossed the river and followed a lane through a flowery meadow. From here a footpath climbed steeply up into the forest; I had to take my 'sac off no less than eight times to keep ducking under an electric fence that surrounded a lonely chalet and it's pastures. At last I left the fence behind, re-entered the forest and crossed a couple of swollen streams, which meant cold wet feet, before I emerged into an open corrie beside a couple of ski-tows. From here I could see the previous day's storm had left a lot of fresh snow covering the path to the col above. As I climbed the easy snow slopes the sound of a falling rock drew my attention to a herd of a dozen chamois crossing the scree away to one side.

The Col de l'Eychauda was a bleak place and I hastened on down into the corrie beyond. At first it was difficult to follow the path as it was hidden under the snow but once I had dropped from the upper corrie into the wider lower corrie I came off the snow and ice and could run easily down the zigzags to the river below. A gentle section took me down a land-rover track; footpaths then cut the corners and led me down to the village of Vallouise. Here a couple of doughnuts and a can of *Coke* set me up for the long climb to the high point of the tour.

The route climbed gently through mixed forest above a raging torrent, the going then grew harder; I had to negotiate overgrown meadows, avalanche debris, rock slides and mud slips, some were easier to cross than others. Where the valley forked I swung south up the left-hand glen. The next hour was delightful as a great path climbed alongside a tumbling stream and small waterfalls, the sun came out and I was flying along, making such good time that I started to think of going on further than the Refuge du Pré de la Chaumette, which had been my original target for the day. If I could go further then it meant that I could possibly complete the Tour inside three days, which was a very tempting target.

Passing the Cabane du Jas Lacroix, a small open bothy, I then faced a dangerous river crossing which led towards the upper corrie and the Col de l'Aup Martin, which was somewhere up there in the clouds. At about 9,100ft this was the highest point on the Tour and as I feared there was still a lot of snow hereabouts. Any sign of the path was soon lost under the deep snow and I struggled on not knowing quite where I was going. As luck would have it the clouds now dropped still further and it started to snow. I was in no immediate danger and had loads of time to play with so I continued slowly onwards. At best the snow was just about ok; I would just sink in to my ankles. At its worst it was horrendous; I was actually in up to my chin at times, I would sink through into a big hole and just my head would be poking out. After a while with no sign of a col, no foot-prints that may lead to it and with snow continuing to fall gently, I decided that I couldn't really justify going on. I climbed onto a rocky island and pulled on my water-proof top and bottoms; put on my hat and gloves and had a drink of water and a couple of cereal bars; I then swore two or three times. I didn't like to retreat but it seemed the only sensible option.

When I set off again after this brief rest I found myself not descending, but climbing. As I had been sitting on my rocky island I'd spotted a faint line across the hillside; it could have been the tracks of an animal, boot-prints or simply a snow-slide. I reached this after much hard work and found what looked like old boot-prints, which I followed until they faded out. Above was a small wall of snow, so I thought I should see what was round the other side, further minutes passed and there was more struggling and floundering. I then thought I should investigate what was round a rib of rock. After more cursing and swearing this was reached and at last, a thinning in the clouds revealed the long sought after col, not much above me, but away on the far side of a shallow gully.

It goes without saying that I was very relieved to reach the Col de l'Aup Martin, but my struggles were far from over. I now had to search out another col, hidden somewhere in the clouds. A compass bearing showed me the right direction but there was no sign of a path; the snow was icier on this side of the col and it was slippery rather than soft, but I persevered and the gods smiled on me. The clouds parted and I could see my col a short way away. After a few more anxious moments I reached the snow and shale on the Pas de la Cavale, at about 9,000ft. It was a splendid view down into the rough corrie below and I now knew that my efforts had not been in vain, the way was clear down to the refuge. At first I could run quickly down the firm snow but as I lost height the snow softened and I kept breaking through the icy crust, which soon skinned my shins. I joined a zigzag path which led steeply down to the stream; unfortunately the bridge had been washed away so I had an icy river crossing before I finally reached the Refuge du Pré de la Chaumette.

I hadn't been able to find out in advance if the refuge was open; it was still early in the season and I half expected to have to use the winter-room. I had therefore come prepared with food for my evening meal and breakfast if need be. Those who know me won't be surprised to learn that my preparations in this respect consisted of buying a large packet of chocolate biscuits when I passed through Vallouise earlier in the day. However, as I approached the refuge I was pleased to see that the shutters were open and indeed the guardian had just arrived to take up residence for the summer; I would eat properly after all. The hut is in a great situation, on a grassy meadow at the head of a pretty glen. A small group of marmots were gambolling about in the weak sunshine; two standing on their hind-legs playfully fighting each other.

I had been thinking of continuing on beyond the Refuge du Pré de la Chaumette; it was still early and my legs could have gone on for more, but my nerves were shattered having endured something of an epic. I couldn't face further unknown adventures on three high cols in quick succession, before I reached the next place to stop. Although I had crossed two high, snow covered cols safely this afternoon, as I was so ill equipped, poorly shod, alone and with no real prospect of anyone coming along, in poor visibility and with snow falling, it's fair to say that I was pushing my luck a bit.

Day 3 saw me off for an early start; a light drizzle was falling and the clouds were again clamped down around the tops. I headed north from the hut on a rocky footpath, up into a wild glen. A short way up the glen I turned off to start the big climb. Drizzle turned to snow as I climbed higher and all traces of the path vanished under a blanket of snow. There wasn't enough detail or clarity on the 1:50,000 map to pinpoint exactly where the col was and visibility had already dropped to around 20 yards. By seeking out both the easiest and the most natural line I found myself in a shallow gully which led comfortably to the crest of the ridge. After a cold night, and it still being early in the morning, the snow was in better condition than the day before and I romped up it effortlessly; a faded way-mark on an exposed rock confirmed that this was the Col de la Vallette.

14: Tour de l'Oisans - difficult conditions for running; was the snow late or was I too early?

The top couple of hundred metres down off the far side were rather unpleasant. On this western side the snow was much icier, and off the snow the ground was made up of frozen banks of shale. This frozen shale was really lethal, a fall on it would have been unstoppable and the razor-sharp surface would have stripped me to the bone. My worn running shoes were not much use on either the frozen snow or the shale, but I kept to the snow wherever possible, leaving a trail of blood across the snow, from my shale shredded finger-tips. After a while I was able to cut right onto an easy angled ramp of snow and this was just soft enough to allow me to jog down into the basin below; as I descended the clouds parted momentarily and I could see both where I had come from and more importantly where I was now headed. This was just across the far side of the corrie where a short easy climb over boulders and snow took me to the Col de Gouiran.

Perhaps because it was a little later in the day now, the snow down the far side was in ideal condition and it lay at an easily runnable angle. I ignored the path and kept on the snow all the way down to the corrie floor, dropping several hundred feet in what seemed like seconds. From here I regained the path, which now contoured round the head of the corrie before climbing steeply on shale again, back up into the clouds.

The col I was heading for faced directly south and the way was generally clear of snow, which meant easy route finding for once and this let me concentrate on my footing. I reached the Col de Vallonpierre just as the snow started to fall more heavily. I didn't pause on top but leapt down the far side anticipating a crisp surface to the snow. Instead I was soon in knee deep snow, which was very tiring and very cold. I couldn't see much of this new corrie but I came to a stream and, avoiding the snow bridges that might collapse, I followed the stream out. When I spotted a black rubber hose-pipe in the stream bed I knew the hut couldn't be far away. A few minutes later a small lake appeared and across on its far side stood the Refuge de Vallonpierre.

On leaving the small refuge I followed the rocky path down below the snow-line and into the valley. It was a delightful lush green area covered in flowers and flowering shrubs, with the occasional orange orchid to brighten the day. A good path led down into the main valley, and into La Chappelle en Valgaudemar, where I stopped for a big bowl of coffee. Now in warm sunshine at last I continued into Villar-Loubière, from where a steep footpath climbed up into a narrow valley which opened out into a wide green corrie. Unfortunately the earlier sunshine proved short-lived and I re-entered the clouds just as I reached the small hut, the Refuge des Souffles. I was pleased to see that I'd taken exactly one hour from the road, after already having had a hard morning, whereas the sign-post and guide-book suggested 2½ hours as the norm.

I stopped briefly at the hut to mix a poly-bag of *Gatorade* then continued on, now on a great path which traversed right round the corrie; in one or two places the path was a little exposed, the rain and swollen streams made crossing the rocks quite treacherous. The path then started climbing up towards the col, zigzagging easily up through the clouds. I reached what looked like a col; there were three small stone wind-breaks on the narrow pass but I couldn't see a route down the far side, I then realised that the route went up rather than down but I couldn't make out on the map where I was. I assumed that this was just a shoulder and followed the faint track which thankfully became more defined and waymarks appeared to show the way ahead.

I could see almost nothing of the ridge above and I soon lost the path again under a blanket of snow. With map and compass in hand I climbed on up the snow hoping to regain the path where it emerged from the far side, but instead I found just a faint ramp leading up the shale. After going along the ramp for a minute or two it didn't look very promising so I returned over the snow and tried the other direction. Again I followed a faint line in the shale and again the way ahead looked nothing like a sensible route. By this time it was snowing gently again and I was concerned to see that my tracks were already being covered. As my tracks were my line of retreat I descended a couple of hundred metres and had another look.

This time I was about 20 yards further to the left than the first time I had passed by and now I caught sight of a short section of path between the snow drifts. This proved that I was on course but I still couldn't work out where the col was. I was sure I must be very close but all I could see looked uninviting to say the least; rocky pinnacles and dripping buttresses. I decided to keep off the shale and instead set to work on the fairly steep, crisp snow. After several more anxious minutes I was very relieved to reach the Col de la Vaurze. The way down to the north was both steep and icy, soon though I was able to jog down the snow on a rough bearing and as the clouds thinned I picked up the line of the path on the right. Rejoining the path I was able to follow this round the hillside and then steeply down into the small village of le Désert.

After studying the map and making some quick calculations I decided to press on; the next col was only around 7,500ft and as the climb to it was from the south I hoped it would be free of snow. The route led up alongside the river into a narrow gorge, the way then steepened and climbed in tight zigzags into the cloud and drizzle. I couldn't see much of the way ahead but the way was clear on the ground and I reached the Col de Côte-Belle without incident, which was proving to be a rare thing on this tour. It had been another tough day and the legs felt the steep descent that led into a lush grassy, flower filled valley. A short jog along the track took me to the gîte at Valsenestre.

Day 4 saw no real change in the weather, it was again cloudy with drizzle in the air as I retraced my steps along the track before turning north up into the corrie. A good path led easily upwards, climbing steadily until it reached the foot of the head-wall. The next section of the route was the only part of the Tour to be marked on the map with crosses rather than a solid line, which indicated that it was hazardous, but after what I'd already been through on Days 2 and 3, I couldn't see how this could be much worse!

The final slope leading up to the col is more steep shale but here the snow came to my aid as it meant I could kick a reasonable foothold and this was far more secure than the shale. Route finding was simple too; I just had to go up, and up and up. On reaching the dismal Col de la Muzelle I could just make out the path some way below, but in between was steep snow. A ramp dropped down to the right and this let me lose height quickly, before turning left and running more easily down the snow to the rocks at the foot. From here I knew that the hard part was over; no more snow, no more shale, no more cols and no more climbing; it was downhill all the way to Bourg d'Oisans.

A path followed the stream down to the Lac de la Muzelle and the refuge just beyond. Marmots whistled and darted away as I ran over the grassy hillock and started the long descent on a good footpath which zigzagged down to cross the river. I followed the river for a while, passing flowering shrubs and tumbling waterfalls, down through the woods and into l'Alleau. More pleasant woodland led easily and gently down valley before coming out where the wide stony river-bed almost fills the floor of the valley. The way led on, first on a footpath then on rough tracks, through scrub and woodland to reach the road for the final couple of miles into Bourg d'Oisans.

It had been surprisingly hard; the run had given me a far tougher time than anticipated but I was feeling very pleased with myself for having completed the tour in 3½ days for the 125 miles and around 38,400ft of climbing, most of it in unusually tough conditions.

Unfortunately my smug feelings of satisfaction were short-lived. As I entered the car-park in Bourg d'Oisans it took a couple of seconds to register that the car-park was empty. My camper-van had been stolen and I was left with just what I stood up in plus the little that I had in my rucksack.

Guidebook: Tour of the Oisans   by Andrew Harper
              (Cicerone Press)

Map: Sheet 6   Écrins / Haut-Dauphiné
              (1:50,000   Didier et Richard)

(Due to the bad weather and late snow 1:25,000 maps would have been far better for crossing the cols in the south and west, the extra detail wasn't really needed on the sections to the north and east.)

Tour du Beaufortain

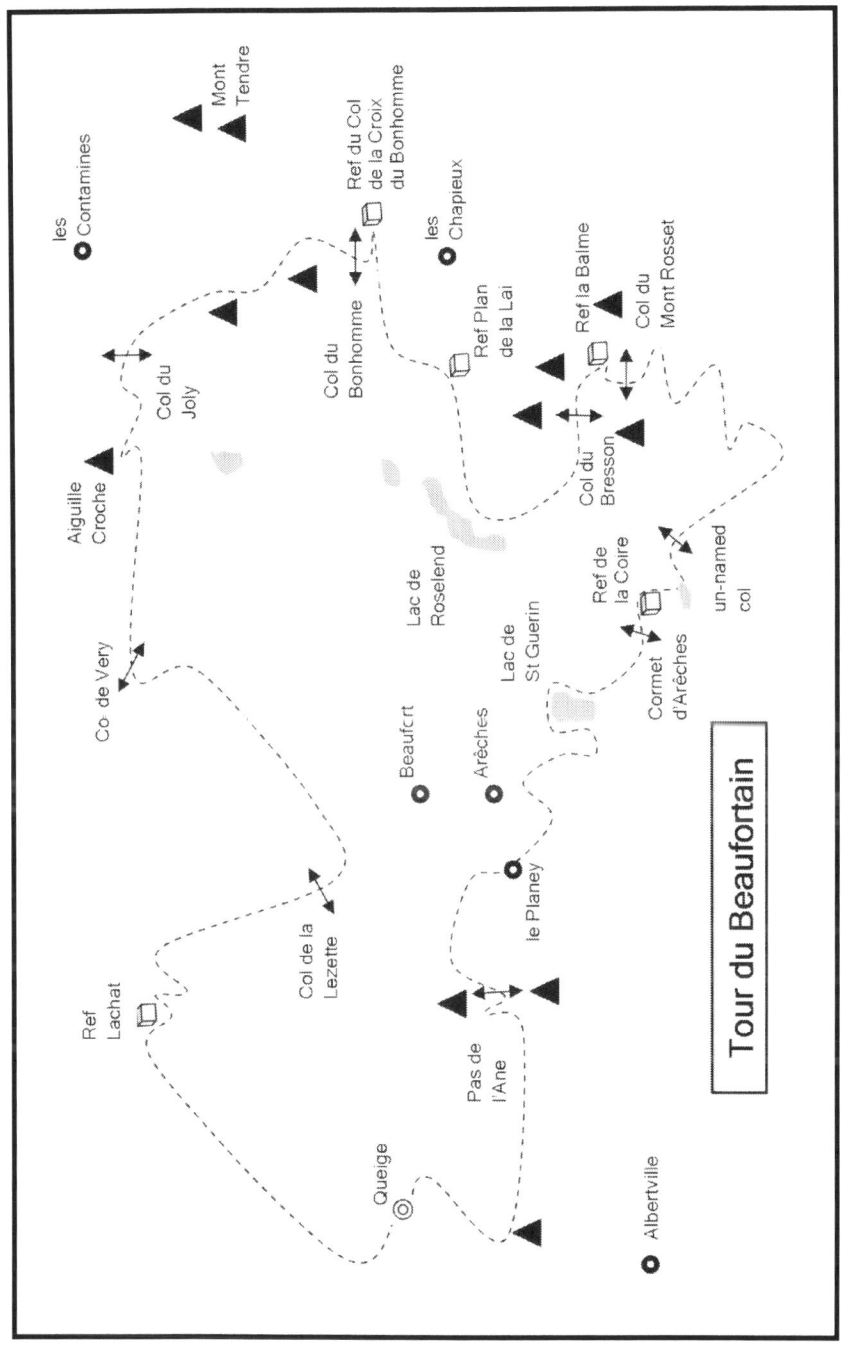

Tour du Beaufortain

A week later and I was reunited with my van, albeit minus a lot of expensive outdoor kit. I headed off for the Tour du Beaufortain, which is shown in a French guide-book as being a circular walk of six to eight days, which I thought I should be able to run in two.

I left Queige early, the '*Meteo*' having promised a warm and sunny weekend. It didn't take long to pass through the small village and start the climb through pastures and woodland. The path then climbed more steeply into forest, where it was pleasantly cool in the shade of the trees.

I jogged past an open bothy by a dry lake; the going was easy, the route well marked, and I was cruising nicely. As the sun rose higher the day warmed up and drew out the wonderful smell of the pines; there were a few squirrels about and prints in the mud showed that deer weren't far away. After passing some ski-tows by the Refuge de Lachat the route dropped down to cross the river before climbing up the far, wooded, hillside. The path here was grim; very wet, very muddy and covered in ankle-twisting tree roots. I was glad to cross the road and continue the climb on a forest track, which eventually brought me out onto a wide grassy saddle beneath more ski-tows.

From the Col de la Lezette I continued on along the land-rover track for a short way before joining a great little path that took me along a wooded ridge and slowly climbed through grassy alps that were filled with cows, all of which had bells round their necks. By now it was very hot and I finally found a small trickle of water which slowly filled my water-bottle. A short while later I reached the Col de Very.

A good path now led off along the ridge before dropping down to contour beneath the rocky crest which terminates in the Aiguille Croche. It was easy going until I neared a lone chalet, where cows had destroyed the path and left a mud-bath instead. After carefully negotiating this I climbed back onto solid ground and up a natural rocky staircase alongside a gushing stream. This led out onto the ridge beside more ski-tows, which form part of the Les Contamines ski area, and I dropped down into the corrie that I had skied three months earlier. After leaving the track a delightful footpath led around the hillside; although the wildflowers were beginning to look past their best, the flowering shrubs brightened the day. One rough section over a small rock-fall was soon passed; the route then led on up the valley.

At the head of the valley the path swung round across more rock-falls and joined the main Tour du Mont Blanc path. It was a busy place with several parties going in each direction and once amongst the crowds I switched to over-drive and stormed up the hill. There was less snow this time than when I had run the Tour du Mont Blanc the previous September and I was up at the Col du Bonhomme in no time.

From the col I set off across the snow, following the many footprints, and catching and passing several walkers struggling up the climb. The ridge continued to cross the rocky corrie on good firm snow and I was soon up at the Refuge du Col de la Croix du Bonhomme. I had planned on stopping here for the night but it was too early so I made do with a bowl of coffee and pressed on. From this large refuge I had a choice of routes, the more interesting being along the Crête des Gittes. The going was quite easy and usually kept to the very crest itself, it was certainly narrow but it would have been hard to fall off. A path then dropped down to the north side of the arête but the snow made this difficult and I preferred to stay on the crest which eventually ran down to the Col de la Sauce.

I ambled down the grassy hillside, cutting the corners off the track, until I came out by the road and the CAF Refuge du Plan de la Lai. Unfortunately the hut was full and while I was offered a bed in an out-house, the Guardian suggested that I might want to try a private gîte a little way up the track opposite. This 12 bed gîte was also full but I was told that I could have a mattress on the floor; not being fussy I said that would be fine.

Next morning it was already warm and sunny when I left before 8am to follow the track up and around the grassy hillside; after a short while the track narrowed to a footpath which gave easy running round into the cool shadow of the ridge. A strong smell from the vegetation had me puzzled for a while, after a few minutes I realised that it was aniseed and it smelt as though someone had dropped a crate of *Pernod*. As I continued round into the next valley the path climbed to meet a track then climbed more steeply up to a grassy saddle. From here the path took me up into a rocky corrie and shortly disappeared beneath thick snow. However, the route was well trodden and I could climb in the old footprints quickly and easily round a corner and up to the Col du Bresson. Looking into the corrie beyond I could see the Refuge de Presset on a wide ledge away to my left but my route was straight down the snow to the floor of the corrie.

The snow conditions made it frustrating; if I kicked my heels in gently they made no impression and I slipped. If I kicked down too hard I broke through the crust and sank in to my knees. Somewhere in between was a happy medium that I struggled to find. Eventually I reached the stream and followed this down the valley, gaining the company of two big shaggy dogs along the way. The dogs left me at the Refuge la Balme as I turned off to climb south, up alongside a stream towards the Col du Mont Rosset. It wasn't long before I was onto snow again and this time there were no tracks to help me; it seemed a long slog up to the col but I enjoyed an easy run down the far side to make up for it.

The path cut round the ridge amongst hundreds of tiny blue butterflies then I joined a track that looped steadily downwards. A rather overgrown path let me cut off one or two of the bends before dropping down into pine forest. As I dropped deeper into the forest the path became clearer but steeper and finally it led me out onto a forestry track, which again gave good running. It was oppressively hot in the forest with no breeze to stir the air and my water-bottle was long since empty. The red and yellow way-marks directed me down another steep footpath before cutting round into a side valley. Near a footbridge three tiny little deer trotted unconcernedly across the path in front of me. I crossed the river and climbed up to the road.

From here I started on a long climb; at first the track led steeply up through forest until I emerged by the river amongst crowds of picnickers. After a short stretch of tarmac I climbed a steep footpath; the tight zigzags gained height quickly alongside the stream, which led me to a delightful grassy bowl. It was then only a few hundred yards to the Lac de la Gouille, which was bone dry, and above this I was soon on an un-named grassy col. It didn't take long to drop down into the corrie beyond where the Refuge de la Coire tempted me in for a short coffee break.

After this rest there was an easy climb up to the busy pass, the Cormet d'Arêches, from where a footpath took off down the hillside giving pleasant running down to the south-eastern corner of the rectangular Lac de St.Guerin. The map showed the path as going round three sides of this rectangle before climbing away from the lakes south-western corner. Spotting the chance of a short-cut I felt sure that there must be a way along the southern end of the lake but of course I really should have learned my lesson by now. I found myself about 300ft above the level of the lake, above an over-hanging cliff with impenetrable forest above me. There was no alternative but to go back the way I had come and thereafter follow the proper route. This 'short-cut' wasted ten minutes and gave me the embarrassment of having to run past a family bar-b-que for the second time as I went back. Once on the correct path it didn't take long to run round, over the dam at the north end of the lake, and back down the far side.

Another big climb took off from the lakeside; a path led steeply up the open hillside, then into forest, before heading round to cross a shoulder to the small ski area above Arêches. An equally steep forest path then dropped down to the village of le Planey far below. Here I ordered a *Coke* and a bowl of ice-cream to set me up for the final climb, some 4,000ft up to the last col of the route. Leaving le Planey a road took me along to the hamlet of la Dray from where a steep footpath climbed through the meadows to a farm on the saddle above. After this it was good going, through forest and across a heath-like area, before heading round into the corrie. The sky was now clouding over and I feared that there may be a sting in the tail, as the col was potentially difficult. The path however was a fitting climax to a great route as it gave a superb run round into the corrie, it then zigzagged up beside bands of low cliffs and only in the upper corrie did I come onto snow. Thankfully I could just see what I took to be a sign-post on the ridge above; a short scramble up some boulders, then a quick climb up the snow and I was on the ridge.

From the col, the Pas de l'Ane, the immediate way ahead was hard to follow due to the low cloud and complex terrain. First I had to swing right, round the rocky hillside, before heading back left to climb a short distance onto the start of a long ridge. The undulating ridge was narrow in places and crossed five or six small tops. It was very like Scotland and I spent the next half-hour trying to think where it reminded me of, in the end I settled for the South Cluanie Ridge in Glen Shiel.

However, this lovely stretch was just postponing the worst part of the Tour, for I finally had to quit the ridge and face a descent of some 6,000ft. The top part was ok; on an interesting path I entered thick forest which seemed to go on forever. At last though I passed under a ski-tow and came to some lonely chalets. After a brief encounter with a vicious dog I had to duck under several electric fences, one of which gave me a nasty shock; however I could now see Queige across on the other side of the valley. A quarter of an hour later I crossed the river and jogged slowly up the road to end a long day, made a lot harder by the heat.

The Tour du Beaufortain is a great route with a little bit of everything thrown in; it is about 70 miles with around 23,000ft of climbing.

Guidebook: None in English, there is a French guide available

Maps: Sheet 3532OT Massif du Beaufortain (1:25,000 IGN)
      Sheet 8 Massifs du Mont Blanc / Beaufortain (1:50,000 Didier et Richard)

Long Runs in Europe

Alpine Pass Route

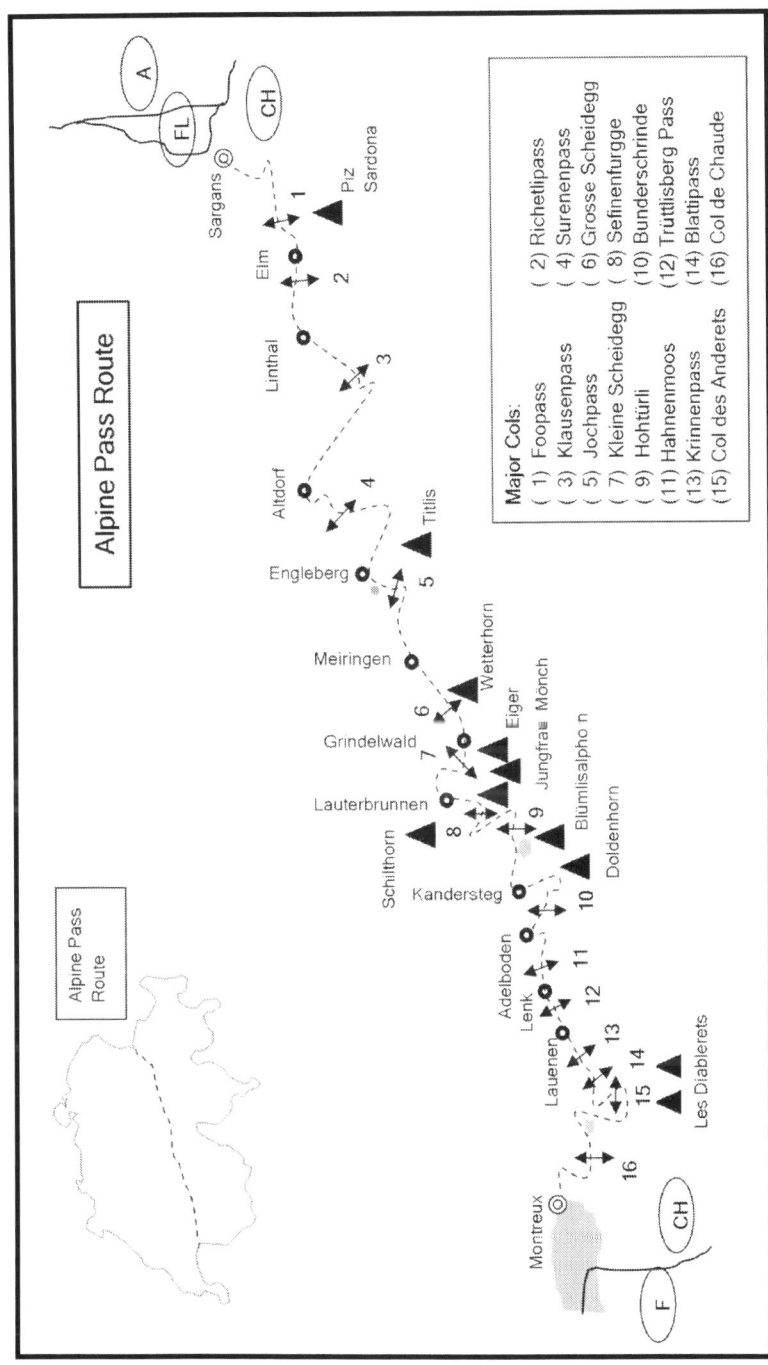

Alpine Pass Route

I'd been looking forward to this run which starts at Sargans, a small town on the border between Switzerland and Liechtenstein, and takes you over sixteen high passes on a journey of some 200 miles with almost 59,000ft of climbing, before finishing in Montreux on the shores of Lac Leman near the Swiss/French border.

Unfortunately after two stormy days I woke to the sound of more rain hammering on the roof of the van but I couldn't afford to delay the run, which I thought would take five or six days, as I had the Sierre-Zinal race coming up and I wanted to make sure I had a few days between the two to rest and recover.

From Sargans railway station I ran slowly through the streets, crossed under a motorway and on to the neighbouring village of Mels. From here I started climbing; a track led up to the hamlet of St.Martin then past a small vineyard from where a footpath led off into the forest. It was warm work climbing in full water-proofs but it was far too wet to take them off. The roar of the river could be heard far below as I splashed along a good footpath and headed up into the valley, the Weisstannental. I soon dropped down through pastures to meet the road which led up to Weisstannen. A mix of track and footpath then continued up the valley to the farm of Untersass at the head of the glen.

From here a path took off across the moraines to climb steeply up into the clouds alongside massive waterfalls. After a while the angle eased as the footpath followed the contour line above the stream, only to start climbing again through a muddy morass around the cattle byre and farm at Fooalp. Above the farm the path led up into a grassy corrie where there was still quite a good show of alpine flowers and the way was clear to the col ahead. I soon found myself on a misty Foopass where the rain was turning to sleet. Dropping swiftly down to the west I passed a couple of lonely farms before gaining a track which dropped down at a comfortable angle through pastures and forests to bring me, after some time, to the small village of Elm. Elm has a somewhat tragic past; in 1881 after days of heavy rain, a mountain that the villagers had been mining for years, suddenly peeled away and collapsed onto the village killing over 100 people. Today it's all green pastures or forest and it's hard to see any sign of where the landslide happened.

From Elm I continued on up the Sernftal; a pleasant track led through pastures which eventually brought me out onto a military road, which continued on up to the head of the valley. I lost the correct route among a maze of paths and ended up on the wrong side of the valley in a military training area, which was littered with shell cases and shrapnel from mines or grenades. In the low cloud it was difficult to work out where I was or where I should have been, however I eventually found the path I was after and climbed the hillside, up into a high grassy corrie filled with sheep and cows. Every animal seemed to be wearing a bell and making a lot of noise. A short distance below the col I came across a bird using the broken wing ploy to try to lure me away from its young, I've seen grouse and ptarmigan do this in Scotland, but I couldn't identify this bird. A couple of minutes later I was on the grassy col of the Richetlipass.

The descent from the western side of the pass was steep and slippery but after a while the path followed the top of an old moraine bank which gave easier running and took me down to the river. It was a long descent from here, first on tracks, then tarmac and back onto forest tracks again, to emerge in the main valley at Matt and moments later Linthal, where I found a cheap Gasthof for the night. It was still raining!

Day 2 and I left before 8am, again dressed in full waterproofs against the unrelenting rain. After a short stretch of road I turned off onto a footpath which climbed steeply through the forest, where I saw a couple of chamois as they bounded away across a clearing. The route now followed a quiet road for several kilometres as it climbed up into the valley of Urner Boden; the road gave faster going than the wet footpaths, and I enjoyed the pretty valley despite the rain. There was fresh snow on the ridges on both sides of the valley which was worrying as it wasn't all that far above me.

Shortly after the village of Urnerboden I was able to take a narrow footpath which cut the corners off the road-climb to the Klausenpass. I took the opportunity to stop and warm up with a coffee and a sticky bun at the café on the col, then it was out into the mist and rain again to search for another wet and boggy footpath. This took me down the western side of the pass to the farm at Ulmer Balm and from here a faint path led across the meadows to a gate and a well engineered path which dropped steeply down beneath towering cliffs. Easy running then led to the beautiful little hamlet of Äsch, which is set amongst woods, waterfalls and green pastures. An easy angled track continued down the valley and out onto the road at Unterschächen. Unfortunately the next ten kilometres were all on the road, following the river down into Altdorf. A statue in the main square is supposed to mark the spot where William Tell shot the apple from his son's head.

From the square I headed for Attinghausen where a footpath started beside the cable-car station. It was an ancient, paved path, sunk down between steep fields. The stiff climb warmed me up again and I saw more chamois in the forest on the long climb up to the top cable-car station of Brüsti. Low cloud and drizzle meant the distant views were disappointing, but the next stretch was interesting. A path led along the crest of the ridge, where cables were fixed for aid, before climbing up into grassy meadows and around into a high rocky corrie. The final signpost below the pass was at a spot called 'Langschnee', which was apt as from here to the pass the path was hidden by late lying snow. The surface of the snow was covered in grit, stones and vegetation, and by using these to run on I could climb it quite easily without slipping. A final short scramble up steep shale took me to the narrow Surenenpass.

The descent on a well drained path meant that I could have a good run down without too much risk of hurting myself, it even stopped raining and the sun tried to come out, which gave me some hope for the rest of the run. It was a long, long descent past a couple of farms and a little chapel, down to the valley floor. A footpath on the far side of the river looked more inviting than the stony track I was on, so I crossed over and saw a sign that read '1hr 30 mins to Engleberg'. After a good 15 minutes of easy running I passed another sign which read '1hr 20 mins to Engleberg'. As a general rule I halve the times given in guide-books or on signposts, so I would have expected the second sign to have read just 1 hour to go. Towards the end of a long hard day little things like this assume a far greater importance and I was not amused. Eventually though I reached the camp-site on the outskirts of Engleberg and a couple of minutes later I was in the centre eating carrot-cake and drinking *Coke*. I asked in the shop if they knew of somewhere inexpensive to stay and I was soon sorted out for the night. The guide-book breaks the route down into 15 daily stages, of which I had covered five in two days; the wet weather had made me slower than anticipated, so I settled on trying to finish in six days. It was raining again when I went to bed that night.

Day 3 saw a great start to the day; it was warm and sunny and I put in a good fast climb through the forest and out beneath the gondola lift. At the top of the steep section the mountain fell back to reveal an amazing grassy bowl with the idyllic Trübsee nestling in the bottom. A good path led on up the hill beneath a chair-lift, past whistling marmots and alpine flowers to the Jochpass from where there were stunning views to the snowy Titlis in the east.

15: Trübsee, above Engleberg

After a quick *Coke* stop, good running led down amongst more marmots and cows to the Engstlensee and then on to the road-end at Engstlenalp. From the farms here a superb balcony path led round the hillside above the Gental before finally starting the long descent to Reuti, then more steeply down through forest to Meiringen. It didn't take long to pass through the village, cross the river and reach Willigen, from where a steep footpath led up through forest until eventually I was forced onto the road which led for some way up the Reichenbach valley.

The weather was staying hot and sunny so I was glad to stop for a couple of iced-teas on the long climb, before a footpath took off again, leaving the road for the cool of the forest. The broad grassy saddle of Grosse Scheidegg could be seen not too far ahead, with the massive Wetterhorn towering above on its left. The path continued to climb to the col and when I reached Grosse Scheidegg I was to find it a very busy spot; the col was teeming with walkers, cyclists and Post-buses. From here I could look across to my days-end at Alpiglen, just below the Kleine Scheidegg.

On the run down from Grosse Scheidegg I kept looking across to Kleine Scheidegg on the far side of the valley, with the Eiger looming above it; the sky was almost cloud-free, the only clouds were those on the face of the Eiger itself. It was a long and dusty descent into Grindelwald, which appeared to be over-flowing with tourists, so I was glad to escape quickly. I dropped down to cross the river at Grund before starting the last climb of the day. An incredibly steep tarmac path climbed between the fields and I was finding it hard work but the end was near. The tarmac gave way to an easier angled footpath which crossed the railway and climbed up through forest to Alpiglen. Here beneath the huge north face of the Eiger I called a halt for the day. The matratzenlager at the hotel was a cheap place to stay and I turned in that night after a good meal hoping that the fine weather would hold.

Day 4 and what a fantastic start! I ate breakfast on the terrace beneath the Eiger, under a perfect blue sky. It didn't take long to make the short climb to the broad grassy col of Kleine Scheidegg; an untidy place with a railway coming up from each side and a third line running up through the Eiger to the Jungfraujoch. It was still early and hardly anyone else was around. The peaks and glaciers of that famous trio; the Jungfrau, the Monch and the Eiger looked superb from the pass and I ran easily down the track beneath them to Wengenalp and then down alongside the railway to Wengen, a delightful little village some way up the eastern side of the Lauterbrunnental.

A short steep descent through the trees took me into Lauterbrunnen on the floor of the valley where a bakery provided my usual running diet of *Coke* and a sticky bun. Little did I know then that I would be back just a few weeks later, racing in the *Jungfrau Marathon;* the race starts at Interlaken, runs a flat loop between the lakes then climbs up through Lauterbrunnen to Wengen and on up to the finish at Kleine Scheidegg. It's a full distance marathon with 6,000ft of climbing, most of which comes in the last ten miles or so, so it's a pretty tough race, my time was 3hrs 31mins.

The Lauterbrunnen valley is narrow and lined with steep cliffs on either side, so it meant a long climb out. A good footpath climbed steeply up through forest, past waterfalls and open glades to finally come out by the railway which I followed into Mürren. This is another lovely little village; there are no cars as it is served by the railway and a cable-car.

A big climb led on from here, up through steep pastures and meadows with fine views back to the Eiger, the Monch and the Jungfrau. It was a beautiful morning and there were dozens of people out walking in what is a superb area. After crossing a stream the path led up a rocky staircase to reach a huge open corrie, the path then gave easy running around the basin to the Rotstockhütte. The col remained hidden from view behind a rocky crest; the path continued easily up into the upper corrie and the col came into sight at last, a final steep wall of shale led up to it. It was a tricky final climb to reach the Sefinenfurgge, where I found several people enjoying the view from the narrow, shattered ridge. I chatted briefly with a lovely American girl, then I was on my way again. Her parting comment was 'With a *Coke* and a smile and he's gone'. The *Coke* was a small bottle of rather warm *Coke* that I'd carried up with me and downed in one. The smile was because I'd just seen her tattoo, which was in a place where not many people would usually see it!

The descent of the first few hundred metres from the col was unexpected; there was a long ladder of steps and a hand-rail, leading down a very steep bank of shale. Rain had washed shale over the rungs of the steps, nearly covering them and making them almost useless. It was dangerous terrain and I was glad not to be tackling it in the wet. At last I was down onto more solid ground and following a good path alongside a stream and into a grassy valley. Once over the river I started on another long climb, up through forests and pastures to a small farm. I stopped to ask for some milk, which was straight from the cow and was delicious; refreshed I ran on and left the farmer to his cheese making.

Above the farm the path headed across pastures then started a very steep ascent up banks of shale and bare earth. It was very hot work on the second 5,000ft plus climb of the day but at last the angle eased and the path zigzagged up black shale to a rocky ridge. On the far side of the ridge the path ran along easily enough but in a somewhat exposed situation. I caught up with a party here; a couple of them were obviously not very happy about the drop to the left, but the path itself was level and it would have been very careless to fall off. It took a while for me to over-take everyone safely as we made the final climb to the pass, sometimes on snow and sometimes on loose shale. Arriving on the Hohtürli, at around 9,100ft I was on the highest point of the Alpine Pass Route and it made all the hard work to reach it worthwhile.

"What an excellent thing it is to stand on a mountain conscious that your muscles have carried you thither, without the aid of any mechanical contrivance; to feel superlatively fit; to be clear of eye and head and strong of arm and leg; to breathe deep breaths of keen cold air and in each breath discern the power and the beauty of the universe; to know a contentment untrammelled by any anxiety; and a peace of mind and spirit which is true happiness." (FS Smythe)

Just above the rocky col sits the Blümlisalphütte; a litre of ice-tea helped me recover from the climb and prepare for the long descent to Kandersteg. Immediately below the col the path led down steep shale but I soon came onto good ground and it gave me a superb run down, looking across to the Blümlisalp Glacier which tumbles down into the valley.

The route was becoming better and better. The descent from the Hohtürli was wonderful as the path continued along the top of a moraine bank before dropping down into a grassy corrie; then it was down to the Oeschinensee, a beautiful little lake hemmed in on three sides by steep cliffs. Short stretches of cable helped on the steep descent, the path then ran off along the northern side of the lake. Overhanging cliffs towered above the path, which eventually dropped down through forest to Kandersteg. The town was very busy and it was only on the fourth try that I found somewhere to stay. This had been a long hard day with the crossing of two tough passes, but it was perhaps the best day of any of the long ones so far.

Day 5 dawned wet and windy but I was planning on it being a relatively short one; I was looking forward to an easy day and an early finish in readiness for a long sixth and final day. From Kandersteg I headed south up the valley on a footpath beside the river as far as the International Scout Centre, where the path led off across the meadows. The climbing then started in earnest, gaining height rapidly through the wet undergrowth and into dripping forest. A track led up alongside the Alpbach until a footpath turned off to climb in tight zigzags up to a narrow break in the cliffs above. It was a miserable morning as I climbed up through the cliffs. The angle of the path then eased a little as I headed for a lonely chalet. From here I climbed into the rain again on a wet path that took me up into a grassy corrie; the col, a narrow notch on the ridge, now came into view as the path led easily across a scree slope and up to the Bunderchrinde.

The descent was not much fun as I ran across wet scree, followed by wet and boggy pastures; the path now resembled a stream-bed and it was slow going. At last I came out onto a solid road which gave easy running for a while, down to cross the river below Adelboden. The road climbed a short way before a track led up beside the river through forest on a long climb, following the cables for a gondola lift. After some time I came out of the forest at the ski-station of Geilsbuel; here I stopped for a coffee and some cake in an effort to warm up. The stop, even though it was just a short one, was a mistake as when I came out into the weather again I just felt very cold and wet and it took me ages to warm up and start jogging again. The climb continued on a private road, with one or two short-cuts to avoid the longest loops. At last though I could just make out the Hahnenmoos Pass through the mist and it didn't take long to reach the grassy saddle. A small group of model plane enthusiasts were huddled in the shelter of the hotel with their radio-controlled planes, but this certainly wasn't flying weather.

From the pass it was another long rough descent to reach the road at Büelberg; the descent continued sometimes on steep footpaths, sometimes on roads, down to the pretty village of Lenk. The next climb started immediately; way-marks led up between two wooden chalets on a path of stones set into the steep meadows, before heading into forest and climbing on a muddy footpath to emerge at an old inn. I headed up an even muddier path, almost losing my shoes several times. It was very, very wet and clinging, which made for slow going. In good conditions the route would have been fine, but today, with no views it was just an endless slog, with cold wet feet, trying to avoid the worst of the puddles. In short, it was grim! The higher I climbed the worse it became; cows now added to the mess and I tried to work out just how far away the col was. The terrain was surprisingly complex, grassy knolls and valleys, and I just blindly struggled on up the path, which was now a stream, a couple of inches deep in muddy water. At last I reached the Trüttlisberg Pass, which is probably very scenic most of the time, but I was freezing cold, soaking wet and covered in mud up to my knees. Just then, if someone had offered me a sun, sea and sangria holiday in Spain I might just have said yes!

The descent was very difficult, simply because of all the rain running down the steep muddy paths and it took me a long time to reach 'dry land', but the road in looping down doubled the distance, so I again took to the footpaths, brushing through the cold wet undergrowth to finally reach the small village of Lauenen. My short, easy day had turned into one of the hardest and I hoped that the weather would be kinder in the morning, although when I took a last look out before bed it didn't look too promising.

Thankfully I was able to wash and dry all my running kit over-night and Day 6 started overcast, but dry. The day began with a short climb, following way-marks across the meadows and up through forest to cross the wooded Krinnen Pass. The descent didn't take long, down footpaths and short stretches of road into Gsteig. From here a steep path led up the opposite side of the valley, through woodland and pastures, past isolated farms and on muddy tracks to reach the Blattipass without too much hard work. I had a pleasant run down the far side, just a short descent over-looking the Arnensee; an easy run then led round the open corrie to a grassy col with a small tarn. From here the path continued round the corrie to a high farm, where I stopped for a couple of glasses of fresh milk. After this brief rest I followed the track round to the next col, the Col des Andérets. A short way down to the west brought me to the restaurant and ski-tows of La Marnéche, from where I picked up a good contouring path which led easily, but muddily, along the northern side of the valley. Looking across to the far side of the valley I could see the long rock and ice ridge of Les Diablerets.

The miles passed quickly and reasonably effortlessly as I contoured along the ridge, before coming out onto a minor road which slowly started to lose height. A mix of footpath and track then led down to the road at the Col des Mosses. After a quick *Coke* stop I continued north along the road for a short way then cut through the camp-site to find a path across the fields. From here the route dropped down a narrow gorge on a private road which led to the eastern end of a reservoir, the Lac d'Hongrin. The lakeside was busy with fishermen as I ran slowly along the road to an impressive dam. A tunnel took me down to the old road and down a green and pleasant valley to cross the river at its foot; from here I was ready to start the final climb of the route.

It was a steep start, up grassy meadows then into forest. After emerging into the open again the way led up through deep mud, round a farm, then back into the woods. Climbing steadily the way became more open and a track led me round to the farm of Alp Chaude; from here the route led easily round and up to the Col de Chaude in just a few minutes.

From this final pass I now had my first view of journeys end as Lac Leman lay glinting in the sunlight some 5,000ft below. After a short distance on the road a footpath dropped steeply down the hillside and disappeared into the trees. When I reached the road again I stayed high and ran on a contouring line round the hillside.

It seemed a long run round until I finally reached Caux, and it was from here that the descent began in earnest, down steep tarmac paths, which were agony on the feet and ankles and pain shot up my shins at every step. On reaching Glion the route continued through the trees down a flight of steps; going down 1,000ft of concrete steps was tough at the end of a long day, but was preferable to following the road. After what seemed like an eternity I passed under the motorway and a few minutes later I was in Montreux. I ran past the funicular station and along the road to Montreux Station to end a brilliant route.

The Alpine Pass Route certainly lived up to my expectations; it was interesting from end to end but the best was undoubtedly the two days between Engleberg and Kandersteg. Life is easy along the route as there is good availability of accommodation and there are plenty of chances to buy food and drink along the way. If you only have the time or inclination to do one High Level Route, this should be the one, it's fantastic!

Guidebook: Alpine Pass Route by Kev Reynolds
             (Cicerone Press)

Maps: Sheet 237   Walenstadt
             Sheet 247   Sardona
             Sheet 246   Klausenpass
             Sheet 245   Stans
             Sheet 255   Sustenpass
             Sheet 5004   Berner Oberland
             Sheet 5009   Gstaad - Adelboden
             Sheet 262   Rochers de Naye
             (1:50,000 Landeskarte der Schweiz)

Alta Via 1

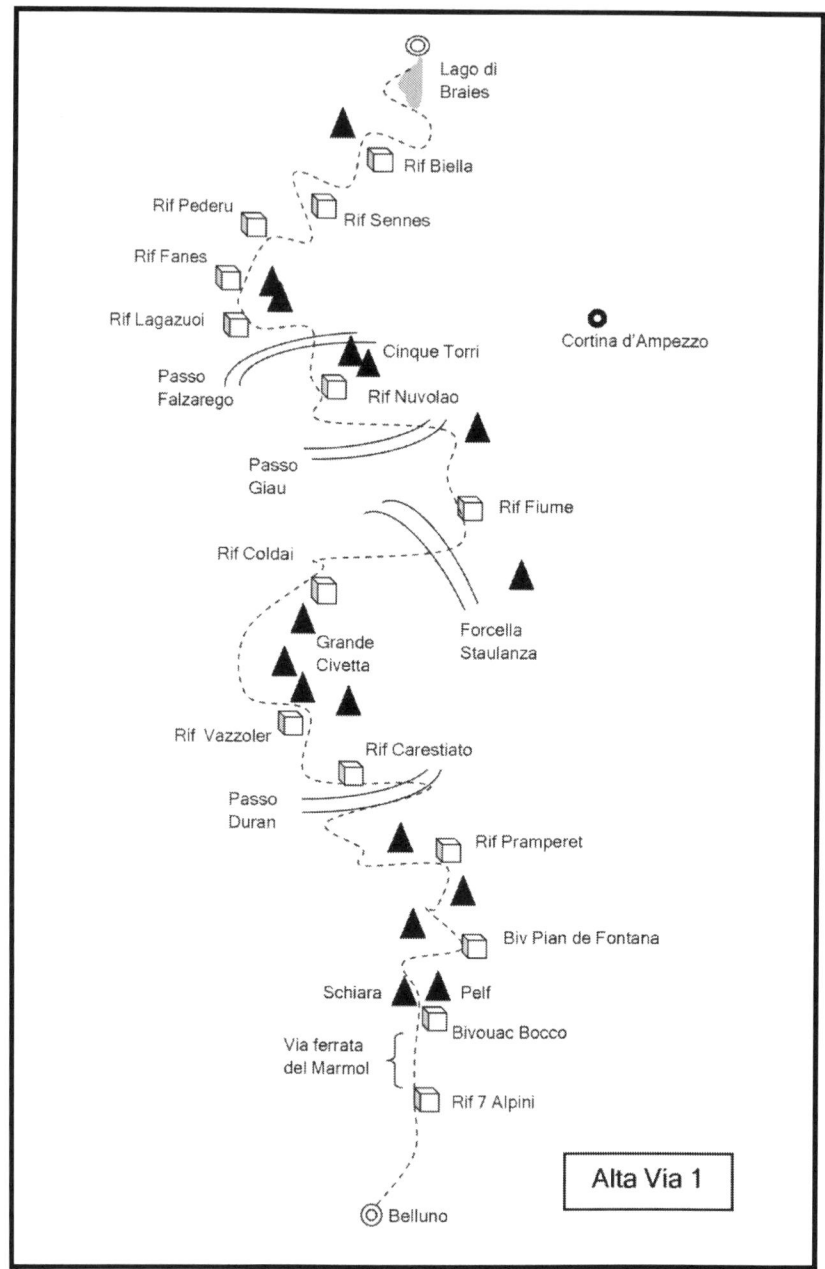

Dolomites High Level Route – Alta Via 1

Although only a short route of about 78 miles, I was undecided how long this one would take to run. I expected it to be very rough underfoot with some steep, aided, climbs and descents, which would certainly slow me down. The guide-book said to allow ten days, so I thought I should be able to do it inside three days, and if I could finish earlier that would leave time on the last day to return by bus to the start point.

The run started at the road-end at a popular beauty spot, Lago di Braies. It was a beautiful morning when I set off and hardly anyone else was around. It only took minutes to run along the undulating path on the west side of the lake; then the hard work started as the path climbed away from the lake, up through dwarf firs and birch trees. It was a stony path but it climbed reasonably easily until I turned off and took a direct route up a loose gully before re-joining the main path, which led on up through the trees to emerge beneath a long cliff. From here the path continued across scree, up a section protected by cable, to arrive on a low col.

A barren valley below the curious rock-strata of Monte Muro gave a brief respite from climbing; then it was upwards again, through a boulder choked gully to reach the col, Porta Sora L'Forn. Passing the Rifugio Biella I dropped down and joined a rough vehicle track which gave superb running around the side of the valley and a short while later I arrived at the Rifugio Sennes, which is set alongside a marshy lake and two or three old farm buildings.

The track continued to descend gradually and I now had to put up with taxis regularly roaring past in a cloud of dust. I couldn't believe it when I reached the Pederu Refuge at the bottom of the valley; it's at the road-end and car-park, and is where the taxis start from; there was a queue of almost 200 people waiting for a ride up, either to the Rifugio Sennes, or the way I was now heading, up to the Rifugio Fanes. After a quick stop at the hut for a *Coke* I set off, initially on a land-rover track, then on a narrow footpath away to the right. This avoided both being run down by taxis and being choked by their dust. The Rifugio Fanes is at the end of the dirt road, where walkers have to walk the rest of the way up the hill; the hut's wooden balcony is decorated with pairs of old wooden skis and some 1st World War shell cases that were recovered from nearby.

Still climbing from the refuge I soon reached the small Lago di Limo and shortly after this the track faded to a pleasant footpath which gave great running over grassy pastures taking me to the Col Loggia. The majority of people continued down into the valley from here, but ahead one couldn't fail to be impressed by the deep slash in the near vertical mountain wall. This narrow col is the Forcella del Lago and the path to it gave reasonably easy running before a final short scramble up through boulders to the pass itself. It was a fantastic situation and the view down the far side was interesting to say the least. The descent was on very loose, very steep ground and neither studs nor boots would give any grip in it. The shrieks of a party descending lower down in the narrow gully echoed up between the steep walls. However, the worst was soon over and the path swung away, passing above the picturesque and very popular Lago di Lagazuoi, to contour the scree before heading up through more boulders to another col, just below the Rifugio Lagazuoi.

Rather than a day in the hills it felt more like a day at the beach; walking over pebbles in bright sunshine, past topless sunbathers, with the over-powering smell of sun-tan lotion in the air. It was particularly hard to imagine that this area saw so such fighting between the Austrians and the Italians in the 1st World War, but the evidence is still there from the man-made caves and tunnels; ruined buildings and trenches; rusting shells and old leather boot soles.

Easy running now led round to the Val Travenanzes, where a marmot playing with its two young in the sun gave me an excuse to stop for a brief rest. Then it was on again, round to the Forcella Col dei Bos. From the col further good running led down on track and footpath to the road. This relief was short-lived as another hot climb started immediately; a good footpath climbed through the trees, out beneath the cliffs of Monte Averau and up to a grassy saddle. It was well worth making the short detour to the Rifugio Scoiattoli for a couple of glasses of iced-tea.

The impressive rocky towers of the Cinque Torri rose from the screes just a short distance away. A further short climb took me up to a rocky crest which soon led to the Nuvolao Refuge. Unfortunately the afternoon now clouded over, obscuring the high peaks and the anticipated views were disappointing. The fun continued however as the descent from the ridge was on a protected scramble, before continuing down another steep, loose gully to finally come out among grassy pastures at a road col, the Passo Giau.

Renewed energy came from somewhere and after crossing the road I went well, climbing a short way to a col and traversing round the valley before climbing a rough path to the Forcella Giau. There was only a short descent from the col before the path led round beneath towering cliffs and across cow filled pastures; this gave easier running than I'd expected, so I made good time round to the next col, the Forcella da Lago. The path continued through scree beneath Becco di Mezzodi to a low col, from where an easy run down a grassy footpath took me to a cattle byre over-shadowed by La Rocchetta. Delightful running in the late afternoon sunshine, through pastures and forest then brought me to the CAI Rifugio Citta di Fiume. Thankfully they could just squeeze me in and I was found a bed in the cellar. A huge meal and a German sing-song ended a great day, which was spoiled only by the poor quality of the Italian maps; after just one days use it was already falling apart at the seams and being so poorly drawn it was hardly worth using anyway.

Day 2 saw me away fairly early on another beautiful morning; it was an easy start, gently downhill through forest to a road col, Forcella Staulanza. After a short run down the road I turned off onto a dirt track. This gave pleasant running, undulating along in the cool of the forest, over a stream, then climbing through a herd of goats up alongside ski-tows to the small ski centre on the Col di Baldi. Poor way-marking and a profusion of paths made life difficult as I dropped down to a farm building before climbing steeply under an already boiling sun to the superbly sited Rifugio Coldai.

The map was useless here and it was only when I read the sign above the refuge door that I was convinced I was in the right place. From behind the hut another rough path climbed up a short gully to the Forcella Coldai. From the col I dropped easily down to the small Lago do Coldai, which nestles beneath the towering cliffs of the Grande Civetta. For the next few miles the narrow path took me along beneath these cliffs, over boulders, scree and some patches of semi-permanent snow, lying as it does in almost perpetual shadow. The rough track led easily round beneath a small hanging glacier, over a shallow col then down through woodlands and meadows before a short climb took me to the Col de Camp.

From the col a good path led round the head of the wild corrie to finally drop down through the trees to the Rifugio

Vazzoler. Two ice-teas revived me and I was soon on my way again, down a dusty land-rover track leading round the next valley. When the angle of descent steepened I took to a rough footpath which climbed up through the trees and headed round beneath the Moiazza Group. There were amazing views back to the Vazzoler hut with the towers and pinnacles of the ridge looming above it.

From the next wooded col I continued on, still on a traverse over scree beneath huge cliffs; it was warm work to gain the next col, the Forcella del Camp. The eastern side was forested and the path more or less contoured round under the cliffs to give easy running along to a forested spur on which stands the Rifugio Carestiato. I stopped briefly to fill my water-bottle then it was on again, down a steep path, which led to a track, the track in turn led through forest and pastures down to a road col, Passo Duran.

After a quick coffee I set to work on the next hard section, starting with a short run down the road to pick up the track by a bridge over the river. It didn't take long to climb through the trees to a low col but the next hour or so was pretty tough; a rough path crossed scree and countless boulder fields, all the time under a cloudless sky, with the hot sun being reflected back off the pale rocks.

The paths were much less crowded than on Day 1 and the chances of finding liquid were few and far between, at last though I came to a couple of old buildings, one of which is an open bothy, and outside was a trough which very slowly dribbled enough water to refill my bottle. Only a few hundred feet remained to be climbed, on a good path through low scrub to a ridge, then easily round the far side to the Forcella Moschesin, a grassy saddle. After a short climb to the east the path ran on below the ridge and led round to the meadows of Pra della Vedova. Another couple of hundred yards saw me at the Rifugio Pramperet.

It was still fairly early but I understood that other than a couple of small, un-wardened bivouac huts there were no further refuges until after the Schiara. The guide-book said the hut had 20-25 beds and this being peak season I was worried it might be full, in which case I might have to make do with one of the bivouac huts, which wouldn't have been the end of the world, but it would have meant a somewhat cold, hungry and uncomfortable night. As it was the Rifugio Pramperet had been extended to provide 45 beds and whilst it was busy they found room for me.

On the third and final day I was away early on another beautiful sunny morning, initially to climb the short distance back up to the meadows of Pra della Vedova before following a good footpath round the head of Val Pramperet, passing several small 1st World War caves that were cunningly hidden in the hillside. It was a rough climb over scree and boulders to the Portela Piazedel. From this rocky col the view ahead was to another wild, lonely corrie and I climbed on, up a grassier ridge beneath the towering Cima di Citta. A chamois stamped it's foot at me in protest before cantering off to safety. Meanwhile I continued on up to the Forcella Sud del Van de Citta.

Another great view opened up before me and I could now see, some 5 miles away, the Forcella del Marmol, the last climb of the route; from that col it would be almost all downhill to the finish in Belluno. To reach the col though first meant a descent of some 3,000ft, down into a beautiful corrie, then through a narrow gap to drop more steeply down to the bivouac hut at Pian de Fontana. Since my map and guide-book had been published one of the other buildings next to the Renzo del Mas hut had been converted to a small refuge so I would have been ok to continue further on Day 2 after all. As it was I stopped briefly for a drink at the trough before continuing the descent.

After only a few minutes I turned off and started climbing on a narrow path which zigzagged up the headwall of the valley, through open woodland, to reach the Forcella la Varetta. It was good, easy running from this grassy saddle, undulating round to the head of the next valley to reach a path junction amongst the trees. This would be the way down for anyone not wanting to make the via-ferrata descent off Schiara. I continued on along a very overgrown path until I finally climbed out of the trees near a ruined cattle shelter. Now on better, open ground the climb continued to a saddle from where I could study the final approach to the Forcella del Marmol.

The narrow col between the rocky bulk of Pelf and Schiara was obvious but how to reach it was less clear. The path had to wind this way and that, over scree and rocky slabs, which gave an easy scramble, until at last I reached the pass. Looking back to the north gave great views of the way I had come, whilst to the south all I could see was a narrow slit of a gully between sheer walls of rock. To descend the gully would clearly have been suicidal. The route actually climbed up the right-hand wall for a short way on an easy but exposed scramble, I then carefully followed the splashes of paint which led me round to the south face of Schiara and down a short way to reach the bivouac shelter Sandro Bocco. This is a neat little nine man shelter, with bunks that fold down from the metal walls of the hut.

The shelter marks the top of the Via Ferrata del Marmol, a great route down about 2,000ft of what seems like near vertical rock. I had a brief stop at the shelter to put on my harness with two long slings, each with a large karabiner attached for clipping onto cables and ladders.

Initially the route wandered down steep ramps, next a scramble down steep rock, then an exposed traverse before descending again.

16: Biv. Bocco, at the top of the Via Ferrata, near the end of Alta Via 1

Sometimes there were short stretches of ladder, often a metal cable; some traverses had a hand-rail bolted on and once or twice a metal spike had been drilled in for a foot-hold. Whilst there was a lot of protection, not all of the descent had been covered and you had to be constantly on your guard.

From the bivouac hut at the top you could see down to the Rifugio 7 Alpini far below, I caught sight of the refuge several times on the descent but it never seemed to come any closer. When the end did appear to be in sight, with grassy slopes not too far away, the route kept traversing and even started climbing a little. Instead of becoming easier the descent became even more difficult; it seemed to be steeper the further I went and the ladders down overhangs were particularly unsettling. I was however thoroughly enjoying myself and the surprising thing was that there was no one else around; this was a beautiful Saturday morning in mid-August and I had the route to myself.

Shortly after passing the cave known as the Porton, and after spotting some fossilised sea-shells in the rock walls, further steep sections down more ladders finally landed me on grassy slopes just a few minutes above the Rifugio 7 Alpini. I celebrated my survival with ice-tea then hurried on down into the wooded gorge above the Ardo river. The path at first was quite steep and rough, it then became easier as I crossed and re-crossed the river several times. The forest kept me cool on the long descent until I finally came out at the road-end at the hamlet of Case Bortot.

With the final four miles into Belluno all on the road I could switch off, relax and cruise down into town in the early afternoon. For the distance of around 78 miles with some 23,000ft of climbing I would usually have expected to complete the route in two days but the terrain is difficult in the Dolomites, much of the way was over scree and boulders and of course you can't hurry too much on a *via ferrata*. Finishing well inside three days gave me plenty of time to return to my van that evening.

Apart from skiing, this was my first visit to the Dolomites, which is a beautiful region; well set up with a good network of paths, mountain huts and *via ferrata*; it also seems to be blessed with better weather than the Alps. I would say that the main requirements for a long run in the Dolomites are: sun-hat and sunglasses; a large water-bottle and the constitution of a camel to see you through the long dry stretches!

Guidebook: Alta Via – High Level Walks in the Dolomites
             by Martin Collins (Cicerone Press)

Maps: Sheet 1   Cortina, Dolomiti di Sesto
      Sheet 4   Belluno, Dolomiti Feltrine
      (1:50,000   Tabacco Wanderkarte)

Alta Via 2

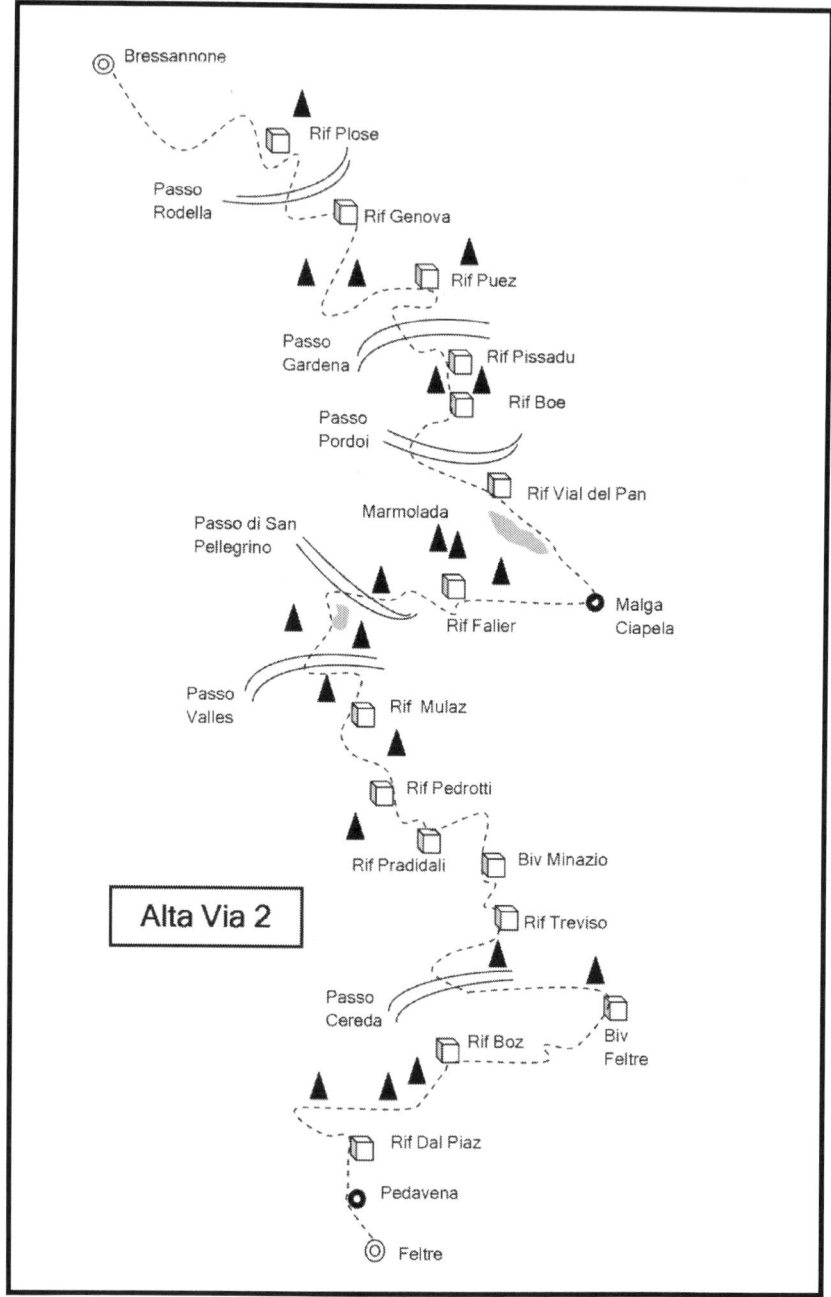

Dolomites High Level Route – Alta Via 2

After three days rest I was ready to start the second of the long ones in the Dolomites. Alta Via 2 starts in the pretty town of Bressanone, a maze of narrow cobbled streets and alleyways and interesting old buildings. I was again undecided how long the route would take to run; the walkers guide-book said to allow 2½ weeks for the 103 miles, which seemed a little excessive to say the least. I knew that that Alta Via 2 was longer, had more climbing and was generally more rugged than Alta Via 1, and in the end I settled on taking 4 to 4½ days. Unusually I didn't start first thing in the morning, this time it was gone mid-day when I set off.

It was quite a hard start from Bressanone as the climb from the town is around 6,200ft up to the Rifugio Plose. The route officially only starts at the refuge but being a purist the energy saving options of taking the cable-car or driving part way up were not for me, instead it meant a short jog through town, over two rivers and then out onto the hill.

Narrow footpaths led up through woodland and across pastures on a dull and overcast afternoon, but it was an easy climb to the small village of San Andrea. From here a footpath zigzagged endlessly up through steep forest, crossing a couple of forestry roads, but other than that there were hardly any landmarks. It was a long, thirsty climb, at last though I could see the top of the ridge through the trees and shortly after I came out into the open for a final climb alongside a stream gully and up to a grassy saddle. The Rifugio Plose lay just a few minutes away beside a tall radio mast.

From the refuge the path continued across a grassy bowl giving me good views out to a magnificent ridge of rocky towers and pinnacles. After passing under one ski-tow and across to another, I followed this second tow down to a small cluster of hotels. Easy running on a dirt track led me round the forested hillside, following the contour line, before a footpath dropped down through a mixture of forests and open glades, and out onto the road at the Passo Rodella.

I could see the narrow pass of Forcella della Putia not too far above the tree-line and after a few minutes running along the road I turned off onto another small footpath. This was a lovely sandy path through the pine trees and it gave an easy run round into the valley below the pass. Once above the tree-line the going became rougher and in light rain the well polished rocks became quite slippery. It was however an easy path and there was no problem in scrambling fairly quickly up to the Forcella della Putia.

Once again the views to the south were of rocky massifs above grassy bowls and forested hillsides. Leaving the col the path traversed easily round to the broad saddle of Passo Poma. Just a couple of hundred yards below here is the CAI Rifugio Genova, a huge old hotel-like refuge where I halted after a short day. Thunder rumbled around the mountains for some time but the weather didn't look too bad and I was hopeful that it would revert to sunshine for the remainder of the run.

Day 2 saw a fine start to the morning, initially to climb back up to the Passo Poma, then contouring and climbing along the hillside, with my next target, the narrow Forcella della Roa, always in view ahead. Now crossing scree and on a rougher path I reached the final climb to the col which, though steep, was not difficult. The view from the pass, a deep cleft in the narrow ridge, was superb; out to the north, the way I had come; and to the south, into a bleak basin of rock and scree. It was only a short descent into this bowl and way-marks led the way through the maze of huge blocks and boulders. Halfway across I spotted a couple of chamois on the scree above and as I drew nearer I realised that it was actually quite a sizeable herd, a couple of dozen or so, they drifted slowly up the hill when I came too close.

Across on the far side of the bowl steep zigzags led up to the Forcella Forces de Sielles and from the col the route climbed a rough ridge. Although there were cables for protection it was an easy scramble and I didn't need to dig out the protection kit from my rucksack. Once over the hard part the path dropped down to a wide terrace which crosses the Alpe del Puez. I was surprised to find a small herd of ponies up here with their foals and they looked beautiful as they raced back and forth across the pastures. The good footpath led easily round, giving pleasant running to reach the Rifugio Puez.

I quickly refilled my water-bottle at the trough and ran on limestone pavement round the head of the valley to emerge onto a barren plateau. The path was easy to follow as it meandered down and across open, flatter areas. There was then a short climb, up past a small lake, to the Passo di Crespeina, dominated by a tall wooden cross. From the col the narrow path continued on, down and round to the Passo del Cir. Below here the route passed through a cluster of little limestone pinnacles, then out onto grassy slopes which dropped down to Passo Gardena among a handful of ski-tows.

After a short break for yet more ice-tea I crossed the road and sought out the path that headed for the Rifugio Pissadu. This promised to be an entertaining section and it didn't disappoint. At first the path led easily round to the east, climbing gently above the road, suddenly the route veered off to climb an unlikely looking gully in an otherwise unbroken wall of rock. The climb was up loose scree and gravel, zigzagging surprisingly easily up the steep gully into the heart of the mountain. As I climbed higher the route trended left and climbed onto more stable rock which gave an interesting scramble. This part of the route was fixed with occasional iron rungs for steps and short stretches of cable. It was a popular walk and the track from the road col up to the hut was very busy with people both ascending and descending. It was frustrating having to queue at the aided sections and although some people did let me through I was at times forced into making some risky overtaking manoeuvres, climbing up the slabs alongside the path. A few minutes later I emerged onto flatter ground and was soon at the crowded Rifugio Pissadu.

Again I stopped just long enough to refill my water-bottle, before passing round the small lake to start a climb along a series of screes at the foot of Cima Pissadu. I was glad the weather was staying fine because navigation would have been a nightmare in poor visibility. The path climbed this way and that, over countless ridges and round rocky basins to then cross one of the most barren places I've ever seen. It was a huge plateau of pale grey rock, in which small clumps of flowers somehow managed to survive. The way-marks led through this maze to finally come out at another crowded refuge, the Rifugio Boe.

Still on gravel and scree I went quickly by, up and over a low col; the rough ground led around to another narrow col and a small refuge. A short climb above the col, beside the top station of a cable-car, was yet another refuge. Whilst the cable-car looked tempting I headed for the col, the Forcella Pordoi, from where a narrow, scree filled gully dropped steeply down to a road pass. The majority of people descended by cable-car; a few descended the gully by clinging to a wire cable that ran along the right-hand wall; even fewer ran straight down the middle.

On reaching the grass at the foot of the gully I stopped to empty the gravel from my shoes; a short run then took me down to the road at Passo Pordoi. This is another ski area and the route crossed the road to climb a low grassy ridge to the top of a group of ski-tows. From the top of the ridge delightful running on a fine path, which was kind to the feet for a change, led along at an easy angle. The Marmolada dominated the view to the south; the highest peak in the Dolomites, it's northern side, which I was now looking at, is covered in thick glaciers.

The superb balcony path ran easily on, past the Rifugio Vial del Pan until the Lago di Fedaia came into view. After a few minutes the path started it's long descent, dropping down in zigzags through the grassy hillside to come out at the dam at the west end of the lake. It didn't take long to run along the lakeside, beneath Marmolada's glaciers, before an indistinct path took me down into the valley. As I dropped lower the path became overgrown, then disappeared, so I had to take to the road for a while before heading off to run directly beneath a ski-tow that took me straight down to Malga Ciapela.

It had been a long tough day and I planned to stop here for the night but everywhere was full and instead I was faced with another hour of hard work. I headed up into a wooded valley until after about three miles I left the route of the Alta Via and made a steep climb up through forest which brought me out into a high, open valley from where an easy climb led to the Rifugio Falier at the far end. Although the refuge was busy they just had room for me. As I was now off the official route of the Alta Via I had two options for the morning. One was to retrace my steps to the junction I'd passed just before starting the climb to the refuge and thus regain the route at the point I'd left it. The second option was to follow path 612 from the refuge, over a high pass and then drop down to rejoin the route near Fociade, this looked to be the best bet and would soon have me back on course.

Day 3 and I left early on a hot and sunny morning. I was soon round the head of the valley and climbing a rough path up into Val Ombrettola, a barren, stony place. Climbing steadily at first the path entered the upper corrie and it now made a very hard ascent up slopes of unstable scree. It was hot, dusty work and I was relieved to finally gain the col, the Passo Ombrettola. Just a few feet below the col, tunnelled into the sidewall was another 1st World War cave and once across the far side I came across rusting barbed wire and the remains of old wooden huts.

There was only a short descent into another incredibly barren, scree filled valley, and after a couple of minutes the path more or less contoured round below the ridge, across endless scree to come out at another col, the Passo di Cirelle. From this col I dropped down around 2,000ft of scree in just a few minutes; heading straight down a broad gully, to emerge onto easier ground. I could now jog across the meadows into the little community of Fociade and here I was re-united with the route of Alta Via 2.

17: Beautiful running terrain in the Dolomites

A dirt road contoured round the hillside, past hay-barns and summer chalets to come out at the road at Passo san Pellegrino, which is yet another pass being developed as a small ski-resort. Leaving the car-park of the cable-car station the route climbed easily up a piste, through forest and across more open ground until I was up onto a low ridge. From here I dropped down past Lago di Cavia and followed a good path, short cutting the track, until I reached another road col, the Passo Valles.

After a short stop for ice-tea and a sticky bun I was soon climbing the broad scar of a path up to a grassy little col before climbing and contouring round the hillside to Passo Venegiotta. The path now climbed up and over a grassy spur before heading off around the rough hillside. I now headed up a steep rocky gully, which gave easy scrambling and had cables for aid over the more exposed sections. A final scramble took me over the lip onto more level ground and way-marks then led me through a boulder-field to the Rifugio Mulaz.

Above the hut a short climb led towards the Passo Mulaz but before reaching it I forked left to climb yet more horrendously loose scree to reach a notch in the ridge at Forcella la Margherita. From the far side the guide-book tried to send me off to the west; it didn't look right and was in fact 180° out. Instead I headed east (left) across the screes on the far side of the ridge and thankfully I soon found a way-mark which reassured me.

It was loose and exposed but I was heading for the highest point on either of the two Alta Via and I didn't expect it to be easy. The path led along the scree at the foot of a rock wall and then turned up into a narrow cleft; here it became even looser and even steeper. I had two choices, either zigzagging up the scree or take to the rock. At first I fought my way up the scree but then sought refuge on the firmer ground alongside. An easy scramble, protected in places, brought me out onto the Passo delle Farangole at about 9,600ft. There was a group on the col in the process of roping up for the descent off the far side, I hadn't intended putting on my protection kit but seeing the others taking great care suggested that perhaps I should do the same. I quickly put my harness on, clipped into the cables and set off. It wasn't difficult to drop down between the rock walls, but it was dangerous with everything being so loose, and I was glad that I had gone to the trouble of kitting up.

Once out of the gully the way continued down a rocky valley. It was very rough underfoot as the route headed up the main Valle delle Comelle. Now climbing gently through grass, with one or two sections somewhat exposed above steep ground, the path led on for some way up to the head of the valley from where it dropped the short way down to more open ground by the river at Pian dei Cantoni. One more climb took me up a rocky gully, which narrowed and steepened at the top, and on emerging from this I found myself on another huge barren plateau, a limestone table called the Altipiano delle Pale di San Martino. Another few minutes through the boulders saw me at the CAI Rifugio Giovani Pedrotti, also known as Rifugio Rosetta, although confusingly there is another Rifugio Rosetta just half a mile away across the plateau at the top of the Rosetta cable-car. Once again the afternoon had clouded over after a warm and sunny start so I was pleased to stop here for the night.

As usual the clouds dispersed and the morning dawned bright and clear. I was away early, anticipating a long hard day. Initially a well engineered path led across the plateau, following the huts water pipe; the path then dropped down a rocky valley in endless zigzags, until it finally led off around the hillside beneath towering cliffs. The path, narrow and exposed in places, led into a side valley, at the head of which could be seen Passo de Ball; it was surprisingly quick to scramble through the boulders and along the easy angled terrace to reach the narrow col. After a reasonably short descent over scree into another boulder-filled valley, the path wound round a rocky spur to reach the Rifugio Pradidali.

There were climbers kitting up outside the hut as I headed up the rocky defile behind the refuge, past an almost dry lake. The way was easy at first but then led more steeply up through a jumble of boulders to a broad shelf and a path junction. I headed off to the right on a rough climb through short outcrops and large boulders, at one point entering a narrow, scree filled gully. Way-marks appeared to offer the choice of either a scramble up the rocks on the left or to simply ascend the gully. I started off in the gully, which was loose and rather unpleasant, so I headed over to explore the rock route. It didn't take long to convince me that I wasn't going to climb it without the aid of a safety-net so I retreated back into the gully, which now seemed much more appealing. Entering onto another broad rock-shelf, the path was indistinct, and I was grateful for the occasional splashes of paint which led me through the rough ground, up rocky slopes and out onto the Passo delle Lede.

Once over the far side it was easy to descend quite quickly and lower down I came out onto grassy terrain. I spotted what looked like lumps of aircraft wreckage and when I reached the bivouac shelter Carlo Minazio a few minutes later my diagnosis was confirmed, outside the hut was a memorial to those who had died in the crash. The long descent continued over steep, rough ground to finally come down through forest to Val Canali. A rough track headed a short way up the valley; I then turned off onto a steep path which zigzagged up through the trees to the Rifugio Treviso. Leaving the hut the path headed south, through trees and rough vegetation, then once out above the tree-line the way continued into a corrie; I climbed over rocks and scree to land on the narrow pass, the Forcella d'Oltro.

After only a short descent the path turned to head round the hillside, it was now a high balcony path which climbed gently beneath the cliffs. After some time of running in thick mist I reached an area of little rocky pinnacles and spires and this was the signal for the path to start it's long descent to the road. It was a tiring run, the stony path was hard on my feet as it took me steeply down through the pinnacles, into forest and finally out into the meadows; this left just a short run down a track to the road at Passo Cereda.

After a good feed of one ice-cream, two doughnuts and three ice-teas I felt ready to face the next long stage; the nearest refuge was eight hours away according to the guide-book and it was now almost 2pm. It had already been quite a hard day and I hoped that the route to the refuge would let me move fairly quickly for once. It only took a few minutes to run along the road and down a track into the hamlet of Mattiuzzi; from here a path started climbing across meadows then more steeply up through forest. On reaching a boulder choked gully the going became hard; a massive rock-fall a few years ago had blocked the route, the path wound its way up the gully, in and out of dwarf trees and amongst huge boulders and other debris.

It was a relief to reach the other side of the rock-fall and enter the sparse forest. However I was soon above the tree-line and following a rough path beneath the cliffs; once again the terrain became harder, climbing more steeply up loose scree. The path, sometimes a narrow ledge, sometimes indistinguishable amongst the rocks, climbed on, protected with a length of chain at one point. It was a slippery and nerve wracking climb up the loose slopes but after a couple of false tops I finally arrived on the Forcella di Comedon, an old smuggler's pass.

The afternoon had again turned cloudy and a thick mist hid whatever was over the other side of the pass, however, the way-marks were plain to see and these took me down a short way before leading round into a grassy hollow, a short way up the far side of which is the Bivouac Shelter Feltre. I was delighted with the time taken to here and now I could afford to relax a little, knowing that I would reach the refuge in good time. The lovely path gave me a spell of easy running as I headed down, past some crystal clear streams and pools, before heading right into a small grassy corrie. Once up and over the rim of the corrie, the way led round the hillside, where sheep bells rang out eerily through the mist. For the next half hour or so the path generally contoured round beneath high cliffs on the right, with an exposed drop down steep grassy slopes to the left.

Strange, crevasse-like, caves were passed as the path led on, winding in and out of gullies with just occasional glimpses of Passo Alvis far away at the head of the valley. Notwithstanding the steep drop to one side, it was easy running with just one 'bad-step' which was protected by a short length of cable. Then, after rounding one last corner and passing a spacious man-made cave, the path finally came out at the broad grassy saddle of Passo Alvis, where the sound of hundreds of crickets filled the air. Just ten minutes down the far side, running over grassy pastures, took me to the CAI Rifugio Bruno Boz, a small and friendly little place, which, according to the visitors book mainly seems to be used by people walking the Alta Via.

With only a short final day ahead of me I allowed myself the luxury of a lay-in; it was almost 8am when I left the hut on another warm but slightly misty morning. I started with an easy run across the grassy hillside, then round to a low col. Dropping a short way down the far side the path then led along and up towards the rocky crest of Monte Zoccare Alto. Now came a long traverse, just below the ridge on a rough and exposed path; part of it was on a narrow ledge hewn out of the rock so that you had to duck your head to avoid the over-hang.

On arriving at another narrow col the path climbed the ridge on the far side, initially up a stair-case hewn out of the rock, then zigzagging towards the summit of Sasso Scarnia. I was soon dropping down through huge boulders before facing another steep descent, down beneath an over-hanging cliff, which finally brought me out onto a more runnable stretch; it was an easy traverse across the southern slopes of the mountain, where the miles passed effortlessly. On reaching a high, rock strewn corrie, the path then made its way across another scree slope and out onto a grassy ridge. After this the rough stuff was almost over. I had an easy run on an old mule track through grassy pastures, which led into a long traverse up an almost Scottish glen, before heading up and over into the next valley. This valley, the Malga Vette Grandi, was greener, broader and filled with bell-ringing cows. It didn't take long to run down to near the farm before cutting off, up the rough track to the final col of the route, the Passo le Vette Grandi. Immediately down over the far side of the col is the Rifugio Dal Piaz.

An old military road climbs up to here, but a footpath cuts off many of the hair-pins and descends quickly into forest to come out 3,000ft later at the small hamlet of Passo di Croce d'Aune. If it hadn't been for the haze the end would now have been in sight as Feltre lay down in the valley about five miles away. A footpath led off down through the trees to continue the big descent, some 5,500ft in all from the final pass, down to the main road in Pedavena. From here a quiet road led down alongside the river, past the Heineken Brewery and into Feltre, a charming old town of typical Italian character.

The run had taken me four full days, which seemed slow for 103 miles, but with the steep climbs and descents making lengthy zigzags the distance is bound to be quite a bit more in reality. The terrain on this one was certainly tougher than the Alta Via 1 and with around 36,000ft of climbing and 37,000ft of rough descents I'd expected a hard time. It reaffirmed my belief that the Dolomites are a superb area for running, with good settled weather, although prone to clouding over for short spells in the afternoons.

Guidebook: Alta Via – High Level Walks in the Dolomites by Martin Collins (Cicerone Press)

Maps: Sheet 9   Bressanone, Val du Funes
       Sheet 2   Val di Vassa, Val Gardena, Marmolada
       Sheet 4   Belluno, Dolomiti Feltrine
       (1:50,000   Tabacco Wanderkarte)

Tour du Queyras (G58)

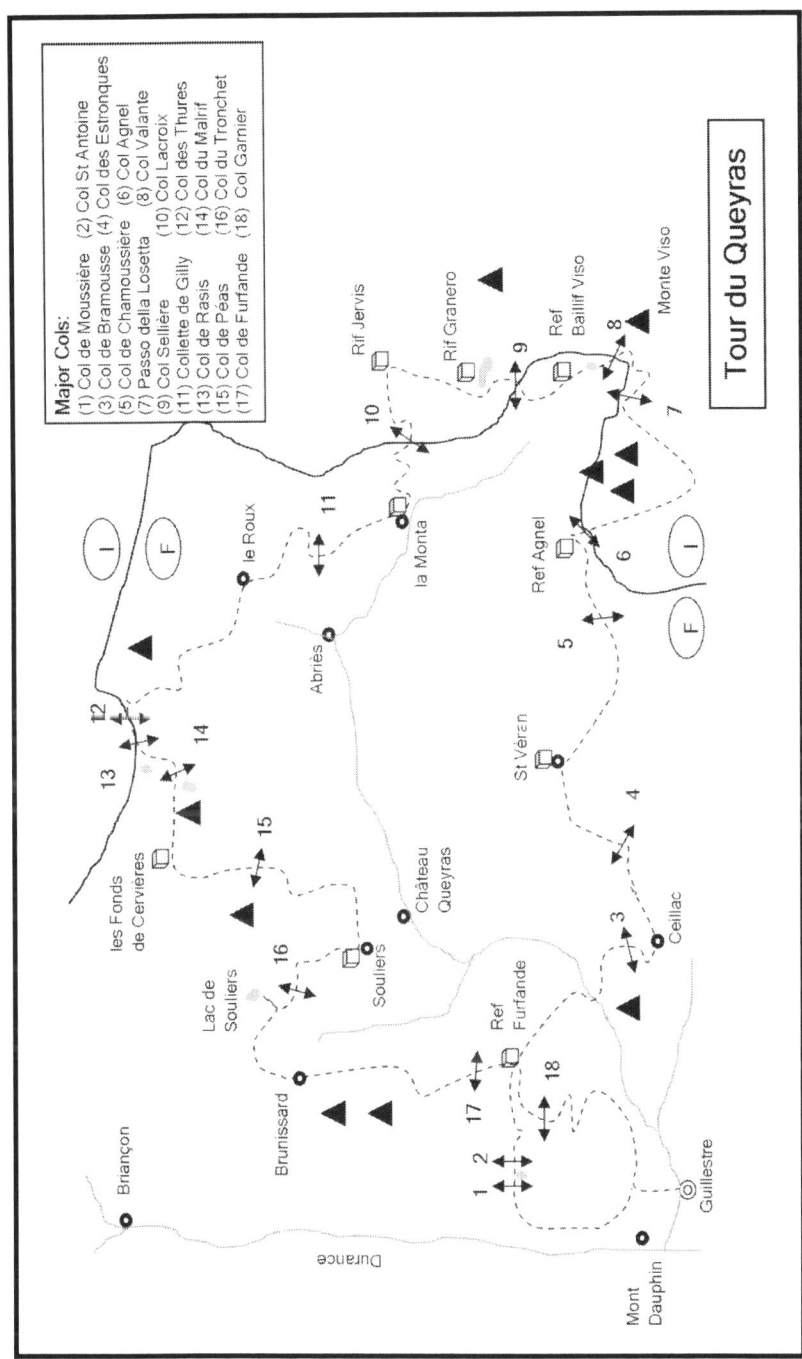

Tour du Queyras (GR58)

I planned to run this one in early June but had to postpone it due to the amount of snow still covering the high cols; it was the end of August when I found myself back in the area ready for the attempt. The previous three days, when I'd been resting after the Dolomite runs, were exceedingly wet and the temperatures fell very low each night. I wasn't surprised when I woke to see fresh snow on the tops on the morning I was to start.

The basic Tour du Queyras is actually quite short, a circuit starting and finishing at Ceillac; the version in the guide-book adds a few miles to the first and last days by starting in Mont Dauphin. This is part of the GR541, which is a link between the GR54 (Tour de l'Oisans) and the GR58 (Tour du Queyras). Once on the route of the GR58 there are a number of optional 'variants', which add both interest and distance. One of the main variants takes the route over into Italy then a short while later back into France, over into Italy again then back to France once more. I decided to run the route suggested in the guide-book with these variants, which would give a run of around 116 miles with 44,200ft of climbing. I hoped to reduce the suggested twelve daily stages down to four.

I left the van at a camp-site in Guillestre, which is on the opposite side of the River Guil to Mont Dauphin, so my run started from here. I dropped down from the plateau on which Guillestre stands, crossed the river and climbed a minor road to the small village of Eygliers and on up the hill to le Coin. From here a well marked path led up the hillside, soon widening into a dirt track, this climbed easily up through forest to reach an open foresters hut. Behind the hut a footpath climbed more steeply through forest, up a steep gully and back into forest. As I came out above the tree-line onto open ground there were superb views back down to the old fort at Mont Dauphin, the Gorges de Guil and the Durance Valley.

An old mule track now climbed the grassy slopes in long zigzags, led round into another high valley before climbing easily to the first col of the route, the Col de Moussière. It didn't take long to drop down the far side into a basin of scattered boulders, the path then led across the rocks and over to the grassy pastures around a small lake. Beside the lake was a makeshift corral of a dozen horses, their young riders, camping wild, were having breakfast outside their tents as I ran past.

From the lakeside a grassy path, sheer bliss after the rough ground of the Dolomites, climbed across the hill and took me steadily up to the Col Saint-Antoine. Easy running took me down into the lush green bowl beyond, the path then climbed up a short way, through the summer chalets and cow-sheds of les Granges du Furfande. I contoured round the hillside, past scattered chalets, to reach the Refuge de Furfande where I stopped briefly for a large bowl of coffee to warm up.

Leaving the refuge the path continued to contour across the grassy slopes before starting the steep descent to the road in the Combe du Queyras. The path dropped down fairly comfortably and gave a good run, through sparse forest to come out at the hamlet of les Escoyeres. From here the route was on a zigzagging dirt road all the way down to the main road in the valley. After crossing the road and the river I followed a narrow footpath which climbed through the trees to Bramousse.

Above this collection of houses a forestry track climbed painlessly, but endlessly, up past the Chalets of Bramousse to finally come out at the broad grassy saddle of the Col de Bramousse. Ski-tows climbed up to the col from the far side. I dropped down a good path, which gave easy running between the chair-lifts then picked up a narrower path which dropped in steep, tight, zigzags through the trees above a rocky ravine; I soon came out onto easier ground which led me past the church and into Ceillac.

It didn't take long to trot through the small village and find the footpath which climbed a short way above the road and effortlessly up the valley. Shortly after passing the chalets at le Villard the hard work started again, on another relentless climb, the path zigzagging interminably up the steep hillside. I was hot, tired and very thirsty when at last I emerged onto the Col des Estronques. Opening up on the far side was another grassy valley and far below I could see the village of Saint-Véran. The path gave reasonably easy running down to a stream, which was followed down through the trees. After a short, steeper section, to the foot of a small water-fall, the way led comfortably down a wide ski-piste through the trees to cross the river at Pont Moulin. A final short climb up a rough footpath brought me into Saint-Véran, a lovely old village whose claim to fame is that at 6,622ft it is supposed to be the highest permanently inhabited community in Europe. Here I found myself a gîte for the night, a fine 200 year old building that used to be the Customs Post many years ago.

It was a cold and frosty start to Day 2, although the sun wasn't far away. From Saint-Véran I headed up the valley a short way and crossed the river which took me up through open forest, climbing up into the bright sunshine. Near a little chapel at the road-end I headed across open hillside, up a path that was booby-trapped with countless marmot burrows. It was a steady climb up to the Col de Chamoussière which soon warmed me up.

From the col the path descended and traversed round into a basin of rock and scree to come out near the Refuge Agnel. I turned up the hill and reached the Col Agnel a few minutes later; the Col Agnel is famous, as this is where Hannibal is supposed to have crossed the Alps with his elephants. Once over the col I was in Italy and I dropped down a good footpath, through steep pastures, cutting the zigzags in the road. At one point I spotted a little weasel amongst the rocks but it disappeared very quickly as I puffed past. Continuing down the grassy path gave good running and eventually I reached the road and a short while later the farm at Granges del Rio. Here a footpath led off up into the Soustra valley, initially climbing alongside a stream, which gave good going for several miles, passing old stone chalets, all the way up to the head of the valley.

18: Easy running in the Soustra Valley, over the border in Italy

The climb now started in earnest, zigzagging up through boulders to come out at the Passo della Losetta. From this high stony pass I now had my first good view of Monte Viso, high above on the far side of the valley.

The route now led down a short way before turning to contour north, around the head of this new valley, to cross the ridge and re-enter France at the Col de Valante. The light snow cover on Monte Viso made it's north-west face a magnificent sight; however, deep snow down the northern side of the Col de Valante was less welcome. The route led down a rocky gully where the snow made life difficult, the path then crossed a horrible slope of unstable scree, which was made twice as hard by the wet snow. I made a slow and careful descent before I finally reached Lac Lestio where a better path gave easier running down to the Refuge Baillif-Viso.

I enjoyed a short rest at the hut, drinking a big bowl of coffee on the balcony while admiring the view back up to the col and Monte Viso. Then it was back to work, continuing a short way down the valley before heading off to climb through colonies of marmots on an indistinct grassy trail. After climbing for a while I then had a chance to catch my breath as the path contoured a short distance round the hill, before climbing more steeply up to the Col Sellière. From here I had another rough and rocky descent back into Italy, where the steep track dropped down to the pretty Lago Lungo. The Rifugio Granero was just a short climb up from the lake. Although it was still warm and sunny, the valley below was filled with thick cloud; unfortunately I had to head down into the valley and into the cloud. It was however an easy run to the summer chalets at Partia d'Amunt and from here a dirt road took me quickly along to Ciabot del Pra.

I was now faced with the last big climb of the day as I had to climb out of Italy and back over into France. The path was well engineered and was reminiscent of a Scottish stalkers path; it climbed the steep forested hillside in countless zigzags and I emerged out of the cloud just a few minutes before reaching the border at the Col Lacroix. A ruined hut gave me some shelter from the cold wind as I had a final bite to eat before setting off on the long descent. The path gave a comfortable run down at a reasonably easy angle, through a large flock of several hundred sheep. The going became steeper as I dropped into thin forest but I was soon out onto more open ground among butterflies and crickets. After another few minutes I was comfortably installed in the gîte at la Monta.

Day 3 saw an unexpected start when the Guardian refused to accept any money from me for my dinner, bed and breakfast. As was usual on these long runs I was wearing my favourite, and by now rather faded, Nepalese t-shirt. When I went to pay and the Guardian saw the t-shirt, he said 'No' it was a present from one Buddhist to another! He told me that he had visited Tibet and Nepal on seven occasions so I had some catching up to do. His touching gesture went a long way to restoring my faith in the French, a faith which had been seriously dented when my van had been stolen two months earlier.

After chatting for a while I set off into a warm but slightly overcast day. I kept an eye out for chamois as I climbed a good path up through sparse woodland; this gained height fast and without difficulty.

19: Monte Viso

Coming out onto open ground the path led across the hill then climbed to the ridge top to follow the Crête de Gilly. It was easy going up here and took me quickly along before dropping down a short way to the Colette de Gilly, where a couple of ski-tows climbed up from Abriès. The frontier ridge that I was aiming for seemed a long way away. First I dropped down a steep hillside and followed a pleasant path through the forest; after an initial steep descent it followed the contour line before dropping down to cross the river and a final climb up into le Roux.

Leaving the small village the route led along a grassy track to a stream junction; after crossing the stream I started on another big climb. The early clouds had cleared away and it was now very hot, with no chance of any shade. I climbed on and on and at last reached the narrow frontier ridge at the Col des Thures. From the pass the path led along the ridge, beneath a small rocky summit, across an awkward slope of boulders and scree before a short climb brought me out at the Col de Rasis, still on the border between France and Italy. This col at 9,576ft has the distinction of being the highest on any of the French GR's.

A short steep descent now took me away from Italy, down a loose slope of scree and schist. From a small lake the path dropped down a steep gully to the foot of a rocky crest. Now onto open ground the path was somewhat indistinct as it mainly just contoured round the basin. I managed to lose the path and reached the difficult slope of scree and boulders below the Crête aux Eaux Pendantes not knowing if the path was above or below me. It was tempting to contour round or to descend slightly to try to reach the ridge but I decided that I had probably lost the path when it turned back on itself in a zigzag. I guessed the path was most likely to be above me so I attacked the rotten slope and after a few minutes of nerve wracking scrambling I spotted a faded splash of paint and was soon back on the faint line of the path, which offered a little more security.

I continued up the path to the 'crête', through a narrow gap in the ridge and contoured across easier slopes to reach the Col du Malrif. A short way beyond the col I climbed up to the Pic du Malrif; this little lump on the ridge seems hardly worth calling a 'peak' but it did give me great views over the Queyras to Monte Viso and out to the high peaks of the Écrins, which I'd run round on the Tour de l'Oisans. From the top there was a short sharp descent through boulders, before I came out onto easier ground which gave me a long run down the valley, beside a clear mountain stream to eventually reach the dozen or so chalets that make up the summer settlement of les Fonds de Cervières. This was a lovely little spot and I enjoyed a short rest, eating apple pie and drinking coffee outside the gîte. It was very tempting to just stay there for the rest of the day; it was so beautiful and peaceful, I even went so far as to look at the map to see how far that would leave me for the final day, but it would have left too much to do so I reluctantly settled up and headed off.

I climbed gently south up the valley alongside the tumbling river, over one false top, then out onto the broad saddle of the Col de Péas. The good path continued down the far side giving easy running across the grassy hillside, through marmots, butterflies and crickets. After a mile or so the way led out on a long traverse, contouring around the hill to reach forest. Easy zigzags then took me down to Souliers. The gîte in this little hamlet was run by Madame Humbert, a wonderful old lady who immediately made me welcome, despite my sweaty state after a hard days running. A little later three Belgians arrived and we were treated to a fantastic meal, all home grown and all home made, and unusually, the meal also included rather a lot of wine. Reading the comments in her Visitors Book, we weren't the only ones to appreciate her magnificent cooking. *Le Grand Rochebrun* at Souliers was the best of all the gîtes and refuges that I stayed in, not just on this Tour, but on all of them, and the competition it had to beat was pretty tough.

Day 4 started with another beautiful morning; it was cold and frosty but the sun was shining on the tops and I knew I would be in for another hot day. The start was easy, following a dirt road up the valley before crossing the river and turning up the steep hillside to climb to the Col du Tronchet. A good path led round the hill on the far side and after a while I made a short detour to visit the Lac de Souliers, which nestles in a grassy hollow.

Dropping back down to the main path this now led on a traverse along the hillside and through forest before descending quite steeply down a stony ravine. This in turn led out to a minor road which took me quickly into Brunissard. I searched out the 'epicerie' for a litre of ice-tea then set off up a forest road, which climbed easily away from the valley floor. The shade was welcome as I jogged along, crossed over a forested spur, had a nasty little descent down a narrow stone chute and crossed a dry river gully. After crossing another stream I came out onto a track that led all the way to the Col de Furfande. However, the track climbed in long loops, so I took to the more direct, steeper footpaths that climbed up through forest, then across more open ground until I arrived sooner than expected on the col.

From the grassy col I was now looking down onto the Refuge de Furfande and a few minutes later I was sitting outside the hut with a big bowl of coffee. It was three days since I had last been here and I had now completed the loop which was the GR58 part of the route, the actual Tour du Queyras, now I just had to return on the GR541 to Guillestre. From the hut the path led past the chalets and instead of turning right to climb to the Col St. Antoine that I had crossed on the way out, I headed south across the grassy basin for a short climb to the Col Garnier, the final col and the start of a very long descent.

At first the path dropped down the hillside at an easy angle to reach forest, the going then became steeper, heading endlessly down before leading round into a side valley to cross a mountain stream. Once over the bridge a short climb took me up above the ravine and over a spur where I came out onto a rough track. With the Gorges du Guil now below me the end was in sight; the track became a minor road at Gros and this road then dropped gently down towards Mont Dauphin.

After a while I spotted a small cairn of stones by the roadside, this marked the start of a faint path which dropped down the rough, steep hillside. I didn't know where the path was going but it was worth the risk to avoid the long slow descent that the road was going to make. I headed down, joined another minor road and was soon at La Font d'Eygliers; from here it didn't take long to cross the Guil. One last climb took me out of the gorge and back into Guillestre to end a fine route.

The last day had gone quicker than anticipated and meant that I finished the 116 miles and 44,200ft of climbing in 3½ days. I think I was still working on the Dolomite scale of things when I decided to aim for four days; having run the route I now think I should have set myself a target of three days, which would have been tough but far from impossible.

Guidebook: Tour of the Queyras by Alan Castle
(Cicerone Press)

Maps: Sheet 10 Massifs du Queyras et Haute-Ubaye
(1:50,000 Didier & Richard)

Tour de la Vanoise

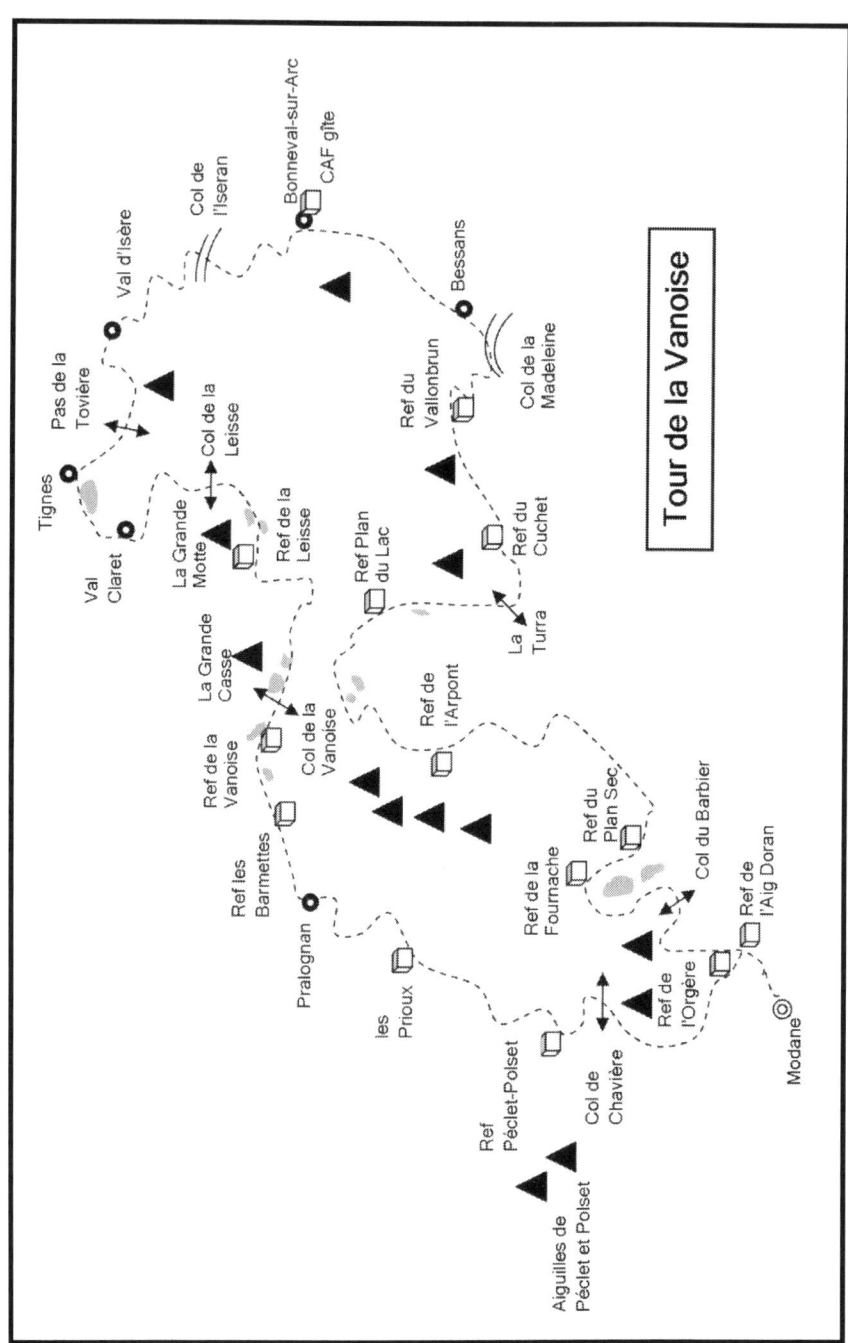

Tour de la Vanoise

This route starts in Modane, and I ran it with my wife Cath, a few years after the other long runs described in this section. It was already late afternoon by the time the train reached Modane so the first stage was just a short one, taking us out of town and up into the hills. For the first night we were aiming for the privately run Refuge de l'Aiguille Doran which was a short way below the PNV owned Refuge de l'Orgère. Familiar red and white flashes of paint led us through the outskirts of Modane, climbing immediately, up into a forest where it was very hot and sticky.

There were signposts at every junction so you were never lost but the finger posts always gave a time to the destination rather than a distance; several of these seemed to have been mixed up as they were installed. We went from being 2 hours to go, to just 45 minutes and then back to 1 hour 15 minutes.

"*Everywhere is walking distance, if you've got the time.*"
(Stephen Wright)

It was very confusing but we were well ahead of both the guide-book and the sign-post times and after about an hour and a half we came out of the forest at a grassy clearing where we found three or four stone chalets, one of which was the Refuge. We were warned to keep the hut door shut to keep out the mice!

As we sat outside resting with a cool drink we heard a clanging of bells and a herd of sheep was driven up by two young shepherdesses and two skinny looking border collies. They stayed grazing among the fresh grass and wild flowers for a couple of hours before being rounded up and driven back down the hill for the night.

We were up early next morning and away by 7:30, which was to become the norm as it was always good to do a few miles before it grew too hot. We set off under clear blue skies, first climbing up to the Refuge de l'Orgère; the path then contoured round the hillside and soon started climbing in earnest, as it did we saw our first marmots of the trip. The shaggy brown creatures let off a shrill cry of alarm, then darted down the nearest burrow to safety. Continuing up through forest we passed a couple of conveniently placed water troughs, crossed a couple of streams and picked our way through the debris of an old rock-fall before coming out into open hillside and grassy slopes.

More contouring on a delightful balcony path took us past a couple of old stone chalets and up to the Col du Barbier. This wasn't so much a col, just a slight dip in a steep ridge, however, having crossed the col we found we had turned a corner and were now headed north. Beneath us we saw two lakes, both dammed for hydro-electric works. We could have dropped down to the first of the lakes to cut off a big loop, but this would have meant losing around 1,200ft of height and having to re-climb it on the far side, instead we stayed high and made our way up valley. The lower of the two lakes, whose dam was shaped like a snow plough, had a pipeline sending tons of water crashing into it. This gave the lake a grey colour as opposed to the upper lake which was green.

It was a lovely path, climbing gently through a wilderness of wild flowers and marmots, with terrific views to the high mountains to the north and the lakes below. Once beyond the higher lake we turned east and dropped gently down the hillside to cross the stream on the Pont de la Sétéria. Across the bridge we had a short climb, tracking back round the far side of the valley, past the Refuge de la Fournache, until we came out onto a dirt road. A short jog down the road took us to the Refuge du Plan Sec where we were glad to stop for an ice-cold *Orangina*.

All too soon it was back to work and we headed along the dirt road, beneath a couple of ski-tows to cross a ridge from where a couple of parapentes had just taken off. Two hang-gliders were waiting for the right conditions for their turn.

The route continued to contour round the hillside, winding in and out of stream gullies, passing one short section protected by chain. In the spring, with snow still covering the path, it would have been useful as there was quite a steep drop to the right, perhaps 1,500ft or so down very steep grass, as it was we were able to jog along the path with no worries.

The path continued, mainly contouring, but at times climbing round corries; always interesting and always with banks of wild flowers bordering the path. At one stage we came across a lone walker coming from the other direction, he appeared to have been adopted by a goat, which was following his every move. Shortly after this we dropped down to a collection of tumbledown chalets, the path crossed a few scattered snow patches as we ran beneath some towering glaciers high above us on our left, whilst to the right below us was the mouth of the Doron Gorge. Almost opposite the narrow entrance to the gorge we came to the Refuge de l'Arpont where we stopped for the night.

We were asked when we wanted breakfast, 4 o'clock or 7 o'clock; this being a climbers hut as well as being used by walkers. We opted for the latter and as we were all in one large bunk-room we hoped the climbers wouldn't make too much noise when they left at 4am.

After a surprisingly quiet night we were ready to leave by 7:30. It was another hot and sunny morning and we made good time climbing gently along the valley, still on a balcony path, keeping high above the Doron Gorge. We passed a lone chamois, and as the path led over a ridge and round into a wild plateau-like landscape dotted with small tarns we spotted a couple of ibex. We ran on, across a snowfield, between the tarns and across several small streams, down more patches of snow to emerge at a small bridge over a glacial stream. The cold blue ice-cliffs of the glacier towered above us as we crossed snow that was criss-crossed with the footprints of a fox. Then it was over another stream, past a couple of delightful lakes and round until we could look down into the head of the Doron Gorge.

Where we started to descend, the guide-book mentioned an 'acorn cup' stone, thought to have been carved by Neolithic man, but despite a brief look at anything that looked a possibility we couldn't find it. The route now led steeply down as we had to cross the Doron River and then climb about the same height up the far side of the valley. Zigzags led down the steep grassy hillside to a small farm where we crossed the river and joined a tarmac road.

A short way up the road we turned off and climbed steeply up the wall of the valley. The path here was quite busy, although the road is not open to cars there is a bus service, a 'navette', that comes up from Termignon and carries walkers up the hill. Once up the climb we followed a path across the grass to the broad col and the Refuge du Plan du Lac. This was the signal for a short stop for a cold drink and a slice of blueberry tart, before heading off, past the lake where a few fishermen were trying their luck.

Dropping down from the col we headed left onto a dirt track which contoured round the hillside beneath the Crête de Côte Chaude. Just before reaching the road-end at la Femma a snow-plough had cut a track through a deep bank of snow; the walls of snow towered about 10ft above us as we ran through. Now on a footpath the route continued to contour across the grassy hillside; after crossing a ridge we turned downhill at a farm, which was guarded by a couple of fierce dogs. From here the path dropped more steeply down through a rocky area into pine forest. It was oppressively hot in the forest as we dropped almost 1,000ft, finally coming out at cross-roads; here we headed up valley, first through forest, then across flowery meadows.

After a few miles the triangular shaped Refuge du Cuchet came into view; first though we had to cross a swollen stream, thankfully without too much of a soaking, then a final short steep climb took us to the hut. We had been told that the hut was unmanned so we had pasta, packets of soup, drinking chocolate, and some bread with us. There was a guardian in residence, but only to supervise, and we did as expected have to cook and feed ourselves.

It was another reasonably early finish and we lazed away the afternoon; as the evening wore on we watched from the balcony as a few chamois grazed their way up the grassy alp towards the hut and a family of marmots stood on their hind legs boxing with each other.

Next day was to be a relatively short stage, with little climbing, as we just continued up the valley of the Arc River to Bonneval. We had worked out the stages in this way to try to avoid having to overnight in the fleshpots of either Val d'Isere or Tignes but it did mean that after this short 'rest' day we would have to face two fairly long, hard days.

It was a nice gentle start next morning, an easy climb along a good balcony footpath that clung to the side of the hill. Once again the wild flowers were a picture and we spotted several chamois along this stretch. It was easy going as we headed gently up the valley to come out at a dirt road in a little hidden valley, directly opposite the Refuge du Vallonbrun.

It was still only 9 o'clock but the time was right for a coffee stop, then it was on again to pass a tiny stone chapel before dropping down steep zigzags to come out on the road at the Col de la Madeleine. A footpath soon led off along the top of an embankment, through a flower filled meadow. We had to rejoin the road for a short stretch before taking to a rough track that ran alongside the Arc. It was turning into another very hot day; there was a beautiful bright blue sky and the only clouds around were the clouds of tiny butterflies that danced a foot or so above the track. Cath spotted an angry snake and I was surprised to see marmots playing in the meadows so close to habitation.

It didn't take us long to reach the hamlet of Bessans where we made a slight detour, crossing the bridge to find somewhere to buy a drink and something to eat. We were soon back to work, re-crossing the river and moving quickly up the valley. After passing through another small hamlet, le Villaron, the way continued through meadows but now we had cliffs towering above us on our left, with house sized boulders piled up around the foot of them.

After more easy miles alongside the river, we saw the hair-pin bends of the road as it climbed toward the Col de l'Iseran, which was one of our objectives for the following day. Beneath the hair-pins we first spotted the church tower, the rest of Bonneval-sur-Arc then came into view. It is a delightful little 'car-free' village which is preserved by banning clutter such as TV aerials and electricity pylons from show.

We sought out the French Alpine Club refuge, settled in, and lazed away an afternoon; Cath stuck needles in my knees to help keep the swelling down. We asked the Tourist Information Office to telephone the next hut, the Refuge de la Leisse, as it was the only hut we had not had a response from and we didn't know if we were expected or not.

Next morning we were again away before 7:30 for what promised to be a long day. Initially the path led steeply up past some hydro-electric works until we came out onto the road. Several cyclists were already on their way up; the Col de l'Iseran, at just over 9,000ft, is the highest major road col in the Alps and is an obvious attraction for any keen cyclist.

We were soon able to quit the road and rejoin the footpath that led through meadows and up past an impressive waterfall. It was already a bright sunny day but the climb took us into a narrowing valley whose high walls cast deep shadows. The lack of sun here kept the snow patches, which were becoming more frequent, hard and icy. Finally we arrived at a larger, much steeper patch of snow, with a long drop below and loose steep shale above. A length of chain partially protected the crossing of the first part of the snow but there was no protection for the second half and we didn't fancy crossing it wearing running shoes. We retraced our steps a short way then cut up to join the road.

Once on the road we were soon round into a more open valley, at the far end of which we could see some quite extensive 'summer' skiing going on. Once over the bridge we took to the hillside on a rising traverse, crossing increasing amounts of snow. A fall would have seen us tumbling down to the road to be run over by a cyclist!

Here in the open valley the sun had been at work so the snow was softer and it was reasonably easy to kick steps. A final scramble took us up a shaly bank and we came out directly at the cairn on the col. This was a miserable looking place; there was a car-park and some ski-tows, a refreshment building and a small chapel. We had hoped to stop for a drink but nothing was open, so instead we started down on the long descent to Val d'Isère.

The soft snow gave us an easy run down; we crossed and re-crossed the road several times as it looped down in zigzags, while we were able to take a more direct line. A path led down beneath a ski-tow, down a piste, then across a footbridge. Cath reached the bridge first, put one foot onto the first plank and keeled over, seemingly in slow motion as the plank simply came away. She ended up in the stream, a bit battered and bloodied but no real harm done. I went across more carefully on my hands and knees as every plank was loose.

Val d'Isère could be seen far below as we dropped down a steep footpath that finally brought us out onto the pistes that are carved through the forest to take skiers back to town. Once onto the main road we quickly sought out a supermarket and went mad with a buying spree of a half litre of yoghurt drink each, bananas and chocolate. We devoured these as we walked along the road through town then stopped at a cafe for coffee and a big slice of fruit tart.

The overeating had a rather unfortunate effect on both of us for the next few hours and we suffered stomach problems as we jogged out of town and started the climb up towards Tignes. It was a very hot afternoon and we climbed slowly up through the forest, both of us having to dash into cover every now and again, before we emerged into a broad, grassy valley, dotted with stone chalets. A final pull led to the boulder strewn Pas de la Tovière from where we looked down on Lac du Chevril and its high dam. We both needed to reach Tignes quickly so we set off down and were soon in the ugly ski resort where we stopped at the nearest bar to drink ice-cold *Fanta* and make use of their 'facilities'.

An easy path led round the south side of the Lac de Tignes, through a small golf course and up to the even uglier resort of Val Claret. I needed another stop here and had downed a large glass of ice-tea before the bar-maid could give me my change. Thankfully the worst effects of our gluttony now seemed to pass and we set off on the long climb towards the Col de la Leisse. It was good to leave the ski resorts and to be back in the mountains again, although a new dirt road had been cut since the map and guide-book were published which meant we were in 'civilization' for a bit longer than expected.

As we climbed higher into the valley we came across more and more snow, so that it was soon completely covering the path. In places the snow was firm and you could jog along with no problem, but then without warning it would change and you would find yourself sinking in up to your knees. It had been a long hot day with some big climbs, which weren't made any easier by our having dodgy stomachs, so we were both feeling tired as we searched for the col.

Numerous false summits came and went but at last we finally spotted the marker post on the highest point; it was a wild and spectacular setting, with the huge glaciated mass of La Grande Motte towering above us. We could see the piste-bashers grooming the slopes ready for the following day; the run they were on seemed to stop just short of a vertical drop of about 1,000ft.

There was no obvious drop on leaving the col; instead a desolate section led on over variable snow with only occasional glimpses of way-marks but after a few minutes the ground finally started to descend and we could start to move more quickly. Looking over the lip we saw beneath us the Lac des Nettes which was virtually frozen over and covered in snow. When we reached the level of the lake we gave it a wide berth, leaving it away to our right so as not to risk falling in.

With the day's end almost in sight we plodded through more soft snow, reaching a chain of small tarns, which this time we kept to our left. Faint footprints led almost alongside the tarns, round to a small dam at the outlet at the far end. From here we turned a corner and a short way beneath us stood the three chalets which make up the Refuge de la Leisse.

One of the huts was the Guardian's place where she slept and cooked, one housed the dining room and the kitchen for self-caterers whilst the third was a dormitory with alpine bunks sleeping about 48 people. The guidebook warned that the toilet and washing facilities here were 'meagre' but either we weren't too fussy or things had changed because we found a good hot shower and very respectable facilities. There were several very tame marmots wandering around, they were happy to come right up to the hut to be fed by the Guardian.

The weather forecast for the following day was not

good; storms were expected in the afternoon with rain and hail. This was unfortunate because it was to be our last full day when we hoped to cover a big distance with a couple of tough climbs, which would end with us sleeping within striking distance of the highest col of the whole route.

Next morning we were again away early. It was a lovely start, dropping gently down into a green valley; we were soon below the snow line and the difficulties of the previous afternoon were long gone. We passed several marmots and chamois on the descent alongside the river, the chamois using snow bridges to cross the river to escape us.

At the little stone bridge of Pont de Croé-Vie we crossed to the far side of the river and started a hot climb on a zigzagging path that took us steeply up the flanks of the Pointe de la Réchasse. Near the top of the steep section, at a memorial cairn for a couple of climbers who were killed nearby, we stopped to admire tremendous views back up the valley that we had just descended.

We decided we should give our new 'in-step' crampons a trial run in preparation for the feared ascent of the Col de Chavière the next day; there was a stretch of easy path still covered in snow, so there was no danger but it seemed a good idea to practice with our new 'running' crampons before we needed them for real. For the first two or three steps they seemed to work well but very quickly both crampons fell off and they simply flapped around my feet, hanging by their straps and were more of a hindrance than a help. Cath started across just after me and one of hers quickly fell off too. We realized that our shoes were far too bendy and there was no way these crampons were going to stay in place. This was a bit of a blow because we were early in the season and it had been a winter with a lot of snow, as evidenced by the amount of snow still lying on the Col de la Leisse.

Trying not to worry about it too much we put the crampons away in our rucksacks and continued on, past some 2nd World War bunkers, before turning into a remote valley between the Pointe de la Réchasse and La Grande Casse. It didn't take long to jog the length of the valley, pass alongside the lakes, mount a small rise and drop down to the refuge. This was an ugly place, there was a huge old building and a couple of new 'porta-cabin' type buildings that looked totally out of place in such a fine setting. We were glad we hadn't planned to stay the night here, however we did stop briefly for more *Orangina* and fruit tart which gave us the opportunity to watch tame marmots scurrying about chasing scraps.

Leaving the hut we headed north-west, in staggering scenery. Above us to our left soared the knife edged peak of Aiguille de la Vanoise, whilst to the right was a glacial lake, Lac Long. There was a rough track up to the hut and in places they had cleared a way through the snow drifts leaving walls of snow some 12ft high. We were able to take short cuts and take a more direct line down the steep moraine bank and were soon at the stepping stones that led us across the Lac des Vaches.

The paths were now much busier; there were hundreds of people on their way up from Pralognan, sweating profusely, as we jogged steadily down. It was a long, hot descent, almost 4,000ft down a dusty path. We passed a hut and were then down into the cool of the forest where we were able to enjoy some shade. Our path led down alongside some ski-tows until we finally emerged in Pralognan. Re-fueling was the first priority so it was straight to the bakers for yet more *Orangina* and some thick slices of quiche.

Aware that a storm was imminent we were soon on our way again, heading initially for a camp-site from where a path led alongside the river and up valley towards the afternoon's objective, the Refuge de Péclet-Polset. We eventually came out of the forest to cross both the road and the river at the Pont de Gerlan. A rough track then took us gently up the valley to a collection of farm buildings and a small refuge at les Prioux. From here we followed the road a short distance, up to the car-park at the road-end. As we went through the car-park a group of four or five lads were doing up their boots, rucksacks full of climbing gear by their side. I guessed they were heading for the same hut as us to do some climbing the following day; this was a good sign as it suggested that the weather forecast, although poor for later that afternoon, would be better again by the following day.

Shortly after starting up the track one of the climbers went by, the first time anyone had over-taken us on the whole Tour. This was like a red rag to a bull and we set off in hot pursuit; the young up-starts were soon burnt off and that was the last we saw of them until they reached the hut, a good while after us.

As we climbed higher the sky started to look more threatening and we could soon hear thunder, which was clearly not far away. We realized we wouldn't reach the hut before the storm broke as it was now very dark and lightning was flashing nearby. As it started to rain, then hail, we stopped to put waterproofs on, huddled by the side of the path as large numbers of people were heading down. We battled on up the path, which was quickly turning into a stream, and at last we spotted a radio mast on top of a small crag. We hoped this meant the hut was close by.

The thunder and lightning was directly overhead and we pushed on hard in an effort to keep warm. Thankfully it didn't take long to crest a rise and tucked around the corner was the Refuge; a fairly new building, sleeping about 80 people in small dormitories of eight. The weather remained cold and wet for the rest of the afternoon and into the early evening and we went to bed concerned about how we would find the Col de Chavière next morning. This was the crux of the route and the guide-book specifically warned that the pass was to be avoided at all costs during an electrical storm. If the weather were to remain bad and we couldn't cross the pass, we would be left with a long retreat down the valley and then some awkward bus and train connections to take us back to Geneva.

Thankfully, next morning the weather was fine, but cold, and it was easy to follow traces of old footprints through the snow. The route led up some gentle ridges, down into shallow depressions and slowly climbed on firm snow up into the open corrie. The view was clear and we could see easy ground nearly all the way to the col; there was just a final short steep section below the col that looked as though it might need care.

Relieved that we would have no trouble crossing the pass we were able to relax but it was far too cold to linger. We pushed on, past a beautiful ice-blue pool and directly up the snow clad head-wall; after traversing a shaly slope we finally reached the narrow crest. It was a fantastic situation with great views back down the way we had come, and to the south, the way we were now headed.

Looking down towards Modane we could see that we had a choice of two routes, these went either side of the Tête Noir. The main route went round the right-hand (or west) side of the 'Tête', however, the guide-book suggested that the left-hand route was better as we were more likely to see wildlife, plus we would pass the Refuge de l'Orgère, where we would find refreshments. This settled it and we dropped down the firm snow at a fast jog, spotting fox tracks, then several chamois and as we dropped lower and left the snow behind we saw our final marmots.

The path led easily down through grassy alps, then into forest to come out at the road-end and the Refuge de l'Orgère.

Here we had our final hut stop of the tour, one last coffee and slice of bilberry tart, before heading out into the forest again. The path was quite steep and we soon rejoined the uphill path that we had climbed five days before. It was a long descent, almost 5,500' down from the col to Modane, so the knees were in a sorry state by the time we emerged from the trees for the final short stretch along the road back to the railway station.

Although the start and finish of the route was rather unscenic, it hadn't taken long to leave civilization behind and reach the hills. It was certainly a good 'tour', with plenty of both wildlife and wild flowers. The guide-book says that the route is just 95 miles with about 23,000' of climbing but both these figures seem to be a little on the low side bearing in mind all the zigzags, the ups and downs on the long 'contouring' paths around the corries and the ups and downs on the approaches to the Col de la Leisse and the Col de Chavière.

Guidebook: Tour of the Vanoise by Kev Reynolds
             (Cicerone Press)

Map: Sheet 11   Vanoise, Massif et Parc National
             (1:50,000   Didier et Richard)

High Atlas of Morocco

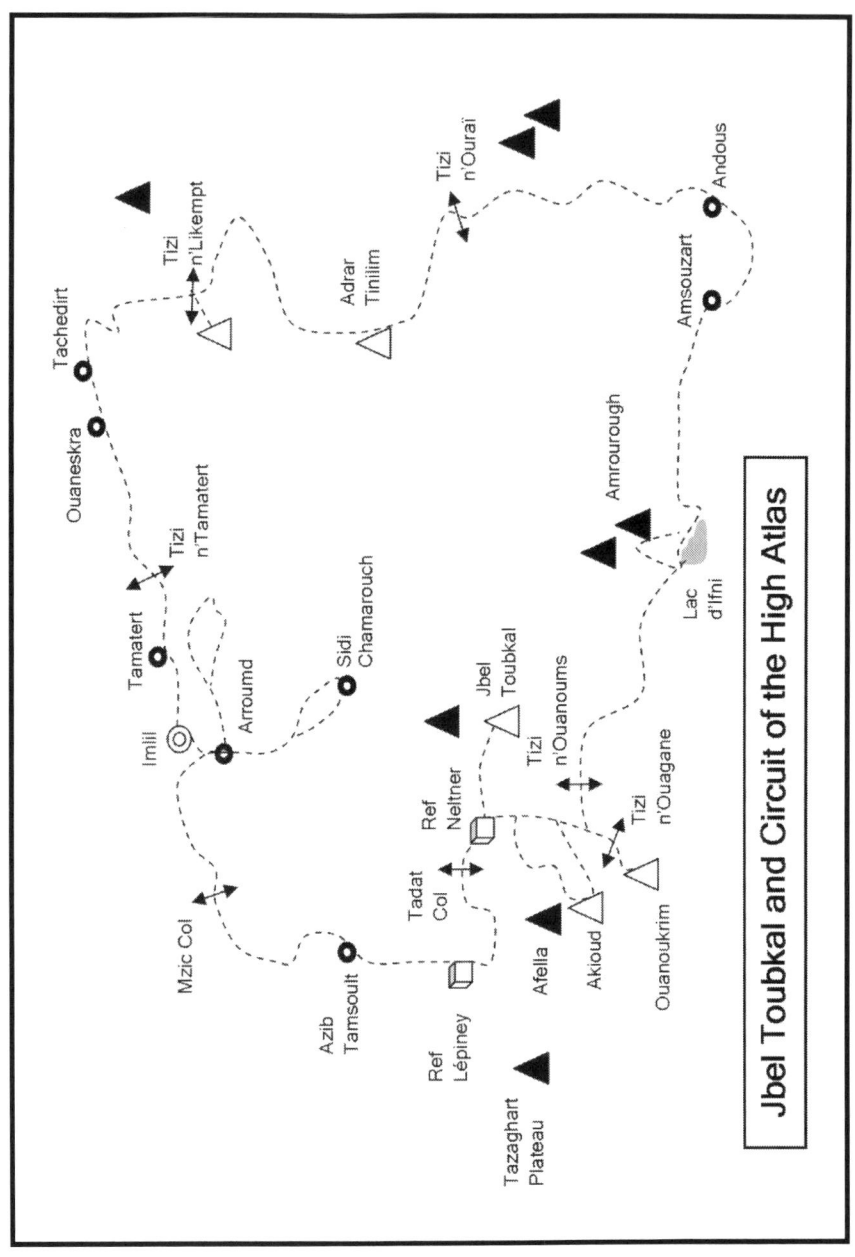

FURTHER AFIELD – WALKING, RUNNING & CLIMBING

Trekking in the High Atlas of Morocco – Jbel Toubkal

"An explorer says; I am not going to let life trample upon me. I am going to trample on myself. What's more, I am going to do it for fun."   (Anon)

I flew into Marrakesh and immediately came in for something of a culture shock on this, my first visit to a truly exotic destination. Our hotel was only about 200 yards from the Djemaa el Fna, the hub of the old town and a fascinating place full of atmosphere. Every evening the square is crowded with Moroccans, Berbers and tourists; you can wander round, stopping to watch a snake-charmer, or perhaps join a circle listening to some musicians or story-tellers, others take up the challenge of various games of chance, such as the 'Find the Lady' three card trick, or watch acrobats perform; colourful water-sellers drift through the crowds but they don't like to be photographed unless you pay them! The fire-eaters always had a good crowd round them and you didn't mind giving them a coin or two when they passed the hat round afterwards. One end of the square is filled with stalls offering a variety of foods, which smelt tempting, but were best kept for the end of the trek, not the start.

Our first day in Marrakesh passed quickly as we explored the town, which was fairly quiet. It was the first day of the Fête de Mouton, a festival celebrated over several days; everyone seemed to be buying a sheep for the forthcoming feast. Many of the mopeds and scooters that passed us had two or three people aboard plus a sheep, slung around someone's neck, on its way to be slaughtered.

Marrakesh was exciting but we were glad to pack the minibuses the following day and leave the oppressive heat and constant hassle to head up into the mountains. A couple of hours drive saw us at the road-end at Imlil. Here the villagers were also celebrating the Fête de Mouton; one of the older lads was dressed in a black sheep-skin and he chased the younger ones, throwing a big bag of flour at any that were too slow to escape.

We were surprised by a shower of rain but this soon passed and we leisurely made our way up the track to

Arroumd, an easy walk of about an hour. Arroumd was to be our base for the next few days and we were pleased to see that we were staying in one of the grander houses, it not only had running water but an inside toilet too! We were offered a large room to sleep in but most decided to sleep outside on the balcony, where we cooked and ate, or to climb the rickety wooden ladder up to the veranda above. Nights were clear and dry so we slept under the stars rather than risk bed-bugs inside.

That first evening, as we ate dinner, the sound of music came floating through the darkness; a couple of us went off to investigate and found the villagers dancing and singing in a small square between the high, window-less walls of their homes. The young, un-married girls stood on one side, while the un-married men of the village stood on the other; they danced in a shuffling motion, first one way then the other. All the time they were singing a very loud, and to our ears, monotonous song, to the accompaniment of several goat-skin drums. Every now and again one of the drummers would walk over to a small fire burning in the corner, and warm the skin of the drum until he was happy it was in tune again. It was a strangely moving spectacle, the whole setting and atmosphere making it almost hypnotic.

The next day we went for a short walk up to Sidi Chamarouch, a tiny settlement built amongst huge boulders, so from a distance it was hard to see it. The only thing that stood out was the brilliant white roof of the small mosque, built to celebrate a local hermit, who, on his death was made into a holy man. We found a great spot by the river for our lunch stop, at the foot of a small waterfall, where we dived in to wash the dust off. Later, returning to Arroumd, we followed the course of the river, which gave some exciting scrambling and bouldering and at the same time introduced us to some of the wildlife of the area. We saw several small lizards with bright blue tails and butterflies of various colours and patterns. That night the Berbers were again out celebrating in the square, singing and dancing into the early hours of the morning.

The following day we headed off up a side valley to the east of Arroumd. A barren, rocky valley led us up into the mountains for the first time. Our goal was a big waterfall, which we had to scramble across to; it gave us a wonderful ice-cold shower. A short way below the waterfall a small copper mine had been excavated from the hillside; a large pile of vivid blue chippings marked the entrance.

After lunch we set off back down into the valley and aimed for a low col across the far side. We reached the col after a short steep scramble up loose scree and as we arrived on a small peak above the col, the rain arrived with a vengeance. Thunder and lightning echoed all around us; people's hair was quite literally, standing on end. The exposed little peak was obviously the wrong place to be in an electrical storm so we dashed off, running quickly down the easy slopes.

We turned in early that night, as the trek all the way round, and then hopefully up Jbel Toubkal, was to start the following day. Next morning, with mules loaded, we set off down the valley for a short distance, towards Imlil, before turning east up the next valley to the village of Tamatert; we were soon surrounded by a number of persistent children asking for 'Bon Bons' or 'Un Dirham'. We climbed slowly up towards the col, the Tizi n'Tamatert, some taking the easier but longer zigzag path, others choosing the steeper but shorter direct route. On descending we again met with rain, which was proving a surprise to everyone. The mornings were usually warm and clear; then around one o'clock or so it would cloud over and sometime in the afternoon it would rain for about half an hour; then it would clear again, giving a clear, dry cloud-free night with superb views of the stars.

From the col we descended towards the village of Ouaneskra, everyone was looking forward to stopping as we were promised mint tea for the first time. As we turned a corner of the track we suddenly saw the small village, built on the steep slopes of a river valley. The village was completely surrounded by trees; each house was built into the slope and into each other. As soon as we were spotted, children rushed out, crossed the river and ran up the hillside to greet us and escort us up the main street and into one of the houses. The house was built of the local stone, the ground floor holding a variety of live-stock; we were ushered up a wooden ladder, through a hole in the floor to the first floor which had just two rooms, one for living and sleeping, the other a small cooking area. Sitting on blankets out on the flat roof, tea was quickly prepared; we all found it refreshing if a little too sweet. In the Berber custom it was made in an elegant silver teapot and poured several times from a great height into a small glass to aerate it. A steady stream of people came to have a look at us; they then drifted away as quietly as they had appeared. Our host kindly brought us small leafy branches, freshly cut from a tree, to help keep the numerous flies away.

Back on the trail we continued up towards the head of the valley and once beyond Tachedirt we started to look for a suitable bivouac site. Finding a small flat area just above the river we each cleared a level patch where we could lay out our *Karrimats* and sleeping bags for the night; while moving rocks to clear a space to sleep, someone unearthed a scorpion, we gathered round to have a look but it was quickly squashed by a Berbers boot. Before preparing dinner we wandered down to the river for an exhilarating cold shower under a waterfall.

The following morning we were expecting a hard walk as we had to cross our first major col, the Tizi n'Likempt (c. 3,550m). People left the bivvy in small groups as soon as they were ready, in order to start on the long drag up the rubble strewn slopes before the sun rose too high. Nearing the col the scree slopes seemed endless, the zigzags appeared to go left and right without gaining any height but eventually, after about 3½ hours everyone had re-grouped on the col. While waiting for the others to make the climb I made a quick dash from the col to the first major peak on the ridge to the west, this gave me a great view down into the corrie where our mules could be seen plodding relentlessly up the trail.

The descent from the col was a good scree run which took us towards Azib Likempt, about 1,000m below the col. We detoured round the village and dropped down to the river, which we then followed up the valley until we came to two huge boulders, where we planned to bivvy for the night. We again attracted attention from the local children who had been working in the fields and terraces; as they were finishing for the day they stopped by the river to re-arrange the drainage channels, diverting the water and causing some concern to those who had already laid out their sleeping bags! We were told that a previous group had been stoned by a mad woman at this site; we managed to escape unscathed although we were a little worried when a lone woman came and hovered close by, looking as though she were up to no good.

The following day the group split up; those with more energy chose to climb Adrar Tinilim, an easy peak of 3,670m, while the bulk of the group stayed in the valley, followed the river and stopped off at one or two of the more inviting pools for a swim on the way.

Tinilim was an easy summit for its height; we climbed the north ridge which gave us the chance to look back on where we had come from and, once on the summit, where we would be going over the next couple of days. Just as we reached the summit a hail storm blew up out of nowhere, so we jogged down, aiming towards the Tizi n'Ouraï. For the first time we now had good views of Jbel Toubkal and it was good to know that with a bit of luck we would be standing on top in four days time. We dropped down to the col and walked a short way down the north side, where we were pleased to find grass to sleep on rather than amongst boulders as at the previous bivvies. The rest of the party arrived a little later, just as the rain came on again for another short shower. As soon as the rain eased off we set about building stone walls to shelter us from the wind which we expected to blow over the col that night. After a good dinner everyone turned in, lying in our sleeping bags watching the stars, the milky-way and shooting stars, before eventually drifting off to sleep.

  Next morning in glorious weather we climbed back up to the col; the transformation in scenery was quite startling as we dropped down to the south then across a ridge, and headed down to the small pre-Saharan village of Andous. Here the houses were made of rammed earth and were of a sandy colour matching the bare rounded hills. We were invited in for mint tea by one of our muleteers, Mohammed, as this was his wife's home village. We sat on blankets on the veranda of Mohammed's mother-in-laws house and were served delicious mint tea from the traditional silver pot. Hearing a disturbance further down the valley we were told that two of the villagers had just made a pilgrimage to Mecca and they were now being fêted as they returned home.

  A large crowd noisily made their way into the village directly under our balcony; a very old shotgun was fired several times just to add to the occasion and there was a carnival feeling in the air. After much singing and dancing the two Haji eventually went off with the crowd to start some serious feasting. Because of the feast we couldn't buy any fresh bread so we settled down to wait while more was baked for us. In the afternoon we had a leisurely walk down the valley, passing through a deserted village, Tanmirselt; we cut some prickly pears but it was fiddly trying to peel them without being caught by the prickles and the end result was hardly worth the effort. In Amsouzart we stopped at a deliciously cool spring, the first time we had felt safe to drink the water without boiling it first. That evening we stayed at a house but elected to sleep in the fresh air, out on the veranda, rather than risk bed-bugs inside. Exploring the village after dinner I crossed the river and climbed a short way up the far side to find two small flour mills driven by water-wheels, it was a scene from the middle-ages.

The following day was to be just a short easy walk up a side valley to Lac d'Ifni. The trail wound pleasantly up the valley among lush terraces. It steepened as it climbed up a huge boulder field, which was presumably formed when the peak above, collapsed and fell into the valley, damming the stream at the bottom and thus allowing the formation of Lac d'Ifni. After several false tops we eventually had our first sight of the lake, which is the only sizeable lake in the Atlas. Due to the snow melt and its great depth the lake stays quite cool all year round, it is about 50m deep over much of its area and the bottom shelves very steeply from the pebble shores. We were told to watch out for water-snakes but unfortunately, or perhaps, fortunately, we didn't see any. Strangely everyone was quite breathless when swimming although we didn't seem to notice a problem with the altitude (2,295m) when we were walking.

In the afternoon, leaving the others to swim or sunbathe, I set off towards a waterfall which was up a steep valley midway along the north shore of the lake. A scramble up the narrow gorge took me to the waterfall but this blocked any further progress as it was too difficult to try and climb up beside it. After retreating a short distance I picked out a likely route that by-passed the waterfall and after an entertaining scramble emerged above the obstacle and continued up towards the peak of Amrourough. On the final ridge I decided that I'd had enough for the day so I turned tail and ran down the scree slopes towards our bivvy site; unfortunately, half way down the scree changed from runnable to unrunnable so I was left with a tiring plod back to the valley floor. Back at camp a welcoming piece of water-melon soon revived me and another swim washed the afternoons dust off. After dinner our muleteers sang for us and they tried to teach us a Berber song; judging by their laughter it was a very rude one.

An early start next day warned us that we would be in for a tough time, and so we were too. An indistinct path picked its way over the rocky floor and then started climbing up the scree towards Tizi n'Ouanoums (3,664m). As the morning wore on the party split into ones and twos, each person finding their own pace. A large flock of sheep and goats were making their way noisily up the trail under the care of a lone goatherd. Nearing the top another mixed flock was lazily picking its way through the boulders, the three teenage goatherds tried to strike up a conversation but their French was as good as my Berber so smiles and gesticulations had to do instead of words. I think they were trying to sell me their largest sheep but I declined their offer of fresh meat.

Eventually, after about three hours, I reached the col, just a narrow gap in a sharply pinnacled ridge; the view back down to Lac d'Ifni was well worth the effort to get up there. On topping the col new vistas opened up, down the far side towards the Neltner Refuge and across the valley to Ouanoukrim and the other 4,000m peaks of Akioud and Afella. After re-grouping on the col the group were left with a short walk down to the Neltner Hut in the valley below. An easy afternoon at the hut gave them a chance to rest for the following day when we would try for Toubkal.

20: Lac d'Ifni (top left) from Tizi n'Ouanoums

Not wanting to waste the afternoon at the hut I decided to go for Ouanoukrim, the second highest peak in North Africa at 4,088m. I ran down the scree from Tizi n'Ouanoums to refill my water-bottle at the stream, then zigzagged up the track to Tizi n'Ouagane. From the col the route took me up a steep but easy ridge, the ground then levelled out onto a scree covered plateau. The summit of Ouanoukrim is made up of two tops; Ras, a twin pinnacled rocky peak which can be seen from the Neltner, and to the south, Timesguida. A hail storm hit me on the broad scree saddle between the two tops but thankfully this didn't last too long. Haze and low cloud limited the views out to the Sahara, but the Tazaghart Plateau to the west looked interesting and well worth a visit on another day. I returned to the Tizi n'Ouagane and jogged down the track to the hut where I arrived tired but pleased with a good hard days walking. The hut was crowded so most of the group preferred to bivouac outside for a better night's sleep.

Next morning we set off for Jbel Toubkal; the route started with quite a tough scramble up steep loose scree but the angle soon eased as the path headed into the corrie. We made our way across the floor of the corrie, slowly gaining height amongst the boulders to arrive at the headwall on the right, or south, side. Here the scree started again in earnest and a scramble up the headwall led us to a poor path, destroyed by the passing of many feet, tired in ascent and careless in descent. Traversing left and upwards we finally saw the summit; a massive iron tripod and a large stone shelter mark the highest point in North Africa at 4,167m.

The whole group made the summit, except one; unfortunately he had been ill earlier on the trek and he never really recovered his strength. Various goodies were pulled out from the depths of rucksacs, saved for this momentous occasion. After a lengthy stop we set off back the same way; those who preferred to scree run making a slight detour to find the top of the longest run. In a little over half an hour the first of us were back at the hut and by the time lunch had been prepared and the kettle boiled the others had arrived. After lunch the group split again; several of us wanted to spend one more night in the mountains, the remainder chose to return to the relative luxury of Arroumd that afternoon.

This meant I had another free afternoon so I decided to try and grab another 4,000m peak. I chose Afella, a rocky peak on the ridge opposite Toubkal. A stiff scramble up tiring scree was hard work so I aimed towards the left-hand ridge thinking it might give an easier climb. Once onto the ridge the scrambling actually became harder and more dangerous so I was forced down into the next corrie over the far side of the ridge. This took me away from Afella, and it was looking as though it would be too risky for me on my own, I decided to divert to Akioud instead. A faint goat track led up across scree and boulders to the ridge from where a fairly hard scramble took me to the summit at 4,010m. As this was my third 4,000m peak in 24 hours I was very pleased.

From the top I had superb views across to Toubkal in the east, Ouanoukrim to the south, the Tazaghart Plateau to the west and north down the valley towards Arroumd. The cliffs of Akioud still held some snow left over from the winter. Dropping down into the corrie I saw a young goatherd and I realised that he seemed to be waiting for me; as I was about to catch him up he set off again without a word, this went on for some time, if I lagged behind he would slow down and wait for me before haring off again. He picked out a perfect route down barren, boulder strewn slopes and through rocky outcrops; he never faltered despite his open sandals and he never had to use his hands. I meanwhile was having to almost jog to keep up and often had to use my hands to help me scramble down. When we reached the path above the river we went our separate ways, having hardly said a word to each other but he had clearly guided me down, and he had obviously been trying to help.

The few of us that remained had the hut to ourselves that evening and we cooked a huge meal using up whatever odds and ends we had left.

The following day was our last in the hills and we planned a tough one to finish on. Leaving the hut we climbed steeply up scree on the west of the valley, heading for Tadat Col, marked by a distinctive rocky pinnacle. After two hours we passed a couple of small copper mines and not far above these we reached the col. A superb panorama opened up before us, looking north-west towards the plains and behind us over to Toubkal and Tizi n'Ouanoums. We dropped down a short way, traversed across the head of this new valley and contoured round to reach another col on the far side. From here good scree led us quickly down to the Lépiney Refuge.

Beyond the hut we met a group of French trekkers, with their muleteers, and they kindly invited us to join them round their fire for glasses of mint tea. Refreshed, we continued our descent, passing Azib Tamsoult, set amongst acres of terraces, and followed a delightful high level path as the valley plunged downwards. Once over the Tizi n'Mzic, our final pass of the route, we could look down onto Imlil where the trek had started some eleven days earlier. By-passing Imlil we joined a dirt road that took us back to Arroumd after a long day.

Next morning we packed our sacs and reluctantly made our way down the track to Imlil where we loaded up the minibuses for the short trip back to Marrakesh. In the afternoon we had time for another visit to the maze of alleyways which form the famous souks. Each type of product or service is gathered in one or two alleys; there is a spice souk, a tailor's souk, one for letter writers, another for butchers, woodworkers, leatherworkers; you wander around passing through each area, each with its own distinctive sound or smell. Before dinner we stopped for a drink on the terrace of the Café de France; it was great looking out over the roof tops of Marrakesh and watching the sun go down behind the minarets. The atmosphere in the square below was building up as darkness fell and it was very relaxing just sitting there watching the world go by, a perfect antidote to the strenuous few days we had just enjoyed.

Next day we took a local bus to Essaouira on the coast; the fresh sea air was an immediate relief and the whole atmosphere was far more relaxing than in Marrakesh. Here you could walk down the street without being pestered; you could look in a shop without being dragged bodily into it and you didn't feel as though you had to haggle over the price of everything you bought. All the buildings looked as though they had been freshly whitewashed, with the doors and windows outlined in blue, giving the impression of a clean, smart and fairly prosperous town. The afternoon and following day were spent swimming and exploring the old walled town and harbour area, but all too soon it was time to return to Marrakesh and head home.

Annapurna Circuit

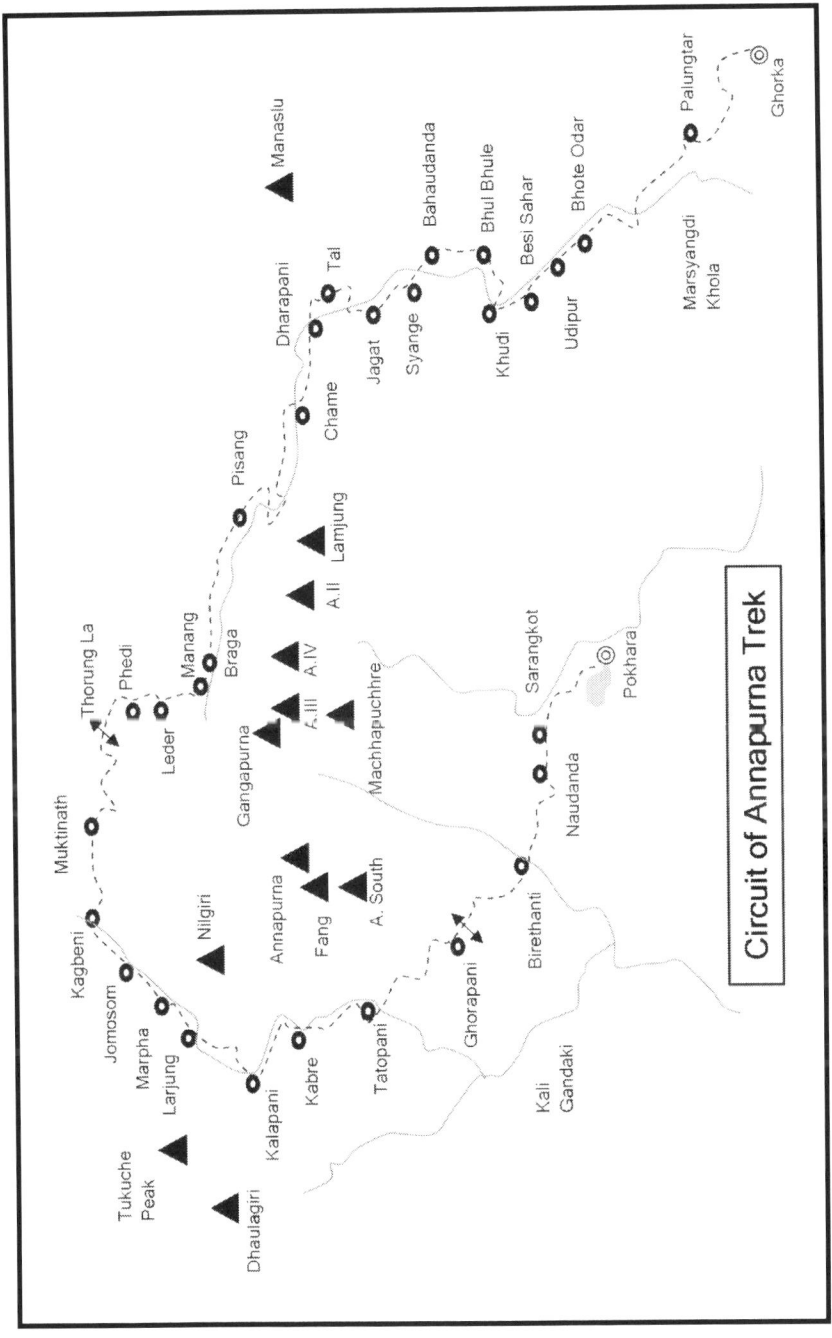

Around Annapurna – A Himalayan Journey

"Going on an Expotition?" said Pooh eagerly "I don't think I've ever been on one of those. Where are we going to on this Expotition?" (Winnie the Pooh - AA Milne)

Generally accepted as one of the greatest treks in the world, the circuit of the Annapurna Massif takes one through a wide range of scenery, peoples and culture in an exciting three weeks of walking.

We flew via Dhaka in Bangladesh, where we had to waste almost a day 'in transit' and were very pleased when we finally made it onto our plane for the short hop to Kathmandu. All bags safely collected, we were ushered onto a minibus for the short journey to our hotel and our trekking group of eight was now complete. After completing our applications for Trekking Permits we set out to explore Kathmandu.

We found our way to Durbar Square, an area of temples, palaces, statues and courtyards. One Palace is that of the "Kumari" a living Goddess. The origin of the legend is lost in the mists of time and various interpretations are now offered, but it appears she is the reincarnation of one of the eight Mother Goddesses and is chosen when 4 or 5 years old if she can fulfil all 32 specific signs. Once selected, she is virtually a prisoner in her elaborately carved wooden palace, allowed out on only six or seven occasions during the year for special festivals; she does however appear at a small window at brief intervals throughout the day. The Kumari then was about six years old; as soon as she reaches puberty she becomes human and a new Goddess is chosen. Just off Durbar Square is Freak Street; it was a hippy Mecca in the 60's and early 70's but the drug trade is now on the decline as Nepal fights to clean up its image.

Our first full day in Kathmandu was spent sight-seeing; first to Bhaktapur, the most medieval city in the Kathmandu Valley. Much of the city was constructed in the 17th century and is a maze of temples, palaces, columns and gateways; interspersed with narrow alleyways. From here we visited Pashupatinath, the most famous Hindu Temple in Nepal, situated on the banks of the holy Bagmati River. Outside the temple vendors were selling garlands of flowers, incense, rice and other "offerings". Firewood was also for sale as there are "ghats" here, small terraces jutting out into the river, where funeral pyres are built for cremations, the ashes are then scattered on the river. Whilst we were there, two bodies lay wrapped in shrouds with the pyres already built in readiness for them. The faithful passed by the bodies with hardly a glance as they walked down the steps to bathe in the river, some scattering garlands of flowers or petals on the water. We were not allowed in the temple itself, being non-Hindus, but we could see it well from the bank across the river, where monkeys scampered about among the stupas.

From Pashupatinath we headed back into Kathmandu to visit Bodnath; one of the biggest stupas in the world and some 500 years old. Around its base are 147 niches each holding four or five prayer-wheels. Devout Buddhists walk clockwise around the stupa, spinning each wheel as they pass and thus sending prayers by the hundred up into the heavens. From whichever direction you look at it the all-seeing eyes of Buddha stare out in all four directions of the universe.

That evening there was a full moon and the Nepalis were all out celebrating at temples throughout the city; we stopped at one where a small group of men were chanting from old parchment books to the accompaniment of drums and cymbals. As people passed by they would walk round the temple, keeping it to their right, ring a bell then make the sign of the cross on their forehead before moving on. All around the temple were rows of tiny butter lamps flickering in the darkness.

Next morning we loaded kit-bags and rucksacs onto a bus and after a couple of stops to pick up our Sherpas, porters, food and equipment, we set off on a six hour journey to Ghorka at the road-end. It was very hot and dusty in the bus as we followed the Trisuli River, where we could see several parties white-water rafting. After some time we turned north off the badly pot-holed main road and climbed up past a big Hydro-Electric plant being built by the Chinese.

It was late afternoon when we arrived at Ghorka and within minutes our fifteen porters had collected their loads and were moving off down the trail. Our team was led by a Sirdar, Ang Kami Sherpa plus two assistants. The cook team was led by Krishna who, just a couple of days before had been in jail. He had been arrested for fighting when drunk during a festival the previous week but somehow our trekking agent had secured his release; we were very glad he did as Krishna did a superb job all throughout the trek. After walking for just half an hour we stopped for the night; Ang Kami had arranged for us to set up camp in the courtyard of the village school.

While the Sherpas put up the tents and laid out our mattresses the cooks built a fire and soon had dinner on the go. We meanwhile were immediately surrounded by about 30 children who asked us for "pens" or "a rupee" and when they found that they weren't going to be given anything they tried to practice their English, which they seem to learn from a very early age. As it grew dark the youngsters drifted off to their homes. We ate dinner under the stars, by the light of the full moon, to an accompaniment of noisy crickets and cicadas. When the candles burnt down at 9pm we turned in.

The following morning we were up at 6am for our first full day of trekking. It was luxury to be brought tea in bed and given a bowl of warm water for a wash. As we ate breakfast the Sherpas took down the tents and packed all the kit ready for the porters. Where we were, high on top of a ridge, it was clear and bright, but below us the valley was filled with thick cloud. We set off and traversed across the hillside through terraces of rice, the trail then dropped steeply down towards the Daraundi Khola. Turning a corner, we suddenly had our first view of the high Himalaya. There in front of us were the snow capped peaks of Annapurnas IV and II and Manaslu. As we dropped down through the forest we entered the cloud and with the noise of the birds and crickets it felt as if we had strayed into a tropical jungle.

The valley opened out and we passed thatched huts and smaller thatched shelters for the cattle; banana trees grew by the side of the track as we passed through a small village and headed over a long suspension bridge. We then climbed steeply up and out of the valley until at around 10am we stopped for an early lunch. In the afternoon we made our way through terraced rice fields until we came to a large village on top of a ridge, Palungtar, where we bought small oranges and dusty *Coca Cola's*. That night we again camped by a village school; this time we enjoyed a big grass field with beautiful views of Machhapuchhre, Annapurna IV and Manaslu. Again we were surrounded by children as soon as we stopped but they were quieter and less demanding than those outside Ghorka and were happy to just sit and watch.

I had a terrible night, couldn't sleep and had to leave the tent four times. I suspected the meat of the previous night but the others who ate it were ok; some didn't risk it, which was probably a wise move on their part. I went without breakfast and felt rough all morning as we walked along in increasing heat. We stopped by a river for lunch but I couldn't face eating anything. Things quickly took a turn for the worse in the afternoon as I had to keep dashing off behind a bush; thankfully there was always plenty of cover. We passed huge spiders, many butterflies of all colours, shapes and sizes and big brightly coloured dragon-flys. Frogs abounded in the pools and puddles but that day was a never ending struggle and I really couldn't appreciate the beautiful scenery we were trekking through. Ang Kami took my daysac from me as I became weaker and weaker; I had to keep lying down by the side of the trail, feeling totally drained. We crossed another river by a suspension bridge with rotting planks and joined a dirt road which had recently been extended up the Marsyangdi Khola.

With Ang Kami's help I managed to scrounge a lift on a lorry which was going our way; I scrambled up on top behind the cab and clung to the spare wheel. The lorry was only going to Bhoto Odar, a mile or so up the track but it was a great help and I gratefully climbed down and staggered into the nearest tea-house to buy a big bottle of mineral water. Slowly I made my way along the track to Udipur where we were to stay the night. While our porters were coming in and the Sherpas were setting up camp, I sat outside the tea-house drinking gallons of lemon tea; after taking a fist full of various tablets I went to bed as soon as the tent was up. Thankfully I slept right through from 5.30 until about 5.00 the next morning and by then I felt almost back to normal.

By now we were learning the way things were done and the hierarchy of our team. Our 15 porters simply carried and when they arrived in camp they dumped the gear and went off to find a tea-house for their dinner of dhal bhat and to find somewhere to sleep. The cook-boys not only carried their cooking equipment but were usually last away in the morning and had to be first at the lunchtime stop; then again they would try to arrive first at the overnight camp in order to prepare dinner. Ang Kami, the Sirdar, arranged the loads for the porters; would find somewhere for us to camp, if not on the ground then perhaps on someone's roof; would pay off the porters once the food supplies had gone down sufficiently; bargained for 'doko' loads of wood and decided on the daily stages we would walk. Ang Kami's two assistants carried their own light packs and acted as guides during the day, put up and dismantled the tents and generally pampered to our every whim.

We were up early again next morning and were walking by 6.30; following the main track up the valley through fields of rice and maize, through the villages of Phalenksangu and Besi Sahar. After about four hours walking we stopped for lunch at a shady spot beside the river. The valley narrowed quite considerably here, the hillsides were too steep even for Nepalis to terrace. We crossed a tributary of the Marsyangdi by a wildly swaying suspension bridge. Passing through a little Gurung village we stopped to rest in the shade of a Pipal and a Banyan tree; these two trees are usually planted together with a stone seat underneath them; a shelf runs along the top of the seat so porters can sit down and rest their loads on the shelf without having to take off their 'doko'. From Khudi we crossed the Marsyangdi by a long suspension bridge which had several planks missing, then, about a mile beyond Bhul Bhule we came to a delightful sandy spot by the river where we waited for the porters to come in. There was an abundance of wild life around here; we saw monkeys in the tree tops, a metre long snake and a praying mantis; after dinner, fireflies darted about the cliff above us.

Next morning we enjoyed a pleasant walk through fields of rice, millet and maize and passed through several small hamlets. At the top of a steep climb we came to Bahaudanda where we stopped for half an hour to look round; then sat in the shade with a glass of lemon tea. It was best to walk early in the day, before the sun made it too hot to do anything but find a shady spot to sit and do nothing. In the afternoon the valley narrowed to a gorge and the track at times almost overhung the river which was 500ft below. The trail was narrow, with a steep cliff on one side and a big drop to the river on the other, so there were often traffic jams. Either we met a train of porters moving slowly under heavy loads, or perhaps a Nepali herding two or three buffalo. When passing any animals on the trail we quickly realised the importance of making sure that we stayed on the inside, just in case they swung their heads or brushed us with their loads; there would be nothing to stop you falling into the racing white waters below. We crossed over to the west bank of the Marsyangdi again and came to Syange, where we met a team of French canoeists who were about to re-enter the river. About a mile further on we dropped down onto an empty terrace above the noisy river and here we camped for the night. The porters took a long time to come in but they eventually appeared. Many more fireflies darted round camp that evening.

The following morning we started climbing as soon as we left camp; the trail switch-backed, sometimes we were just 100 feet above the river, then we would climb to almost 1,000 feet above it, but we could always hear the rivers roar through the trees. After passing through Jagat we stopped for a *Fanta* at a Tibetan run "hotel", which was set in a clearing surrounded by brilliant red poinsettias. Crossing the Marsyangdi again, this time by a good suspension bridge, we climbed steeply up the opposite hillside, now in the full heat of the day. As we progressed further up the valley it started to open out again and at one point the river disappeared completely, buried under the rocks of a massive landslide, only to reappear a little later in a flat basin, which was once the site of an ancient lake. Here we saw corn, barley and potatoes being grown and clumps of bamboo grew beside the path. We stopped for lunch at Tal, which looked like a one-horse Wild-West town. Later the route followed an undulating path cut into the cliff until we came to the wide scar of a landslide which had totally obliterated the path. We had to cross the rubble with great care, as a slip could have sent us into the river below. Safely across we descended to Karte and crossed the river into Dharapani. Here we saw stone entrance chortens for the first time; we also had to report to the Police Post, where we signed-in and had our Trekking Permits checked.

Ang Kami had trouble finding any flat ground to camp on and eventually we had to settle for a stony and rutted maize field. The porters were late coming in, and as it turned very cold as soon as the sun went down we waited in a tea-house to keep warm. After another good dinner we went straight to bed as it was far too cold to do anything else.

Almost immediately on leaving camp the following morning we saw a group of six langur monkeys but they were very shy and quickly went into hiding. We entered another small village through an entrance arch and passed a huge prayer-wheel some 4ft high; we then came to a 'mani' wall, along which were dozens more prayer-wheels. The path passes on both sides of any sacred walls or buildings so one can always pass it on your right no matter which direction you come from. A stream ran down the middle of the village street and in a couple of places it had been diverted by a wooden conduit to turn small water-mills to grind the grain.

The trail took us across steep forested slopes, constantly climbing up and down. It was cool in the trees and a very cold wind was blowing down the gorge. As we came out of the gorge and looked back we had a great view of Manaslu, at 8,163 metres it is the seventh highest mountain in the world. Ahead of us Annapurna II soared up almost vertically to a shapely summit. We stopped at Kodo for lunch and hanging from the balcony above our heads was a dead langur monkey; we tried not to let it put us off our food. We had to check-in again at the Police Post in the village where we noticed a much stronger Tibetan influence; more prayer wheels and mani stones; the ponies with their high saddles and colourful saddle cloths; the men wearing big felt Tibetan boots. In the afternoon we continued up the forested gorge to Chame, the administrative centre for the area.

On crossing the river we headed downstream a short way below the bridge to reach a small hot spring. The warm water bubbled out of the bank into a natural rock hollow beside the main river. The hollow formed a rock bath-tub just the right size for one person; the water was a perfect temperature, about the same as you would have for a bath at home, and it was great to soak off the dust and grime of the last few days. We again had trouble finding somewhere to camp that night but we eventually settled on a rough field about a mile further up the track. As we climbed higher and the valley narrowed, the evenings turned very cold as soon as the sun went down, so straight after dinner we were glad to climb into our sleeping bags.

There was a heavy frost overnight so we enjoyed an extra half hour in bed; even so, we were still up at 6.00. It was very cold in the shade at the bottom of the valley and we watched the sun move slowly down the ridge-top towards the valley floor until at last it reached us and started to thaw us out. It was a beautiful walk that morning, through pine forests and past a few silver birch trees. As we progressed up the valley the dramatic Paungda Danda rock face soared above us. This is a clean slice of rock almost 5,000ft high; curving round the bend in the valley so gracefully it looks as if it has been sliced with a knife. Meanwhile, to our left, we had views through the trees to the snow covered summit ridges of Annapurna II. In a clearing among the trees I came to a lean-to made of pine logs and covered in pine branches. Two enterprising young Tibetan girls had set up a tea-house and I was happy to stop and chat and drink a couple of glasses of lemon tea before making my way onto Pisang where we planned to stop early and camp for the night.

The entrance to Pisang is quite dramatic as the trail leads through an entrance chorten and past a long 'mani' wall housing 150 prayer-wheels. The houses here were flat-roofed, very solid looking stone buildings, each flying strings of prayer flags. Just beyond the far end of the village was a small square chorten containing a large prayer-wheel, which was revolving continuously; a stream having been diverted through the base of the building to turn a wooden paddle that turned the wheel. We found a sheltered spot to camp, surrounded on all sides by low trees; Annapurna II soared above us, it's northern face breathtakingly steep. This was the best day of the trek so far; I was now fully recovered from my bug, felt fit and strong and we were right up amongst the high mountains. I wandered up to Upper Pisang and explored the narrow alleyways, chortens and the abandoned monastery. Back at camp it was already really cold so we lit a large camp-fire until dinner was ready. Krishna, our cook, surprised us with a delicious steamed pudding that he had decorated with whipped egg white, it was amazing the meals he could conjure up over a wood fire.

21: Chortens beneath Annapurna

The following morning we were offered a choice of routes; either the easy, direct, lower road which the porters and cooks would follow, or the high road. We chose the high trail to Manang. It was bitterly cold when we were called for bed-tea (minus 5°c) and there was another heavy frost on the tents and the ground. After a hurried breakfast we backtracked to Pisang, past a 300m long conduit, carved from tree trunks, which diverted water from the main stream to the village water-mill. We crossed the river and climbed to Upper Pisang from where our trail worked its way through dwarf pine and scrub before climbing in steep zigzags to about 12,000ft.

We rested on the ridge-top and watched two huge Lammergeyers soaring on the thermals. Across the valley rose Annapurnas II and IV whilst above us were Pisang Peak and Chulu. It was another beautiful walk with stupendous views opening up at every turn of the path. After passing several 'mani' walls and stupas in the forest we came to a small village, we couldn't see a tea-house but thankfully a young girl, who couldn't have been older than four, came out and asked "Tea?". A couple of us gratefully followed her into her house; through a courtyard, which was covered in a carpet of fresh pine branches, up a ladder made from a hollowed-out tree trunk, to the veranda where we sat on a carpet she laid out for us. We had a couple of glasses of lemon tea and watched Lammergeyers gliding effortlessly, directly in front of us. Reluctantly we left this idyllic spot and carried on in the sunshine. Eventually we dropped down alongside the Marsyangdi Khola again and followed it up past Braga, a larger village set high on a steep hillside, until we reached Manang.

Manang is about 11,500ft above sea-level and we planned to stop for two nights to help us acclimatise. Ang Kami arranged for us to stay in a tea-house but there wasn't room for all of us so we pitched a couple of tents on the roof. The view from the roof was tremendous, looking straight onto Annapurna III and the Gangapurna icefall. I had a slight headache and wasn't sure if it was due to the altitude or the sun but the following day was a day of rest and acclimatisation so we were pleased to be able to have a lie in. Over breakfast we watched a couple of Americans who had climbed the cliffs above town and then parapented from the ridge; the local children rushed to see them landing, amazed at the mad foreigners. A couple of us decided to walk up to a monastery we could see high up on a narrow ridge. After a long climb we realised it was deserted and falling into decay. Below us we could see another square white building in a side valley, so we set off to explore this one too. A Lama saw us approaching and came to the door to greet us, he explained that usually there were three monks there but one was down in Manang. We were shown round the many prayer-wheels, garishly painted frescoes on the walls and the altar lined with carved statues of Buddha and rows of butter lamps.

Back in Manang we went to visit the Himalayan Rescue Association's Aid Post where three doctors do a voluntary three-month tour of duty, covering the main trekking months of October to December. Every afternoon they give an interesting talk on Altitude Sickness and they explained that their patients are roughly 50% trekkers and 50% locals. There is another aid post run by the H.R.A. over in the Everest region at Pheriche, where they have done much to advertise the risks of going too high too quickly. After dinner and another of Krishna's excellent steamed cakes we had a sociable evening of trivial pursuit, cards and dominoes before falling into bed at the very late hour of 8.30.

It was well below freezing again next morning and as we only planned a short stage we could afford to stay in bed until the sun had hit the tents and melted the frost. We were moving up to Leder at 13,800ft; for safe acclimatisation we could only make small gains in height and the 2,300ft climb was enough for the day. It was a pleasant path that climbed away and left the Marsyangdi valley, which we had followed for so long. Although overcast we had great views of Annapurnas III and IV, Gangapurna and Tilicho Peak. The track led north-west up the Jarsang Khola, which was a long way below us. This region is usually very dry as it is in the rain shadow and only scrub juniper and gorses grow up here. However it soon started to snow quite heavily and it quickly turned very cold so we pushed on up to Leder where we found just a couple of stone huts. Everyone crowded in out of the snow to thaw out with glasses of tea, we were all looking forward to crossing the Thorung La as we knew it would turn warmer again once we dropped down the far side. The snow stopped later but no one ventured far from the tents that day.

Day 12 was scheduled to be only about a two hour walk up to Phedi, at around 14,300ft. We allowed ourselves the luxury of another late start and set off in bright sunshine following a track which climbed into the barren valley; later crossing the river by an old covered bridge. Up on the hillside we saw a small group of goral or ibex but they quickly moved off. Reaching Phedi by mid-morning we soon had the tents pitched beside the hut, which is the last building before the pass. There were already several parties camped here preparing to cross; I had a slight 'altitude' headache so took a couple of pills and went off to bed to rest, it was too cold to sit around outside even though the sun was shining. After an early dinner we went to bed, knowing we faced an early start next morning.

We were up at 2.30am; it was very dark and very cold (about minus 10°c). After a quick breakfast we started the climb to the Thorung La. It was pitch dark as we climbed steeply up the track by the light of our head torches; it was far too cold to stop and in the dark there was no view, so we climbed non-stop, breathing heavily in the thinner air. We were soon onto snow but the track was quite clear and as we neared the col the ground levelled out. Just as dawn was breaking, around 5.15, I was walking on my own some way ahead of the rest of our group when I saw a dark object just off the trail, which I thought was a rock, then I realised it was a porter and his load. He was sitting there almost senseless and frozen stiff so I took my duvet out of my rucksack and fastened it around him; I then started pummelling his arms and legs, back and chest. He couldn't move at first so I kept rubbing him to try and restore some circulation. After a few minutes our cook-boys came along and together we pulled the porter to his feet and tried to make him walk. After another couple of minutes Ann, our leader, arrived so we were able to dress him in more warm clothes; we also forced a little warm lemon drink and a Diamox tablet down him; supported by the two of us we managed to help him up to the top of the pass. It was fully light by this time and thankfully the porter's companions now came back to look for him; they took over from us in helping him down the far side of the pass.

The Thorung La was an impressive place, surrounded by high, snow covered peaks; we stopped briefly at the cairn, took a few photographs and then hurried on down. As we descended from the col at 17,700ft the porter showed signs of improvement and he was soon able to continue down under his own steam. The track rapidly lost height into the barren, arid valley above Muktinath. About 1½ hours below the pass we stopped at the first tea-house and lay in the sun drinking endless cups of lemon tea. Continuing on down, just outside Muktinath we arrived at a large temple, one of the most important to both Hindus and Buddhists in the whole of Nepal. We wandered around the walled gardens and into the various temples, with their beautiful altars and colourful frescoes. In one of the temples, underneath the altar, were two small holes in the rock through which ran a stream and next to which burned a flame of natural gas. It is this combination of fire, water, rock and earth that makes the place so sacred.

Even though it had been a hard carry for the porters they soon arrived; it had been too cold for them to stop, they had no option but to keep walking to stay warm. After dinner that evening some of us decided we deserved a "night on the town". The local beer was quite tasty and went down well; we tried the rakshi but this smelled and tasted like paint stripper, none of us could face it so Ang Kami was more than happy to finish off several half empty glasses.

After the rigours of crossing the pass, the following day was to be an easy one. It was bitterly cold until the sun eventually rose over the high Annapurnas that towered above our camp. Leaving Muktinath we walked down through desert-like country where virtually nothing grew. It was an easy three hours down to Kagbeni, the most northern village that foreigners are allowed to visit, as it is not far from the Tibetan border. Kagbeni is only a small place; a cluster of mud walled houses with chortens, stupas and a monastery. Prayer flags fluttered in the strong breeze and a Lammergeyer soared overhead, casting a huge shadow on the ground. From here we could now see the Nilgiri peaks to the south, which rise to over 7,000m and the beautiful Dhaulagiri, at 8,167m. The steep sided valley leading to Kagbeni is lined with caves high up the almost vertical cliffs.

Leaving Kagbeni the following morning we entered the gorge of the Kali Gandaki; this is an important and ancient trade route between India and Tibet, the path follows the river as it carves its way between Dhaulagiri and Annapurna, the sixth and tenth highest mountains in the world. With only 22 miles between the summits the mountains tower 22,000ft above the river, making this the deepest gorge on earth. We followed the trail south along the wide river plain, hemmed in by steep cliffs; at one point we heard a rumble and a large part of the cliff crashed down in a landslide. The river meandered across the flood plain and we searched for fossils, which are plentiful around here.

An hour or so down the gorge we came to Jomosom, where there is a small airstrip and a Nepalese Army High Altitude and Mountain Warfare Training Centre. Staying on the western bank of the river we reached Marpha around mid-day; our cook team failed to appear so we stopped in a tea-house for dhal bhat followed by delicious locally grown apples. The floor of the valley here provides good growing ground and there are acres of orchards and fields of cabbages. Marpha was a delightful little town; all the streets were paved and very clean; there was even a sewage system running under the paving slabs. On the hilltop there was another small monastery and behind it, on the cliff, sacred inscriptions had been carved into the rock and painted.

We continued south along the river; in places the path had fallen away and the track had been built out on stilts and poles to bridge the gap. As the day wore on a strong wind started to blow up the valley, whipping sand into our faces; this is caused by the heating of the Tibetan plateau sucking the air through the narrow gorge. At night, as the plateau cools, the wind turns about and blows back down the valley. A couple of hours walking after lunch found us at Tukche, where we waited for the porters to arrive. As a treat Ang Kami found us a lodge to stay in for the night and it was good to be able to spread out the gear and eat inside where it was warm and light. As we were now losing height each day it turned warmer again and it was good to be back into shorts and T-shirts, although it still felt cold as soon as the wind picked up mid-morning. Next morning we enjoyed a pleasant walk down the valley to Larjung, an old village of narrow alleyways and tunnels, the houses are built within enclosed courtyards to provide protection from the daily winds.

We continued down the narrowing gorge and at a bend in the river, crossed back to the west bank at Kalapani. Due east from here are the dramatic peaks of Nilgiri, Annapurna and Fang and during a tea stop we heard a loud rumble from the Dhaulagiri icefall above us. The area changed again here; we saw no more prayer flags flying from the roof tops and fewer prayer-wheels and chortens. All the time we were in the Kali Gandaki we met long trains of ponies and donkeys, as many as fifty at a time. Most of the animals wore bells and the leading animals wore foot-long red and white plumes on their bridles; being in the confines of the gorge you could hear them coming from almost half a mile away. In the afternoon there was another huge landslide; the wind blew clouds of dust and from a couple of miles away it looked as though the whole valley was on fire. When we reached the area a little later rocks were still tumbling down into the river.

After lemon tea and delicious apple pie in Ghasa, which is at just 6,600ft, we walked to the next small hamlet where Ang Kami arranged for us to set up camp on the roof of a house. The gorge narrowed the next day; we crossed the river by a new wooden bridge and as the track had been wiped out by a land-slide we stayed in the river-bed before re-crossing the river and climbing the ridge to Kabre. There was a Festival taking place so the children had a day off school; the men and boys wore garlands of flowers and had a special tikka mark on their forehead, even the cattle had tikka marks, wore flowers around their necks and tassels on their horns. Across the streets were strings of flowers.

By now, after over two weeks of trekking, food began to play an increasingly large part in our thoughts. On arriving at Tatopani at mid-day we sought out the best tea-house and were amazed at the variety of food on the menu; chocolate cake, apple crumble and a tasty lemon custard tart were all soon tucked away and as it was so good we decided we would go no further that day, we gave ourselves the afternoon off. Tatopani means "hot water" and refers to the hot springs which are found here so we all wandered down to the river to soak in the hot springs where they flow into the river. While soaking in the hot water beneath bright sunshine, three or four monkeys came down to the river to watch us; as soon as the sun dropped below the ridge the temperature plummeted and we hurried out. That evening we watched the sun setting on Nilgiri South, while bats flew about among the trees.

The following day we were up early; we faced a long climb of over 5,000ft as we now had to climb up out of the Kali Gandaki valley, which we had been following for the past few days. We were heading towards Pokhara where the trek was to end. From the far end of town we crossed a rickety suspension bridge and set off on a fairly steep climb up to Ghara. By now the sun was up and it was very hot again; as we climbed higher the summit pyramid of Dhaulagiri rose above the ridge behind us. The terrain was now very green and fertile; with terraced rice fields as far as the eye could see. We continued, climbing steeply through a forest teeming with white faced monkeys, until we finally arrived at Ghorapani, which is a large village situated on the ridge-top at 9,300ft, here we set up camp. About 1,500ft above Ghorapani stands Poon Hill, which is a famous view point, so we arranged for an early call next morning.

Bed-tea was brought to us at 4.45 and we left camp by torchlight so we could be on top of Poon Hill in time to watch the sun-rise. It was well worth the effort as we gathered on the hill-top along with a small crowd of trekkers from all corners of the globe. Away to the north-west stood Dhaulagiri and

Tukuche Peak, then the gorge of the Kali Gandaki; to the north were Nilgiri, Annapurna, Annapurna South, Hiunchuli, Gangapurna and the twin summits of the graceful Machhapuchhre; beyond that to the north-east were Annapurnas IV and II. It was hard to believe we had been the whole way round these huge peaks in so short a time. After spending about an hour on Poon Hill we jogged back down to the tents for breakfast and packed up the gear.

The track wound steeply down a paved footpath through thick forest, alive with birds and troops of monkeys. From Banthanti the trail contoured round the hillside, through rice fields and banana trees to Ulleri where the track suddenly dropped 2,000ft down a steep stone staircase to the river below. We crossed two small suspension bridges in quick succession and were soon at Tirkedhunga where I met an ex-Ghurkha; he wanted to chat and on finding I lived in Scotland he proudly told me he had been to Edinburgh twice to take part in the Military Tattoo.

We continued to follow the river down a steep valley between heavily terraced hillsides. Another half an hour's walking brought us to Birethanti; we camped that night on an empty paddy field above the village, from where we watched the sun set on Machhapuchhre, the snow clad cliffs turning a vivid pink for ten minutes before darkness fell.

An early start next morning meant we were up in time to watch the sun rise on Machhapuchhre before we crossed the Modi Khola, which drains from the Annapurna Sanctuary. The track climbed steeply through forested hill-side to emerge on the ridge-top at Chandrakot. From here we contoured round a very green and fertile valley before slowly climbing to Khare at the head of the valley. Here we met a new road which the Chinese were pushing out from Pokhara; unfortunately we had to follow the dirt-road for a short while but we left it at Naudanda, as we kept to the high ridge from where we could look down on our ultimate destination, Phewa Tal, the lake at Pokhara. It was good to leave the dusty road and follow a pleasant path to Kaskikot, a small village of only a dozen houses. For our last night in the hills we camped in the school yard with another great view of all the high peaks.

Next morning we continued along the ridge to Sarangkot, which is almost directly above Pokhara, watching red kites flying both above and below us. We then regretfully left the ridge and headed for home. We had been on the trek for three weeks and now, just one hour from the finish, we lost the track for the first and only time. We had quite a battle climbing down steep terraced paddy fields and overgrown disused tracks until, thankfully, we finally emerged by the lakeside. We camped by the shore of Phewa Tal and the afternoon soon passed in an orgy of eating, drinking and shopping for souvenirs. The following morning we were at the air-field by 7am; the plane soon came in from Kathmandu and after a quick turn-around we were on our way home. It only took half an hour flying, following the backbone of the Himalaya, to take us back to Kathmandu.

We enjoyed a couple of easy days exploring Kathmandu; I particularly relished the chance to browse in the bookshops, one, the Pilgrims Bookshop, displayed many old second-hand mountaineering books and on expressing an interest I was shown through the back into a smaller room where there was an Aladdin's cave of hundreds of rare first editions going back over 150 years. Unfortunately prices were high but I was able to pick up a few interesting and cheaper editions.

Later I had a walk out to Swayambhunath, about four miles outside of Kathmandu. This is one of the oldest stupas in the world; it's foundations are said to date back 2,000 years, though the present buildings date from the seventh century. Standing on a hilltop at the head of a flight of 250 steps are temples, a monastery and sanctuaries along with the main stupa itself. There are countless prayer-wheels, a huge thunderbolt and above all, the all seeing eyes of Buddha on the central stupa. Devout Buddhists were performing a "puja" making sacrifices, burning incense and lighting small butter lamps. Running around in the trees on the hillside were dozens of small rhesus monkeys, giving the temple it's alternative name, "The Monkey Temple". The following morning, we headed for the airport for the long flight home.

My first visit to the Himalaya was a terrific experience and every bit as good as I had hoped. The scenery was fantastic, varied the whole time, with no two days alike. The people were very friendly; our team of Sherpas, cooks and porters were always smiling and ready to help and I knew that I would be back again and again.

A First Alpine Holiday – Climbs around Arolla

One summer four of us decided it was time we learnt how to climb safely in the Alps, so we booked onto a course run by Plas-y-Brenin, the National Centre for Mountain Activities. We were based around Arolla in Switzerland for a couple of weeks.

We enjoyed a leisurely drive down and booked into our campsite in Evolène, a charming little village made up of old wooden chalets along a picturesque main street. It seemed that every house flew the Swiss flag and the flag of the Canton and every house was bedecked with colourful window-boxes full of bright red geraniums; many of the women wore their national dress. Just above the village is a steep crag, the 'Guides Crag', and sticking out of it is a huge piton, it must have been 10ft long, and as a piece of art it was very impressive. That afternoon we met our Instructors; Nick and Mick were both qualified Guides, while the other two, Dave and Tim, were 'Aspirants', trainee Guides part way through their long period of training.

Next morning we jumped into the minibus for a short drive up the valley to just beyond Arolla, parking a short distance below the Arolla Glacier. A short walk up some loose moraines took us onto the glacier where we spent the day. Each of our instructors ran a session; movement on steep snow; climbing steep ice; crampon technique; and belaying on ice. The glacier is dominated by Mont Collon, which towered above us while we practiced the various skills which would see us through the next two weeks. We tried climbing without crampons on steep snow and ice, then practiced the art of cutting steps rhythmically and in the most energy efficient way possible. Then we moved on to wearing crampons and how to move up, down and across steep ice. We next practiced belaying; how to put in ice-screws and set up belay systems, which we tried out with a short but steep little climb. By mid-afternoon the surface of the glacier was very wet, with small streams running across, so we rapidly made our way down to the glaciers edge, where we rejoined the track down the moraine.

The following day was spent entirely on rock; learning and practicing the skill of moving together on a short rope, putting on running belays and generally settling into a 'team'. We again drove up to Arolla, this time heading up a jeep track alongside a ski-tow on the west side of the valley. We were surprised by the driver's skill and tenacity in driving the minibus as far up the mountain as was physically possible to save us all an unnecessary walk. When we could drive no further we walked for about an hour, which saw us up on the col, the Pas de Chèvres.

Here we split into four ropes; two headed south from the col and two headed north, we then spent the morning scrambling up an interesting ridge. In the Alps, speed equals safety, so we concentrated on the three of us moving together, spending as little time as necessary belaying, only moving singly when the ridge steepened or an individual move was too hard to climb while moving together. The route gave us a good mornings sport, scrambling over firm rock, up and down several gendarmes, with moves of grade II or III. On reaching the Pointe du Pas de Chèvres we dropped down to the col beyond and then had a slightly unnerving few minutes as we descended a very loose gully. Once safely down we contoured back round to the Pas de Chèvres.

After a short break we climbed north from the col and spent an hour or so abseiling and being lowered. We thought the latter was somewhat undignified but the Instructors kept stressing that the ability to move quickly is essential in the Alps; when long distances are involved and the weather can turn quickly against you, a short lower may be quicker than trying to down-climb something or set up an abseil.

That evening it was decided we would move up to a hut the following afternoon; this meant we could enjoy a lazy morning around Evolène, and we packed and re-packed our rucksacks a couple of times to make sure we had everything we needed for a three-day trip.

The road to Arolla was familiar to us now as we drove up and left the minibus parked on the outskirts of the village. After crossing the turbulent river we climbed a good path, initially steep and through pleasant woodland then the angle eased a little and the hillside became more open and exposed to the full strength of the sun. A Swiss flag came into view first, then, following the paint marked rocks, a short while later we came to the Cabane de la Tsa. Leaving our boots and ice-axes in the lobby we collected a pair of hut-slippers from the rack and went off to find our bed spaces. Later in the afternoon we wandered up the hill a short way to recce the start of the route in preparation for the morning. After a good filling dinner we were early to bed as we knew we would have an early start.

For the following day it was decided that one pair, already dubbed 'The A Team', would climb Pointe d'Tsalion by the West Face Pillar route, this was quite a severe rock climb and our little group was represented by Nigel. Meanwhile the rest of us would climb the next peak along, the Dent d'Tsalion, by the west ridge, which was noted in the guide book as being one of the best rock scrambles in the Arolla district. It was certainly steep but if you stayed on the crest of the ridge the rock was sound and free from stone-fall.

We set off from the hut after a quick breakfast and made our way by the light of our head-torches to the foot of the climb. We reached the bottom of the ridge in about an hour and by this time it was daylight, though we remained in shadow for some time before the sun rose above the summit ridge and we were able to enjoy its warmth. As well as our three ropes there were two continental teams on the route. They were very impatient when trying to pass us, or when we tried to pass them, and they had us worried at one stage when they knocked down some large boulders, which came crashing down in our direction.

After a really enjoyable scramble, we all met up on the summit, which wasn't big enough for more than two people to stand on at any one time. From the summit we followed the ridge south to reach the foot of the obvious pinnacle which is seen so well from the valley. This is the Aiguille de la Tsa; the pinnacle itself is only about 250' above the glacier and we climbed it on good rock, pleased to find piton and bolt belays in-situ.

On returning to the glacier we fitted our crampons and contoured round to the Col de la Tsa, crossed over a short rocky outcrop and came out at the Cabane de Bertol. The hut is in a very impressive position; there are sheer drops on three sides and it can only be reached by climbing several fixed ladders and cables between the glacier and the hut itself.

Thankfully we didn't need to be up too early next morning as we planned to spend the day practicing crevasse rescue techniques on the Glacier du Mont Miné, which was only a stone's throw from the hut. We roped up and made our way across the glacier until we found a suitable crevasse. Nick and Mick then demonstrated how one should extricate oneself from a deep hole. We all had a go, dropping down into the crevasse and trying to climb out unaided; it was very easy to say, or to read in a book, "prusik out" but it was a lot, lot harder than it looked.

Although we had all prusiked before, we now discovered that it was a totally different thing when you have to climb up and over an over-hanging ice lip. Once the rope starts to cut into the snow you're in trouble and it makes self-rescue nigh on impossible. We were then shown an assisted rescue, in which your rope-mates help you climb out by setting up a pulley system, after having first dug an ice-axe, dead-man or rucksack anchor deep into the snow and made fast the rope. Again we all had a chance to practice, both from within the crevasse and being the rescuer on the surface. If the rope is kept tight enough when on a potentially dangerous glacier, and if everyone in the party is paying attention, it should be possible to arrest a fall before a person falls all the way in, and this of course was what we were aiming for, but it was important to practice all the techniques, just in case!

During the day the cloud level dropped and it started to rain, so we packed up and made our way to the Col de Bertol, crossed this to the west and dropped down onto the Glacier de Bertol. We soon left the glacier and followed the obvious path which zigzagged steeply down to the upper reaches of the Arolla valley leaving an easy walk out back to the minibus.

We planned to leave on another three-day hut trip the following day, so we again enjoyed a lazy morning around the campsite, not leaving until 1pm. After leaving the main road in Arolla some exciting driving took us a good way up a jeep track on the west side of the valley. When the driver decided he could take the bus no further we set off on foot, on a steep but well made path alongside a dried up water-course. Within a few minutes, without warning, we saw a surging torrent of water above us, streaming down what only seconds before had been a dry bed. Someone had obviously opened a sluice gate, which regulated the stream below the glacier.

After crossing the moraines we climbed the glacier, jumping the open crevasses and generally keeping to the left of the glacier. A couple of hours after leaving Arolla we reached the Cabane des Vignettes, a large hut sited on a narrow arête, with a small heli-pad recently added to one end. When the helicopter lands it's rotors must be only inches from the wall of the hut and it must take a very good pilot to land there.

An early night was called for as we needed to be up early next morning for a real 'alpine start'. The Guardian called us at 4:15 and we crept upstairs for a hurried breakfast. Outside, we climbed down the ladder onto the snow where we put on our harness and crampons then set off by the light of an almost full moon. The 'A Team' were to do a different route again, while the other three ropes were to climb a route on the north face of L'Eveque. In the dark we followed a trace of a path round the edge of the Glacier du Mont Collon and crossed about 2km of glacial plateau. As day was breaking we reached a glacier falling from L'Eveque and we slowly climbed this snow slope, our other two ropes keeping more to our left. On this occasion I was climbing with Dave and Owen and we attacked the face from a fairly central position. First we crossed the bergschrund by a dubious snow bridge; we then climbed a short, almost over-hanging, ice wall of about 15ft. This brought us to the face proper; Dave led up a rope length, hammered in a couple of ice-screws and brought Owen and I up to the belay. We each cut ourselves a small ledge to rest on while Dave led out another rope length. Once he was safely up and had put in another couple of ice-screws we removed our protection and followed.

The climbing was steep and exciting; using only the front points of our crampons and whacking in our axe and hammer we quickly joined Dave. Towards the top of each pitch our calves were screaming and we were glad of the rest at each belay. Four rope lengths took us to the summit rocks, where we found a snow gully which led us easily up through the rocks and onto what we had thought was the summit. However, once out and on top we realised that we were only on a subsidiary summit, we had to descend a short way down the far side to a shallow col, from where a rocky scramble took us up to the true summit.

All three parties met on top but we couldn't stop for long because the snow was already softening in the bright sunshine. We descended the north-east ridge for a short distance to bypass the steeper ice of the north-face; we then dropped down to rejoin our tracks from earlier. As we made our way back to the Cabane des Vignettes we had to stay more to the centre of the Glacier du Mont Collon in order to avoid avalanche debris which covered part of our morning's path below Petit Mont Collon. It seemed a long way back across the plateau before we started the climb towards the col and so arrived back at the hut. We were back shortly after mid-day and enjoyed a lazy afternoon drinking beer while sunbathing on the heli-pad. Nigel and the 'A Team' returned an hour or so after us; they were muttering rude things about guide-book writers who promised sound rock, when what they found was actually very loose and unreliable.

A long day was scheduled for the following day so we all had another early night. Around midnight though, the whole hut was wakened when a terrific storm hit the mountain. Hail hammered against the hut and lightning lit up the dormitory like daylight, however, it was fine again by morning and an early start saw us ready to leave by 5am. The 'A Team' were due to traverse round to the North Face of the Pigne d'Arolla to climb it direct, while the rest of us planned to make a traverse of the Pigne d'Arolla; cross the Col de la Serpentine; climb the east ridge of Mont Blanc de Cheilon; descend the west ridge; cross the Glacier de Cheilon; go over the Pas de Chèvres and so return back to the minibus in Arolla.

One of the lads decided he needed a rest day so he stayed at the hut to descend with the 'A Team' when they came back after their climb. The rest of us started the traverse in one rope of two and two ropes of three. From the Col des Vignettes we passed beneath an icefall and moved south-east to where a steep snow slope climbed towards the summit. The sunrise over the eastern peaks was magnificent as we slowly toiled upwards. Nearer the top the angle eased off and the slope was split by several deep but narrow crevasses that we could easily jump. We were soon on the saddle from where easy snow took us to the summit. It was still very cold so early in the morning so we didn't rest long, but retraced our steps to the saddle before dropping steeply down to the west into a snow bowl, which looked as if it would give superb skiing. Once we reached the Col de la Serpentine we could clearly see the steep ridge leading to Mont Blanc de Cheilon; it looked hard and on seeing this a couple of the lads decided to call it a day and go straight down to Arolla missing out the final peak. Dave, Owen and I continued, with Nick and Julian on the other rope.

The sharp arête reared above us as we climbed the narrow east-ridge, where we ran out a couple of rope lengths, after which we were past the worst of the steep ice and moving together we climbed off the snow onto a rocky ridge. The route was not obvious and we moved up and down over a couple of pinnacles searching for the best way. In places it was very loose and combined with the steepness it meant we had to move very carefully. We reached a small col; above this a final short steep section gave us a good scramble up to the summit.

From this high point we enjoyed a great view and we took the opportunity to eat a quick snack before setting off along the west ridge. Here a mixture of rock and snow eventually led us down to the Col de Cheilon, from where a short steep snow slope, now starting to soften after a morning's sun, dropped down to the glacier. The glacier was quite heavily crevassed but all the crevasses were open and easy to avoid. We could see the Cabane des Dix about 2km away, standing on a bank of moraines above the glacier, so we moved fast, sensing that the end was in sight. We spent a welcome half hour at the hut drinking tea or beer; well rested we then just had to cross a mile of moraine covered glacier until we came out below the Pas de Chèvres. A scramble through boulders took us to the foot of the fixed ladders, these in turn took us up the steep cliff to the pass from where we had only a couple of miles, all downhill on a good track, back to the minibus. It had been a long but very satisfying day.

For our final climb we decided to try a 4,000m peak in an adjacent valley. We left at 11 the next morning, drove down to Sion, along to Sierre, then up the numerous tight hairpins to Zinal. From the village we took the minibus as far as we could up the track beyond. Following a recent land-slide the old track to the Grands Mountet hut was no longer passable and a new route had been made, which climbed steeply up the hillside over-looking the Glacier de Zinal. After climbing almost 3,000ft the path contoured round the hillside and across a boulder-field. The long hot climb had strung the group out and with bad weather threatening we raced over the final mile to the hut, the first of us just making it before the rain started. The rest of the team straggled in a little later having been caught out in a short sharp hail-storm, while wearing just shorts and t-shirts. This hut, the Grand Mountet, was probably the best we stayed in; the meals were good, there was a shower, a real toilet and to top it all, the Guardian's daughter was a real cracker.

When we planned this part of the trip it was agreed that two ropes would go up and down the north ridge of the Zinalrothorn, while the other two ropes were to traverse the mountain, going up the south-west ridge and descending by the north ridge. I was pleased to find that I had been promoted to the 'A Team' and was to try the traverse with Nigel and his rope. Unfortunately, after speaking to a couple of lads who had just returned from doing the traverse, and on hearing the weather forecast, our Instructors decided that all four ropes should go for the easier north ridge ascent so my promotion to the 'A Team' was short-lived.

We were all up early and away from the hut before 5am. For the first hour we climbed up a faint track through the moraines alongside the western bank of the Mountet Glacier. As daylight was breaking we were ready to leave the rocks and move onto the glacier itself, so we stopped to strap on crampons and put away our head-torches. A long climb followed, jumping many crevasses. The altitude of 3,500m was now making itself felt and we gained height slowly until we reached the bergschrund. Here we took the opportunity of having a short stop and a second breakfast before crossing a fragile snow-bridge and climbing up the headwall, which led to the foot of the Arête du Blanc. The narrow crest of the snowy ridge was only inches across and a false step would have sent us back down to the glacier a lot quicker than we had climbed it. With such exposure beneath our feet, rather than moving together Nick led out a rope length and cut himself a small stance, he then carved out an ice bollard to belay us on. A second, then a third pitch followed, and we were glad when we left the arête behind and gained the rocky ridge, which gave us a greater sense of security.

We tried to keep to the crest of the ridge but were sometimes forced to traverse out onto the western side to avoid some difficult gendarmes. The way was not obvious but an occasional piton confirmed we were on the right line. After some exciting scrambling, still wearing crampons to help on the odd patch of snow or ice, we reached the final gap in the ridge below a steep rock tower. Though over 100ft high, and by the look of it almost vertical, the climb of the tower was easier than expected and once up we were left with just a short easy section up to the summit at 4,221 metres.

For all the trainees this was the highest peak any of us had ever climbed, although I had been higher when I'd crossed the 5,400m Thorung La in Nepal. After shaking hands all round we were glad of the chance to have a short rest and a bite to eat. The view was superb as we looked across to the Matterhorn only 5 miles away to the south. Nearer to us were the Ober Gabelhorn and the shapely Dent Blanche, whilst almost 50 miles away we could see Mont Blanc.

As it was continually drummed into us that when climbing in the Alps you can't afford to squander too much time, particularly when the snow is softening rapidly, we were soon roping up again and retracing our steps; as we scrambled quickly down the rock tower we were glad not to be on the neighbouring peak where the sun was setting off avalanches and rockfalls at an alarming rate.

There were some unnerving moments as we traversed across some steep smooth slabs just below the crest of the narrow pinnacled ridge; our Instructors kept urging us on, they wanted us down and off the glacier as soon as possible. We were soon back at the top of the Arête du Blanc but rather than descend the crest on soft snow we dropped straight down the steep face. This took us quickly down to the bergschrund and back onto the Glacier du Mountet.

22: Rod on the summit of Zinalrothorn, Matterhorn in the distance

The snow was soft and kept balling up under our crampons, which made walking difficult, but it wasn't long before we were down off the glacier and were able to relax, unrope and take our harness and crampons off for the final time. We made our way down the moraine and with the hut almost in sight, after two weeks of accident-free climbing we had our first and only mishap when Owen stumbled on the rocks and hit himself in the face with the point of his ice-axe. Luckily it just missed his eye and he ended up with nothing worse than a small cut and a big bruise. We reached the hut around three in the afternoon and enjoyed a lazy couple of hours until dinner where we celebrated a successful adventure with a couple of bottles of wine.

In the morning we just had to drop back down the hill to the minibus. Somehow the descent turned into something of a race, which wasn't easy when wearing rigid plastic climbing boots and carrying a heavy rucksack. From simply jogging we were soon racing down the steep zigzags. As we flew down the track, people who were on their way up stepped to one side and stood open-mouthed, staring in disbelief at the mad Englishmen. Pooling all our food we ate a second breakfast at the minibus while waiting for everyone to re-group, then it was back to Evolène to pack up camp and start the long drive home.

It was a great trip; we had all learned a lot and hoped to be back in the Alps again on our own, to put what we'd learnt into practice.

The High Valleys of Everest

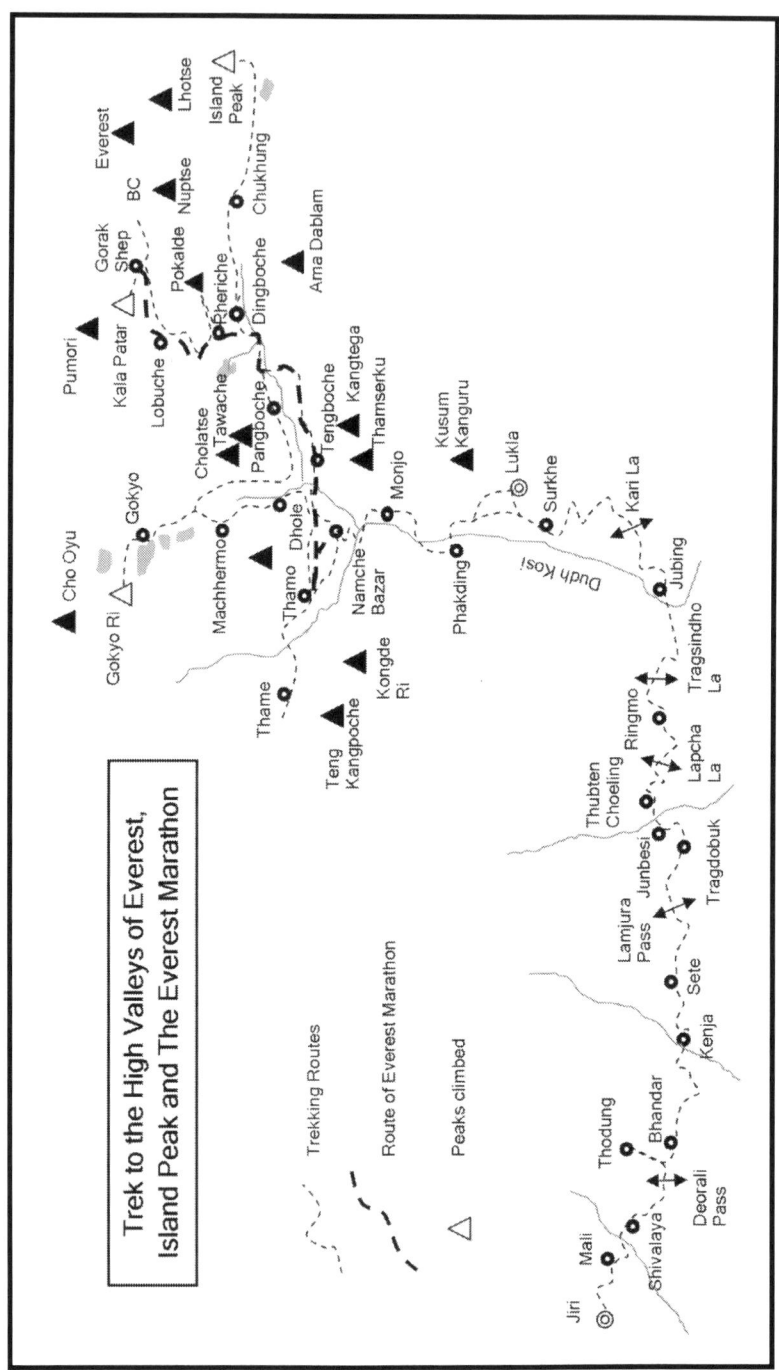

The High Valleys of Everest and the Climb of Island Peak - 6,189m

The long flight from Heathrow to Kathmandu, via Dhaka, was on time but sadly several kit-bags failed to arrive; this was not an auspicious start to the trip although I was pleased to see that mine was there in the pile. We were a group of fifteen, off trekking in the Khumbu, visiting Everest Base Camp and hopefully then going on to climb Island Peak.

The following morning we toured Kathmandu, visiting the familiar tourist sites. Firstly the medieval city of Bhaktapur; then Pashupatinath, a temple on the holy Bagmati river where an orange shrouded corpse was laid out on a 'ghat' awaiting cremation. Finally we visited the massive stupa at Bodhnath. This is one of the largest stupa in the world and the centre of Tibetan culture in Nepal; from high up on the stupa we had good views north to the snow covered Langtang Himal. Red robed monks walked slowly clockwise around the perimeter, spinning the many prayer-wheels as they went.

While we drove around the city we met several squads of riot Police, all were wearing helmets, bamboo vests and carrying long stout truncheons. The King was about to announce a new constitution and the people were concerned it won't give them all the freedom they wanted, as a result a general strike had been called for the following day which was when we were due to fly to Lukla. Those who had lost their rucksacks spent the afternoon desperately trying to either hire or buy the various bits of kit that needed to be replaced. Meanwhile, I wandered round town soaking in the atmosphere which attacks all your senses at once. The constant noise of horns and bells, from cars, buses, bicycles, bicycle rickshaws and the three wheeled motorised 'tempos'; people calling to you to look at their wares or tugging at your sleeve to show you a carpet or prayer-wheel. The smells of spices and herbs, the rotting fruit and vegetables, cooking smoke and incense all combined into a heady mixture.

Back at the hotel we packed our kit ready to leave early the following morning. As the weight was restricted we had to keep our kit-bags, which were going in the hold, to a minimum, which meant we had to wear our heavy climbing boots, carry our heavy waterproofs and cameras, and carry our climbing gear as hand luggage. It was all a bit farcical as the weight going onto the plane was of course still exactly the same.

We were at the airport early, with tickets for the third flight of the day, but after a long wait it became apparent that the Lukla flights were running behind schedule. When the second flight returned, instead of loading us on, we were told there would be no more flights that day. The weather in Kathmandu was hot and sunny with hardly a cloud in the sky and we heard that it was also fine in Lukla, but there was turbulence en route and the pilot decided not to go back; this meant we were first reserves for the following day. We knew Lukla flights were prone to delay; at that time the dirt airstrip was only about the size of a football pitch and is hemmed in on all sides by high mountains; the pilot has to bring the plane down in a tight spiral and if it's windy or there's bad visibility he has sole responsibility for deciding whether to go on or turn back, which seemed fair enough.

> *"Passengers Please Note: In Nepal we do not fly through clouds, as here they often have rocks in them!"*
> (old sign at Kathmandu airport's domestic terminal)

After returning to the hotel I took a walk out to the Monkey Temple at Swayambhunath. It's a fascinating place in spite of all the tourists and associated tourist stalls selling brightly painted masks and puppets, jewellery, prayer-wheels, religious 'thangkas', postcards, stamps, coins and of course, *Coca Cola*.

Next morning we were up at dawn again to head back to the airport; it was cold and misty but it started to clear which gave us hope of being able to leave, only for it to close in again worse than ever. Thankfully we had been given tickets for the first flight of the day and three Fokkers were fuelled and waiting on the tarmac. Eventually we were given the all clear and boarded the twin engine, 20 seater STOL plane. The flight only took 30 minutes and was an experience in itself. The list of big mountains we saw started with the Langtang peaks to the north of Kathmandu, then east towards Gauri Sankar, possibly Menlungtse in Tibet, then Everest itself and Lhotse. A sharp turn north took us up into a narrow, very deep, wooded valley where an impossibly small cleared strip eventually became apparent in the hillside village of Lukla. The engines were cut back and we dropped down to the strip, bounced about wildly on touchdown and rattled along the stony surface to come to an abrupt halt by swinging sharp right onto the parking bay. It was only once we were out of the plane that we saw how steep an angle the strip lay at, and just how short it was, probably no more than 100 yards.

Within minutes the kit was unloaded so the plane could return to Kathmandu and make a couple more trips while the weather stayed fine. Our porters loaded some dzos, a cow/yak cross-breed and organised the rest of the loads. Finally we were on our way, following a major trail north up the river valley. There was not a lot of climbing as we later had to drop down to cross the river; the trail just meandered in and out of side valleys. We crossed the Kusum Khola on a wooden bridge; at the head of the valley loomed the huge west face of Kusum Kanguru, said to be the hardest of the designated 'trekking peaks' in Nepal. Although called a trekking peak it doesn't imply they can simply be walked up, Kusum Kanguru for instance is technically difficult it's just that the formalities are kept to a minimum meaning less red-tape and expense.

The day was warm and sunny and by early afternoon we reached Phakding; after crossing the Dudh Kosi by a narrow suspension bridge we waited in a tea-house. Our porters and dzos weren't far behind and once they were unloaded our Sherpa crew quickly pitched the tents and set up camp. As soon as the sun dipped below the high ridge at 3.30 it turned very cold so tea and biscuits were served in the warmth of the tea-house next door.

Our Sirdar was Ang Kami; he organised the porters, yaks, cooks, food, where we camped and the length of the daily stages. It was good to see him again as he had also been Sirdar on my Annapurna Circuit trek a couple of years previously. I had a short walk through the village and up the hillside, then it was back to the warmth of the tea-house for dinner and we were all in our sleeping bags by 7.30.

Next morning we were woken with 'bed-tea' at 6.30 and a few minutes later a bowl of warm water was brought to the tent door for washing. Four of the group were already unwell; two with sickness and diarrhoea, one with throat trouble and one with a chill. When we left Phakding we were well wrapped up against the cold; we could see the sun shining on the peaks above but the valley of the Dudh Kosi was very narrow and the sun didn't reach us until we had been walking for almost an hour. All morning we were accompanied by the roar of the river as we followed the Namche Bazar trail. The path was not very wide considering how important a trade route it is and we found it hard to pass trains of yaks and dzos; it wasn't too bad if they were coming down the trail as we could stop and let them through, but when we caught up with some and tried to overtake we had to choose our spot carefully and slip past quickly without either being speared by their horns or worse, being knocked over the edge several hundred feet into the river below.

We stopped in the small village of Monjo for an early lunch; as we left later we met a young Sherpani collecting water to take back to her tea-house, she was just strolling up the path, carrying a very heavy load, and playing a mouth-organ non-stop. We were now up at about 10,000ft and were already puffing just walking slowly up the hills.

A short distance above Monjo we entered the Sagarmatha National Park where, for a fee of 250 rupees, we were given a permit which we had to show along with our trekking permit at various check-points en route. One of the conditions of the permit was that we were fully self-sufficient with our fuel supply; it's illegal to buy wood or to take it from the hillside, so we cooked on gasoline fuelled stoves.

As we continued up the Dudh Kosi we crossed and re-crossed the river by precarious suspension bridges and a wooden cantilever bridge until we reached Jorsale from where we crossed the Bhote Kosi and started a long 2,000ft climb up through forests until we reached a lonely tea-house. From here we had our first glimpse of Mount Everest, about 25 miles distant, at the head of the Imja Khola. Finally we reached Namche Bazar and were glad to stop at a tea-house while we waited for the rest of the group to catch up. Namche Bazar is at 3,446m (11,350ft) so we were all starting to feel the altitude, especially when we tried to overtake porters or yaks, which required a sudden spurt of effort; we planned to spend two nights in Namche to help us acclimatise. Namche Bazar is the capital of the Solu-Khumbu region and is set in a natural amphitheatre; the houses, 'hotels' and shops are built up the steep hillsides, with a few small fields in the only flat ground available. The town takes its name from the big market held there every Saturday.

Luckily, the following day was a Saturday and after a late breakfast we were able to visit the market and explore the town. Everywhere you looked there were people; many were wild looking Tibetans dressed in dirty sheepskin jackets and trousers with tall woollen boots, their long hair threaded with red braid and wound round their heads. The Tibetan and Sherpa women wore their traditional costumes of a long black dress covered with an embroidered apron. Dozens of children ran about with their bottoms out of their torn trousers, they were wearing wellingtons, flip-flops or going barefoot. It was very crowded; at one point a heavily laden Sherpani knocked into me, I almost fell onto a pile of about ten dozen eggs, which would have been very expensive! The variety of produce was amazing, from sacks of rice, corn, all sorts of fruit and vegetables, cheese and butter; the meat had to be seen to be believed, for fifty yards there were legs of buffalo, whole yak heads, whole goats and sheep, there was also livestock; chickens, goats and small cattle. There were also clothes, hides, tea, bottles of rum and beer, salt, kerosene and candles, in fact virtually whatever you wanted. A weather-beaten old Tibetan wanted to trade two yaks' tails for my *Rohan* shirt but I declined.

In the shops of Namche you can buy used climbing gear, sold off after expeditions, but they know its price and they also know that if you need climbing gear up here then you'll pay their prices rather than go all the way back to Kathmandu to collect more. There were stalls of hand knitted jumpers, scarves and hats, hand-woven carpets and saddle-rugs, antique Tibetan prayer-wheels, jewellery, yak bells and the tall cylindrical churns used to mix butter-tea.

In the afternoon we climbed the hillside to visit the Sagarmatha National Park museum, which is housed in a newly constructed building on top of the ridge. The museum was basic; much more impressive was the view from outside. South back down the Dudh Kosi where we had come from, whilst to the north-east were Everest, Lhotse and Ama Dablam. On our way back down we called in at the Police Post where we checked-in and had our permits stamped.

Back at the tents we sorted our gear for the rest of the trek. We knew we wouldn't need our climbing gear for some time so we packed all the ice-axes, helmets, crampons, harnesses, ropes and karabiners into a couple of kit-bags for a porter to take up to Dingboche to await our arrival. Meanwhile our Sherpas had been busy, buying the mass of food required to feed the whole group for the next couple of weeks.

Next morning we woke to a cold but clear day. As we ate breakfast in the bright sunshine we watched a group of Himalayan Tahr sunning themselves on a large rock above the village. Knowing the walk up to Thame wouldn't take long, a few of us climbed the hillside for another look at Everest; this time visibility was better and we had a clear view of the final summit cone, just peeking out above the Nuptse/Lhotse ridge.

Also looking good was the snow covered Ama Dablam, a fantastic snow and ice tooth. After a short while we returned to camp to collect our rucksacks and set off to catch up with the others.

The high level trail led off to the north-west, far above the Bhote Kosi; it wound easily round the hillside through shrubs and pine trees with birds and butterflies flitting about. On the way we met some Tibetans who were returning home over the Nangpa La, a journey of five or six days; we heard them coming from some way off as they were singing cheerfully. We were amused to see one poor fellow stumbling along at the back; any profit he had made from trading had obviously been spent on a little too much chang and rakshi.

Above Thamo the trail started to climb and we became more spread out as some of the group were suffering more than others; either from colds, stomach troubles, the altitude or a combination of all three. Near here we passed a hydro-electric building, but most of the workings had been washed away in a major flood which had also torn huge chunks out of the landscape. We were told that a new scheme was underway at Thame to replace it. At a place where the gorge narrowed we crossed the Bhote Kosi and had a short steep climb up the far side on a dusty trail, which led round into a high valley beneath the sheer snow and ice walls falling from Kongde Ri and Teng Kangpoche. Kongde Ri is virtually the same height as Island Peak and to think that we could possibly be going so high was beyond belief.

At Thame, where Sherpa Tenzing grew up, there were a few houses scattered among the stone walled potato fields; high up the hillside above we could see a large monastery or 'gompa'. As our Sherpanis served afternoon tea the peace was shattered by several large explosions; we were all quickly out of the tents to see what was going on. More explosions followed, from only a couple of hundred yards away, which sent chunks of stone flying in all directions. Here we realised was the site of the new hydro-electric scheme.

While chatting with our Sherpas we found that one, Phurba, had been with Messner to Everest, Makalu and Dhaulagiri, so to come with us to climb Island Peak was something of a rest for him. Our Sirdar, Ang Kami, had also been on several big expeditions and had carried loads to the south summit of Everest. A game of frisbee with some local kids kept us warm when the sun went down, then, after an early dinner we all drifted off to our tents.

The valley faced east so it was good to eat breakfast in the warmth of the sun before climbing the hill to visit the 'gompa'. We took off our boots at the entrance and filed inside it's dark recesses. Along the roof beams were brightly embroidered 'thangkas', there were dozens of butter-lamps on a shelf in front of a large gilded Buddha and all along the far wall were row upon row of prayer books. A pile of strangely shaped yellow hats, worn by the monks during ceremonies, stood in a corner by the only small window; alongside were conch shells and long trumpets, together with a couple of large drums hanging from the rafters. After an interesting time wandering around we returned to camp to collect our rucksacks and set off to catch up with the porters.

For a couple of hours we retraced our steps along the previous day's route. We passed the school in Thamo again, where the kids were sitting on benches enjoying their lessons outside in the sunshine. We continued back down the valley towards Namche but then turned off the main trail and climbed a long hill, up past a small airstrip, which was built to serve the Japanese built Everest View Hotel, which had already fallen into disrepair. After passing through an area of huge boulders and caves the village of Khunde came into view.

This high village is set in a huge amphitheatre and is the site of the first hospital built some years ago by Sir Edmund Hillary. The hospital has a small operating theatre, short stay and long stay wards, and a separate kitchen for use by the patient's families, as food is not provided by the hospital. The hospital is funded solely by voluntary contributions so they charge a fee of just five rupees for locals and two hundred and fifty rupees for foreigners. Foreign groups often donate items of equipment and one of our party had previously raised funds for a *Gamow Bag* for the Khunde hospital; the patient is sealed into a large bag, air is pumped in which brings the pressure up and has the same effect as taking the patient down to a lower altitude. In the few months that they had had the apparatus it had already been used several times and may well have saved lives.

By the time we left the hospital the sun had gone down and it was very cold so we lost no time in dropping down to the village of Khumjung where we camped for the night. Here was the longest 'mani' wall that I have ever seen; it must have contained thousands of the carved stones. Clouds drifted in and filled the corrie so after dinner we were soon in bed.

Next morning we woke to another beautiful day, though it was still very cold, and the sun didn't appear over the ridge until we had been walking for half an hour or so. It was a great mornings walk; as we turned a corner the awe inspiring sight of Ama Dablam came into view, to its left were Lhotse and just visible was the snowy summit of 'our' mountain, Island Peak (Imja Tse). After contouring round the valley we had a gradual climb up to a tea-house where we rested for a while, drinking lemon tea and watching eagles and griffon vultures soaring on the thermals.

After a steep dusty descent towards a bridge over the Dudh Kosi the trail climbed slowly up through rhododendron forest, where snow and ice still lay in the almost perpetual shade. Looking back we had great views across to Kangtega and Thamserku, the ice flutings falling almost sheer to the glacier below. We camped that night at Dhole, in a potato field beside the river. To help acclimatise some of us climbed the ridge above camp to watch the sun go down; at the head of the valley stood Cho Oyu, the eighth highest peak at around 8,200m on the border of Nepal and Tibet; to the east was Tawache, south Thamserku and Kangtega, while to the west was a string of smaller mostly un-named and un-climbed peaks. As soon as the sun went down it was freezing so after dinner we were in bed by 7.30; this meant we faced another twelve hour night. It may have been Tilman who said that one of the biggest dangers on a Himalayan expedition is bed sores.

Thankfully our camp faced east and the sun was already warming the tents when we were brought our bed-tea next morning. The days walk was only a short one as we needed to acclimatise slowly; after a short climb up onto the ridge we contoured and gradually gained height, passing through Luza before continuing on up the Dudh Kosi until we reached Machhermo. The scenery here was much bleaker than the previous day as the rhododendron forest had given way to scrub juniper. On the way we passed several small 'yersa', summer settlements used when yaks are grazed up here in the summer months. We were now at about 14,500ft and as it was important not to gain too much height each day we only needed to walk in the mornings, leaving the afternoons free to go for a short walk or climb before dropping back down to camp.

That afternoon I wandered up the side valley and climbed up onto the ridge amongst stunning mountain scenery. When I returned to camp everyone was quite subdued; a

Frenchman had been carried down from Gokyo suffering from pulmonary oedema. The sensible thing was to descend still further but Em (a doctor), Brian (translator) and the two Johns (our trek leaders) were having a hard job trying to persuade them. After a while his friends agreed and a porter was enlisted to carry him down to Dhole.

Another short day was planned for the following day as we continued up the valley to Gokyo. The trail dropped towards the river before climbing up onto the terminal moraine of the Ngozumba Glacier which falls from Cho Oyu. A short steep climb took us up alongside the roaring melt water; we crossed a wooden bridge, then another climb through boulders brought us out alongside the lateral moraines, which were some 200ft high. We soon reached the first of the five Gokyo lakes and saw a couple of Brahmin Ducks swimming amongst the ice. The trail was not too steep as it was bounded on one side by the moraine ridge and the other by the mountain wall. After passing the second lake, the third and largest lake soon came into view; it was a beautiful deep blue, even deeper than the blue sky in which there wasn't a cloud to be seen. A small settlement of three lodges had sprung up here to cater for trekkers; we set up camp on a great site away from the others, directly above the lake.

After lunch a few of us walked further up the valley towards the fourth lake and climbed up onto the moraines from where we had tremendous views of Cho Oyu and down onto the dry, rubble strewn glacier below. On the way back to camp we called in at one of the lodges where a multi-national group of Canadians, Australians, Norwegians and Israelis had set up a mini ghetto-blaster and were holding an impromptu disco, it certainly livened up a cold afternoon. After the usual good dinner most people were in bed by 6.30; it was minus 20° in the tents and was becoming difficult to stay warm.

Gokyo sits at 15,700ft and next morning most of the group elected to climb a small peak, Gokyo Ri, which is a little over 18,000ft and overlooks the lakes and glacier. The path zigzagged slowly up the grassy hillside and as we climbed higher the grass gave way to rock. It was harder and harder to maintain a comfortable rhythm and keep going without having to stop for a breather; it was however a beautiful morning, once the sun had risen over the ridges to the east. At last after almost two hours of hard grind we reached the summit, which was decorated with prayer flags. The climb was well worth the effort; the summit of Everest looked magnificent as we looked across to the south-west face, the west ridge and the south col route. Next came Nuptse and Lhotse, then, a little further away was Makalu, and round to Kangtega again. Just eight miles to the north was Cho Oyu and stretched out beneath us was the entire length of the Ngozumba Glacier; it was covered in rubble so very little ice was visible and the string of bright blue/green lakes stretched away to the south.

On the descent from Gokyo Ri a huge Lammergeyer glided around my head for some minutes, coming very close at one point. By the time we were back down at Gokyo our camp had been packed up and the porters and yaks had left. We retraced our steps down past the lakes, over the bridge, down through the moraines and along-side the infant Dudh Kosi. After a short while we crossed the river to the small village of Na, which nestled at the foot of the glacier's terminal moraine. It was another cold night but probably only minus 10°.

23: *Our tough little Sherpanis, always smiling*

A good walk next morning took us back down the valley of the Dudh Kosi, this time keeping to the east side of the river. The trail generally contoured round the steep barren hillside; it was a narrow, dusty track that overlooked the river some 2,000ft below and a stumble could have been fatal. As we neared the entrance of the valley we slowly lost height and started to pass mani walls, small stupas and tall poles flying prayer-flags. With the lower altitude we entered an area of dwarf rhododendron bushes and here we saw several redstarts. We passed a couple of water driven prayer-wheels and reached Phortse, where camp was set up on a small terraced potato field. Drifting up from a gompa below was the sound of horns and trumpets and beating drums.

It was a beautiful morning as we followed a high level track round into the main Imja Khola valley. We saw several pheasants, small groups of tahr and flying below us, eagles. On our right was a 3,000ft drop to the river; across the valley among the trees on the ridge top we could see the newly re-built Tengboche Monastery. As we rounded a ridge the huge south-west face of Ama Dablam came into view; a hanging glacier far up on the face seemed about to peel off at any moment. Later, around another corner the Nuptse/Lhotse ridge came into view with the summit of Everest just visible over the top. We stopped early and camped that night at Pangboche; we had planned to continue to Dingboche but one of the group was ill and we knew there was no way he would make it that far.

Some of us took the opportunity to visit the gompa, where the Head Lama of Tengboche Monastery was on a rare visit. We each bought a silk 'khata', a ceremonial scarf, to present to the Lama. Almost everyone from the village turned out to meet the Lama and they all wore their best hats for the occasion. We entered the courtyard and climbed a rickety flight of steps, which led us into a larger room where the Lama sat on a dais, lit only by the light of a small window; we joined the queue and approached one by one to offer our scarves, together with a small donation for the monastery.

After blessing the khata the Lama returned it and hung it round my neck. In another room of the monastery we were shown what are reputed to be the scalp and hand of a yeti; however, subsequent research in America suggests they are not!

Next morning we only had a short walk as we were finishing off the previous days stage, and it didn't take us long to reach Dingboche. Here we had our first real sight of Island Peak, which was dwarfed by Lhotse, but was nevertheless an attractive snow and ice mountain of a very worthwhile size. Camp was set up in a field behind a lodge and with plenty of time and space to prepare, Hero, our cook, served up an 'interesting' dinner. It started with a strong clear garlic soup with spicy poppadums; the main course consisted of roast potatoes, cinnamon rolls and apple pie; the sweet was a hot lemon pudding with a crumb topping, which had been brought out from the UK. It was all superb but Hero certainly had a strange idea of European tastes.

It was very cold next morning when we set off but we hadn't gone far up the hillside when the sun reached us. It was a steep climb up the ridge above Dingboche; we then contoured round towards the Khumbu valley. Some of us stopped for lemon-tea at Dughla; Dai came back from a visit to the loo looking rather upset, he had dropped his expensive glacier glasses into the pit and was unable or unwilling to fish them out! I came to the rescue, not by retrieving them but by lending him my spare pair. We were now faced with a short steep climb up the terminal moraine of the Khumbu Glacier; the climb went quickly and we re-grouped on top amongst dozens of small cairns built to commemorate the Sherpas and porters who had died on Everest and the surrounding peaks. From here the trail dropped down to follow a glacial stream alongside the lateral moraines. On the way up to Lobuche we had fine views of Pumori and to the right, the huge wall of Nuptse. Although still early, we stopped at Lobuche, which is at 16,500ft, and about 2,000ft above our previous camp. With time to spare I climbed up onto the boulder strewn ridge above camp; as the sun set I watched Nuptse turn wonderful shades of golden pink.

Next morning we set off on a short walk up the valley, between walls of moraine to Gorak Shep; a couple of us sat and drank tea in a lodge while we waited to see who else would arrive but after half an hour there was still no sign of anyone so we set off up Kala Patar. This is a small hill on the flank of Pumori; at 5,550 metres it gives good views across the Khumbu Glacier to Everest's south-west face and the Khumbu ice-fall, which leads into the Western Cwm. Unfortunately the morning was cloudy and overcast and we were denied any real views.

After dropping back down to Gorak Shep we met some of the others and a few of us climbed up onto the Khumbu Glacier and walked towards the site of Everest Base Camp. We knew that Base Camp was deserted as all the expeditions which had been there earlier had already left for home, so we didn't miss much by not going further up the glacier. We did however enjoy the walk among the pressure ridges, which pushed up fragile 'sharks fins' of ice some 20ft high. On our way back down the glacier a serac fell from high up on Nuptse, which brought down a huge avalanche. As the afternoon wore on the clouds parted and by evening the sky was clear giving us another very cold, starlit night.

In the morning the tents were covered both inside and out with frost, it had been minus 20° again during the night. After breakfast most of the group again tried to climb up to Gorak Shep and climb Kala Patar. This time the weather couldn't have been better and the view across to Everest was fantastic; the Lho La, a high pass leading into Tibet, was just across the glacier, Pumori looked spectacular as was Nuptse and a host of other unnamed peaks. It was very cold on top and we had a long way to go so after taking several photos I dropped quickly down a rocky ridge, which led more directly to Gorak Shep and returned to Lobuche.

After having lunch and waiting for a couple of hours those of us at Lobuche decided to continue down and a long walk saw us back at Dingboche by early afternoon. By 4.30 there were still only six of us sitting safe and sound drinking tea in the mess tent and with only an hour of daylight left we were beginning to wonder whether or not we would see the others again that day. Everyone finally made it in to camp in a fairly exhausted state, just as it was turning dark.

Because of their late arrival and exhaustion, it was agreed that we would all have a mornings rest then move up to Chukhung after lunch; this was only 1½ hours further up the valley. From Chukhung the following day we climbed along banks of moraine and after crossing a sandy, dried up lake bed, we reached Island Peak base-camp around mid-day. It was a dismal place where the wind swept through, driving dust into everything. The gloomy atmosphere wasn't helped when we found a plaque to three people who had died when an avalanche struck their tents during a storm a couple of years earlier. In the afternoon six of us collected our climbing equipment and set off up the hill with our two leaders and some Sherpas. It was a steep but easy climb to a small level area at around 18,000ft where there was just enough room to pitch our tents. It was of course very cold and a strong wind was blowing so after collecting a few rock crystals and watching a spectacular sunset we retreated to our sleeping bags.

Island Peak takes its name from the fact that it is indeed almost an island; it is virtually surrounded by the Lhotse and the Lhotse Shar Glaciers. The peak was first climbed in 1953 by members of the Everest expedition; Evans, Wyllie, Gregory and Sherpa Tenzing all made the first ascent while testing their oxygen sets.

Our hardy Sherpanis were up at 4am the next morning, melting ice to bring us bed-tea at six. It had been a long sleepless night and it was almost a pleasure to leave our sleeping bags and start to prepare. After a quick breakfast we set off with light rucksacks, initially up a very loose rocky gully then trending right and upwards until after about an hour we came to the end of the rock and stepped onto the glacier. We put on our harnesses, crampons and helmets and roped up. Two Sherpas, Ang Kami and Phurba, set off first; Kevin and I, led by Tugden followed; the two Johns, our trek leaders, each led another rope of two clients. The way led across a beautiful glacier surrounded by high mountains. Tugden set a slow and steady pace as he wound in and out of hidden crevasses; we jumped across one or two open ones and eventually stopped below a steep 300ft ice-wall, which led to the summit ridge.

Our rope stopped for a snack while Ang Kami and Phurba climbed the ice-wall, fixing two ropes as they went. When we were ready to follow we tied a prusik knot around the main rope to protect us should we fall; then with ice-axe in one hand and the other sliding the prusik loop, we climbed slowly and somewhat breathlessly up to the narrow crest of the ridge.

24: *Approaching the summit of Island Peak*

Here we were midway between the south summit and the main summit of Island Peak; we turned right along the narrow, corniced ridge where a fall would have meant a drop of around 2,000ft on one side or 500ft the other. Ang Kami fixed a second rope on the snowy arête, this wasn't really needed but we would have been grateful for it if it had been any windier. Ahead the final snow slope broadened out to the summit.

Towering above us was the huge face of Lhotse while some distance away was the pyramid shaped summit of Makalu. Baruntse, Tawache, Kongde Ri and Ama Dablam all stood out clearly in the bright blue sky. We were at 6,189m (20,304ft) the highest any of us had been before. After half an hour on the summit we were feeling the cold so as soon as the third rope reached the top we retraced our steps back along the ridge and dropped down the fixed ropes. It didn't take long to reach the snowy basin below the ice-wall and crossing the glacier soon had us warmed up again. At the first rocks we un-roped and took off our crampons and warm clothes; then it was away again, almost at a run down the loose scree and rubble back to high camp. We enjoyed a brief stop for tea and to collect the rest of our gear before descending to base-camp; a short way below high camp we passed the second group who were moving up for their attempt on the summit; we wished them luck and headed down. That night the temperature again fell to below minus 20°.

The following day we enjoyed a lazy day in and around base-camp; the Sherpanis kept bringing us food and hot drinks at regular intervals. At base-camp the cooks supplemented the petrol stoves with yak-dung fires; this gave the tea an interesting and not particularly pleasant taste. I went for a walk up onto the moraines above camp and looked down onto the Imja glacier 200ft below. There were several fresh footprints in the soft sand on the crest of the ridge but I couldn't decide what had made them, I still say they were yeti shaped! Only a short way down the valley the glacier came to an abrupt end in an ice cliff, which dropped down into a lake; as the glacier crept slowly down large chunks of glacial ice broke off into the lake to form mini ice-bergs.

We were visited in camp by a small marmot-like creature and a pair of Tibetan snow cocks as we waited for the second group to return; the last ones came in just as the light was fading but they too had all made it to the top and had enjoyed a great day.

Next morning we started the long walk out; it was a lovely stroll back down the valley through Chukhung and Dingboche all the way down to Lower Pangboche where we camped in a small potato field. On the way down we had passed a scene straight out of Hitchcock's 'The Birds', a huge flock of yellow billed choughs filled the sky turning it quite dark.

We also saw several redstarts which were singing and feeding among the juniper bushes. As we were now down at only 3,900m we had a frost-free night and it was a relief not to have to sleep in long-johns and thermals.

The following morning we had another beautiful walk; initially contouring the hillside and then descending to a rickety suspension bridge over the roaring Imja Khola. Once across the river we entered forest and climbed easily in bright sunshine among pines and rhododendrons. A rustling in the leaves drew my attention to a small musk deer just off the path, it was obviously young and nervous and it quickly skipped off into the undergrowth. A short while later I spotted three more, one of which was darker and had quite long tusks, so was presumably the male and leader of this particular group. After another short sharp climb we emerged into a clearing on the ridge top where the village of Tengboche has sprung up around the monastery.

All the early Everest expeditions used to call at the monastery so the climbers and Sherpas could receive a blessing from the Head Lama; the original building was totally destroyed by fire in 1989 but it had now been almost re-built. It had been restored surprisingly quickly considering that all the stone is shaped by hand and porters had had to carry in all the wood from several miles away. It would be hard to find a better place for meditation; the monastery sits on a spur jutting out into the main valley and is surrounded by high peaks on all sides. At the head of the valley is the huge Nuptse-Lhotse wall, with the summit of Everest just showing over the ridge; towering above us was Ama Dablam; across the valley stood Cholatse and Tawache while a short way down valley were the peaks above and beyond Namche Bazar. Another young musk deer trotted through the courtyard while we were resting; the birds and animals around here were quite tame, feeling safe in a Buddhist stronghold where they have never been hunted. Leaving Tengboche we had a steep descent to the river some 2,000ft below, through delightful pine and rhododendron forest.

After crossing the river on a fragile suspension bridge we passed through Phungi, with its row of water driven prayer-wheels, and immediately started on a long climb up through forest. One of our yaks went on strike here; it was given food and water, partially unloaded, then fully unloaded but still it refused to move. It seems that yaks do this occasionally and no amount of persuasion will make them change their mind. The kit was shared out amongst the other yaks and we continued the climb. After a long afternoon we eventually rounded one last corner and there was Namche Bazar nestling in the hollow below. Phurba called to us from a lodge; after tea and apple pie we set up camp behind the lodge.

Next morning Hero made us huge plates of delicious Spanish omelette and rosti for breakfast. As we were about to leave, Ang Kami's wife arrived and she served us chang, the Sherpa beer brewed either from rice or millet. It was very drinkable but at 8.30 in the morning it was a little early to do it justice. After the chang Ang Kami's wife presented each of us with a 'khata' scarf.

It was very hot that morning as we dropped down the hill and enjoyed our last look back to Everest, Nuptse and Lhotse. It was a long but easy walk down the Dudh Kosi, crossing and re-crossing the river, either on wildly swinging suspension bridges or over cantilever log bridges, through pine and rhododendron to Phakding. Another couple of hours walking saw us on the final climb up onto the ridge from where we looked down onto Lukla and the end of the trek. Low cloud filled the valley that evening and a steady drizzle set in.

Hero surpassed himself with a fantastic spread for our farewell dinner; we had soup, roast chicken, salad, rice and vegetables followed by a hot pudding and then a huge birthday cake for one of the group. Ang Kami kept the chang flowing, refilling our glasses every time we took a drink; so it soon became difficult to keep track of just how much we had drunk. After dinner the whole group; trekkers, Sherpas, cooks, porters and yak drivers spent a lively evening singing and dancing until very late.

Next morning dawned cloudy and damp and we were concerned that the planes wouldn't be able to fly. Lukla is not a pretty place and we had no great desire to be stranded there for even one day. After breakfast Ang Kami again kept pouring us glasses of chang, which we were beginning to enjoy, and he presented each of us with another 'khata'. An anxious couple of hours passed as the clouds refused to lift but at last we heard the sound of an approaching plane and an army cargo flight touched down in a cloud of dust. Two civilian Fokkers followed within minutes and we knew we were ok.

The take-off was amazing; a very bumpy 100 yards downhill at full throttle, the ground then simply dropped away beneath us and we were airborne. The 35 minute flight was interesting, if a little turbulent at times. We heard later that these two flights were the only ones to make it through that day; we had been lucky, several other groups were stranded at Lukla for a few days.

We were able to enjoy a couple of days in Kathmandu; time passed very quickly and of course food played a large part as we searched out the best restaurants and cake shops. When not eating I browsed the bookshops where I managed to pick up some fairly rare mountaineering books. One morning a couple of us hired bikes and cycled out to Bhaktapur, a city that has hardly changed over the last two centuries; it is filled with temples and shrines, squares and fountains.

25: Devout Tibetan

It was a special holy day so all the women and young girls were dressed in their finest and were performing ritual offerings, a 'puja', at the many shrines. On the way back to Kathmandu we stopped to watch fruit bats roosting high up in the trees and called in at Pashupatinath, where two cremations were taking place on the burning ghats that jut into the river. The relatives seemed very calm and didn't appear to mind the onlookers, or the monkeys, that roamed among the shrines.

Eventually the time came to return to the airport for the flight back to London, again via Dhaka, where we endured a ten hour wait in transit. It had been a superb trip but it was good to be home and to see the familiar landmarks as we flew in over London.

The Everest Marathon

After living in my camper-van for eighteen months, and running many of the best high-level routes in France, Switzerland and Italy, I decided to take advantage of my fitness, endurance and acclimatisation and entered the Everest Marathon.

We were an unlikely looking group who gathered at Heathrow Airport in November 1993; certainly not the super-fit superstars that I expected to see. On arrival in Kathmandu we were presented with fragrant garlands of marigolds; a short drive then took us to a reasonable hotel within walking distance, or a cheap taxi ride, from the centre of the city.

After a couple of days exploring this wonderful old city we climbed onto two old buses and left Kathmandu just after dawn. It was a long ride, made longer by a forced stop of almost an hour when a vehicle ahead of us ran off the road, which was just a dirt track above a roaring river. After crossing the Lamosangu Bridge a Swiss-built road took us to the road-end at Jiri. We met our Sirdar, PK, here and he impressed immediately as he had the gear unloaded and the porters away in double-quick time. It was a pleasant two hour walk along easy trails and I felt great, like a dog let off the lead at last. The fresh air of the foothills and the openness meant I could cruise along and I strolled ahead of the group to reach Mali where I found the tents had already been pitched and were waiting for us. I sought out the cook tent and a mug of tea and some biscuits were soon thrust into my hand. With two mess tents pitched end to end we could not quite squeeze the whole party into them for dinner, it was a lesson soon learned, if you wanted to be warm, be there on time to grab a seat near the middle.

Next morning we were walking by 7.15. We had a huge number of porters to carry all our tents and gear and they headed off while we ate breakfast in the open air. For the next few days the route headed generally east, going across the grain of the country so that we were forever climbing and descending ridges. On this, our first full day on trek, we headed down the valley through lush terraces, through small settlements, over an old covered bridge and into the valley of the Kimti Khola. Here we crossed the river by a big suspension bridge into the village of Shivalaya. The obvious trail climbed up the valley to Sangbadanda where we stopped for lunch in the schoolyard. Keen to do some proper running training again

I changed and ran back down to the bridge at Shivalaya. Running back up the trail to Sangbadanda was a little harder than expected; the altitude was already making a significant difference. A worrying thought was that the race would be starting around 9,000ft higher than I was running at here.

During the long lunch break we all had to introduce ourselves to the camera crew who were following the race to make a documentary for TV. In the afternoon the trail climbed a dusty path up to the Deorali Pass, where some of us made a short detour to climb a ridge leading to Thodung. We climbed up through the clouds to a mist shrouded cheese factory; the poor weather denied us the celebrated views but I knew the extra ascent would only be good for acclimatisation and could prove vital when it came to race-day. It didn't take long to drop back down to the pass and once there I started jogging down the path; one of our Sherpas joined me and suddenly we were flying down the hill. Having already had a run I was not expecting this little work-out; I wondered if he was going to be in the race as he could certainly move fast over the rough paths. When we came to some freshly painted stupas I took the chance of a quick rest, using a visit to the small monastery as an excuse. Then it was on again at a run, down to our camp at Bhandar. The porters straggled in, tents were pitched and after dinner most people were soon in their sleeping bags.

We were up early again next morning, which started with a long walk through forest, over a couple of rivers and up into the small village of Kenja where we stopped for the usual long lunch break. I was again among the first to arrive and so had time for another run, at a deliberately slow pace; it felt easy on the flat and downhills, but the climbs still felt hard. That afternoon gave us one long climb up a ridge, past a few houses; women were working in the fields, tending goats or winnowing grain. We stopped in the village of Sete; the climb had spread the group out so it was some time before all made it into camp. To keep warm we crowded into a tea-house for a while, waiting for the tents to go up and for dinner to be cooked.

Next morning the climb continued up the ridge, through a forest of pines. Russell and Alan, two Kiwis, dashed off ahead; I followed them to the lunch stop just below the Lamjura Pass. Russell and Alan were about to set off to climb a ridge above the pass; it was tempting to go with them, but I thought they might make it competitive so I decided to run on my own instead. I ran up to the pass, then back down the trail, past the lunch stop and a quite a way back down the hill. At around 11,500ft it was hard work on the climb back up to the lunch stop but I convinced myself that it was doing me good. I also thought that perhaps I was starting to psych out some of the opposition who had yet to even try to run at altitude.

During lunch our Japanese ladies played hopscotch with a couple of the local kids. When we were ready to move on we climbed back up to the pass; the summit marked by piles of carved mani stones while a few tattered prayer flags fluttered in the breeze. There was a long descent off the far side, down through forest to Tragdobuk, then a short while later we turned up a side valley towards Junbesi. PK had found us a river-side field to camp in; unfortunately it was a very rough, ploughed field, which the Sherpas tried to flatten as best they could before they pitched the tents. After dinner several local girls came to the camp to sing and dance for us.

Next morning the group split; half decided on an easy low level traverse round the end of the ridge, the rest wanted to climb up to the large monastery at Thubten Choeling, about an hour above Junbesi. It's an active monastery which seemed full to bursting of lamas and very small, very ancient nuns. A couple of monks were painting an intricate thangka; others were praying and chanting endless mantras. It was a complicated route up to a pass above the monastery; a Sherpa guided us as the path wound its way up through the mist, through forest and across open hillside. Eventually we came out into a small clearing at the Lapcha La; again the col was adorned with tattered prayer flags and cairns of mani stones.

Cath and I left the others at the col and ran down the steep trails together, revelling in the joy of moving fast again, dropping steeply down to cross the river at Ringmo. We then made the short climb up to the Tragsindho La, from where a short descent took us to our campsite by the Tragsindho Monastery. We had a late lunch in camp and spent a lazy afternoon around the tents. A few of us later ran back up to the pass and along a wooded ridge, where deer flitted among the trees. I was pleased to see that I thrashed Russell on the climb to the pass, unfortunately he thrashed me on the descent and of course the race would be predominantly downhill.

It was a murky start to the next day; we were in a damp, clinging mist and had to walk quickly to keep warm. A long descent of almost 5,000ft down a steep track took us to the Dudh Kosi. This was our lunch stop and yet it was only 9.30! The early stop gave us plenty of time to rest but a few of us opted for another training run. A couple turned back fairly soon after crossing the river but Cath and I carried on up the hill and contoured round on a good path through the terraced fields. A short sharp climb then took us to a ridge on the far side. Once we had caught our breath we returned along the trail, back across the suspension bridge to rejoin the others. The film crew had filmed a couple of the others running over the bridge and after we'd had lunch we were asked to go back over again so they could film us running over the wildly bouncing bridge too. With the posing finished we crossed the river yet again and climbed up to the small settlement of Jubing. From here we climbed more steeply up to a low col from where a path contoured round to Khari Khola. The tents were squeezed tightly onto narrow terraces and what should have been a superb site was actually quite bleak as we were surrounded by low clouds which clung, limpet like, to the hillsides.

It was another cold, wet start the following morning; quite a steep climb took us up through forest in a thick mist. We were supposed to be able to see monkeys but although we could hear some we couldn't see a thing in the almost jungle like atmosphere, with creepers and old man's beard hanging from the trees. We warmed up in a tea-house and played with three lovely, snotty nosed kids; that just left an easy walk to Phuiyan. It was still cold and damp so our cooks 'borrowed' a lodge where we could eat lunch in comfort. In the afternoon it left just a stroll down to Surkhe. We had trouble here in more ways than one. There was no site big enough to take all our tents so several people were put into lodges for the night; the rest had to climb carefully up to the tents which were packed tightly onto narrow terraced fields. Some of our porters then picked a fight with another group of porters and we overwhelmed a tea-house, upsetting the Germans who had already staked their claim.

Feeling guilty at not having run, Cath and I escaped the hassle, changed into running shoes and set off. The trail climbed steeply and it was hard work heading up the Dudh Kosi valley with the river lost in the cloud below us. The sky cleared a little after dinner and rather than squeeze into the stuffy, overcrowded lodge I preferred to sit outside and watch the stars trying to break through.

Next day in better weather we followed the trade route up the Dudh Kosi, often far above the river. We had another early lunch stop by a bridge over the Kusum Khola. Kusum

Kanguru, the hardest of the designated 'trekking peaks', stood majestically at the head of this side valley. I set off for a long run, up the main path, across the river at Phakding then way up the valley almost as far as Monjo. By the time I had run back again I was ready for an icy bath in the river and some lunch. It was good to see that Cath and a couple of the other girls had also gone for a short run but in general I was surprised at how few of the others were either willing or able to go for a run.

After lunch we walked up the now familiar trail, past painted mani stones and idols carved into the rock beneath multi-coloured prayer flags, and back into Phakding. We were easily tempted into stopping at a tea-house for lemon tea and apple pie, then it was back out to cross the Dudh Kosi and continue comfortably up the valley. The afternoons walk was just a stroll along the trail to Chumoa where we had a good site on flat ground. It had been great walking all day and it was good to be back into bright sunshine again after a few dull wet days.

We woke to another cold but beautiful morning and realised that there was a lot of fresh snow on the surrounding peaks. We were told that the snow was down as low as Gorak Shep, which was a worry with the race only a week away. It was however an easy walk up to Monjo after which we entered the Sagarmatha National Park. After crossing and re-crossing the river several times we continued up the boulder strewn river bed, until, at the last bridge a steep climb led off, up a hot dusty ridge to Namche Bazar.

We enjoyed a lazy afternoon in Namche; later almost everyone connected with the race walked the last 6 miles of the race route out to Thamo and back, as this was the only part of the route that we wouldn't cover on our outward trek. Before dinner the afternoon clouds broke up so Cath and I climbed up to the broad saddle above Namche. We sat on a boulder eating white *Toblerone,* watching the sun go down; the summit of Thamserku briefly unveiled itself and life just couldn't get any better.

The following day was Saturday, market day. We all had to climb up to the col by the National Park Office and Museum for the official team photos, with Everest some 25 miles away, it's summit just visible above the Nuptse-Lhotse ridge. Once this chore was done we dropped back down to Namche to tour the thriving market, squeezing past piles of eggs, sacks of grain and rice, boxes full of Kukri rum, mounds of vegetables, various scrawny looking livestock and rows of 'fresh' meat. It was relaxing sitting on the terrace of a tea-house, eating delicious cool yoghurt with muesli, while watching the bustle of the market going on below us.

The morning soon passed, and after lunch we set off for the short walk to Tengboche Monastery. Once back up at the National Park HQ on the col, the path led off on a contouring route up the Dudh Kosi, following the race route through Sarnassa then dropping steeply down a dusty path to cross the river. The hot sun made us all lethargic so we spent an hour sunbathing by the river before setting off again, up a very steep and dusty trail through pine and rhododendron forest to reach the monastery on the ridge above. The famous monastery had been rebuilt following the fire of 1989.

At Namche many of the porters had been paid off, most of our kit was now carried by yaks; those porters that remained had been issued with warm clothes, which we were pleased to see, as it turned cold very quickly once the sun dropped down behind the mountains. It was a cold and frosty night and bed-tea wasn't brought round until 7am, which was a rare luxury and meant we hadn't too long to wait before the sun crept over the ridge and found us. There had been a very heavy frost overnight which left the tents frozen almost solid and the yaks were covered in rime and looked frozen stiff too. It was an easy downhill start; past water-driven prayer-wheels and down through forest to a bridge over the Imja Khola. From the river a short climb followed by a traverse up the valley, took us through Pangboche and half an hour beyond this we stopped for lunch in a potato field. The morning's walk had really spread the group out and it took a long time for everyone to come in; illness and altitude were now making themselves felt.

After lunch Cath and I walked up to Pheriche to recce more of the race route. From the HRA medical post we climbed up and over a ridge, where we had good views out to Island Peak, which I'd climbed 3 years earlier. Once down in Dingboche we took refuge in a tea-house until camp was set up.

It was great not having to pack up camp next morning as we were to spend the day acclimatising in and around Dingboche. We all enjoyed a welcome lay-in and an unhurried breakfast in the sun. A few of us climbed to the ridge above the village to do some posing for the film crew. They particularly wanted shots of some of the races expected 'stars', especially Pierre (the previous year's winner) and Russell, who were shot running together, also Cath and Viv. Later Cath and I wandered a few miles up the valley towards Island Peak and only when the sun started to dip behind the mountains did we walk back down to Dingboche. I now started feeling guilty about having had such a lazy day so I went out for a run for half an hour; it was very hard work and I was concerned about how I would survive the race, which was now only four days away.

The following day was only to be a short stage; it started with an easy climb up onto the ridge above Dingboche followed by a comfortable walk along the broad terrace before dropping down to Dughla, at the foot of the terminal moraine of the Khumbu Glacier. We had a long lunch break then most of the group set off for the easy walk up to Lobuche. As we had plenty of time to spare, Russell, Alan and I decided to make a detour for some extra acclimatisation. From the snout of the glacier we climbed steeply up the hillside, which was rough and open at first, but nearer the top it became rockier and gave an easy scramble. Alan stopped some way below the top while Russell and I climbed on, finally coming out onto a rocky pinnacle at around 19,000ft, just a short way below the ridge leading to the 'trekking peak' of Pokalde.

26: Looking down on the first few miles of the Everest Marathon route from high on Pokalde

We were both pretty breathless but the view from the ridge made the effort well worthwhile. It was a tremendous sight with the Khumbu Glacier stretching out far below us; we could look down on the first 5 miles of the race route all the way from Gorak Shep down past Lobuche to Dughla. Finally we set off down, collected Alan and together we jogged down to the glacier. It was almost dark as we climbed the moraine onto the rubble strewn ice but Russell led us quickly on a good course across to the far side; we then dropped down off the moraine bank and found the path which led to the tents.

We spent two nights at Lobuche to help us acclimatise so there was no need to be up early next morning. Most people seemed fit enough for the walk up to Gorak Shep, which is where the race was to start in another couple of days. I headed up and went into a lodge for tea with the Ghurkha team but no one else turned up so I set off to climb Kala Patar, an easy but steepish walk up to a small summit below the awesome Pumori. At 18,500ft the air was certainly thin but once again the views made you forget any shortness of breath; the south-west face of Everest, the Khumbu ice-fall, the Lho La (a col on the Nepal/Tibet border) and beyond to Changtse in Tibet, it was all wonderful and used up a considerable amount of film.

After 20 minutes or so on top I jogged down to Gorak Shep and back down the trail to Lobuche. The cold that night meant everyone went to bed almost as soon as dinner was finished. The following morning, with race day now imminent, we had to undergo a laughable medical and an even more hilarious race briefing, which left many of us feeling aggrieved at being treated like children. Everyone passed the medical, although many of us were concerned about one of the Japanese ladies; she looked rather ill and was much quieter than her usual ebullient self. We were all very fond of her and wanted her to be able to race so it was a relief when the Doctors finally gave her the all-clear.

Martin Stone, a very experienced long-distance fell-running specialist was at the race, working with the film-crew; he was planning what he hoped to be a record-breaking run from Everest Base Camp all the way back to Kathmandu. Debbie, Cath and I had agreed to try to help once our race was over and we chatted about this for a while, agreeing what we needed to do to help with pacing and providing supplies for the three days it was likely to take. Later we ambled slowly back up to Gorak Shep and settled down to a lazy afternoon. I felt cold and tired and a bit below par all afternoon and evening but Cath was fantastic as she tried to cheer me up and made me eat. I hoped I'd have a reasonable night's sleep and that my illness would turn out to be pre-race nerves rather than anything serious.

Race day came around at last; for the previous three or four days I'd been itching to run but now it was here I really didn't feel like doing it. We were called at 6am with tea and porridge in bed, then it was up to pack the kit-bags and pile the sleeping bags separately as these were to be taken down to Namche that day by fast porters. So it was that a very mixed bunch of 75 people from all corners of the world lined up on a sandy, dried-up lake bed, ready for the off at 7am. It was probably about minus 10°c but it didn't feel that cold and I didn't need too many layers on. As expected Pierre, the previous year's winner, hared away, keen to establish an early lead. I quickly found that I'd done up the chest strap on my rucksack too tightly. At the first big effort, climbing up out of the sandy basin and onto the moraines, I found I could hardly breathe. I had to slow down, take the sack off, adjust the straps and put it back on ....not a good start.

As I went through the first control at Lobuche I was back in about 12th position, running alongside two Ghurkhas. From here it was easy running, down past the memorials and into Dughla, then steeply down to the flat ground beside the river and into Pheriche. From Pheriche the route dropped down to cross the river then a short climb had me gasping again, passing one of the Ghurkhas now, but still on the shoulder of the other.

27: Ama Dablam, a great back-drop to a marathon

I chased the Ghurkha all the way down to Pangboche and to the bridge over the Dudh Kosi but he pulled away again as I slowed to take my sack off and fish out a small bag of jelly-babies to set myself up for the climb.

By the top of the climb, going through the half-way point at Tengboche Monastery, I had re-caught the Ghurkha and felt reasonably comfortable and happy with the way the race was progressing. The descent from the ridge top was fast and furious as we both cut corners off the steep track, dodging through the trees, until, nearing the foot of the descent we caught up with a Sherpa who had started too fast. The three of us crossed the bridge together but a short way up the big climb I pulled away from the other two and worked really hard to try to open a gap. It was by now very hot, very thirsty work but I managed to drop them and jogged into the checkpoint at Sarnassa where it was good to see my tent-mate, Graham, dishing out encouragement along with tea and *Mars Bars*.

After Sarnassa we had easy running on a reasonably level path that more or less contoured round the hillside. Just before reaching Chorkhung, the point above Namche, I was delighted to pass an American, one of the pre-race favourites, so now I was up to 8th. They told me at the checkpoint that Russell was some 8 minutes ahead, which was a lot to try to make up. Mentally it was quite hard to pass by just ¼ mile from the finish but we still had some six miles to go; a very long six miles out to Thamo and back. The path was an undulating one and yet it seemed to be uphill all the way out and also uphill all the way back. It was good seeing the race leaders on their run in to the finish at Namche and they all had words of encouragement as they went past, none though were within catching distance for me. I had a bit of a shock when I reached the turn-around point at Thamo and saw that one of the Ghurkhas had almost caught me so I had to dig in and try to move away again. It was great to see Cath so well up and not too far behind me as I made my way down to the finish in Namche. It was a relief to cross the line in 8th, 1st Brit, but I was a little disappointed with the time of 5 hours 2 minutes, I'd hoped to be about half an hour quicker. Pierre Gobet won for the second time, almost an hour ahead of me. A Nepalese Olympic runner was 2nd with Kiwi Ray Brown 3rd. Ghurkhas filled the next three places, and then came Russell some 10 minutes ahead of me. Cath had a wonderful race to finish 14th overall, setting a new women's record of 5 hrs 32 mins. It was a great performance and a timely boost to her morale.

During the long day we had a warm lodge to stay in with endless supplies of tea and noodle soup; the whole party was dispersed into various lodges for the night; our sleeping bags came down from Gorak Shep with fast porters; the rest of the kit-bags and tents followed the next day.

Some people opted to leave Namche the day after the race but I and a few others decided to stay a second night before catching up with the bulk of the group somewhere near Lukla. The day passed quickly in an orgy of eating, visiting the market, shopping for souvenirs and we even managed to find a hot shower. Those of us who had stayed in Namche faced a longish walk the next day; I set off down the steep hill, feeling stiff from the hard race. We dropped down to the Dudh Kosi, walked back through Monjo and after passing through Phakding we caught up with the rest of our group beside the bridge over the Kusum Khola. An easy afternoon saw Cath and I take the lower trail, passing below Lukla, all the way down to Surkhe. We had a long wait in a cold tea-house so I tried to warm up with a bowl of noodle soup; the owner of the lodge must have needed a laugh as I'm sure she put in ten times the normal amount of chilli powder; the sweat poured off me as I forced myself to finish the whole bowl.

Meanwhile, Martin had started his record attempt from Everest Base Camp that morning and it was almost dark when we met him on the path near Surkhe. We ran with him for a short way and made arrangements to meet him again somewhere near the Lamosangu Bridge as early as possible on the Tuesday morning, about 36 hours away! Thereafter, backed up by a hired car, we would help pace him on the long run to Kathmandu. In the darkness Debbie, Cath and I climbed the steep track up to Lukla where we eventually found our campsite.

Just after I'd gone to bed a tired looking Martin arrived in camp, he had gone on for another couple of hours after leaving us but knee problems on a long climb had forced him to abandon the attempt. He then had to return through the dark on difficult paths to find us. The weather was fine the next day and we were all able to leave Lukla as planned; it's a grim place to be stranded waiting for a plane to appear.

As we were no longer needed to help Martin with his run, Cath and I enjoyed a couple of lazy days in Kathmandu, eating cakes, drinking 'lassi' and searching round bookshops. One evening we came across a little Tibetan restaurant where the food was great and was washed down with chang from an evil looking chang pipe. Three suspicious looking Tibetans sat at the neighbouring table sucking chang through a bamboo straw; they looked as if they were plotting the freedom of Tibet, if so, good luck to them.

The last morning saw us wandering slowly through the exotic streets, browsing, bargaining and buying. We finally had to leave and caught the short flight to Dhaka; again we had a long wait 'in transit', but at last we were called for our flight home via Dubai and Paris.

28: Shopkeeper in Bhaktapur

The Pindos Mountains of Greece

We were looking for somewhere different for a trip to the mountains; running was out, following a recent arthroscopy, but Cath and I settled on Greece where we hoped to find spring sunshine and some easy walking. We phoned Cath's friend Hélène, who is part Greek, and she sent us a useful letter full of good advice along with a copy itinerary of a trek she had once led in the Pindos. With no real plan we flew to Athens, carrying with us a guidebook, Hélène's' letter and a photocopy of the Pindos Traverse chapter from *Trekking - Great Walks of the World* (by John Cleare - Unwin Hyman Ltd). Sadly, we had been unable to find any maps.

On arrival in Athens we booked domestic flights up to Ioannina, away up in the north of the country. It was only a short hop of about 50 minutes and at Ioannina we were met by an intense heat and an immediate problem in not being able to speak any Greek. We dashed around looking for food, fuel for the stove and most importantly a map, but decent maps are almost impossible to come by and we had to set off with only a vague idea of where we were going. From Ioannina we caught a bus 30 miles up to the road-end at Monodendri; a small hillside village built of grey stone. Surprisingly everywhere in Monodendri seemed to be full but we found a farm a mile or two away that offered us a decent room and the farmer made us very welcome.

Breakfast was taken at a small taverna in Monodendri. Fed and watered we first headed for the 14th century monastery of St.Paraskevi, built on the edge of the Vikos Gorge, with huge cliffs towering above and below. It only took minutes to return to Monodendri where we sought out the Vikos Gorge path, way-marked from beside the old church; well paved it led steeply down through scrub and woodland into the gorge. Sheer cliffs rose some 3,000ft above us as we followed the occasional daubs of red paint; we were often among the boulders of the dry river bed but more usually a short way up the left-hand side of the gorge. The path crossed scree slopes and meandered through woodland.

Where the Megas Lakkos ravine came in, water appeared in the gorge so we stopped to refill our water-bottles, as we did so three snakes slithered off and dropped down into the water to safety. For the whole day we were among beautiful wild flowers, birds, frogs, butterflies and small lizards which shot away at an amazing speed. After passing a shrine by a polluted spring the walls fell back and the gorge opened up; strange limestone pinnacles marked the start of the gorge proper. At the Voidhomatis Springs we followed the obvious trail which climbed steeply away to the left. As we climbed up we were surprised to meet three canoeists dragging their plastic boats down the rough path; from the springs downstream it looked like the river would give exciting paddling.

Unfortunately the obvious track tricked us as the village we climbed up to on the plateau above wasn't Papingo as expected but Vikos; Papingo was a long way away on the other side of the gorge and we should have crossed the river back at the springs. We were tired and hungry after a hot walk so we ate at a small taverna before dropping back down the path to the river; we crossed the dry river-bed immediately above where the river emerged from the cliff and made a long, hot and dusty climb up interminable zigzags. At last the path eased and we traversed a steep scree slope, through a small forest, across terraces and so into Mikro Papingo. We soon found a room in a lodge and it was good to sit out on the terrace in the shade of the vines watching the sun go down on the limestone towers above.

Next day we wandered down into Megalo Papingo, where we managed to buy a reasonable photocopy of a map and a rough plan of the area; we also bought some food to supplement what we had taken out with us. After climbing back up to Mikro Papingo we started the climb up to the hut on the Astraka col. It was another hot and sunny day so we took full advantage of the several springs along the way. A footpath leads off from near here to the mouth of the Provatina Cave, famous for its vertical shaft of 1,400ft, one of the world's longest single drops. On reaching the hut on the col we were surprised to see a guardian in residence; the old hut had been destroyed by Albanian bandits a couple of years previously and now that it had been rebuilt the guardian 'lived-in' from April through to October. There were superb views north across to Ploskos and Gamila, with Astraka high above to the right and a ridge running out to Lapatos on the left; below were two tarns 'stanee tsoomanee'. As we sat outside the hut, by a strange trick of the light the sun cast a rainbow on a small cloud above Astraka.

Rested, we dropped down to the tarns and hid our 'sacs among the boulders; we then climbed under a very hot sun up to the 'Drakolimni', Dragons Lake. This is a beautiful little tarn surrounded by wild flowers; huge banks of crocuses were pushing up through the snowdrifts. The views down the far side were to forested ridges above the Aoos Gorge. As we rounded the lake a large snake dropped down into the water to hide. We returned back down the hillside to our 'sacs where we soon had the stove going for a dinner of *Beanfeast* and *Smash*. It turned quite cold and windy but other than that it was a superb bivvy site surrounded by grassy knolls, rocky peaks and snow. The guidebook actually warned us not to camp by the tarns because of vicious sheep dogs but the hut guardian had told us that the shepherds hadn't arrived at these high pastures yet and we would be safe for another two or three weeks. An almost full moon lit our bivvy site so it was just about light enough to read by. It was a great night out and we woke at 7am to another beautiful morning.

29: *Cath beneath the Astraka Hut -just visible on the col between Astraka (L) and Lapatos (R)*

Another very hot day was in prospect as we cached our gear, then set off up the stony valley past the largest of the lakes; we climbed over boulders and patches of snow between the gullies and buttresses of Astraka and the limestone pavements of Gamila. It was now three weeks since the operation on my knee but it was still swollen and sore, which made crossing the rough terrain quite difficult. It didn't take long though to reach the Robozi Tarn on the col above; from here we headed across the rocky basin to a ridge that led to Gamila. There were masses of crocuses in bloom around the edges of the snow drifts and more hardy buds were pushing their way up through the snow. From the summit cairn, at around 8,300ft, the ground fell away steeply to the Aoos Gorge; we had great views down to the wooded ridges and ravines and across to Mt.Smolikas. We ran easily down the snow then dropped down under a scorching sun, back to the tarn where we refilled our water-bottles. After a quick lunch we were soon on our way again, picking a route through the boulders and snow, putting up a huge hare in the process. We soon reached the ridge above and from here the ground eased and we wandered comfortably round the rocky basin up to the summit cairn on Astraka.

There were enormous cornices along the edge and we had extensive views all around. A grouse like bird took off as we retraced our steps back across to the cairn before dropping down more steeply to regain the col. All day long we had been surrounded by beds of crocuses, gentians and dozens of other wild flowers, there were also butterflies of every description. Back at our cache of gear we made soup, Cath then ran up to the hut for beers. By now the weather was looking far from good; dark clouds had dropped down around Astraka and rain looked imminent. Thankfully the clouds moved on during the night and we were treated to another great display of stars.

Next morning again dawned bright and clear but we had breakfast in bed while we waited for the sun to hit the bivvy bag. After packing up we set off back up to the Robozi Tarn on the col. This time we seemed to choose a better route and it was a pleasant walk up, through crocuses, gentians and forget-me-nots, through grassy knolls to a cool stream and a welcome drink. Dropping down the far side gave lovely walking to some shepherd's huts. The path then dropped into a ravine, climbed up the far side and across the hillside to a small spring, which issued from under a slab of rock beneath towering limestone cliffs. Around the spring grew mint and other wild herbs; making the most of the rare surface water. A few minutes later we turned up into a side valley; this gave us a short climb before we came out onto the summit plateau. The small tarn here was teeming with frogs and as we rested we watched swifts darting about eating flies from the surface of the water. Sitting there in the sun we heard the sound of bells from a herd of sheep or goats, this was quickly followed by the barking of dogs. Three fierce looking dogs then appeared on a knoll a short distance away so we lost no time in arming ourselves with stones before setting off on the long descent. Unsure of the correct route we entered a narrowing gully and a steep, slippery section slowed us down but we could now see Tsepelevo below us and we finally came out by a small chapel and a lone pine, before dropping down into the village square.

Alexis, the storekeeper, spoke excellent English and he put us up at his 'hotel' once we had had a beer on the terrace of his taverna. He told us there was no need to pay for things as we went along, he just asked for a Passport as a deposit; he seemed genuinely surprised when Cath produced hers, he didn't seem to think that a woman should have a Passport of her own! Next morning we packed a light 'sac for a walk up to the Beloi viewpoint overlooking the Vikos Gorge. Alexis kindly put us on the right route; climbing steeply away from the village, past a shepherd moving a small flock of sheep. The old path was well engineered and climbed alongside a rocky gorge until we reached a dead maple tree, here Alexis was insistent that we turn right, to climb the rough hillside until we finally came out onto a tarmaced road. The road contoured round then dropped down to enter the delightful little village of Vradeto. The solid, grey stone houses and church were deserted but a lovely old lady sat knitting in the shade of a tree outside her taverna, so we stopped and joined her.

A short distance from the village the road petered out and a footpath headed across the limestone, through some wonderful wild flowers where I had a quick sighting of a bright green chameleon. After squeezing through a narrow gap in the rocks the path ended dramatically on a rocky table, beyond which the ground fell vertically some 3,000ft into the Vikos Gorge; it was a great sight as we were able to see almost the whole length of the gorge, right up to the small village of Vikos which we had visited by mistake some days before. After exploring along the top of the gorge we returned to Vradeto then down to Tsepelevo.

The following morning we caught the bus to Vrisohori, about 25km up the road, heading deeper into the hills. Thankfully Alexis had returned on time from his weekly trip to the market in Ioannina so we were able to add a fresh loaf of bread to our loads. The little road-head village of Vrisohori nestles among the trees in a hollow and we stopped briefly for a drink before setting off in the heat of the day. The path was way-marked and climbed away from the village, past a small chapel overlooking the Aoos Gorge. The path climbed on, winding in and out of little gullies and wooded ravines with occasional '03' signs to reassure us.

It was hot work, climbing endlessly on a narrow path through beech and firs. A spring issuing from beneath a low cliff didn't quite fit with our vague route description and as we anticipated passing another we ignored this one and went on with almost empty water-bottles, which was not a very smart move on our part. A short distance on from the spring the path climbed into a ravine and this led to a grassy corrie where we found a muddy waterhole, fit only for sheep. Two paths headed off from here, but the map and guidebook were confusing and after exploring a short way we decided to head off up a steep, unmarked path. After 20 minutes or so we thought we must be heading for a different col, the path was still ok though so we carried on and guessed it might lead us back to the tarn on the Robozi col. However, the path then took off downhill and seemed to be heading for the Aoos Gorge rather than climbing to a col so we reluctantly headed back to the waterhole in the grassy corrie. It was by now time to call a halt for the day but having missed our opportunity at the spring it meant we had only about half a litre of water. I climbed up into the rocky valley to prospect the route and see if I could find any melt water running from the snowfields, meanwhile Cath collected some dirty snow in our pans and mugs which gave us just enough to make our usual *Beanfeast* dinner.

It was a comfortable bivvy on grass beside a large boulder; I was just nodding off to sleep when Cath nudged me awake to say she could hear someone coming. This was more serious than it sounds as we had been warned by the owner of the taverna in Vrisohori that Albanian bandits may climb up to us, slit our throats and steal our money. As it was the third time in a week that bandits had been mentioned we took the warning reasonably seriously, after all, we knew they had recently raided the Astraka hut. After a few anxious minutes it became clear that the footsteps were neither coming closer nor were they receding, a change of note then made it obvious that the sound was only a bird, probably a stonechat, and nothing to fear. An owl then started calling and lulled us to a fitful sleep. It was a breezy but starlit night and we woke early to another bright clear morning.

After coffee and croissants we set off up the valley of boulders and snow drifts to come out into a huge scree bowl beneath towering cliffs. On this northern side of Tsouka Roussa there was still an amazing amount of snow and we soon lost all sign of the path. The map and guide gave no clue as to which notch on the crenulated ridge was the col and without knowing for certain where the route went we couldn't justify the risk in climbing the icy snow in training shoes and without ice-axes. A slip would have meant a very long fall into the rocks below so after searching for half an hour we decided the sensible thing was to retreat back down to our bivvy site and from there head back to Vrisohori.

It seemed to take no time at all to reverse our long hot climb of the previous afternoon, down the ravine, through the forest, up into the beeches and down to the track. We headed down bare gullies, past a lonely chapel and back to the village. When we eventually found someone who could speak English we learnt that the next bus was three days away and as we were due to fly from Ioannina the following day it left us no option but to start walking the 25km back to Tsepelevo. Thankfully, just as we were leaving the village a lorry carrying stone for new houses came up the road and a short time later it returned empty and we were able to hitch a lift. Only a few minutes later the driver pulled over at a roadside taverna for his lunch; we joined him in the smoky 'transport cafe' and were brought freshly made, spicy rissoles and bread as nibbles to go with our beers. We noted that our friendly driver needed several ouzos to calm his nerves from driving the winding mountain roads before setting off again; we were dropped back at Tsepelevo mid-afternoon.

Next morning we caught the bus to Ioannina, passing through Kipi on the way. There are several wonderful old pack-horse bridges near here, the most impressive of which is a graceful, three arched bridge. Once back at Ioannina we had time to explore the old walled town before flying back to Athens and home.

Although it was a bit of a problem not being able to read or speak any Greek at all, everyone we met had been most welcoming and we agreed that the mountains of Greece were well worth a return visit.

The High Tatra of Poland and Slovakia

For our visit to the Tatra Mountains in Poland we had to fly to Katowice, from where we caught an airport bus to Krakow. By the time we arrived in the centre of Krakow it was very late and after trying several hotels it seemed they were all full. A woman, who looked like she was soliciting, stopped us and asked if we wanted a private room; fearing being mugged, raped or being sold into slavery we declined as politely as we could with our non-existent Polish. However, after trying several more hotels with no success we went back to find her and accepted her offer. Her husband drove us out of the city centre to an old block of flats where we were led into the living room, furnished with two bed settees. It was fine, cost us about £12, and was a lot better than sleeping at the bus station or on a park bench. In the morning it was surprisingly easily to negotiate buying tram tickets to the city centre where we caught a bus out to Zakopane.

Zakopane is 'The Capital of the Tatra', about 60 miles south of Krakow, just inside the Polish/Slovakian border. It was an interesting drive, through forests and meadows, where horse-drawn ploughs worked in the fields and horse-drawn carts trundled along the country lanes. On arriving we headed straight for the Tourist Information Centre, who booked us into a 'pension' for a couple of nights. A short walk to the outskirts of the town found us at our B&B, a new house but built in the traditional Zakopane style. It was clean and cheap and, more importantly, the owner had a ten year old daughter who could speak a few words of English and could translate for us.

We were soon changed into running kit and headed up the road to the foot of the hill; a metalled road led up through forest to Kuznice where we found we were supposed to pay a fee of one zloty to enter the National Park. As we were only out for a run neither of us had any money with us but I sweet-talked the woman at the kiosk and she let us through. The paths leading away from Kuznice were well sign-posted, way-marked with paint flashes and were generally like cobbled motorways!

The paths were very busy; people were everywhere, so we were glad to run slowly away up the hill. A small path climbed off to the right, up into forest, and to escape the crowds we took it, even though it wasn't way-marked and it wasn't on the map. We should have known better of course; the path ended at a small chapel and monastery, which we would not have found otherwise, but we had to retrace our steps after having made a couple of half-hearted attempts to fight our way through the forest. We ran back down to rejoin the motorway below and a short while later another path climbed away to the right, this was the one we wanted and it took us up into some beautiful forest and then out onto an open ridge. The path wandered around the hillside, seeming to go further than the map suggested; we then turned off the main path and dropped down into the Dolina Biatego. A good path followed the stream back down to the outskirts of Zakopane. Here, on the edge of town, at the very foot of the mountains, two frighteningly steep ski-jumps have been built to follow the natural contours of the hill.

Next morning we headed back up to Kuznice again, past gangs of school children collecting bin-bags of litter as their contribution to 'Clean Up the World' week. We had to queue for ages to catch the cable-car; however the wait was quite entertaining as people kept pushing past and others tried to stop them, it would have been even more fun if we had understood the arguments. We finally did make it, and climbed in two stages from about 1,000m up to Kasprowy Wierch on the ridge at almost 2,000m.

We emerged on top in thick mist and heavy drizzle so it was on with the waterproofs and out into the elements to seek out the start of the 'yellow' route. From the main ridge we ran down a well marked path (a chair-lift on our left, although the map had it marked on our right) and from the bottom of the chair-lift another way-marked path led round into the corrie between several small tarns. It was a steep climb up through boulders to a col at Karb; from the col we followed the path south, climbing a steep, shattered ridge to reach a small rocky top, Koscieiec at 2,158m. The crowds on the narrow trod through the slabs and crags made it slow going as we dropped back down the ridge to the col. In the cold wet weather we then dropped more quickly down to the lake, Czarny Staw; this means 'Black Lake' and there is a Czarny Staw in virtually every corrie so it can be a bit confusing. The steep ridge around the corrie was narrow and rocky and reminded me very much of the Black Cuillin on Skye.

From the lake-side it didn't take long to drop the short distance down to the Refuge at Murowaniec; a huge old place, full to the rafters with walkers gently steaming as they dried out. After a coffee, with the rain easing, we started down, first climbing up and over a shoulder, then down to a path junction.

We took the 'yellow' route again, being the more open, and this led down towards the stream on the valley floor. Near the foot of the descent we met the local Mountain Rescue Team, they had just immobilised a woman's injured leg and were assembling a stretcher to carry her down. There were only six in the team so we stopped to ask if they needed an extra pair of hands for the carry; they didn't seem to need us so we dropped a little further down and saw that they had driven their vehicle a good way up the hill and the carry was only a short one.

From here it didn't take us long to run down to Kuznice where we piled into one of the waiting minibuses which took us back to Zakopane. Back in town we bought a better quality map, which at 1:30,000 we could safely navigate by. We were fortunate at dinner; when the elderly waitress saw us struggling with the menu she took us in hand and suggested some traditional Polish dishes, which were very filling and just what we needed after a long cold wet run.

Next morning, carrying rucksacs with kit for two or three days, we returned to Kuznice, paid our park entrance fee, and climbed on the 'green' path which headed east up into the forest. Thick mist and a heavy drizzle set in as we climbed up through the trees, through dwarf conifers and along below a ridge to finally drop down to the hut at Murowaniec. After a short stop for coffee and to warm up we followed a narrower path through more forest, contouring round into the Dolina Panszczyca and down to the Czerwony Staw. Once above the lake the ground became more open and rocky and a well made path climbed to the head of the valley, which ended in a small corrie, ringed with high, rocky peaks. A steep but easy path zigzagged up to the narrow col of Krzyzne. Once over onto the south eastern side of the ridge it was less rocky but very steep and the long descent was hard on the knees. At last the angle of the path eased and it turned to head up into the boomerang shaped 'Valley of the 5 Polish Lakes'. At this stage, in thick mist, we couldn't even see one lake but we then joined the 'blue' path and, turning east along this we dropped down to the shore of Wielki Staw; we jogged past a Polish Alpine Club hut, came to Przedni Staw and on its far shore we found the Five Lakes Refuge.

It was mid-afternoon when we arrived at this large wooden hut and tried to book in, only to find that reception wouldn't open until 5pm; when we saw a queue forming we joined it. At last 5 o'clock came and a friendly Pole told us that the hut was full and we would have to sleep on the floor along with perhaps 40 others! We were given tokens so we could be issued with some blankets (we had no sleeping bags) but these couldn't to be issued until 7 o'clock and meant yet another queue. The friendly Pole came to our aid again and helped us obtain three blankets each and also a possible reservation for the following night. Corridor spaces were quickly taken and we ended up sitting on the floor of the dining room to claim our 'space' until about 8 o'clock when people started to drift off to their beds/floor space.

It was a warm and rather uncomfortable night so we were up early and away from the hut without breakfast. Outside we found a beautiful, bright, frosty morning, which made the rocks even more slippery than usual, but the sun soon cleared the ice and dried things off. Our path started right on the shore of the lake and climbed east, easily up alongside steep cliffs for a while, then over into another corrie to cross a shoulder at Kepa. From here another fairly steep descent led down, first through open hillside, then mature forest, to come out a short distance below the hut at Morskie Oko. Morskie Oko is said to be the prettiest of all the lakes in Poland; a metalled road runs all the way up to the hut but thankfully the road is closed to private traffic.

30: Morskie Oko Refuge at the head of the lake

It was only 9.30 when we reached the hut and a lovely old lady quickly sized us up and realised we needed breakfast;

wonderful ham and eggs and jugs of coffee were soon placed in front of us, she must have been a mind reader as our attempts to learn Polish never progressed beyond three words and hardly anyone there spoke any English. She also helped us book in for the night and showed us up to a very comfortable room up in the rafters.

Leaving most of our gear we went out for a short run; climbing up past Morskie Oko, then turning off the main path into a side valley. Here amongst the boulders and dry tarns we saw a few marmots and heard their usual warning whistles. We now faced a short, steep climb along a loose path up to a narrow col, the Wrota Chatubinskiego. This ridge forming part of the Polish/Slovakian border was marked by small red and white cairns. The ridge was narrow and rocky and the only way to return was back down the same way, so, after carefully descending the steep top section we were able to cruise easily back down to the hut for lunch.

The old lady in the dining room again came up trumps and guessed what we needed, quickly bringing a big bowl of soup. Later we headed out again, for our third lot of exercise for the day. We walked round the shore of Morskie Oko then steeply up, past a waterfall to the upper lake, another Czarny Staw. High cliffs dropped steeply down to the lakeside giving it a black and forbidding atmosphere. Large patches of snow still lay deep in the gullies which split the cliffs falling from Rysy, at 2,499m Poland's highest summit. We dropped back down to Morskie Oko, completed the circuit of the lake and returned to the hut for dinner and an early bed.

Rather than wait for breakfast we again left early to take advantage of the fine weather, which we were finding was usually best first thing in the morning, before cloud drifted up from the plains below. Using the same path we had climbed the previous morning, we again climbed easily up above Morskie Oko, past the turn off to the col on the border, and under a hot sun climbed up to the col at Szpig Iasowa Przel. It was a great place to stop for a breather, watching a small group of chamois that were lying out in the sun on a grassy spur below us. From the col we could now see 'round the corner' to the other lakes in the valley of the 5 Polish lakes.

Leaving the col we were faced with a tricky descent; thankfully a section of fairly exposed scrambling was fixed with several lengths of chain for protection. Cath was a little apprehensive so I went down to check it out, then climbed back to report on how it was. On closer inspection it was easier than when viewed from the top, so Cath quickly said 'Let's go!' and down we went, down a sloping ramp, along a ledge then down steep slabs, where a few extra footholds had been carved into the rock, to finally come out at the foot of a rocky gully.

From here the path zigzagged down to cross the valley floor between Czarny Staw (yet another one!) and Wielki Staw, the 3rd and 4th lakes respectively, counting from the top downwards. Turning off the 'yellow' route onto the 'blue' took us along past the lakes and more marmots, back down to the Five Lakes Hut. By now it was almost mid-day, so we called in for a combined breakfast/lunch of the only thing we seemed to be able to order, which was indigestible tripe soup. It wasn't great to run on.

Leaving the hut we jogged down past the cableway that's used to supply the hut; then dropped steeply down flights of steps to join the path alongside the river, this took us through the forest to waterfalls by the road at Wodogrzmoly Mickiewicza. From here we climbed back into forest on an easier track, climbing gently in and out of valleys until we finally joined a dirt road in Dolina Suchej Wody, which in turn led to Brzeziny, where we caught a minibus back into Zakopane.

We decided on another early start next morning and left the pension without breakfast at 7.30, heading up the familiar road to Kuznice where we joined the short queue for the cable-car. It was a beautiful, cold, clear morning and we were whisked up to Kasprowy Wierch. Once outside we saw the views that we had missed the first time; south into Slovakia, whilst to the north were some of our previous routes spread out beneath us.

We ran west along a fairly broad ridge, following the red and white border posts, climbing over small tops or by-passing them, either on the Slovak side or on the Polish side. As the morning progressed the clouds closed in and the wind picked up, so we preferred to be off over the northern side of the ridge and in its shelter. Ignoring the first three paths heading north off the ridge, we continued along to the summit of Ciemniak where the ridge and border made a sharp turn to the south. From the summit the 'red' route gave a reasonably gentle descent down open hillside, then through dwarf firs to the dirt road in Dolina Koscieliska. This left us with an easy jog across sheep filled meadows out to the road at Kiry. As usual there was a fleet of minibuses waiting and it didn't take long to fill one and return to Zakopane. The cost for the four or five miles back to town was about 20p.

As we were back in town fairly early we called in at the Tourist Information to try to book a hut for a couple of nights but we were told that all the huts in the area were fully booked for the next few months and it was impossible to reserve a bed, although we could of course sleep on the floor if there was space. Under the circumstances we decided to stay on in our pension and just make day trips out to the western end of the range, using the great system of buses that plied non-stop back and forth between the road-heads.

When we saw the weather next morning we weren't at all sorry that we'd agreed not to spend the next three days up high; it was very wet and windy and was not the weather to be trying a route which involved several sections of chains or to be out on exposed ridges. Instead we climbed up to Kuznice again, in the pouring rain, and stopped for a coffee in the bar to warm up. We got chatting to a fellow Englishman, he too had been told that the huts were fully booked right through to October and he'd even be told that the cable-car was fully booked too. We found the last bit a little hard to believe as both times we had used the cable-car neither we nor the majority of the other passengers appeared to have pre-booked. Today though, no one was going up, booked or not, as it was far too windy for it to run.

With the rain easing a little we followed the 'black' path we had used on our first afternoon, deliberately staying in the shelter of the forest as much as possible. It was lovely once we had left the main cobbled path behind and started climbing up into a clearing on the ridge, before contouring across the hillside then dropping down a slippery staircase to a small wooden chalet at the head of Dolina Strazyska. We were more than glad of the chance of another warm up before heading out into the rain again. Still heading west on the 'black' we climbed up over another wooded ridge, straight across the Dolina Malej Laki, up and over another wooded ridge and so back down to the dirt track in the Dolina Koscieliska. We jogged out through meadows back to the road at Kiry where a minibus was ready and waiting to take us back to the centre of Zakopane.

It was another very wet and windy start the following day, so we left the pension already dressed in full waterproofs. We had no sooner started walking down towards the town centre when a passing minibus stopped for us and took us to the main roundabout where the minibuses start out from. We asked around for a bus to Dolina Huciska and within a few minutes there were enough people gathered for a bus to leave. As a result we were soon at the road-end but it was still raining heavily.

Our starting point this day was in the furthest west of the valleys of the Polish Tatra; a deep limestone gorge with caves hidden by thick forest. A gentle climb took us up alongside the river to an area of open meadows where we found a dozen small wooden shepherds huts, at the far end of this clearing was the Polana Chocholowska refuge. This is the hut we had tried to book but we were assured that it was full; indeed there were still a few people lying on the floor, in their sleeping bags, when we called in for a coffee. Thankfully by the time we came out the rain had stopped and we followed the 'green' route through the forest, climbing easily at first, then more steeply to emerge into an open corrie, covered in dwarf firs. The warning whistle of marmots kept us company as we climbed to the col where we looked down into Slovakia on the far side. Slovakia looked good walking country with a lovely path linking high tarns in remote mountain corries. From the col a short climb up the ridge took us to the summit of Wolowiec. From here we followed the border posts along the ridge, with steep drops away to our left in Poland but easier slopes dropping down to small tarns in Slovakia.

A few easy scrambles led down to a col then a short climb took us up towards the peak of Lopata. A short way below the top however, the path contoured round the hill on the Slovak side, a legal detour into the country to avoid the top. Why we had to avoid the top was unclear as it didn't seem to be at all difficult. A 1:10,000 map showed a footpath from the summit that headed back down to the Chocholowska hut and it may simply have been to deter people from taking this option, keeping them instead on the prepared, way-marked, paths. The ridge was fairly easy and gave fast going; there was a 'Scottish' feel to the day as we dropped down to another col, past another substantial, but unmapped, footpath before we faced a steepish climb up newly constructed steps to Jarzabezy Wierch.

Luckily the weather was staying dry but clouds drifted up and down over the tops. A cold wind kept us moving quickly along, still following the border, down and along to the next top, Konezysty Wierch. Here we turned north off the main ridge and met our first people of the day; it was very unusual to have gone for so long without seeing anyone, generally all the paths had been very busy despite the weather. The broad ridge gave an easy start to the descent but after passing over Trzydniowianski Wierch the going became harder and very trying as we passed through a tangled area of dwarf pines. We had to step down over the roots, duck down under the branches and even climb down some roots.

Once out of the dwarf pine we continued down the steep path; as we descended we could hear a loud grunting noise coming from the forest across on the far side of a small valley, this continued for several minutes and sounded very much like a bear. There are known to be a handful of bears in the area; only a couple of years earlier a bear had been found wandering around outside the cinema in Zakopane. Alternatively, what we heard may have been deer rutting, if so, they start several weeks earlier than in Scotland.

At last the tough descent came to an end and it didn't take long to head out down the track, back alongside the river to the road-end. By this time in the afternoon the valley path was busy and we didn't have to wait long until there were enough people to fill a minibus to take us back to Zakopane.

The following morning we returned to Krakow with a day to spare before we flew home. We explored the old town, visited the 'Dragons Cave' beneath the castle, and browsed the market in the old indoor market place in the main square. The following day we visited Auschwitz, about an hour and a half away by bus. I was amazed at how big the concentration camp was; I assumed that much of it would have been destroyed before the Allies could liberate it but only the gas chambers and ovens had been partially blown up. It was very moving, and beyond most people's comprehension as to just how bad it must have been.

So that was the end of our first trip to Poland. One of the things that struck us most was the sheer number of people out walking in the hills; the second was the ubiquitous rainwear, a 'pac-a-mac' type coat with a pixie hood that cost about 30p.

The Tatra were well worth the visit and with all of the Slovakian side of the range still to explore I hope that one day we will be able to return.

Mongolia - Sunrise to Sunset

It was Christmas Eve and the last post before Christmas brought with it a couple of Christmas cards and an envelope marked '*Bufo Ventures*'; '*Bufo Ventures*' organised the Everest Marathon where Cath and I had first met so of course I opened the '*Bufo Ventures*' letter first and inside was a flier for a race that was to take place the following June.

The leaflet described the 'Mongolia Sunrise to Sunset' as the world's most beautiful 100km run, set beside a huge lake in northern Mongolia, in one of the world's most pristine and remote National Parks. After reading it through I knew where we would be heading for our summer holiday; it was too good an opportunity to miss, to run the longest race either of us had done in such a beautiful wilderness area. There were two options; to run the 100km or to cut short and run the usual marathon distance of just over 26 miles. For both of us the challenge had to be to go for the 100km, we both knew we could run a marathon anytime.

We had six months to make ourselves race-fit so we planned plenty of long runs and races. Initially things went according to plan and I trained well in January and February; in March Cath and I did a 50km race together through the Yorkshire Dales. A couple of weeks later I raced in the *Great Lakeland 3-Day;* a three day, solo, Mountain Marathon. This went well, proving I was strong and running well again and I was fairly confident I would last the 100km distance.

Unfortunately things then took a down-turn; we ran in the 24 mile Yorkshire 3-Peaks race on a dreadful day when a gale was blowing, the rain was pouring down and eventually around 20% of the 250 competitors suffered hypothermia to varying degrees. Within the first couple of miles to Pen-y-ghent my left Achilles was feeling sore; it hurt more and more as the race progressed, over Whernside and down to the road beneath Ingleborough. I considered pulling out at the road crossing before the climb of Ingleborough but I told myself I was just being a wimp because it was so cold and wet; instead I battled on. I felt strong climbing Ingleborough but the long descent over wet rocks and through deep puddles was agony and by this time I was limping badly.

In hindsight I should have quit as soon as it started hurting and perhaps the damage could have been minimised, but I didn't, and that was the end of my chances in Mongolia. With race-day still two months away I tried everything I could to fix my Achilles. I was icing it, taking anti-inflammatory pills, massaging it with anti-inflammatory gels, stretching, seeing a Physio for ultra-sound and using a 'Tens' machine.

All this was to no avail and by the time we left the UK I had hardly run for two months. Meanwhile Cath's training was going well; she had good runs in the Swaledale Marathon and the 'Old County Tops' race (a tough 37 miler from Langdale that takes in Helvellyn, Scafell and the Old Man of Coniston).

We flew to Beijing; our flight-path took us out over Scandinavia, St Petersburg, Mongolia and Ulaan Baatar. It never really turned dark as we flew into the sunrise and as we started our descent we saw the unmistakable sight of the 'Great Wall' as it snaked its way along the top of forested ridges for mile after mile.

As this was our first visit to China, we made sure we had a couple of days to explore Beijing; we enjoyed wandering down the back lanes taking in the atmosphere. One thing that impressed us were the exercise stations, which were set out on street corners throughout the city. The stations were nearly always in use no matter what time of day it was. Young and old, would be constantly swinging, stretching, stepping or cycling. None of the machines were broken and there was no litter or graffiti anywhere.

We spent almost a whole day walking just five miles, from Qianmen, which is at the south end of Tiananmen Square back to our hotel. The first of the 'sights' was the impressive South Gate at Qianmen. We then headed up through Tiananmen Square, and past the Mao Zedong Mausoleum, where Mao has laid since his death in 1976. It is said that a waxwork figure was made in case the preservation didn't work too well and it is now unclear whether the devotees filing past are looking at the real thing or merely a wax copy. Still heading north through the square we came to the 'Monument to the Peoples Heroes'; a troop of young flag-bearing children stood solemnly beneath it as a guard of honour.

We reached the Forbidden City, crossed one of five marble bridges and climbed to the top of the Tiananmen Gate. The temples and pavilions have been well restored and look as impressive now as they would have done when they were first built some 600 years ago. It was good to reach the gardens at the north end where suddenly all was green again; beautiful old gnarled trees, fishponds and strangely sculptured rocks.

North of the Forbidden City is the Jingshan Park; we climbed the small hill, up through woodland to the temple on the summit, where we looked out over the golden rooftops of the Forbidden City. The hill was man-made, using the soil excavated when they dug the moat that surrounds the Forbidden City.

Later, we watched the moon rise as we ate dinner in the hotel courtyard; dozens of kites climbed high into the darkening sky, they climbed unbelievably high and stayed aloft for half an hour or so before they finally fell back to earth.

Next day we headed for the airport to meet the others who were heading to Mongolia for the race. There were several delays as our flight was put back again and again; eventually the plane arrived, but there was still no sign of us leaving. Things then took a nasty turn as someone in the group made a comment about the delay that was meant in good nature but was either mis-understood or mis-interpreted by a Mongolian airport official. He took great offence and for a while it appeared as though none of us would be allowed to leave that night. The official eventually calmed down but only after receiving three written apologies. Having heard how friendly Mongolians are this was not an auspicious start.

Yet another delay was announced and it was clear that we weren't going to reach Camp Toilgot that night as planned. Finally, almost eight hours late, we took-off for Ulaan Baatar, the mystical capital of Mongolia. It had been a stormy afternoon and evening in Ulaan Baatar; the town is ringed by hills and the bad weather was causing a problem for the pilots who didn't want to fly. Bad weather seemed a perfectly reasonable explanation for the delay but it would have been better if we had been told this when we were waiting, rather than afterwards. We were soon to find out just how stormy it was as lightning appeared to strike the wing and we were bounced around more than we liked as we descended into Ulaan Baatar. Mongolian formalities were soon completed and we were taken to the Chingis Khan Hotel in the centre of town. The bad news was that we had to be back on the coach again by 5:30, which meant we had just three hours sleep.

Bright and early next morning we returned to the airport. Bearing in mind the difficulties with the delayed flight people had moved very quickly to sort things out; laying on a coach to the hotel, hotel accomodation for forty people, a coach back to the airport, and then 40 'take-away' breakfasts for 5:30 in the morning. All this was quite an impressive feat and quickly restored our faith in Mongolian hospitality.

Our 'plane was an old twin-propeller Russian AN-24 that was chartered to fly us to a dirt strip some three hours north, just inside the border with Siberia. The whole 'plane rattled like crazy as we bounced down the runway, which was not an encouraging sign. As we climbed higher it was beautiful looking down on rolling green hills and wide expanses of grassland, with virtually no sign of human habitation for miles and miles. We landed with a bump on a dirt strip in the centre of a broad grassy valley. The first thing I noticed as I stepped off the plane was the incredible smell, the air seemed so pure, scented with herbs and wild flowers.

There were no permanent buildings at the airstrip, just one lonely 'ger' and a wooden toilet shed. Half a dozen jeeps were parked by the side of the run-way and the locals soon had our bags loaded for the 5km drive to the lakeside where we would catch an old ferry to take us up the lake to the camp. The group walked or jogged across the meadows, through the little settlement of Khatgal, to the ferry. We passed herds of yaks and cows; wild-looking horsemen trotted past as if in a great hurry. Khatgal itself consisted of about a hundred wooden cabins and felt 'gers'; there were only a couple of more substantial permanent buildings.

The lake, Khovsgol Nuur, is spectacular and boasts a number of surprising statistics. For example:

⇒ it is almost 100 miles long and up to 20 miles wide, it even showed up on the 5 inch globe we had bought for our daugther Molly;
⇒ there are 96 rivers flowing into the lake, but just one flows out of it;
⇒ it is the 14th largest source of fresh-water in the world, holding between 1% and 2% of the world's fresh-water supply;
⇒ it is the deepest lake in Central Asia;
⇒ in winter it freezes to a depth of four foot and trucks drive down over it from Siberia.

Although it was a warm, sunny day it felt cold sitting out on the deck of the battered old ferry that took us 25 miles up the lake. The huge body of cold water seemed to chill the air by several degrees as we sat watching the stunning views and tried to work out where the race route might go.

After about an hour and a half the boat nosed onto a shingle beach and we all clambered down the steep gang-plank for our first sight of Camp Toilgot. This 'tourist-camp' consists of about a dozen round felt 'gers', a few wooden 'gers', a large wooden 'dining ger', toilet block and an office. It was situated on a grassy meadow on the west shore of the lake, sandwiched between another small lake and a low wooded hill. A mile or two further west, running on a north/south axis parallel to the lake, was a range of hills reaching to almost 10,000ft; the camp itself is at lake level, about 5,300ft.

We were allocated a 'ger', the traditional felt tent of the Mongolians, who, being a nomadic people, need something that is substantial and weatherproof for the freezing winters but mobile enough to move easily in the spring and summer when they move on looking for grazing. The frame is a wooden trellis; wooden roof supports rest on top of the trellis and fit into something like a cart-wheel, which is supported by a couple of posts. The whole frame is made entirely of wood; no screws or nails are used.

It was interesting chatting with the other competitors. All corners of the world were represented, from Alaska to New Zealand, most of Europe, South Africa, Japan, Thailand and of course, Mongolia. Many of the Europeans were ex-pats working in Shanghai or Hong Kong. One of the Swiss arrived the hard way; he cycled the 600 miles from Ulaan Baatar and only arrived a day or two before the race.

That afternoon a group of us went out for a run for an hour or so. This gave us the chance to 'recce' the start of the race route; it also showed us what effect the altitude might play when racing. For me though it was an important test of how my Achilles might stand up to a long run. On top of a small hill, deep within the forest, we found a wooden wigwam shaped cairn, an 'ovoo'. By tradition these are placed on the high points of passes and hills and one should go round them three times, in a clockwise direction, adding something to the cairn, to ensure good luck. Once out of the forest we ran a short way north along a jeep track before heading back to the lakeside by a small settlement of 'gers'. We then followed the shoreline back through the forest to our camp. Unfortunately my Achilles was very painful and I had to treat it with massage and the 'Tens' machine as soon as I was back.

Next day we didn't want to do too much and risk tiring ourselves out before the big race so Cath and I went for a gentle walk for an hour or so to familiarise ourselves with the first few miles of the race route; we knew we would be starting in the dark so it helped to know the way in advance. I'm no horseman but in the afternoon we went out for a ride round the small lake; generally the horses were pretty easy to manage but as luck would have it mine seemed to be a bit frisky. He wanted to run on ahead with the more experienced riders while I was content to just walk along at the back with the other nervous beginners.

Later I took a mountain bike and went out for a couple of hours, heading south down the lakeside, following the jeep track that was the race route between 42km and 54km on the way out and 88km to 100km on the way back. The track stayed fairly flat as it was always within about 50 metres of the shoreline. It was a lovely ride through grassy meadows that were dotted with wild flowers; flocks of sheep and goats and herds of cows and yaks grazed all around me; many of the horses had pretty young foals running at their side. Dotted around were little groups of 'gers'; at one a wrinkled, weather-beaten, old lady had penned a small flock of sheep and she milked them as I rode by.

After dinner the local five-piece band, 'Dalai Eej', came to sing, play and dance for us. A couple of the guys worked around the camp and the little dancer was one of the girls who looked after the 'gers' and lit the stoves for us. It was a very professional performance, the singing was very good but one of the men also did some 'throat singing', which was unusual to say the least.

The following day all the runners had to have a medical to show we were fit to race. One of the Doctors was Nat, whom Cath and I had met back in 1993 at the Everest Marathon. Nat specialises in the lower limb and works at a teaching hospital in London so he was the ideal person to look at my Achilles. After a thorough examination he said that if he had seen me at his clinic he would have advised me not to travel and to cancel the holiday. Instead of being 'tendonitis', an injury to the sheath around the tendon, it looked as though the main problem was with the tendon itself, 'tendonosis'. The treatment for this was different, which is probably why the injury hadn't healed.

In the end he said there was quite a risk of doing further damage and possibly rupturing the tendon if I raced the 100km, I should content myself with running the marathon and take it very easy at that. Whilst this wasn't welcome news it came as no real surprise; it was in fact a weight off my mind as I no longer had to decide what to do. Now the 100km was no longer an option, I would just jog round the marathon instead.

That afternoon we enjoyed another short walk and before dinner we had the pre-race briefing. The Mongolian entrants were introduced to everyone; one was a Mountain Guide who had summited Everest and one of the girls had run the marathon at the Atlanta Olympics. After a big dinner we sorted our race kit for the final time and turned in early.

It was 3:15 when we woke to hear the multi-talented Tyler playing reveille on his bugle. It was of course pitch dark, there was a hint of rain in the air but it was not too cold. Just before 4:30 we gathered under the 'Start' banner, then we were off. It was still dark but thankfully the drizzle had stopped, so it was on with the head-torches and straight into the forest. From our 'recces' we knew the trail was very narrow for the first couple of miles and in several places it was blocked by fallen branches and tree roots, which made it difficult to over-take, thus it was important we had a good start and not be trapped behind anyone going too slowly.

I lost Cath immediately; I knew she was ahead of me and whilst I was supposed to be taking it easy, bearing in mind I was only doing the marathon and she was planning on running the 100km, I was worried that she had set off too fast. We were soon spread out on the trail as we wound our way up and over the first small hill, then, as we came out of the forest onto the jeep track it became lighter and we were able to put away our head-torches. I caught Cath again after a few minutes and we ran together for the next few miles.

The track led north along the lakeside, across grassy meadows and past 'gers' where the inhabitants were still fast asleep. The first check-point was at the 12km mark, at the foot of the climb to the first pass. It was too early to need anything at this check-point so Cath and I ran through; the track then turned away from the lake and started to climb in easy zigzags through open woodland then across more open ground. As we neared the top of the climb I looked back and watched the sun rising over Khovsgol Nuur, and beyond it, Siberia.

We overtook the Mongolian Olympian as we climbed this first pass and we were aware there was another Mongolian lady still ahead, although we weren't sure if she was planning on running the marathon or the 100km. Once on the pass the trail turned south and we ran along a ridge for a short distance before dropping quite steeply down the far side, across grassy meadows and back into forest again. Through the forest the path was quite wet and boggy; we then crossed a dry river bed and headed back into forest, following splashes of eco-friendly green paint that marked the full length of the course. We were almost back to the jeep track by the lake-side when we turned west once more and headed deeper into the forest.

Cath dropped me again here and I didn't expect to see her after that. I was finding it very difficult to run with any rhythm; there was a shot of pain every time my left heel hit the ground. I swallowed an energy gel and drank a lot of water at the second check-point, then started on a long drag of a climb that didn't seem to fit the route profile. According to the profile, which I had studied so much in the previous six months, the steep climb to Khirvesteg Pass started almost as soon as you left the second check-point. On the ground though I seemed to be going for miles; only climbing gently, as the path followed another dry river bed.

At last I met a lone horseman who was waiting to show me the way across the river. Once over the rocky bed the path disappeared and we had to fight our way up a very steep hillside; I found the climb very hard, nevertheless I did catch someone here, although I was almost immediately overtaken myself, this time by Marc, the guy who had cycled out from UB.

Nearing the top of the climb I heard the tapping of a woodpecker, then, as I came out into the small clearing on the pass I had a good view of the woodpecker itself. It was a painful run down the far side of the col; there was no real path, we just headed down into a steep sided valley on uneven ground that was hidden beneath knee deep wet grass. At last the angle eased and beside an old log-cabin I met a lone Mongolian who was manning a water-station. This was a good sign; I now had just 10km to go. Below the water-station I reached a jeep track, which led through open forest at a perfect angle, just heading very gently downhill as it was leading back towards the lakeside. I was able to run reasonably well again here and surprisingly as I came out into the open meadows by some 'gers' I found I was catching a couple of runners. I stepped up the pace as much as my heel would let me and soon after reaching the jeep track I caught and passed a young German and just ahead of him was Cath.

Cath was going well but I caught up with her and we ran together for a few hundred metres, I then left her so I could get to the finish before her. This of course was the marathon finish; it was only the 42km point for her, not even half way yet. I prepared some spare kit and put together some food and water for her to take with her on the next leg of the race; I also wanted to find out if any other ladies had gone through and how far ahead they were.

As it transpired only one lady had come in, a Mongolian, but she had stopped at the marathon distance, so Cath was now leading the women's race in the 100km. I finished the marathon 5th in 5 hours 32 minutes, which was a reasonable result under the circumstances. It was a little frustrating though when people congratulated me and said that 5th was good, when I knew that if it hadn't been for the injury I could easily have run as much as an hour faster; I had achieved 5th when, under doctors orders, I had been 'taking it easy'.

Cath quickly turned around and headed back out onto the course, this time on a loop heading south down the lakeside. I meanwhile wandered back to our 'ger' for a lie down. After a couple of hours rest and several bowls of tea I loaded up my rucksack with food, water and dry clothes and set off on a mountain bike to look for Cath.

The Mongolian who won the 100km race went through the first 42km in what would have been a new course record for the marathon distance, he ran about 4 hours 15 minutes, he then went on to smash the 100km record, coming in half an hour ahead of the next person in a time of just 11 hours 12 minutes. We heard that he had been in the Khovsgol area for the past couple of months, training specifically for the race. This will have been a huge advantage as he will have known the course intimately and he will have been well acclimatised. He wanted not just to win, but to win in style; he was looking to secure sponsorship for himself and his family and to gain a place in the Mongolian team for the Athens Olympics in 2004.

I was about 10km from camp when I came across a Mongolian and an English lad who were fighting it out for second and third places. I followed the two of them back to the finish, offering them food and water; it was the Mongolian who held on to take second, with Andy only a minute behind in third. Back in camp I checked the radio reports and found that Cath had just gone through the check-point at 76km so I jumped back on the bike and went out again to meet her. As I headed back down the track I met the guys in 4th and 5th, both were English lads now based in Shanghai, who did very well to finish in around 12½ hours and 13 hours. Further down the trail I came across the Swiss, Marc, who was suffering with stomach problems and was forced to walk in for 6th place.

I had just arrived at the Jankhai check-point and hadn't even climbed off the bike when Cath arrived. She too was suffering with stomach problems, which made running very uncomfortable so she was forced to walk for much of the last

40kms. I cycled slowly back up the jeep track, offering food, water and encouragement as Cath walked and jogged across the grassy meadows; the race route stayed close to the water's edge where it was easier to take a straight line route, avoiding the little climbs and loops of the track.

We passed through herds of yaks and dozens of horses with long legged foals standing unsteadily by their side, through 'ger' camps, and past pairs of huge golden coloured ducks swimming out on the lake. Two young girls from a 'ger' ran along with Cath for a couple of hundred metres, before finally giggling and waving goodbye. Cath came in to finish 1st lady and 7th overall in a time of 15 hours 16 minutes; a brilliant effort.

Meanwhile, strange tales were coming in about what was going on out on the course; one 63 year old Japanese man is supposed to have slept for 20 minutes, in a squatting position, at one of the aid stations; as he crossed the finish line he proceeded to recite Japanese poetry.

Next morning there was a very relaxed feeling around the camp. After a short walk to loosen up a group of us took some horses and went out riding again. We rode a few miles north, following the lakeside path, looking for a Tsaatan camp. The Tsaatan people live a very nomadic life based around their reindeer herds, which provide them with virtually all they need; from milk and meat to skins and transport. 'Tsaa' means 'reindeer' in Mongolian. Unlike the Mongolians, Tsaatan nomads don't live in 'gers', they live in reindeer skin tepees which they move around as they go in search of the mosses and grasses that the reindeer like best. After riding for an hour or so we came to the fly infested camp, right on the shore of the lake. There were a couple of tepees and lying panting in the sparse shade of some trees, was a small herd of reindeer. The family welcomed us into their tepee, cooked a big pile of pancakes and passed round a bowl of reindeer-milk curds and cheese. I found the riding fun but I was very glad when we reached our camp again and I could dismount. I could hardly walk at first and I realised I was not a natural horseman.

Some of the group were fortunate in being able to stay for another week; they planned to trek on horse-back up to the north end of the lake and back. For us though our time was up and we had to head home. When we had flown in we landed on the dirt strip at Khatgal with about 50 passengers and their baggage, but the 'plane couldn't take off from such a rough airstrip with the same heavy load, so going back we split into two groups. Some went back down the lake on the ferry and then flew out from Khatgal. Others volunteered for a very bumpy jeep ride instead. The rough jeep track was 'entertaining' and the drivers of the three vehicles were soon racing each other. This was all very well when we were side by side tearing across flat open grassland but not so much fun when the tracks merged back into single lane and someone had to 'give way'.

We finally reached the small town of Moron after having raced across the open steppe; there was very little other traffic. The airfield at Moron has a concrete runway and the 'plane from Khatgal arrived with the rest of the group shortly after we arrived in the jeeps. We loaded up and flew back to Ulaan Baatar and the Chingis Khan Hotel. Next morning we flew back to Beijing where we again had a couple of free days. We visited the famous Silk Market, the Summer Palace and the Lama Temple. The temple is now home to a group of monks from Mongolia and Tibet and is used by China as a symbol of its tolerance of religious freedom.

We also booked to go on a tour to the Great Wall; we opted to visit an un-developed part of the wall at Huanghua rather than be swamped by thousands of tourists at the more popular, fully rebuilt sections. Unfortunately it was a grey and drizzly day with mist right down to road level so we could see very little when we arrived. When the mist did clear for a minute or two we could sense how spectacular it once was but now it all seemed rather dreary. Once on the wall we headed away from the road in thick mist; there were no views at all. At most of the watch-towers along the way, enterprising locals had taken control of the ladders and insisted on charging people to climb them. After this had happened two or three times we tired of their games and couldn't be bothered arguing with them anymore so we just gave up and feeling rather disappointed we made our way back down to the road and returned to Beijing. Next day it was back to the airport for the long journey home.

Mongolia is certainly a wonderful country where we met many lovely people. I knew I wanted to return to explore the mountains, plains and deserts of that beautiful land.

To the Top of Europe: Mount Elbrus – 5,642m

It had been a long time since I'd climbed any big peaks so I searched the internet for trips to Mount Elbrus and found a cheap package with a Russian company, *Pilgrim Tours*, which I hoped would give me a reasonable chance of success and would not take me away from home for too long. When friend and neighbour Paddy heard my plans he quickly decided to join me and go for the second of his 'Seven Summits'; he had already climbed Kilimanjaro a couple of years earlier. We had fun trying to sort out our visas; I managed to do mine through the post but Paddy had to travel down to London to collect his from the Embassy only days before we were due to fly.

We flew into Moscow's Sheremetyevo Airport and were pleasantly surprised to find that all our bags had arrived safely and we needn't have worn our climbing boots after all. A driver was waiting to meet us and we set off into the busy Moscow traffic to be dropped at the 'Rossia' Hotel. The hotel is not pretty but it is huge, with around 3,200 rooms on 21 floors, which has put it into the 'Guinness Book of Records'. The hotel was ideally situated, right at the heart of the city, overlooking Red Square, the Kremlin and the picturesque St Basil's Cathedral. We headed out to explore Moscow and were amazed at the number of expensive cars on the road and at the variety of shops, there was the usual mix of big name brands; it could easily have been London or Paris.

Next morning we met up with two others from our group, Barry and Paul, who, like Paddy, had recently climbed Kilimanjaro, so this was to be the second of their 'Seven Summits' too. We headed south through Moscow to the domestic airport. On time, we were called for our flight and led out to a rather ancient aeroplane, which had obviously undergone several re-sprays and changes of owner in its long career. The take-off and initial climb were very bumpy but thankfully, after we had broken through the clouds, things settled down and most of the unsettling rattling stopped. The flight south towards the Caucasus took just over two hours; we touched down in Mineralnye Vody and were off-loaded onto an ancient German bus which took us to the 'Arrival Hall', although this looked more like a giant cattle-shed. The whole place was in decay and it had definitely seen better days.

Marianne, who was to be our guide for the week, met us here; she led us out to a waiting minibus and we set off for the mountains. Our driver and Marianne were both constantly talking into mobile phones and it eventually transpired that we should have collected the fifth member of our group at the airport. At one stage, after having been driving for two hours, we actually did a u-turn and started back towards Mineralnye Vody. Thankfully our driver soon did another u-turn and we again headed for the mountains. A short while later, amongst a cacophony of tooting horns we pulled in beside a parked minibus and there we found Jonathan; our group was now complete. Jonathan, an Israeli, had come direct from Turkey, he'd been trekking with his girl-friend in Turkey's Taurus Mountains; he had then climbed Mt Ararat as acclimatisation for Elbrus.

At last we turned off the main road and headed up into the Baksan Valley, which would eventually lead us to our base near the road-end, at Cheget. We had to make a brief stop as we passed through one small town to register our visas with the local Police. Back in the minibus we climbed higher up the valley into ever-thicker mist and rain so that soon we couldn't see the interesting rock formations on either side of the road. Cows, goats and a few sheep grazed along the roadside as we climbed still higher beside a raging glacial torrent.

We finally pulled up outside Logovo Lodge, a wooden chalet, where we were to be based for the week. Next morning it was not very inspiring; rain poured down and clouds filled the valley. The plan was that we would climb Cheget Peak, which is on the opposite side of the Baksan Valley to Mt Elbrus. At about 11,800ft it would be a good acclimatisation walk and it should have given us great views across to the twin summits of Elbrus. In view of the weather Marianne kindly organised a minibus to take us the five miles down the valley to Cheget, rather than making us walk.

As we climbed out of the minibus it was pouring with rain, it was also cold and windy so we had to put on full water-proofs straight away. On too went hat and gloves as we rode the slow and rather ancient, single seat chair-lift, which reminded me of the first stage of the old lift in Glencoe. Lightning was flashing close by as we rode the lift up; huge claps of thunder rolled around the hills above us.

The higher we went the thicker became the rain until it was soon falling as very wet sleet. From the top of the first chair we were supposed to take another ride a bit higher but the second chair-lift wasn't running. Apart from ourselves and a small party of Japanese there was no one else around. We were in thick cloud as we headed off up the steep dirt track that climbed to the top of the second chair-lift. From the top station we left the track and climbed on a narrow path into ever thickening snow and dense cloud. The snow was now lying and it was truly a miserable day.

After walking uphill for about an hour and a half we reached a narrow ridge and here we stopped. Marianne thought the lightning was so close it would be too exposed and too dangerous for us to continue along the ridge and up onto the summit, which was still a short distance above. Instead we waited for Barry and Paul, who were bringing up the rear; as we waited we gazed out over the precipice into Georgia. Needless to say, there was no view of Mt Elbrus, which was disappointing as it was difficult to take a good photograph of the hill once we were actually on it.

After standing around in the wind and snow for about twenty minutes, we turned about and headed back down the track, our footprints barely visible as the heavy snow continued to fall. We made good time down to the top station, then dropped quickly down the dirt road, to reach the top of the lower chair-lift. While waiting for Barry and Paul to catch up, a couple of us went in and had a cup of tea with Sergei, the old chap who was operating the chair-lift. Back on the chair-lift, as we lost height the snow turned back to rain and it was a very cold, wet party that emerged through the mist to reach the cluster of buildings around the bottom of the lifts.

Marianne took us into one of the restaurants where we were fed a huge lunch; I didn't really feel as though we'd done enough to earn such a substantial feed but I ate it anyway, thinking it might be difficult to eat properly when we stayed higher later. With the rain still pouring down, the minibus collected us and we were again saved the five-mile walk back to the lodge.

Later in the afternoon Paddy and I went back out into the rain for a short walk, we just wandered up to the road-end at the Azau Cable-car Station. Several cabins lined the small 'square'; most were cafés and each of them had a bar-b-que smoking away out the front. We chose a café and went in for a coffee and a pastry; we obviously looked foreign so a woman came over to serve us and rather than speak Russian she spoke to us in German. After that all dealings were in German, which made life easier as we couldn't speak any Russian. However, almost as soon as we had finished our coffees she came over and gave us the bill, then, although we were quite happy sitting in the warm and dry chatting, she held the door open for us, making it clear that we should go. We seemed to have been thrown out but we didn't know why, it wasn't closing time as the locals were still sitting there eating and drinking.

On reflection it was a mistake to speak German; we should have stuck with English. During the Second World War Germany had fought Russia for control of the Caucasus and they even managed to plant a German flag on top of Mt Elbrus. A brave local climbed to the summit a few days later and tore it down. The older people in the valley probably still remember and I guess that Germans are not their favourite tourists.

We wandered back down the road in the teeming rain; the clouds were right down and we could see that the snowline had dropped to only a few hundred feet above the floor of the valley. The weather looked set and the prospects did not look good, it was clear that there was a lot of fresh snow higher up and even if it did clear soon it could still take a day or two for things to settle and let us go safely for the top. As we were working to quite a tight schedule we did not have too many days to spare and our chances did not look good.

After dinner at the lodge we chatted with two very weather-beaten young English lads who had just arrived. They must have only just been out of their teens, yet they had been roaming around the Caucasus for a few weeks, on their own, with no guide. They had just come back from summiting on Elbrus, having camped up at the old Diesel Hut. It seemed as though they had had a great time, enjoyed all sorts of adventures, including one of them being snow blind for two days because he forgot his sunglasses. I think we were all a bit envious of them, thinking back to the daft things we had done at their age but wouldn't dream of doing now.

As I took a last look out of the window before I went to bed I was amazed to see stars shining brightly from a totally clear sky. We hoped that the storm had passed and it would be fine for us after all. Next morning I was awake early, eagerly looked out of the window and saw bright blue sky with golden sunshine lighting up the ridge on the south side of the valley. It was bitterly cold, there was ice on the puddles and the snow line was only a few hundred feet above the road, but the sun was shining and there wasn't a cloud in the sky.

After breakfast we set off on the short walk up the road to the cable-car station at Azau. Another guide came with us; his party consisted of three Japanese men. The guide looked just like Reinhold Messner used to look some twenty years ago; the look can't have been an accident, he must have worked hard on it. 'Reinhold' as he became known, wandered about the lodge practicing the saxophone and whenever he met Marianne on the hill he grabbed her around the waist and they would dance a waltz. As we came in to the top of the first stage of the cable-car we were amazed to see a man prancing about on the snow, dressed only in a pair of swimming trunks.

We went straight through onto the second stage, which took us up to the Mir Station at about 11,400ft. Here too were a man and a rather elderly, overweight woman, prancing about on the snow in their swimming costumes. It was bright and sunny but it was freezing cold with a biting wind. The exhibitionists were all Russians; it just seems to be something they like to do on the slopes of one of their highest mountains. We walked from the cable-car to the nearby chair-lift and as we waited for the chair a pretty young girl stripped down to her bikini and she too danced in the snow. She drew quite a crowd and was being appreciated much more than the woman down at Mir!

The chair carried us easily up the hill towards Garabashi and as we rode we couldn't take our eyes off the twin summits of Elbrus, which seemed to be so close that we could walk there in only an hour or two. From the top of the chair there was a short walk to Garabashi where we found 'The Barrels'; a row of eight huge barrel-like huts, they look like the 'tank' part of a petrol-tanker. We set off from 'The Barrels' on an acclimatisation walk and were overtaken a couple of times by 'Snowcats' laden with Russian tourists out to see Elbrus close up. It was a straightforward walk on snow from 'The Barrels' up to the Diesel Hut, which is a relatively new hut but seems to be little used as it is so cold in there. The Diesel Hut replaced the Priut II hut, which was sited a little higher on a rocky ridge at about 13,700ft. The Priut II burned down a few years ago but it's walls still stand and a tent was pitched inside, giving the campers a sheltered spot out of the wind.

Just above the old hut is a huge boulder, which is covered in about forty memorial plaques. This was a grim reminder that although the mountain looked easy as we strolled about in the sunshine, in bad weather it could be a killer. Paul had phoned home earlier and his wife told him that a party of eight Polish climbers had been missing on Elbrus for three days. From the weather we'd seen in the valley over the past couple of days we knew the conditions would have been atrocious higher up.

After resting at the Diesel Hut, we turned and headed back down the hill. Marianne had carried a pair of 'blades' in her rucksack and she now clipped these on and skied down. Back at 'The Barrels' Marianne took our orders for lunch, using her mobile she then phoned ahead to a little café in the main square at Azau to tell them we were on our way.

By the time we had dropped back down the chair-lift and the two stages of the cable-car it was mid-afternoon and we had all worked up quite an appetite. As the sun was out, bringing with it coach-loads of tourists, stalls had been set up in the square; they were piled high with the local knit-wear of gloves, hats, socks and jumpers, there were local felt hats too. We headed back down to the lodge where we spent the rest of the afternoon sorting our gear and packing our rucksacks with all that we would need for a three or four day stay at 'The Barrels'.

We left the lodge after another leisurely breakfast, made the short walk up the road to the cable-car station and rode up the two stages of the cable-car; we then had to wait for half an hour for the chair-lift to start running. It was a clear, bright day but I thought it was too cold to be just standing there waiting so I asked the guides if they knew when the lift would start, they said "Soon, this is the East you know." I then asked about walking up, but was told a very firm "No."

At last the generator spluttered into life and the ancient chair-lift sluggishly started to move. We climbed on, carefully clutching our over-laden rucksacks on our laps, and rode back up to 'The Barrels'. We settled in to our 'barrel'; there were five beds, each with a lumpy mattress, a couple of thin blankets and a dirty pillow. We were pleased to find that there was an electric light and a very efficient radiator, but it was best not to examine the wiring too closely or we would probably have turned them both off and not risked using them. We had a great view out of the window at the end of the 'barrel', it looked west into the sunset, and we could also see out to the twin summits of Elbrus.

At lunch we discovered a flaw in Marianne's far from perfect English. There was some confusion about the time, did she mean 1 o'clock, or in one hours time. This made us look again at the timings that Marianne had given us for the ascent and these now made much more sense. Instead of the climb taking 10 hours like she had said, she meant that we should be on top by 10 o'clock, assuming that we started at 3:00am as planned; this would mean 7 hours climbing rather than 10 hours as she had seemed to suggest.

After lunch we walked back up to the Diesel Hut, then continued on, climbing more steeply up the snow to an outcrop of rocks at around 15,400ft, known as the Pastukhov Rocks. The climb took about three hours and for the first two and a half hours I felt fine but the last half an hour was hard work. I wasn't feeling ill, just very tired and lethargic. Paddy, Jonathan and I climbed with Marianne and we were the only ones to make it to the rocks. Barry and Paul, climbing with a new guide, Anton, and the three Japanese with their guide 'Reinhold', all failed to reach our high point at the top of the rocks. As we went past them on our descent, they all turned round and headed down too.

That evening we had a very big dinner, with loads to eat and drink. During the night I paid for it, I felt awful, my stomach was churning and I felt sick. Next morning I was up early for the cold walk out to the 'long-drop'. It was another beautiful morning, freezing cold but with bright blue sky and not a cloud in sight. A short while later I had to face another walk out to the 'long-drop' and I decided I'd better start taking the *Imodium*. After a late breakfast we set off up the hill again to the site of the ruined Priut II Hut. We took it easy as we wanted to rest as much as possible in readiness for the summit the following day, but we were aware that the extra acclimatisation was necessary and should only do us good.

Later that afternoon Marianne asked whether we wanted to take the 'Snowcat' up to the Pastukhov Rocks, this would mean a big saving of two or three hours climbing and would make a successful ascent much more likely. Paddy and I, and Barry and Paul all said yes but Jonathan wasn't happy. I had initially been in two minds about taking the 'Snowcat' but after considering it carefully I decided that I had already climbed up to the rocks so I wasn't missing anything out; for $50, although expensive, it was well worth helping a 'once-in-a-lifetime' opportunity to succeed. We had always been aware that this was going to be an option, so it didn't come as a surprise to find we would have to pay for the ride up.

Marianne tried to put Jonathan off climbing the whole way but he was quite upset and felt that if taking the 'Snowcat' was necessary to climb to the summit then *Pilgrim Tours* should have made it clear in their itinerary and they should have included the cost in the overall package. With everyone feeling the tension we had a lazy afternoon, an early dinner and were in bed by about 7pm.

Good to his word, Jonathan refused to take the easy option, he was up at 1:30 the next morning, and left the 'barrels' at 2:30, with Anton, to start his ascent. The arrangement was that the rest of us, Barry, Paul, Paddy and I with guide Marianne would take the 'Snowcat' up to the Pastukhov Rocks where we would meet Jonathan and Anton at about 4:40. Marianne would then lead Paddy, Jonathan and I, while Anton would look after Barry and Paul. Our alarms went off at 2:30 and we slowly roused ourselves and dressed in layers and layers of warm clothes. It was a long way below freezing, probably about minus 20°, but it was otherwise a clear, starlit night. I managed to force down a couple of yoghurts and a cup of tea for breakfast, which was not really enough to set me up for a long day at altitude, in sub zero temperatures.

At 4 o'clock we climbed up onto the open back of the 'Snowcat' and huddled down for the 40 minute ride up to the Pastukhov Rocks. The diesel fumes made me feel ill but I kept telling myself that it was better than walking. About two thirds of the way up, on the steeper part above the Diesel Hut and the ruins of the Priut II, it looked for a while as though we would have to jump out and walk. The 'Snowcat' was having trouble climbing the steep snow, which, at that time of the morning was frozen hard as ice. It was quite scary as the 'Snowcat' slid sideways across the mountain or at times started to slide backwards down the steep icy slopes.

At last we caught the other 'Snowcat', which was carrying 'Reinhold' and his Japanese party, and we followed them up to the pre-arranged meeting place, passing Jonathan and Anton, who had made really good progress, so that all three groups arrived at the Pastukhov Rocks at around the same time.

The Japanese were ready first and they set off followed a minute or two later by Paddy, Jonathan and I with Marianne, then Barry and Paul, with Anton. It was so clear, that with an almost full moon and the starlight, we hardly needed to use our head-torches. There was a slight breeze but it was nowhere near as windy as it had been during the night when we could feel the 'barrel' moving beneath us as we tried to sleep.

We started off from the Pastukhov Rocks with Marianne leading our little group and setting a very sensible, steady pace. The climb started immediately, up a steepish ice slope, which led up under the lower, eastern summit. As we were about to join a line of wands that would lead us towards the col between the two summits we looked out to the east to watch the sun rise, always a magical moment.

The wands led us off on a traverse towards the col and at first I felt fine. Our group over-took the Japanese party and was now in the lead; Paddy and Jonathan were both going strongly but I soon needed more frequent and longer rests. I told Paddy that it was starting to look as though I might not make it. I was clearly not acclimatised, yet he and Jonathan were both going well and taking it all in their stride.

31: An early start on Elbrus

There are the ruins of a small hut on the windswept col and we had a short rest there, but we were soon moving again, now climbing between the twin summits, on a rising traverse heading in a northerly direction, across a steep snow slope. After a short but steep climb we came out onto a ridge; from here we had great views north towards the plain where there was no snow in sight, whilst to the south we saw hundreds of miles of stunning, snow capped peaks, including the beautiful Ushba, dazzling in the bright sunshine.

I slowly made my way up behind the others and at last we reached the crest of the broad ridge. Away to our left we could now see the western summit, which seemed to be only a short stroll away. We stashed our rucksacks and walked easily along the ridge to the summit; at 18,510ft the highest mountain in Europe. Sadly our arrival on top coincided with the arrival of a thick bank of cloud and any hope of a good view disappeared.

> "I think that maybe we do not climb a mountain because it is there. We climb it because we are here"   (Jon Carroll)

About ten minutes later the Japanese party arrived; the actual summit was quite small so we dropped down out of their way and let them climb to the top. They were obviously very happy to have made it and stood in heroic poses shouting 'Banzai' at the top of their voices while a Russian photographer snapped away.

I was still feeling worn out and sick and Jonathan was cold, so after about 20 minutes at the summit we dropped back down the ridge and collected our rucksacks. Unfortunately we heard via Marianne and her radio that Barry and Paul had had to turn back at the col. Paul had not been going too well earlier in the week but today it was Barry who had had a hard time and although Paul would probably have made it he seemed quite relaxed about missing out on his chance for the top.

On reaching the col we stopped by the ruined hut for another short rest. We had lunch with us, which included a small carton of orange drink; I took one sip and was immediately violently sick. I felt a little better after that and Marianne was happy for Paddy and I to go on ahead while she looked after Jonathan who had very little experience of using an ice-axe and crampons; and he had of course climbed the whole way without resorting to the 'Snowcat'.

As we descended the traverse beneath the east summit and dropped back down to the Pastukhov Rocks, the snow was softening in the bright sunshine. Our crampons were starting to 'ball-up' so we put them away and stripped off our warm clothes. The long descent continued, past the Pastukhov Rocks, down past the Diesel Hut for the last time, and finally, after a nine and a half hour day (6hrs up and 3½ hrs down) we reached the 'barrels'.

Barry and Paul were both very philosophical about having had to turn back; I doubted if I would have taken it quite so well. As we were back earlier than expected we realised we still had time to drop down to the valley so we quickly packed our kit and walked down through the volcanic landscape to the cable-car station at Mir, we caught the last lift down and slowly wandered back to Logovo Lodge.

We left for Mineralnye Vody the following morning. It was another clear, cold day of bright sunshine and it was a beautiful drive alongside the noisy river. The valley must be nearly 40 miles long with steep volcanic mountains closing in at first, but then, slowly, the mountains become hills, the hills then dropped back and we came out onto a vast plain, which was virtually flat except for a few steep volcanic cones. At Mineralnye Vody airport we were taken up to the Intourist Lounge; a woman came to us, collected our tickets and checked us in while we sat in the lounge; a porter then came and took our rucksacks and checked those in for us too. It was only when we were escorted down to the 'gate' that we met the rest of the passengers; the locals clearly didn't enjoy the same level of service that we did when checking-in, we were treated like VIP's! It was good to see a *Pilgrim Tours* driver waiting to collect us in Moscow; dropping us off at the 'Rossia' again.

We had a couple of spare days to explore Moscow; as we wandered the streets we found a great little map shop which was piled high with maps of every scale imaginable; these seemed to cover the whole of their vast country, except for the one little bit that we were interested in, the Caucasus. We struggled to make ourselves understood as no one spoke any English but we noticed that some squares on a huge master map had been blanked out; we guessed this either meant they had sold out, or what was more likely, that the maps for these areas were restricted and therefore unavailable.

During our aimless wanderings through the city's streets we also came across a 'traditional' Tibetan restaurant so we headed back there for dinner one evening. The *'Tibetan Kitchen'* was certainly a good find, the food was excellent and amongst other dishes we worked our way through a huge pile of momos. It was late as we headed back to the hotel; there was a lively street scene with mime artists, buskers and even a six-piece classical group playing in one of the under-passes.

It had been another great trip; the cost was certainly far more reasonable using a local company rather than a UK one, and we achieved our goal. Now just six more of the seven summits to go!

Mount Khuiten: Mongolia's Highest Mountain – 4,374m

To celebrate my 50th birthday I returned to Mongolia. The trip was sold by *KE* as being to the world's most remote peak, Mount Khuiten, which is Mongolia's highest mountain at 4,374m. Khuiten is in the Altai Tavan Bogd range of mountains, in the far west of Mongolia, on the border with China and Russia. China, Russia and Mongolia all meet on the summit of one of the other peaks we hoped to climb, Nairandal.

We flew via Moscow to Ulaan Baatar, capital of Mongolia, which we reached early the following morning. Tom, our *KE* trip leader and a qualified Mountain Guide, met us at the airport, along with Oggi, a lovely Mongolian lady who was to be our 'city guide'. That first afternoon Oggi took us sight-seeing round UB; first stop was the Gandantegchenling Monastery. There had been some 5,000 monks at the monastery in the early 1900's, but in 1938 the communists suppressed religious activities and destroyed around 900 monasteries. About half of the temples in the Gandantegchenling Monastery were destroyed; the other half were used to house Russian officers and their horses. Many monks from Gandantegchenling were among those killed. It was only in 1990, when the Russians left, that Buddhism was able to flourish again and some of the temples have been restored. There are now around 900 monks studying at the monastery.

Leaving the peace and calm of the temple complex we headed for the Natural History Museum. The most interesting displays were the dinosaur skeletons, of which there was a big collection, many of them mostly complete; there were also several nests of dinosaur eggs. Later we stopped at a Bank to change US dollars into Mongolian tögrögs and we all ended up with a huge wad of notes.

Next morning we packed our 'sacs for a day-hike up Tsetseguun, in the Bogd Khan National Park, situated just a few miles to the south of Ulaan Baatar. We were told that Tsetseguun was the highest peak in the park at 2,256m but the map shows a slightly higher top, Tusheegun Uul (2,268m) about a mile away. Thought to be the world's oldest protected area, the Bogd Khan National Park was founded in 1778.

The weather was cool, cloudy and a bit breezy as we left UB; we were soon away from the built-up area and driving among rolling green hills, dotted with gers and big herds of horses, sheep and goats. After a while we crested a hill at the top of which was a large 'ovoo' which was built from old crutches; the theory was that if you had just recovered from a broken leg, if you added your old crutch to the ovoo it would stop you breaking that leg again. Dozens of blue prayer flags flew from the ovoo, the blue to match the beautiful blue Mongolian sky.

As we walked round the ovoo three times, a large pack of mangy looking dogs appeared out of nowhere; having read about the dangers of Mongolian dogs I picked up a handful of stones but thankfully they didn't come too close. Back on the bus we drove for about another hour, passing through the small mining town of Zuunmod before turning up into the valley towards the National Park and the road-end beneath the ruined monastery of Manzushir.

It was good to be out and walking in the hills again after so much travelling. We set off through the trees, the path was way-marked with squares of yellow paint as it climbed steadily up through open forest, then past a low rocky outcrop, not unlike Harrison's Rocks, a sandstone outcrop to the south of London.

After a couple of hours, the angle started to ease off and the trees thinned out; in the distance we could see the rocky 'tors' that formed the summit of Tsetseguun. When we left the edge of the forest Tom tied a bright red plastic carrier-bag to a bush so we could spot the way back in; he knew from past experience that from a distance it would be difficult to find the path and the correct way down. Several eagles were soaring on the thermals above us and there was a lot of insect life buzzing around including butterflies and grass-hoppers.

From the edge of the forest it was only another ½ mile to the foot of the summit 'tors', which are similar to the 'barns' on Bynack More in the Cairngorms. Here we found another large 'ovoo' covered in hundreds of prayer flags; two locals reached there just before us and they were burning incense beside a prayer-wheel. The skull of a horse lay on the rocks alongside.

Most of us made the scramble up to the highest point; the rock was quite rough and 'grippy' so it was reasonably easy if a little exposed. We scrambled back down to the 'ovoo' before re-tracing our steps, searching for our red 'flag' which marked the way back into the forest. On the way down we filled our rucksacks with around 60 or 70 plastic water-bottles (and a couple of glass vodka bottles) that people had dumped by the path. Why they couldn't carry them down empty when they weighed nothing was a mystery to us all. Other than the two locals we met at the summit, there was no one else about and we had the whole mountain to ourselves all day.

Once back at the bus, Oggi produced ice-cold beers and *Cokes*, then flasks of tea and coffee and cakes galore; it was clear that we weren't going to starve on this trip. While we lazed in the sun, eating and drinking, Tom told us stories about the legendary mountaineer Don Whillans, and about Ron Fawcett and Johnny Dawes, ace rock-climbers from the Sheffield scene. Later we wandered up the hill a short way to look at the museum and the ruined monastery; another of those destroyed by the Communists in the 1930's but which has now been partially re-built. With rain threatening, we raced back down the hill to the bus, passing some inquisitive marmots on the way. Once back at the hotel we packed our kit in readiness for a move to the mountains the following day.

The 'plane, an old Russian twin propeller model belonging to *SCAT Airlines,* took us almost 2,000km or 3½ hours due west to Olgii. At first we were flying through thick cloud so we didn't see much and the ride was very bumpy at times; then the clouds parted and we could see we were flying along the edge of a desert then over some large lakes. It looked wild, beautiful and very empty; after we had been flying for about 3 hours, snow covered mountains appeared ahead.

Once we'd landed at the small air-field in Olgii we rounded up our kit and piled into a number of jeeps. We were expecting a five or six hour drive to the road-end, but road-end suggests that there was a road; there wasn't of course, it was at best a dirt track but often no track at all, we just drove straight across the grassy plain. The scenery was fantastic; at first we travelled through a wide grassy valley, crossing and re-crossing the river several times by deep fords. At one point we stopped to watch an eagle catch and eat a marmot.

After driving for several hours we stopped beside the river to eat a huge picnic. It was an idyllic spot, just a herd of sheep and a far off ger for company but we couldn't stop for long as we wanted to reach the road-end and pitch the tents before dark. As we continued on, heading almost due west into the setting sun, we passed several large herds of sheep, goats, horses and even small groups of camels. We had to check-in at a Police Post then about half an hour later we finally arrived at the two gers that marked the entrance to the Altai Tavan Bogd National Park.

The scenery here at the road-head was very similar to Scotland, and on about the same scale, as the peaks rose around 1,000m above the camp. It was 10pm and just turning cold and dark, so we quickly pitched camp beside the gers. We were fed a substantial 3-course meal that we didn't finish until almost midnight. This was the first time that we met Sandagash, who was coming up to base-camp to cook for us. Her son, Eldos, was also joining us; he was on holiday from being a student in Kazakhstan, he drove one of the jeeps and hoped to climb Khuiten with us.

At the time we were there, Mongolia was celebrating the 800th Anniversary of the founding of the Mongolian State and as part of their celebrations we had heard that the President was attempting to climb their highest summit, Mt Khuiten. As it happened, he was due to leave the area on the day we planned to walk in to set up our base-camp, and for some reason we were not allowed to leave the road-head until he and his party had come through. As we weren't allowed to leave we had an easy morning around camp, watching the girls milk the yaks and make cheese. There was no sign of the President by 11am, there was still no sign of him or any of his party by 2 o'clock; by this time we were tired of waiting so, hoping we wouldn't be arrested, we set off on the 10 mile walk up to base-camp.

Our tents, kit-bags and much of the food was carried on two camels; they set off first but we soon over-took them. As we reached the top of a grassy col, we spotted across on the far side of the corrie a long line of about 15 vehicles that carried the President and his party. The first vehicle stopped, and out jumped Eldos' father who used to be Head of the National Park and now worked for the World Wildlife Fund. The column bumped slowly past, several people waved from the jeeps. Eldos pointed out amongst others: the President's wife, the Local Governor, Mongolia's Champion Wrestler, the first Mongolian to climb Everest and the Chief of the Secret Police. However, there was no sign of the President himself, he was presumably in the back of one of the two Land-Cruisers which had blacked-out windows.

Excitement over, we continued on our way, climbing up and over another grassy col, from where we had great views down to the Potaniin Glacier, the longest in Mongolia. Tucked in the ablation valley beside the glacier were two gers that Eldos and his crew had put up for the summer climbing season. Since there are no good maps of the area, all we had to go on was a photo-copy of a map Tom had drawn by hand; this helped us identify most of the peaks we could see across and up at the head of the glacier. We pitched our tents behind the gers and settled in.

After a cold night we woke to find a covering of snow on the tents but the sun soon burned it off. We had a quick breakfast then set off for a short walk and some training on the glacier. We headed up the ablation valley between the moraine and the mountain-side; after a couple of miles we came to a small 'ovoo', which we all walked round the regulation three times. On the 'ovoo' were two argali skulls complete with their massive horns, and an ibex skull with it's longer, thinner horns.

After walking for about an hour and a half we came to a dried up lake-bed where we readied the ropes and practised roping up and moving together. Once Tom was happy we scrambled up over the moraine bank and down to the edge of the Potaniin Glacier; here we strapped on our crampons and jumped across a stream onto the glacier itself. Roping up into two teams, Tom leading one, Jason the other, we wandered around on the glacier for a couple of hours, practising moving together, walking in crampons on flat and steeper ground and using the ice-axe. When Tom was satisfied we could look after ourselves we headed back down to where we had first crossed onto the glacier.

Once off the glacier we changed into our light-weight boots and made a cache of the heavy kit; mountain boots, ice-axes, crampons, harnesses and ropes, were dumped to save us having to carry them all the way back up again the following day. This left us with a short walk down the valley and back to base-camp where we enjoyed a lazy afternoon, reading and dozing, packing and then re-packing the things we needed for high-camp. After dinner we turned in early; it was only 8:30, broad daylight on a beautiful evening, which we hoped was a good sign for the time we would spend up at high-camp.

The alarms were set for just after 4am, so we could have breakfast and be away for about 5. It was still very dark, but not cold, as we took the tents down and added these, along with our sleeping bags and *Thermarests,* to our loads. Although we set off by the light of our head-torches it was soon light enough to see without them. Our route repeated the previous days walk; up the valley between the hillside and the moraine bank, past the 'ovoo', past the dried up lake-bed, then up and over the moraines to where we had cached our boots and the climbing gear. After changing into our mountain boots and kitting up, we jumped the stream back onto the glacier and roped-up into the same teams as before.

The heavy 'sacs make it hard going but Tom set a steady 'Guides' pace as we climbed up the middle of the glacier, initially just walking on bare ice. As we climbed higher there was more snow and whilst some of the crevasses were open and could be jumped easily, one was big enough to make us retreat. Instead we followed the line taken by a French party that had passed us a little earlier; we had briefly met the French party the day before and were surprised to see them now, so relatively late in the day, as they were aiming to climb Khuiten and descend, without using a 'high-camp'.

It was hot work as the sun beat down, but a big bank of cloud hung around the summit of Khuiten itself. We steadily climbed higher, passing the wreckage of a crashed helicopter. We were told it belonged to the Russian army; it came down in 1989 having been caught in a cross-wind when out on a wolf-hunt, so none of us felt much sympathy for them.

As we neared a rocky island, the 'rognon' in the middle of the glacier, the snow became softer, the glacier steeper and it was hard work. With the combination of altitude (around 3,600m), heavy snow and heavy packs we were quite tired but at last, round the back of the top of the 'rognon' we found a fairly flat spot on which to pitch the tents.

No sooner had we arrived, then the wind picked up and it started to snow. We quickly levelled three platforms for our tents. Tent pegs were useless; we had to tie the guy-ropes to large rocks and place rocks all around the valance. It was a struggle in the rising wind and with the temperature dropping rapidly but as soon as we had our tents pitched we set about levelling three more platforms for the other rope who arrived half an hour later. They had been slowed by one of the team whose crampons wouldn't stay on, then they lost one of the small nuts when trying to fix it!

As soon as the others arrived, while they were still catching their breath, we took their tents and pitched them for them. Finally we could dive inside our tent and sort the kit out. The tent soon warmed up, even though heavy snow was piling up on the sides. Very strong, cold winds continued all afternoon and we had to keep clearing snow off the tents as the weight threatened to damage them. We were all concerned about the French party; we couldn't see them and knew that if the wind was so bad where we were, it would be twice as bad on the exposed summit ridge.

Tom and Jason had the stove going all afternoon making soup and hot drinks; later we ate dinner, filled our flasks and turned in for an early night. The plan, weather permiting, was that we would climb Mt Khuiten the following day so we set our alarms for 2am when we intended to review the position. When the alarm woke me I lay awake for a while, listening to the howling wind and occasionally pushing snow off the tent walls, but there was no sound from any of the other tents and it was clear that in weather like that we wouldn't be going anywhere. The sound of rock-falls and avalanches reverberated throughout the night. There was still no word at 4am, nor was there any improvement in the weather, so now we knew that Khuiten was definitely off for the day. Instead we enjoyed (or should that be endured?) a lay-in until 8 o'clock.

After such a grim night, three of the group decided that they had already had enough and they just wanted to go down; Jason had to lead their rope down so Tom was left with more people than was comfortable on the remaining rope.

Those of us who decided to stay agreed that we wanted to try for Nairandal. We all tied-in onto the one rope and it was a very long line of us who trudged away from the tents at around 10:30. This was not the 'alpine start' we had planned; the snow was already softening but the wind was moderating and there were some patches of blue sky, which gave us hope.

Tom set a good steady pace across the glacier, avoiding one or two crevasses. The over-night snow had covered most of the holes so people would sometimes drop through unexpectedly, but we were tied close to each other and it was easy to pull anyone out before they dropped too far. We made a steady climb, up across a bowl, which then steepened at it's head as we climbed up to a subsidiary summit to the left of Nairandal. There was one final, short, steep wall to climb, then we popped out onto a narrow snow ridge. From here we had great views down into China and Russia. The terrain in China looked similar to the Mongolian mountains we were in but over in Russia it was much lower and greener, the ground dropping quite quickly away from our summit ridge.

We followed the ridge along and up until we reached Nairandal itself; here the borders of Mongolia, China and Russia all converge on the summit. Now in sunshine and with only a light breeze, we were able to stop to eat and take photos. We were all relieved to have climbed Nairandal, because it meant we had actually climbed something; if the weather turned bad again, at least we wouldn't be going home empty handed.

Leaving the summit we continued along the ridge before dropping down to a col; from the col we had a short climb up to another little rocky peak. Again we had fantastic views over into Russia and down to our tents beside the 'rognon'; we left this final 'top' and dropped back down to the col, we then went more steeply down into the bowl to rejoin our route from earlier. By now the snow was very soft and it was balling-up badly under my crampons; it was frustrating to see that most of the others had new crampons, which were sold with anti-balling plates, and they were having no trouble at all.

We were back at high-camp by about 1pm; there were just four tents now as Jason and the others had left. Adrian and I were disturbed to see that a huge puddle of icy water had formed under our tent in the short time we had been away, such is the power of the sun at these altitudes. We dug a channel, which did drain the water away, but this left us with several inches of icy mush as a base which didn't look too inviting to sleep on. We decided we would be better off moving the tent to one of the sites vacated by the others so we quickly emptied the tent, placing all our gear on the rocks of the 'rognon' where it soon dried off in the hot sun and cool breeze. We lifted the tent over to the new, drier spot and soon had it well pitched and protected with a wall of snow, ready to survive any further storms that the mountain might throw at us.

It was very hot inside the tents as we relaxed; I spent a while cannabalising part of my rucksack, using some of the stiff plastic back-board to make improvised 'anti-balling' plates to fit between my boots and my crampons. After an early dinner we were soon in our sleeping-bags, hoping the weather would hold and allow us to go for Mount Khuiten in the morning. Alarms were set for 2:30am, when we would check on the weather, if it was good we hoped to leave by 4am.

It was pitch dark when the alarm went off and the only sound was Tom in the tent next door, firing up the stove. I was glad to have a bit of a lay in, knowing it would take quite a while to boil enough water for all of us. Eventually I emerged from my sleeping bag at 3am and grabbed a mug of tea and a bowl of muesli; by the time we'd all strapped on our crampons and tied-in to the rope, it was just about 4am. Tom led us off through the darkness, across the crevassed bowl, nine little pockets of light spread out along the length of the rope. We seemed to make good time, moving well across the reasonably firm surface of the glacier, which for now was at a nice easy angle.

Away in the east the sky finally started to brighten; the angle of the slope steepened, and after just over an hours climbing we reached the foot of the col. We now faced a steeper climb as the day dawned, heading straight up towards the col. Just before reaching the col we turned and headed off to the left, to climb a steep ridge, kicking steps into the soft snow. As we climbed higher the wind increased significantly, blowing in ever stronger gusts. The ridge seemed to go on for ever but we finally came out onto flatter ground which we knew was the start of the summit ridge. We could soon see the summit about half a mile away, but up here the wind was even stronger; severe gusts were sending plumes of spindrift blowing everywhere, we could hardly see our feet, or more importantly, the ground.

32: Mount Khuiten from Nairandal

We had to battle our way along the ridge, the footsteps of the French party were just visible from when they had summitted a couple of days before. We reached the top at 6:40, just as the sun was rising in a beautiful orange/pink glow. There was nothing to mark the summit; we half expected to find a Mongolian flag left by the President's party, but if he did leave something behind it had either blown away or the French had taken it as a souvenir.

In the violent wind Tom wouldn't let us stop on top, so there were few photos, he just wanted us safely down off the mountain. We set off in reverse order; Eldos leading, retracing our steps along the summit ridge, with Tom bringing up the rear. When we reached the top of the descent ridge it was steep enough for us to have to turn and face inwards; it was slow going on the descent as the steps we'd formed on our way up often collapsed as we climbed down, it was only when we were back at the col that we could relax and catch our breath.

With the worst of it now behind us, the rope changed ends again; Tom re-took the lead and led us down to the bowl. From here, with the benefit of daylight, we were able to take a more direct line across the glacier and back to the tents.

It was still only 8:40, so the round trip had taken us just 4hrs 40 minutes, instead of the 7hrs we had been told it might. The plan was that once back at high-camp we would stop for a brew but the weather looked as though it might turn for the worse again. We quickly struck the tents, packed up camp and were soon roped up and heading back down the glacier towards the comforts of base-camp.

It felt like a long slog back down the glacier, carrying heavy packs in soft snow. People stepped into small hidden crevasses at regular intervals but no one was allowed to fall in too far, there were plenty of people on the rope to give support from either side. The further down the glacier we went, the wetter and mushier it became, there were several large surface streams that needed to be jumped but at last we reached the spot where we had first climbed onto the glacier. While not perfect, my home-made 'anti-balling' plates had worked well and had proved to be quite an inspiration, it would certainly have been a much harder day without them.

We were finally able to un-rope and swap our heavy mountain boots for our hiking boots; we then had a difficult climb with big packs, up and over the unstable moraine bank. Once down at the dry lake bed we were left with a very pleasant 'blast' back down the valley to the base-camp gers. There were a couple of camels grazing loose nearby and a Swiss couple had pitched their tents close to our camp. We pitched our tents and Sandagash produced another huge dinner, we then spent a lazy afternoon around camp, washing in the ice-cold glacial stream, reading and sleeping.

That night the rain set in and it continued uninterrupted for 12 hours. Nobody seemed too keen to do anything next morning, so we sat around the stove in the ger, trying to keep warm, chatting and drinking endless cups of tea, pleased that most of the group had achieved the trips main objectives. After lunch a few of us headed back up the hill to carry down the remaining kit, as the ropes and a few pairs of mountain boots had been left by the edge of the glacier and now needed carrying back down. Although we set off in rain and a cold wind, it soon stopped and the sun came out.

Throughout the rest of the afternoon, as we lay sunbathing, we could hear stone-fall from the peaks across the glacier. Up at the head of the glacier, around Khuiten and Nairandal, it looked very grey, as though it was raining up there, rather than snowing. We were very lucky that we had the day of reasonably good weather for climbing Mt Khuiten when we did. The day ended with a beautiful, but very short sun-set, which was followed by a clear, cold night.

We woke to an almost cloud free morning and a fantastic blue sky. Jason led one group who wanted to go down the valley, beyond where the President's party had camped, past the end of the glacier, to climb a grassy hill which looked as though it should be a good viewpoint. The rest of us went with Tom to climb Malchin, the third of the trips scheduled peaks.

We were now well acclimatised and made quick work of the now familiar walk up to the dried-up lake bed; from here we climbed steep scree slopes under a roasting hot sun. It was very loose underfoot with only a hint of a path to follow through the scree, but as we rose higher we had great views across to Khuiten, Nairandal and the site of our high-camp by the 'rognon' in the middle of the glacier. For once the summit of Khuiten stayed clear of cloud and we were happy for the Swiss couple and their Mongolian guide who had chosen a great day for their summit attempt. At last we reached the short summit ridge, where there was a huge bank of snow to our right, but we stayed on the rock and followed the ridge along to the high-point at the far end. As we reached the small summit we had great views north and out into Russia.

Buried in the summit cairn we found a couple of plastic water-bottles, thinking they were rubbish we were about to pick them up and bring them down, until we realised that they contained a small amount of money and some prayers, so we left them where they were, tucked away in the cairn as an offering. After the obligatory photos we returned along the ridge, then ran quickly down the scree, losing a lot of height very easily, so that we were soon back at the dry lake bed. On the walk back to camp we spotted a mountain hare, a couple of ground squirrels, marmots and loads of butterflies and small birds. There were also a lot of wild flowers, including eidelweiss, although these were now past their best.

After lunch I set off down the valley to the site of the President's camp, where a new monument had been erected to celebrate the successful ascent of Khuiten by the President's party. The monument was an ugly concrete pillar, the writing on it was already coming off after only a week, and someone had written graffiti on the monument, which was dated just the day after the monument was erected. Laid out in stones on the ground in front of the monument was an outline map of Mongolia; there were five larger rocks in a group in the far western corner, these five rocks signified the Five Holy Peaks of the Altai Tavan Bogd range. Four eagles stood on the rocks just beyond the monument, sunning themselves, but they took to the sky when I moved too close. I then wandered back up to camp, followed a little later by four young Poles who set up their base-camp nearby.

We had been offered the choice of walking back to the road-end or riding out; everyone thought it would be more of an adventure to ride. Generally Mongolians don't like to walk anywhere and this would be another part of our Mongolian experience; in the late afternoon our horses arrived along with the baggage camels.

Next morning there was no great rush as we only had to make our way the 10 miles or so back to the road-end. We watched as the camels were loaded; these were far better natured than I expected, apparently Asian camels are much less aggressive than their African cousins. It took a while for Eldos to match the horses to the various members of the group, only one or two of whom had ridden before but we finally set off on the trek back to the road-end. Near the President's monument the ponyman's dog, which looked as though it was part wolf, caught the scent of a marmot, it raced off on the chase, easily caught the marmot, and then carried it away to eat it undisturbed.

After riding for about an hour and a half, the pain in my knees was excruciating, probably because the stirrups were too short for me, so when we reached the high point of the col, beside a small lake, I dismounted and walked for a mile or two to restore some circulation. A little later Alan also dismounted, though not through choice; his horse spooked at something and suddenly raced off, Alan was thrown, landing first on his shoulder, then on his head. He looked shaken and refused to continue with the horse that had thrown him, so he swapped mounts and rode a more docile one the rest of the way back. I re-mounted too, which made the river crossing much easier, and after another hour in the saddle I was very pleased to see the road-end gers in the distance.

Once at the gers it was difficult to dismount as my knees had seized up but I was glad to see that everyone else had trouble dismounting and they couldn't walk normally either. Tea and borsch were ready for us as soon as we arrived, then it was tents up for the last time. There were piles of yak dung drying around the gers; the dung is used for fuel and was being stored for the winter. Up at base-camp we had burnt wood in the stove; the wood had been carried in all the way from Olgii as there are no trees within miles of where we were. After dinner we watched a storm coming in from the mountains, it was moving very fast and I'd never seen so much lightning before.

Next morning we loaded the jeeps and set out on the long drive back but after only half an hour we stopped at the ger of one of our drivers. He had a big family; his parents were there, along with his wife and their many children. They brought out a huge spread which included fermented mares milk and Kazakh tea, which is made with milk and salt. We were served pastries and biscuits and several types of home-made cheese. We ate what we could, then climbed back into the jeeps. Our next stop was only an hour down the road, here we met a Kazakh eagle hunter. His bird was a three year old Golden Eagle, which he let us hold on a gloved arm; the bird was huge, very heavy, and had a wicked curved beak, in winter the bird catches marmots which the family eat.

After climbing into the jeeps we continued on our way, stopping again about an hour later. We made a short detour up the hillside to some rough cabins that the nomads move into in the winter, when it's too cold and too snowy for them to stay living in their gers. Carved into the rocks above this little winter settlement are hundreds of petroglyphs. These show men with bows and arrows, horses, snow leopards, antelope, deer, elk, and even elephant and hippopotamus. The carvings are very crude and are said to be about 2,000 years old.

We climbed back into the jeeps for the final leg of the journey; after driving for a couple of hours my jeep ground to a halt, having run out of petrol. Thankfully one of the other jeeps realised we were missing, so they turned round and came back to see what the problem was. We siphoned a litre of petrol out of their tank and this was just enough to get us to a small village, with a petrol pump, which was the first we had seen all day. As the jeeps were refueling, it was found that one of them had a blocked water hose and the same jeep also had a flat tyre. All four drivers, and the guys manning the petrol pump, rallied round and had both problems fixed in no time at all.

Eventually, the track we were driving on became more substantial and we arrived at a surprisingly big village, nestled against the foot of some big hills. This was Sagsai and as we pulled up at the Blue Ger Hotel the whole village seemed to be out watching a frantic game of basketball that was being played on a dusty court. We took over three gers, each richly decorated with rugs and embroidered silks.

The old Russian 'banya' was fired up for us; there was no shower, just a huge barrel of ice-cold water and a ladle to scoop it over you, then we dashed into the boiling hot sauna. This soon soaked off a weeks dirt and the dust from the days journey. After a fantastic dinner the group drank their way through several bottles of *Chingis* vodka and drank the bar dry of beer; I stayed on orange juice and was one of the few without a sore head in the morning.

Next morning we were soon at Bayan Olgii and from there we flew back to UB. On our last day we took the opportunity to visit a festival celebrating 800 years of the Great Mongolian State. The main attraction was some 500 horsemen of the Mongolian army who were re-enacting a battle. It was an impressive sight as the warriors swept back and forth across the grassy plain, showing off their skills in horsemanship and archery; two of the three 'manly skills', wrestling being the other.

Next morning there was quite a scrum at UB airport but Oggi saved the day and somehow we made it through on time. It had been another great trip and confirmed what I had learned on my first visit to Mongolia; the people and the country are wonderful, and I can't wait to go back again.

Ecuador – Failure on Cotopaxi & Chimborazo

There were just three of us booked onto this trip; we hoped to climb four peaks, getting progressively higher. We were to start with Imbabura at around 4,630m, followed by the more technical Iliniza Norte (5,126m), then Cotopaxi (5,897m), said to be the world's highest active snow-capped volcano, and finally finishing with Chimborazo, Ecuador's highest mountain at 6,310m. Keeping within the 20 kilos weight limit wasn't easy bearing in mind we had to take ice-axe, crampons, harness, helmet, climbing gear and full winter kit. We were bound for Quito, via Madrid.

Passing through customs and immigration was surprisingly quick and we were soon being welcomed to Ecuador by the local guide for *Enchanted Expeditions*, who were arranging the trip. A 20 minute ride through Quito took us to the hotel *Sierra Madre*, in the new part of town.

After a poor night's sleep, we went for a look round Quito, which sits at 9,200ft above sea-level, and we could already feel the altitude when going up and down stairs. The 'old' town was very colonial looking, and it was a lovely relaxed sort of place to wander round. It's a World Heritage site so they go to great lengths to keep the city free of the usual modern clutter, such as ensuring there are no telephone and electricity wires trailing across the streets. One of the highlights was the 400 year old Jesuit church; it was built using local lava rock, so it looks dull and grey from the outside, but inside there is over a ton of 23 carat gold-leaf which covers almost the whole surface of the walls, pillars and ceiling.

Later we drove about 25 miles north of Quito to visit the Equator at La Mitad del Mundo. It was here in 1736 that the Frenchman Charles de la Condamine discovered that the earth bulged in the middle. Unfortunately, about 20 years ago, when GPS was invented, it was found that the line depicting the Equator was in the wrong place, the real Equator was actually about 240 yards further north! Quickly tiring of the tacky souvenir shops we were pleased to head back to Quito to meet Jacobo, who was to be our Guide for the trip. Jacobo had just returned from leading a group on Cotopaxi, but they had been forced to turn back a couple of hundred metres below the summit; his clients being tired and the snow almost knee deep.

Next morning we headed up the Pan-American Highway to Otavalo. It was cloudy, with no views of the big peaks, but it was Saturday, which meant we were able to visit Otavalo's famous weekly market. The guide-book warned to be on the look-out for pick-pockets but we had an enjoyable hour wandering round, and it actually felt very safe and un-pressured; there was no hassle, no aggressive sales techniques, instead everything was done with a sense of fun and a big smile.

We headed back to the Landcruiser and drove up to the road-end at Laguna de Cuicocha. The lake, some 600ft deep, is in the hollow of a collapsed volcanic crater; the two islands in the middle are new volcanic cones that are slowly rising up and taking over the lake. In heavy rain we set off for an acclimatisation walk; everyone was wrapped up in full water-proofs as we followed a footpath through the trees to the crater's rim, where we could look down over the two small islands in the lake below. The path was narrow and covered in over-hanging vegetation of all sorts of weird and wonderful plants. In some places the path ran along the edge of the crater, with an almost sheer drop into the water below, in others the path was so eroded into the ground that we couldn't see over the top, we were walking in a trough some 6ft deep. We were now up at 11,000ft and we could feel the altitude on the uphill sections. After about an hour and a half we reached a view-point, which was about half-way round the crater; the second half was easier as it was mostly downhill. Towering above the lake was Volcán Cotacachi, the mist parted occasionally but most of the time we couldn't see much at all.

Back at the Landcruiser we headed down the road for an hour until we reached a lovely old hacienda, *Hosteria Chorlaui*. Here we were able to dry our kit and prepare for our first big hill the following day. We were away early for the short drive to Ibarra; as we drove past the military airstrip we were surprised to see that it was packed with people walking and jogging, apparently they open it to the public for a couple of hours every Sunday morning so they can exercise there.

Leaving Ibarra we started climbing on a cobbled road, steeply up the hillside, through scattered communities where almost every house had a cow or two tethered outside, usually a pig or two, perhaps a couple of sheep and there would be a handful of chickens running round too. As we climbed higher, the road became rougher; the cobbles ended and were replaced by hard-packed mud. The mud was very slippery after the previous day's rain and we finally ground to a halt when the tyres couldn't find any grip. We had a dangerous few minutes reversing, slipping and sliding back down the track until we regained the cobbles and were finally able to find enough room to turn round and park up.

We were in warm sunshine when we set off; initially climbing the dirt road we'd tried to drive up. Ahead of us loomed Imbabura, at just over 4,600m, and we were now at around 3,500m. After a short while we turned off the track and took to a footpath that climbed up to a water catchment tank. Ahead we could see the path we would take; it cut through the grassland in a straight line, straight up, there were no zigzags, so it was a steep climb. The mud path was hard packed, but very slippery. We stopped to re-group after an hour, then again after two hours. By now we could see that we were about to start climbing up and around the rim of a collapsed crater. Here Matthew twisted his knee and decided to go back. Jacobo, myself and Robin carried on, but Robin soon dropped back.

As we climbed higher, around 4,300m, we left the grass behind and climbed more on rock, which involved some easy scrambling but there were always plenty of good holds when you needed them. Near the first 'top' we over-took a group of lovely young American girls with their two guides; the girls had been in Ecuador for four months learning Spanish at a language school and it was great to chat with them and share their 'tostadas' while we waited for Robin to catch up.

We continued on but Robin soon decided to call it a day and turn back, while Jacobo and I carried on to the top; we climbed along the rim of the crater then up onto the highest point. After a bite to eat we retraced our steps to pick up Robin and continue down. We could see the weather was turning again and were keen to descend as soon as we could. Robin was slow and kept falling a long way behind, twice Jacobo and I over-took the American girls, and twice they over-took us as we were forced to wait.

Back at the road-end we again waited for Robin, but the time was well spent as we watched a beautiful humming-bird feeding from a flower. Once down at the car we rejoined Matthew, who was feeling very sorry for himself, then headed back to Quito for another night at the *Sierra Madre*. It was great to feel that I was acclimatising well, I had felt a little out of breath at the top but it was still early days and it looked promising that I would be alright on the higher peaks to come.

At breakfast next morning, Matthew announced that he was going home, he was worried about his knee and hadn't settled in Ecuador, which left just Robin and I with Jacobo for the rest of the trip. We also learned that an Iberian Airlines flight from Madrid had over-shot the runway and crashed just the day after we'd arrived. Quito airport is right in the middle of town, it has a very short runway and at almost 10,000ft it is difficult for larger planes to land there. It wasn't the first time it had happened and with the plane still blocking the end of the runway the airport was temporarily closed to the bigger planes; local planes were ok as they didn't need so such tarmac. The feeling was that Iberian might stop using Quito, which would mean we would have to go to Guayaquil on the coast and fly home from there.

With Matthew gone, we packed and headed off in the Landcruiser. Our first stop was at the offices of the *Ecuadorian Alpine Institute*, where we signed a legal disclaimer, saying that we knew mountaineering was a dangerous sport and that if we killed ourselves it would be our fault and we wouldn't sue the *EAI*, or words to that effect.

Jacobo drove us south for a couple of hours, down the Avenue of Volcanoes, and as the weather was initially bright and sunny we could at last see several snow capped peaks, including Cayambe, Cotopaxi, Iliniza Sur and Iliniza Norte, the last of which was where we were heading. We stopped briefly in Machachi to shop in the market for food, then, not long after Machachi we left the tarmac road and started climbing, initially on a cobbled road, then up a good dirt track. We stopped at a small hostel at the foot of the Ilinizas, changed into our mountain clothes and left any kit we didn't need.

Leaving the hostel the dirt road climbed quite steeply up towards the 4,000m level and where the road finally ended we parked up. It was hot and sunny as we set off for what we thought would be a three hour walk, initially up gentle slopes on a good sandy path through woodland. As we climbed higher the clouds rolled in again and thunder echoed all around us. We climbed on at quite a good pace, and as we climbed higher the rain started to fall; higher still and the rain turned to snow. As the ground became steeper we found ourselves on an exposed ridge, there was a lot of lightning which seemed far too close for comfort. After a few minutes of this we decided that the open ridge was not a good place to be so we left the path and contoured across the slope, just below the ridge top.

This was, in a word, horrible! The ground was soft, shaly earth that you either sank into or slipped down at every step. We were forced to kick steps as though we were climbing on snow. Thunder and lightning continued for the next half hour as we traversed the rotten slope. Thankfully, as we climbed higher things became a little easier as we moved onto snow and it was easier to kick steps in the real thing. The snow, thunder and lightning were ever present as we continued to climb up to the col between the two peaks, Iliniza Norte and Iliniza Sur. As the slope eased we rejoined the path that contoured round a bowl and brought us to the Rifugio Nuevo Horizon at 4,650m. It's a solid, stone built hut, painted bright yellow; inside there are some bunks plus a small sleeping-shelf up in the rafters. The door was open when we arrived so we had to shoo out a bird and tidy up after a fox that had been in and rummaged through the rubbish. We were annoyed to find so much rubbish; no one was going to collect it from the hut, so why hadn't whoever left it taken down what they had carried up?

Jacobo soon had the stove going and brewed tea and a big pan of pop-corn. After a while the weather cleared a little and although it was still snowing, we now had great views down into the valley. With a long cold afternoon ahead of us we crawled into our sleeping bags and dozed for a couple of hours, Jacobo then cooked dinner, and we were all back in bed by 7:30. On my last look outside, I spotted a huge fox, which was almost as big as Tasha, my much loved border collie.

It wasn't a long climb to the top of Iliniza Norte, so we didn't need an 'alpine start'. The sun came up and we waited for it to warm the hut a little before we got up, excited about the prospect of the first of the three big mountains we had come for. When we left the hut we were blessed with bright blue skies and hot sunshine. At first the way led up and across a shale slope to a col; from the col we headed right towards a rocky ridge. After crossing the ridge we contoured round onto the far side in order to avoid a huge rock tower, the snow was soft and difficult to traverse. At one stage Robin dropped a glove, which quickly disappeared down a steep snowy gully, we agreed to try to find it on our way back.

As we climbed higher it became quite tricky on the fresh snow and not far below the summit, on a particularly exposed section, Jacobo fixed a rope. After that we had just 100m of easy scrambling up a shallow gully, until we came out at the small summit where there was just room for the three of us to sit. The climb had taken about two and a half hours from the hut. The summit was adorned with a small metal cross, and sadly the clouds started to roll in so we had no real views, although we had had good views earlier of Cotopaxi rising up above a sea of cloud. From where we were it looked very high, quite difficult, and covered in a lot of snow.

After a short rest we retraced our steps back down the gully and across the fixed rope. Jacobo then untied the top end and threw that end down the gully to protect the next steep section of the descent. The snow was turning even softer by now and we had to be careful as we often had to traverse above some big drops. We dropped down one particularly steep gully by climbing down a rock wall on one side; we then continued the traverse until we finally found the glove Robin had dropped earlier. This detour to find the glove had taken us much further down the mountain than we wanted and it left us with another nasty traverse and a climb back up before we rejoined our outward path. From here it didn't take long to re-cross the ridge, drop back down to the col and down the shaly face back to the hut.

33: Cotopaxi from high on Iliniza Norte

Packing quickly we headed back down to the Landcruiser, but the usual afternoon rain just caught us, giving us a good soaking before we could reach the car. It was an exciting drive back down the muddy track, Jacobo lost control once but thankfully the car suffered only minor damage. After collecting our spare kit from the hostel we were soon back on the main road and a short drive took us to a hacienda for the night, *La Estacion*, near Machachi.

Jacobo was a regular at the hacienda so we were well looked after, very well fed and importantly we were able to dry our kit. The following day was a lazy one as we only had to transfer a short distance in readiness for the next hill, Cotopaxi. We stopped again in Machachi to buy fresh food for when we were at the hut; then a short drive took us up another rough cobbled road. When the cobbles ended we bounced our way along a dirt road that took us to the entrance of the Cotopaxi National Park. Once we had shown our permits it was just another couple of miles to Tambopaxi, a little collection of huts, set in the middle of no-where, and just a couple of miles from the foot of Cotopaxi. Driving through the park we came across our first llamas and saw several herds of fine horses.

We packed our climbing gear then set off in the Landcruiser for a very rough drive up the dirt road from about 3,800m to the road-end at 4,600m. From the car-park we could see the José Rivas hut just 200m higher; while it looked very close we were told it would take 45 minutes to an hour to reach it. I did it comfortably in 30 minutes, so was quite happy with the way I was acclimatising. On the way up to the hut we passed several 'day trippers', Cotopaxi is a very popular mountain, and lots of people want to reach the hut to see the volcano from close up.

After a big lunch, using our food, the hut only provided hot water for drinks, we wandered another couple of hundred metres up the hill to around the 5,000m mark to help us acclimatise. We left our axes, crampons, helmets and harnesses at the hut to save carrying them up again the next day then dropped back down to the car; the usual afternoon storm came in and we were stung by hail.

One group who had just visited the hut took mountain bikes down off the roof of their vehicle and set off on the 1,000m descent of the ash road, just as the hail was at its worst. We drove down to Tambopaxi and spent a peaceful afternoon in front of a log fire.

A leisurely start next morning saw us packing our kit for a night at the hut, with the climb of Cotopaxi scheduled for the following day. It didn't take long to climb back up to the hut; we then headed a little further up the hill again to help with our acclimatisation. The afternoon was spent resting as the hut filled with more climbers; Jacobo then introduced us to his friend and fellow Guide, Franklin. It was good to see that we would have two Guides as it meant that if either Robin or I were going badly, the other should still be able to continue.

We went to bed early, after setting our alarms for 11:30, with a view to starting out just after midnight. I didn't sleep well; I lay awake listening to the wind howling and rattling the tin roof of the hut. After a hasty breakfast we set off, up the now familiar path to the glacier. It was of course pitch dark and heavy clouds obscured the stars. Considering where we were it didn't actually feel that cold; this though was soon to change.

At the edge of the glacier we strapped on our crampons and roped up; me with Franklin, Robin with Jacobo. The snow hadn't frozen much overnight, it was still quite soft as we climbed the glacier by torchlight. As we climbed higher, the wind blew stronger and stronger; we were frequently forced to just stop and hang on. Occasionally we could see a deep crevasse but generally we just plodded on, in a world of our own, all wrapped up against the increasingly fierce elements. We could see the lights of other parties stretched out above and below us and after perhaps two hours we met a party coming back down, they had already had enough. The slope we were on was steep soft snow, which kept giving way as we tried to kick our feet in; it also seemed to be taking the full force of the wind.

We had been told that the round-trip should take between six and eight hours. After struggling on for about four hours and having reached about 5,600m, with another 300m or one and a half hours still to go, the general consensus was that this was no longer fun, in fact it was now rather dangerous, so without too much hesitation we turned around and retreated. After descending for about an hour, daylight started to break through the driving snow and hail.

We reached the safety of the hut about 6am, almost totally encased in ice; everything from boots, gaiters, trousers, jackets, gloves, balaclavas and head-torches were covered in a thin veneer of ice and it took several minutes before I was able to undo my gaiters and boots and take them off. We defrosted, ate a second breakfast, packed and dropped back down to the car. Of the ten parties that had set out from the hut, we knew for certain that nine had retreated because of the weather. When we left, one party was still out on the hill, but we doubted they would have been able to reach the top and assumed they were on their way down.

"Ever tried? Ever failed? No matter.
Try again. Fail again. Fail better."   (Samuel Beckett)

Whilst we were very disappointed, it wasn't too much of a problem as we were still in good shape to try for Chimborazo in a couple of day's time, and we had climbed to about 5,600m, which could only help our acclimatisation. We stopped briefly at Tambopaxi to change into warm dry kit and to collect our kit-bags; as I packed my kit-bag the ice from around my headtorch finally came off in one almost perfect mould of the torch, this was some two hours after we had descended, which shows just how cold it had been up there.

We drove out through the park's south entrance and joined the Pan-American Highway for a couple of hours drive down to Riobamba in the Chimborazo Province. The drive was a quiet one as we were tired from the early start and the effort of the climb.

We stayed just outside Riobamba at the *Hosteria Abraspungo*, another lovely old hacienda. The walls were covered in old mountaineering photographs from Whymper's era, there were also several good mountain paintings, which were much more European in style than the colourful, more naive, local paintings sold in the markets. All the kit was laid out to dry under the wide veranda; it was warm down here, but still wet as the afternoon rains came on again.

Next day was a 'rest day'. We visited Ecuador's oldest church, built in 1534, and Laguna de Colta, a lovely little lake surrounded by tall reeds that the local people use to make hats and baskets. Back in Riobamba we wandered round the old town and enjoyed fresh fruit juice, served with ice that had been carved from a glacier on Chimborazo, then wrapped in straw to stop it melting as it was brought down to town. I was amused to see a notice at the entrance to the market that read "No Bicycles – No Llamas".

Back at the hacienda we packed in readiness to leave for Chimborazo the following day. The weather was looking reasonably hopeful; whilst we still had rain every afternoon, it was generally just a brief shower and we even saw a little sun. Chimborazo itself though remained hidden by thick cloud.

Dinner was late that night; Ecuador were playing their near neighbours Paraguay in a World Cup qualifier and Jacobo didn't want to miss it. The result: Paraguay won 5:1; Ecuador sacked their manager; Jacobo was grumpy.

In the morning we headed back to Riobamba to collect Franklin, our second Guide, and then drove to the foot of Chimborazo. The road climbed quite steeply and as we climbed higher we passed small herds of graceful vicuna, these are slimmer and have a longer, thinner neck than llamas. Soon all vegetation disappeared and we turned off the tarmac road and headed up a dirt track, through a lunar landscape of bare volcanic soil and rocks until we finally reached the road-end at the Carrel Hut.

We spent an hour or so at the hut, at around 4,600m, where Jacobo and Franklin cooked us a fine meal. Later we headed up the path, following a glacial stream, up to the Whymper Hut, which sits at around 5,000m. The hut was less busy than the one below Cotopaxi and each group was able to have their own room. We went straight to bed to try to sleep as much as possible before the alarms went off at 10pm; the aim was to set out for our ascent of Chimborazo at 11pm.

Again I struggled to sleep; I kept waking myself up with 'cheyne-stokes' breathing, where I stopped breathing for a second or two, then woke up gasping for breath. As I lay there dozing, the wind roared round the hut and whistled through the tin roof; I wasn't optimistic that we would be leaving at 11 as planned.

Of the three groups, ours was the only one to be up and ready on time and after a quick 'breakfast' we set out. The night was initially clear and well lit by the moon and the stars, but the wind was very, very strong. We wore helmets from the start, as we climbed up a faint path through the scree and over a little snow. Franklin set a steady pace and we all climbed well and were enjoying it as we were so well acclimatised. However, the wind remained very strong and Jacobo was worried about the risk of stone-fall. As we climbed higher we could see from the colour of the snow that stones came this way quite regularly, the snow wasn't white here but a reddish colour.

After following the path for about an hour and a half, and making what appeared to us to be good time, we halted and Jacobo went on ahead a short way to the foot of a rock-band. The route traversed to the right underneath this rock-band, after which we would turn left and head steeply up to a ridge. The route followed this exposed ridge all the way to the summit.

Unfortunately, here below the rock-band was as far as we went. Jacobo said it was too dangerous; firstly from the stone-fall, which was caused by the wind actually blowing rocks off the rock-band; and then once above the rock-band there was a strong possibility one of us could be blown off the steep exposed ridge.

Reluctantly we turned around and headed back to the hut; the hut was reached about 2am and we went straight back to bed. Again I just dozed as I kept waking myself up when I stopped breathing. Later, when we were having another breakfast, we found that a young Frenchman had set off with his Guide during a brief lull at 3am. They climbed fast and made the summit in just four and a half hours, against a guidebook time of eight to ten hours. The Frenchman's friend had decided not to go as he thought it too dangerous and unlikely to succeed. The other group at the hut also failed to make it.

By 11am the weather was worsening and the wind showed no sign of abating. We did have one spare day so we had time to try again but everything pointed to that being a waste of time. The weather was forecast to turn really nasty so we agreed our climbing was over and we headed down to Baños for a day of R&R before heading home. Nearing Baños, we crossed the lava flow that had come down from Volcán Tungurahua the previous year; we were told that the earthmovers, which were still trying to clear the road, found that many of the rocks were still warm to the touch, over a year after the eruption.

Arriving in Baños at just 1,800m soon cleared my altitude head-ache and we booked into a German run hacienda on the edge of town. Next day we hired mountain-bikes to follow 'the route of the waterfalls', initially on a tarmac road, but soon diverting onto the 'old' road. It was a lovely, mainly downhill ride alongside the river amongst lush vegetation and all sorts of exotic birds and butterflies.

Later we visited one of the famous thermal baths of Baños; we chose an outdoor one with three pools; one was cold, the next warm and the main one was very hot. It was great to lie back, soaking in the warmth, while looking up at the waterfall and jungle covered slopes towering above us. Dinner that night was guinea-pig, a local delicacy, but not really to my taste.

Next day we were back in the Landcruiser for the four hour drive back up the Pan-American Highway to Quito. A short flight from Quito took us to Guayaquil on the west coast, where we transferred onto a larger plane for the flight home.

It had been a good trip, not quite what I was used to, in that we were never up in the wilds for very long, only being away for a couple of days before heading back to civilization and a warm hacienda. Nor was I all that used to failing; not just once, but twice. I would have loved to have looked down into the crater on Cotopaxi and it would have been great to set my own new height record on Chimborazo, but this time it was not to be.

GLOSSARY

Banya	(Russian) Steam-bath or sauna
Chang	A (usually) mildly alcoholic drink in Tibet and Nepal – made from barley
Dhal Bhat	(Nepalese) Dish of lentils (dhal) and rice (bhat)
Doko	(Nepalese) Conical basket used to carry large loads on the back, the weight is taken on a strap round the forehead, rather than the western style by the shoulders
Dolina	(Polish) Valley
Dzo	(Nepalese) Male offspring of a cross between a yak and a cow, generally smaller than a yak
Ger	(Mongolian) Round tent made of felt, easy to dismantle and transport
Gompa	(Tibetan) Monastery
Haji	One who has completed the Hajj to Mecca
HRA	Himalayan Rescue Association
Khata	(Tibetan) Traditional ceremonial scarf, symbolizing purity and compassion, usually in white or ivory and made of silk
MBA	Mountain Bothies Association
Munro	Scottish peak over 3,000ft, and included in tables devised by Sir Hugh Munro in 1891. There was never a specific definition of what constituted a 'Munro' it was down to Sir Hugh's personal choosing. The original tables have been revised by the Scottish Mountaineering Club following the re-survey of heights and to address anomalies.

Glossary

Ovoo	(Mongolian) Shamanistic cairn, usually of rocks, built on peaks and high passes; travellers usually add a stone as they pass to seek protection
Prusik	Knot tied around a climbing rope; designed to slide one way but locks when weighted, used to climb a rope, for example out of a crevasse
Puja	(Hindu) Religious ritual performed as an offering to various deities
Rakshi	Alcoholic drink in Tibet and Nepal - distilled from millet or sometimes rice
Rognon	(French) isolated rock outcrop on a glacier
Sirdar	(Nepalese) Lead Sherpa who manages all the other Sherpas and Porters in a climbing/trekking group. Responsibilities include hiring and paying local porters; making decisions regarding the route; purchasing local food during the trek or expedition; assigning responsibilities to the other guides; dealing with officials or the police.
Staw	(Polish) Lake or tarn
Stupa	Buddhist religious monument, usually dome shaped, many contain ancient relics
Thangka	(Tibetan) Silk painting, usually depicting a Buddhist deity or scene
Top	Scottish peak over 3,000ft and included in Munro's tables, but not designated as a 'Munro'
Via ferrata	(Italian) Literally 'iron-way'; fixed supports, cables, ladders to aid climbing a steep cliff
Wierch	(Polish) Hill
Yersa	(Tibetan) Summer settlement

INDEX

A'Bhuidheanach Bheag..............71
A'Bhuiheanach 96
A'Chailleach (Fannaichs) ...130
A'Chailleach (Monadh Liath) 97
A'Chioch..............93
A'Chralaig..........111
A'Ghlas-bheinn ..113
A'Mhaighdean....126
A'Mharconaich.....70
Adrar Tinilim 294
Afella 298
Aiguille de la Tsa320
Aiguilles Rouges 176
Aircraft wreckage ..81, 84, 125, 265, 402
Airgiod Bheinn.....74
Akioud...............298
Alltbeithe Youth Hostel....116, 168
Alpine Pass Route 240
Altai Tavan Bogd397
Am
  Basteir...........140
  Bodach (Aonach Eagach).......53
  Bodach (Mamores) ..58, 160
  Faochagach ..122, 133
Ama Dablam ..336, 343
Amrourough 296
An
  Cabar 133
  Caisteal ...24, 167
  Cearcallach 96
  Coileachan.....131
  Dorus 141
  Garbhanach ..58, 161
  Gearanach ..58, 161
  Leth-chreag ...115
  Riabhachan ..117, 169
  Sgarsoch..........72
  Sgor...............32

Socach (Glen Affric) 114, 168
Socach (Glenshee)...75
Socach (Loch Mullardoch) 117, 169
Stuc 147
Teallach 128
Annapurna 304
Aonach
  air Chrith.......107
  Beag (Loch Ericht).........67
  Beag (The Aonachs).....62
  Dubh 52
  Eagach (Black Mount) 48
  Eagach (Glencoe) 52
  Meadhoin 110
  Mor 62
Arolla 318
Arroumd...........292
Astraka 360
Athens 359
Avenue of Volcanoes 414
Azau Cable-car Station..........388

Baksan Valley....387
Baños...............421
Baruntse..........343
Beard, Eric........121
Bearnais Bothy ..121
Beijing..............376
Beinn
  a'Bheithir 56
  a'Bhuird 93
  a'Chaolain 156
  a'Chaorainn (Cairngorm) .92
  a'Chaorainn (Laggan) 95
  a'Chlachair 68
  a'Chlaidheimh 126, 147
  a'Chleibh..........22
  a'Chochuill 45
  a'Chreachain ...39

a'Chroin...24, 166
a'Chuirn..........42
a'Ghlo...........73
Achaladair.......39
Alligin 123, 147
an Dothaidh 39
an Oir 156
Bheoil............68
Bhreac..........92
Bhrotain..........85
Bhuidhe 21
Chabhair..24, 166
Dearg (Blair Atholl).........72
Dearg (Ullapool Rd) 134
Dorain 39
Dubhchraig 22
Each.............29
Eibhinn 67
Eighe (Kinlochewe) ..125, 144, 147
Eunaich 45
Fhada (Ben Attow)110, 113
Fhada (Glencoe) 51
Fhionnlaidh (Glen Cannich) ..114, 168
Fhionnlaidh (Glen Etive)..........55
Garbh.............73
Ghlas............34
Heasgarnich 37
Ime................19
Iutharn Bheag .76
Iutharn Mhor ...75
Liath Mhor 122
Liath Mhor Fannaich....131
Mhanach.........42
Mheadhoin 92
na Lap 66
nan Aighenan ..45
Narnain 19
Sgritheall 105
Sgulaird..........56
Shiantaidh.....157
Tarsuinn........126
Teallach...95, 147

Tulaichean ..24, 106
Udlamain 70
Ben
  Alder 68
  Attow............114
  Avon.........92, 93
  Challum 37
  Chonzie 30
  Cruachan 44
  Hope 137
  Klibreck.........137
  Lawers 34, 147
  Lomond 18
  Lui 22
  Macdui ..86, 87, 89, 163
  More (Crianlarich) 24, 165
  More (Mull) ..139, 155
  More Assynt...136
  Nevis..............60
  Oss 22
  Rha 137
  Starav 46
  Vane 19
  Vorlich (Loch Earn) 27
  Vorlich (Loch Lomond)......21
  Wyvis 133
Bethesda..............9
Bidean
  an Eoin Deirg .119
  nam Bian .50, 147
Bidein
  a'Choire Sheasgaich 120
  a'Ghlas Thuill .128
Big Grey Man of Ben Macdhui..........85
Binnein
  Beag 58, 161
  Mor 58, 161
Bivouac
  Feltre............266
  Pian de Fontana 255
  Sandro Bocco.256
Bla Bheinn 146
Blencathra 150
Blümlisalphütte..246
Bob Graham Round 150

Bogd Khan National Park 397
Boots Across Scotland........105
Braeriach ..84, 88, 162
Braigh Coire Chruinn-bhalgain 73
Brandreth 152
Brévent 177
Broad Cairn 79
Bruach na Frithe 140
Buachaille
  Etive Beag50, 147
  Etive Mor .49, 147
Bynack
  Beg 91
  More ..91, 92, 94, 398

Cabane
  de Bertol 320
  de la Tsa 319
  de Prafleuri....181
  des Dix 324
  des Vignettes .321
  du Jas Lacroix 226
  du Mont Fort..180
Cac Carn Beag 80
Cader Idris 13
Cairn
  Bannoch 79
  Gorm ..88, 91, 92, 163
  Gorm Hill Race .88
  of Claise..........78
  of Gowal 79
  Toul...84, 88, 162
Cairngorm 4,000's 162
Caisteil...............63
Calf Crag 151
Camp Toilgot.....378
Capercaillie.........81
Carn
  a'Chlamain 73
  a'Coire B oidheach 80
  a'Gheoidh 76
  a'Mhaim 86, 88
  an Righ............74
  an t-Sagairt Mor 79, 80
  an Tuirc 78

Aosda 76
Ballach 97
Ban 97
Ban Mor 83
Beag Dearg 62
Bhac...............75
Cloich-mhuilinn 85
Dearg (Loch Ericht).........67
Dearg (Loch Ossian) 66
Dearg (Monadh Liath)..........97
Dearg Meadhonach.62
Ealar 72
Eas 94
Eighe 114
Ghluasaid 112
Gorm..............32
Liath (Beinn a'Ghlo) 73
Liath (Creag Meagaidh) ...95
Mairg..............31
Mor Dearg 60
Mor Dearg arête 61
na Caim 71
na Con Dhu ...116
na Criche.......131
nam Fiaclan ...119
nan Gabhar 73
nan Gobhar ..117, 118, 169
nan Sac 76
Sgulain 97
Caucasus 386
Cayambe 414
Ceann Garbh 134
Chamonix to Zermatt 179
Changtse 354
Cheget Peak......387
Chimborazo411, 420
Chno Dearg 65
CIC hut 61
Ciemniak 371
Cinque Torri 252
Cirque de la Solitude 194
Ciste Dhubh 110
Clachaig
  Gully 54
  Hotel 54

Cnap a' Chleirich .93
Coetmoor Mill 9
Coinneach Mhor.125
Collie's Ledge 144
Cona Mheall 134
Conival 136
Cornice ..23, 53, 61, 69, 95, 119, 342, 362
Corrour Bothy ..84, 162
Corrour Station ...66
Corsican High Level Route (GR20) 192
Cotopaxi....411, 415
Craig Coire na Fiar Bhealaich 106
Craig of Gowal 79
Creag
  a'Chaorainn ...112
  a'Mhaim 107
  an Dail Mhor....94
  an Dubh-loch...79
  Dubh 117
  Ghorm a'Bhealaich 118
  Leacach 78
  Meagaidh 95
  Mhor (Glen Lochay) 37
  Mhor (Glen Lyon) 31
  nan Damh 107
  Pitridh 68, 69
Creagan a'Choire Etchachan 86
Creise 47
Creux du Van 215
Crianlarich 3,000's 165
Crib Goch 14
Crow Craigies 79, 80
Cruach Ardrain ..24, 166
Cuidhe Crom 81
Cuillin ridge....... 146
Culra Bothy ...67, 68
Curved Ridge 49

Dale Head......... 152
Dartmoor 11
Dent
  Blanc 325
  d'Tsalion 320

Derry Cairngorm 86, 88
Devil's
  Kitchen 13
  Point 84
  Ridge 59, 160
Dhaka 329, 346, 358
Dhaulagiri 314
Diamox 312
Diesel Hut......... 390
Dingboche .339, 352
Diollaid a'Chairn ..67
Dollywagon Pike 151
Dolomites
  Alta Via 1 251
  Alta Via 2 259
Dotterel.............. 96
Driesh 79
Druim
  Mor 78
  Sgarsoch.......... 72
  Shionnach 107
Drumochter 70
Dughla 340, 353

East Herts Border VSU 10
Ecuador............ 411
Eididh nan Clach Geala............ 134
Essaouira.......... 300
Everest Marathon 347, 380
Evolène 318

Fafernie.............. 79
Fairfield 151
Falls of Glomach 113
Fenêtre d'Arpette 179
Fionn Bheinn 132
Five Sisters of Kintail....110, 147
Forcan Ridge 108
Fords of Avon bothy 91
Frostbite............. 13

Gairich 103
Gamila 360
Garabashi 390
Garbh
  Chioch Bheag.102
  Chioch Mhor ..101

Geal
  -charn (Drumochter) 70
  Charn (Glen Feshie)........ 83
  -Charn (Loch Ericht)......... 67
  Charn (Loch Laggan)....... 68
  Charn (Monadh Liath).......... 97
George Hann VSU 10
Gerry's Hostel ..119, 122
Ghorka 303
Glas
  Bheinn Mhor....46
  Leathad Mor ..133
  Maol 78
  Mheall Liath ...130
  Mheall Mor..... 130
  Tulaichean 74
Glen Feshie......... 83
Glenshee....... 76, 78
Gleouraich 106
Glyder
  Fach 10
  Fawr............... 10
Goatfell 158
Gobet, Pierre..... 356
Gobi desert 399
Gokyo 337
Gokyo Ri......... 337
Golden Eagle..... 409
Gorak Shep 340, 354
Grand Combin ...181
Grande Civetta ..253
Great
  Calva 150
  Dodd 150
  Gable............ 152
Great Lakeland 3-Day 375
Great Wilderness Challenge 128
Green Gable...... 152
Grey Knotts........ 152
Gulvain 99, 101

Helicopter ride..... 61
Helvellyn ..149, 151, 376
High Raise 151

Index

Hillary, Sir Edmund 335
Hindscarth 152
Hohenschwangau 209
Hotel
 du La Sage 183
 Inchnadamph . 136
 Weisshorn 184
humming-bird ... 413

Iliniza Norte 411
Iliniza Sur 415
Imbabura .. 411, 413
Imlil 291
Inaccessible
 Pinnacle 142
Ingleborough 375
Ioannina 359
Island Peak 329, 353

Jbel Toubkal 291
Jean's Hut 87
Jiri 347
Junbesi 349
Jungfrau Marathon 244
Jura High Route . 211

Kala Patar .. 340, 354
Kali Gandaki 313
Kangtega 336
Kathmandu .. 302, 317, 329, 347
Katowice 366
Khovsgol 378
Khumbu Glacier . 353
Kilimanjaro 386
KIMM .. 20, 31, 33, 172
King Ludwig Way 205
Kirkfell 152
Kleine Scheidegg 244
Kongde Ri 343
Koscieiec 367
Kusum Kanguru .. 331, 351
Kuznice 366

L'Eveque 322
La
 Dôle 217
 Grand Motte .. 285
Lac d'Ifni 296

Ladhar Bheinn ... 104
Lady Shamrock .. 154
Laguna de Cuicocha 412
Lakeland 3,000's 148
Le
 Chasseron 215
 Grand Rochebrun 276
 Soliat 215
Leabaidh an Daimh
 Bhuidhe 93
Lho La 354
Lhotse 341
Liathach 123, 125
Lobuche 340, 354
Loch Mullardoch 114, 168
Lochearnhead Scout
 Station .. 9, 23, 24
Lochnagar 80
Logovo Lodge 387
Lopata 373
Lowe Alpine MM ... 69
Luinne Bheinn ... 104
Lukla 329, 357
Lurg Mhor 120

Machachi 414
Machhapuchhre . 304
Makalu 343
Malchin 407
Mam
 nan Carn 76
 Sodhail .. 114, 168
Mamores 58
Mamores 3,000's 160
Manang 310
Manaslu 304
Maoile Lunndaidh 119
Maol
 Chean-dearg .. 122, 133
 Chinn-dearg .. 107
Marmolada 262
Marrakesh 291
Marsyangdi Khola 310
Matterhorn 184, 325
Mayar 79
Meall
 a'Bhuiridh 47
 a'Choire Leith .. 35

a'Chrasgaidh .. 131
an Fhuarain Mhoir 114
an-t-Snaim .. 96
Buidhe (Glen
 Feshie) 83
Buidhe (Glen
 Lyon) 33
Buidhe
 (Knoydart) . 104
Chuaich 70
Coire Choille-rais 96
Corranaich 35
Dearg 52
Dubhag 83
Garbh (Ben
 Lawers) 34
Garbh (Glen
 Lyon) 31, 32
Ghaordie 37
Glas 38
Gorm 131
Greigh 34
na Dige 165
na Teanga 99
nam Peithirean 131
nan Ceapraichean 134
nan Con 137
nan Eun 46
nan Tarmachan 36
Odhar 78
Megalo Papingo . 360
Meikle Pap 80
Midges 168
Mikro Papingo 360
Mineralnye Vody 386
Moel
 Eilios 13
 Siabod 11
Moine Bhealaidh .. 93
Monadh
 Liath 97
 Mor 85
Mongolia - Sunrise
 to Sunset 375
Monodendri 359
Mont Blanc 181, 190, 325
Mont Blanc de
 Cheilon .. 181, 323
Monte Viso 273
Moruisg 120

427

Moscow 386
Mount
  Ararat 387
  Elbrus 386
  Everest ..332, 340, 354
  Keen 81
  Khuiten ..397, 404
  Smolikas 362
Mudge, Angela 80
Muktinath 312
Mullach
  an Rathain.....123
  Cadha Rainich 114
  Clach a'Bhlair ..83
  Coire Mhic
    Fhearchair..126
  Fraoch-choire.111
  Lochan nan
    Gabhar........94
  na Dheiragain
    ....114, 169
  nan Coirean ..58, 160
  Sithidh 116

Na Gruagaichean..... 58, 161
Nairandal 403
Namche Bazar ..332, 351
Nethermost Pike 151
Neuschwanstein
  Castle 208
Nuptse 340
Oban 154
Ochil Hill Runners 80
Old
  County Tops ..376
  Man of Coniston
   376
Olgii 399
Otavalo 411
Ouaneskra 293
Ouanoukrim 297
Ovoo .379, 398, 401

Pap of Glencoe 52
Paps of Jura 156
Pas de Chèvres 319, 323
Pastukhov Rocks 392
Peak Assault..10, 13
Pen-y-ghent 375
Pic du Malrif 275

Pigne d'Arolla ..181, 323
Pilgrim Tours 386
Pillar 152
Pindos Mountains
 359
pine marten 123
Plas-y-Brenin 318
Ploskos.............360
Pointe d'Tsalion .320
Pokalde 353
Pokhara............316
Poon Hill 316
Potaniin Glacier .400
Poucher,Walter ..141
President of
  Mongolia 400
Priut II hut........390
Pumori 340
Quito................411

Raise................151
Ras 298
Red Pike 152
Refuge
  Agnel............272
  Alfred Wills 189
  Baillif-Viso 273
  Bertone.........174
  Carrel 419
  Ciottulu di i Mori
   194
  Col de la Croix du
    Bonhomme ..173, 235
  d'Anterne 190
  d'Asinao 200
  d'Usciolu 199
  de Capannelle 198
  de Carrozzu ...193
  de Furfande ..271, 276
  de l'Aiguille Doran
   279
  de l'Alpe........225
  de l'Arpont 281
  de l'Orgère ..279, 288
  de la Coire.....236
  de la Fournache
   280
  de la Leisse ...285
  de la Muzelle..231
  de Lachat 234
  de Manganu...196

de Péclet-Polset
 287
de Plate 188
de Prati 198
de Presset 235
de Vallonpierre
 229
des Souffles...230
di l'Ortu di u
  Piobbu.......192
du Cuchet......282
du Plan de la Lai
 235
du Plan du Lac
 281
du Plan Sec ...280
du Pré de la
  Chaumette.227
du Vallonbrun 282
Elizabetta 174
Five Lakes 368
Grands Mountet
 324
José Rivas 417
Lépiney 299
Morskie Oko ..369
Murowaniec ...367
Neltner 297
Paliri 201
Pietra-Piana ...197
Polana
  Chocholowska
   373
Whymper 420
Riffelberg.........185
Rifugio
  7 Alpini 257
  Biella 251
  Boe 261
  Bruno Boz 267
  Carestiato 254
  Citta di Fiume 253
  Coldai 253
  Dal Piaz........267
  Falier 262
  Fanes 251
  Genova 260
  Giovani Pedrotti
   264
  Granero 273
  Lagazuoi 252
  Mulaz 263
  Nuevo Horizon
   415
  Pederu 251

Pissadu 261
Plose 259
Pradidali........265
Pramperet 254
Puez 260
Scoiattoli.......252
Sennes 251
Treviso..........265
Vazzoler........254
Robinson 152
Rock & Run MM ...60
Rotstockhütte....245
Round of Loch
  Mullardoch.....168
Ruadh
  Stac Mor
    (Fisherfield)126
  stac-Mor (Beinn
    Eighe) 125
Rysy 370

Sagarmatha
  National Park ..332,
  351
Sail
  Chaorainn 112
  Liath.............129
  Mhor.............125
Saileag 110
Scafell........149, 376
Scafell Pike 149
Schiara............255
Schiehallion 31
*Scottish Islands
  Peaks Race* ..139,
  154
Scottish Mountain
  Trial 20
Seana Bhraigh...135
Seat Sandal 151
Sgairneach Mhor .70
Sgiath Chuil 38
Sgor
  an Iubhair ..58,
    147, 160
  an Lochain Uaine
    ....84, 147
  Bhan 56
  Choinnich........66
  Gaibhre 66
  Gaoith 83
  na h-Ulaidh 54
Sgòran Dubh Mor 83
Sgorr
  Dheorg 56

Dhonuill 56
nam Fiannaidh .52
Ruadh............122
Sgurr
  a'Bhealaich
    Dheirg 110
  a'Chaorachain 119
  a'Choire Ghlais
   118
  a'Dubh Doire .114
  a'Ghreadaidh .141
  a'Mhadaidh....141
  a'Mhaim...58, 160
  a'Mhaoraich ...105
  Alasdair.........143
  an Doire Leathain
   107
  an Fhuarail 111
  an Lochain.....107
  an Lochan Uaine
   86
  an Tuill Bhain.126
  Ban 126
  Breac............130
  Choinnich 119
  Choinnich Beag 64
  Choinnich Mor..63
  Dearg 142
  Dubh Mor 144
  Dubh na Da
    Bheinn........144
  Eilde Beag 161
  Eilde Mor .58, 161
  Fhuaran 110
  Fhuar-thuill....118
  Fiona 128
  Mhic Choinnich
   143
  Mhor............123
  Mor (Fannaichs)
   131
  Mor (Loch
    Quoich) 102
  na Banachdich141
  na Carnach ..110,
    147
  na Ciche........101
  na Ciste Duibhe
   110
  na Fearstaig ..118
  na Lapaich (Glen
    Affric)........114
  na Lapaich (Loch
    Mullardoch)
    ....117, 169

na Ruaidhe 118
na Sgine 108
nan Ceannaichean
  ....120, 147
nan
  Ceathreamhna
  n 114, 169
nan Clach Geala
 131
nan Clachan
  Geala 117
nan Coireachan
  ....100, 101
nan Conbhairean
 112
nan Each.......131
nan Eag 145
nan Forcan 108
nan Gillean ..140,
  194
nan Saighead.110
nan Spainteach
 110
Thuilm 100
Shenavall..........127
Sidi Chamarouch292
Sinclair Memorial
  Hut 84, 162
Skiddaw 148, 150
Sligachan Inn 140
Slioch...............126
Snechdach Slinnean
 97
Snowdon 14
Spidean
  a'Choire Leith.123
  Coire nan Clach
    ....125, 147
  Mialach 106
Spittal of Glenshee
 74
Sron
  a'Choire 95
  a'Choire Ghairbh
   99
  Garbh 115
  Garbh Coire.....96
  na Lairige........84
  Riach..............86
Stacan Dubha 92
Steall Hut......58, 60
Steel Fell 151
Steeple.............152

429

Stob
 a'Choire
  Dhomhain ..115
 a'Choire Leith ..63
 a'Choire Mhail 160
 a'Choire
  Mheadhoin ...64
 a'Choire Odhair
  (Black Mount)
 47
 a'Choire Odhair
  (Knoydart) .104
 an Cul Choire...63
 an Fhuarain 55
 an t-Sluichd.....93
 Bac an Fhurain.94
 Ban (Grey
  Corries).......63
 Ban (Mamores)
  ....58, 160
 Binnein....24, 165
 Choire Claurigh 63
 Coir' an
  Albannaich ...46
 Coire a'Chairn ..58,
  161
 Coire Altruim ...49
 Coire an Laoigh 63
 Coire an Lochain
 165
 Coire an t-
  Saighdeir.....84
 Coire Bhealaich 63
 Coire Cath na
  Sine............63
 Coire Dubh 96
 Coire Easain 64
 Coire Etchachan
 92
 Coire Leith 53
 Coire Lochan..115
 Coire na Cralaig
 112
 Coire nam Beith
 51
 Coire nan
  Dearcag.....115
 Coire nan Lochan
 50
 Coire Raineach ..50,
  147
 Coire Sgreamhach
  ....51, 147
 Coire Sgriodain 65

Coire Sputan
 Dearg..........86
Dearg 49
Diamh 44
Dubh 50
Dubh an Eas Bhig
94
Garbh 166
Ghabhar 47
na Bròige.49, 147
na Doire..........49
Poite Coire Ardair
95
Stuc
 a'Chroin 27
 Garbh Mhor 94
Stuchd an Lochain
32
Stybarrow Dodd.150
Swaledale Marathon
376

Tadat Col 299
Tambopaxi........417
Tatopani 315
Tatra Mountains.366
Tawache 343
Tengboche
 Monastery ..339,
 356
Thamserku 336, 351
The
 Barrels..........390
 Cairnwell.........76
 Cioch 143
 Cobbler..........20
 Grey Corries ..60,
 63
 Saddle 108
Thorung La 312
Tigh Mor na Seilge
112
Tignes 284
Timesguida 298
Tizi
 n'Likempt 294
 n'Mzic 299
 n'Ouagane.....297
 n'Ouanoums ..296
 n'Ouauraine...295
 n'Tamatert 293
Toll Creagach ..114,
 168
Tolmount 79, 80

Tom
 a'Choinich ..114,
 168
 a'Choinich Beag
115
 a'Choinnich....133
 Buidhe 79, 80
 na Gruagaich ......
 123, 147
 na Sroine 63
Toman Coinich...130
Top of Eagle Rock 81
Tour
 de l'Oisans
  (GR54) 224
 de la Vanoise .279
 des Fiz 188
 des Portes du
  Soleil.........219
 du Beaufortain
 234
 du Mont Blanc
  ..172, 179, 235
 du Queyras
  (GR58) 270
Troon 159
Tryfan................10
Tsaatan 384
Tsetseguun 397

Ulaan Baatar ..377,
 397
Ushba 394
Val d'Isère 284
Via Ferrata del
 Marmol 256
Vikos Gorge 359
Volcán
 Cotacachi 412
 Tungurahua ...421

Watsons Dodd ...150
Weisshorn.........183
West Highland Way
47
Whernside 375
Y Garn 10
Yewbarrow........152
Yorkshire 3-Peaks
375
Zakopane 366
Zermatt............185
Zinalrothorn ..183,
 324

Made in the USA
Charleston, SC
12 April 2013